Dreamweaver® 4
Fireworks® 4 Studio:
A Beginner's Guide

About the Author

Kim Cavanaugh is the Technology Coordinator and Web Design Instructor at Congress Middle School of Math, Science, and Technology in Boynton Beach Florida.

Mr. Cavanaugh achieved a life-long ambition in 1995 when he became certified as a teacher and began working at Congress Middle School. In 1999 he was appointed as the school Technology Coordinator and began working exclusively in instructing students in the use of the Internet for research, training members of the school staff on the use of technology in their classrooms, and developing curriculum for multimedia, business, and design software applications. In addition, he has also served as an instructor for the School District of Palm Beach County, covering such diverse topics as Windows 3.1, 95, and 98, Microsoft Word and PowerPoint, Internet Explorer, Netscape Communicator, and has presented numerous workshops on the instructional use of technology. Mr. Cavanaugh is also a Master Trainer for FloridaLeaders.net—an initiative funded by the Gates Foundation to train school principals on the use of computer-based instructional and productivity tools.

Mr. Cavanaugh began developing a groundbreaking course in web design in 1999 with the goal of teaching the three primary web authoring titles from Macromedia—Dreamweaver, Flash, and Fireworks—to middle school students. The lessons presented in this book are a result of his vast experience as trainer, teacher, and curriculum developer.

Mr. Cavanaugh lives in West Palm Beach, Florida with his wife and daughter and loves all things associated with life in South Florida—especially warm weather, the Miami Dolphins, inshore fishing, and Jimmy Buffett tunes.

Dreamweaver® 4 Fireworks® 4 Studio:
A Beginner's Guide

Kim Cavanaugh

Osborne/**McGraw-Hill**

New York   Chicago   San Francisco
Lisbon   London   Madrid   Mexico City
Milan   New Delhi   San Juan
Seoul   Singapore   Sydney   Toronto

Osborne/**McGraw-Hill**
2600 Tenth Street
Berkeley, California 94710
U.S.A.

To arrange bulk purchase discounts for sales promotions, premiums, or fund-raisers, please contact Osborne/**McGraw-Hill** at the above address. For information on translations or book distributors outside the U.S.A., please see the International Contact Information page immediately following the index of this book.

Dreamweaver® 4 Fireworks® 4 Studio: A Beginner's Guide

1234567890 FGR FGR 01987654321

ISBN 0-07-219260-7

Publisher   Brandon A. Nordin
Vice President & Associate Publisher   Scott Rogers
Acquisitions Editor   Jim Schachterle
Project Editor   Janet Walden
Acquisitions Coordinator   Emma Acker
Technical Editor   Deb Maupin
Copy Editor   William McManus
Proofreader   Pat Mannion
Indexer   David Heiret
Computer Designers   Carie Abrew, Roberta Steele
Illustrators   Michael Mueller, Lyssa Wald
Series Design   Gary Corrigan
Cover Series Design   Greg Scott
Cover Illustration   Kevin Curry

This book was composed with Corel VENTURA™ Publisher.

With all my love to the beautiful brown-eyed girls in my life—Kayleen and Katy.

Contents at a Glance

Table of Contents

Acknowledgments

No project as complicated and as time-consuming as writing and publishing a book happens without the contributions of a number of very dedicated people, and this book is certainly no exception.

First, thanks to all of the dedicated staff at Osborne/McGraw-Hill for their efforts in helping to produce the best book possible. In particular I would like to thank Jim Schachterle, not only for his faith in my ability to produce this book, but also for all of his guidance and suggestions along the way. Thanks also to Emma Acker, Betsy Manini, Bill McManus, and Janet Walden for their efforts in shepherding the book to its completion.

To my great friend, fellow trainer on so many projects, and the technical editor for this book, Deb Maupin, thanks as always for your intelligent insights, your support, and your many helpful suggestions.

To my fellow educators in Palm Beach County, a big thank you for your help, and your enthusiastic support of the use of technology in education. Thanks to Ken Meltzer, Gary Evans, Teresa Wing, Larry Liss, Kris Swanson, John Long, and Bill Gullion for all of their help and encouragement in my own personal discovery of the excitement that technology can bring to the classroom. Finally, a very special thanks to Lee Keller, our original Macromedia evangelist, and Tykisha Grant for her help as the original ideas for this book were being formulated.

No book about a Macromedia product should fail to note the outstanding support that the company provides through its web site and the active participation of product support specialists in the many newsgroups that follow their products. If all software companies took the same approach to customer support that Macromedia does, there would be far fewer frustrated users (and authors) than there are in the world.

To my family, thanks for putting up with all the times that I disappeared—either to the computer or in thought—as this project was under way. Thanks to Katy for sharing the family computer with me, and for all of the Mario breaks we took together when I needed to get away from writing. And, of course, to my wonderful wife Kayleen, thanks so much for your love, support, understanding, and patience.

Introduction

In 1999, as I began developing a course for middle school students on the principles of web design, and specifically on the terrific Dreamweaver and Fireworks programs available from Macromedia, I was increasingly frustrated by my inability to find *one* book that presented web design principles in a thoughtful, sequential, and thorough manner. Certainly there were (and are) any number of well-written books available that cover the software and all that it is capable of, and yet none of them presented their material in a manner that was consistent with what I knew to be sound educational principles.

This book fills that need for a web design reference that begins with the basics, then leads you through a series of step-by-step tutorials to build your skills and comfort level to the point that you can confidently use the software to create unique and dynamic web sites of your own. In addition, because this book is written by a teacher, as opposed to someone who is an expert on the software but who knows nothing about the way people really learn, you can be sure that the lessons and tutorials make sense *and* anticipate your questions every step of the way.

Who Should Read This Book

Macromedia's Dreamweaver and Fireworks programs are the industry leaders in the creation of web sites and graphics for use on the Web, and yet they come with the undeserved reputation as being too difficult for the average user to learn on their own—what I call the "Macromedia Myth." Although the software is unparalleled in its ability to quickly and efficiently develop entire web sites, to visually design pages that are compliant with standard HTML code, and to produce graphics that look great while being small enough to load quickly, many new users are put off by the way that the tools for doing those things are organized, and choose to settle for less capable software as a result.

This book is designed for the person who wants to use what is considered to be the best "What You See Is What You Get" visual web-authoring tool available today—Dreamweaver 4, and its companion graphics creation and optimization program Fireworks 4—without giving any credence to the myth that the software is too hard to understand. Anyone who has basic experience in using computers can easily follow the exercises in this book and in a surprisingly short time can be designing and posting their own creations to the World Wide Web.

What This Book Covers

Many books claim to present an approach that is like being in a classroom setting, but few actually deliver on that promise. Throughout the development of this book, my approach has been to literally imagine myself in front of a classroom full of bright, motivated students (no dummies here!), who are eager to learn about Dreamweaver and Fireworks, and who are excited by the possibilities that the Internet affords. You can think of this book as a combination of lectures and hands-on activities, presented in self-contained modules and projects that support new concepts and tools as they are introduced.

Part 1, "Dreamweaver 4 and the World Wide Web," contains ten modules that lead you through a series of projects covering not only how the program is used, but also covering many of the fundamental principles required for a full understanding of how the Web works, including both technical and practical considerations in web design.

In Module 1, "Fundamentals of the World Wide Web," you will learn how the Internet and the World Wide Web are organized, how the coding structure that makes web pages possible actually works, and how the Internet browsers function to read the code that you will create with Dreamweaver. You might consider this module as "Internet 101," as it explains the basic underlying structure of the computer coding language, HTML, which makes it possible for web pages stored on a computer halfway around the world to display on your computer at home.

Module 2, "Planning and Organizing Your Web Site," explains why the planning process for creating web sites is actually more important than the design of the pages themselves. At the conclusion of Module 2, you will understand why the simple question, "What is the goal of my web site?" drives almost every design, layout, and site management decision you will make in defining your web site, and how Dreamweaver is used to help you focus on both the practical and technical aspects of site design.

In Module 3, "Understanding the Dreamweaver Interface," you will be introduced to the Dreamweaver authoring environment and the primary tools that are used for designing your web pages. The Properties Inspector and the Objects panel are the two primary tools for inserting and modifying content, and in this module you will come to appreciate how efficient this interface is and how quickly you can use it to lay out your pages.

Module 4, "Layout and Alignments: Building Your First Web Page," delves into the actual creation of your first web pages, and provides you with an understanding of how files are named and titled and how the properties of the page are defined in Dreamweaver, including text and page colors. Included in this module is a guide to the use of colors in web design, with some practical tips for creating pages that are easy to read and that make the maximum possible impact.

"The Printed Word: Working With Text" is the topic of Module 5, and in this section you will begin adding text to your pages and gain an understanding of the capabilities and limitations of text for the Web. This module will teach you not only how text is entered on a page, but will also show you how formatting can affect the viewer's experience, and present some of the issues involved with text alignment and how it displays in different browsers.

In Module 6, "Adding Visual Interest: Working with Images," you will learn how the use of graphics and images can lead to a more dynamic experience for your intended Internet audience. You'll learn in this module not only how to insert basic images, but also how to create sophisticated rollovers that respond to a viewer's mouse pointer, and be introduced to one of the newest features of Dreamweaver—Flash text and buttons—that continues the tight integration between the Macromedia family of products.

Module 7, "Controlling Page Layout," covers the use of the new layout tools in Dreamweaver 4, and introduces you to the concepts that are fundamental to creating pages that look great on any computer. By understanding the way that tables are used for page layout and alignment, and the advanced features available with objects such as tracing images, you will be able to produce web pages that have an interface that is easy for your viewers to navigate.

In "Advanced Page Design: Frames and Cascading Style Sheets," which is Module 8, you will learn how web page design can be taken to the next level through the use of the more advanced techniques afforded by frames, and get a peek into the future of the Web by working with cascading style sheets.

Module 9, "Automating Your Work: Tools for Consistent Content," covers another new feature of Dreamweaver 4, the Assets panel, and how it is used to keep track of all of the items that you have employed in your site—from links, to colors, to library items and templates that can be used over and over not only to make your work easier, but also to assist in branding your site so your viewers find a consistent experience when they visit.

Module 10, "Forms and Functions: Interactivity in Web Design," explores the use of programming techniques and the requirements for creating interactive elements in your site design. At the end of this final Dreamweaver-only module, you will understand how forms are created, the programming required to make your forms function properly, and be introduced to some of the capabilities of the Extension Manager—Dreamweaver's tool for extending the capabilities of the program by offering free extensions at the Macromedia web site.

In Part 2, "Graphics Creation and Optimization with Fireworks 4," you will find seven modules that introduce you to all of the capabilities of the fabulously easy-to-use graphics program, Fireworks 4.

Module 11, "An Introduction to Fireworks 4," explores the Fireworks interface and explains in detail how the program works and how to access the features of the software through the panels that organize tasks based on their function.

In Module 12, "Working with Bitmap Images," you will learn how GIF and JPEG files, the two most common formats in use on the Web, are created and how you can modify existing photographs and graphics in new and exciting ways.

Module 13, "Creating and Modifying Objects with Fireworks Panels," takes you further into the many uses of the software by exploring vector-based drawing tools, how objects are arranged and combined, and how special effects such as drop shadows, glows, and bevels are applied.

Module 14, "Working with Text and Text Effects," details the different ways that text can be created and converted to graphical images with the Fireworks Text Editor, and how advanced techniques such as attaching text to different shaped objects is possible.

"Creating and Organizing Complex Objects," which is Module 15, explores more advanced techniques available through the use of masks, and Fireworks' Styles, Symbols, and Layers. By using these tools you will be able to compose highly sophisticated graphics in a short period of time.

In Module 16, "Optimizing and Exporting Fireworks Files," you will learn essential skills required for preparing your images for the Web by discovering how Fireworks allows you to fine-tune your images to achieve the fastest download times possible while maintaining image quality.

Module 17, "Creating Animated Files with Fireworks," covers in-depth both the practical and technical aspects of the creation of animated images. You will learn not only how animations are created, but also be introduced to the new animated symbols features of Fireworks 4.

In Part 3, "Bringing It All Together," the exceptionally well-integrated features of Fireworks and Dreamweaver are explored as one, with an emphasis on how the two programs work together to create dynamic content for the Web.

Module 18, "Creating Interactive Images," leads you step-by-step through some of the more complicated and exciting ways that the two programs can be used together. Not only will you learn how the programs easily create the JavaScript necessary for advanced features such as rollovers and image maps, but you will also be introduced to one of the cutting-edge features of Fireworks 4, pop-up menus.

Module 19, "Integrating Fireworks and Dreamweaver," continues to explore some of the ways that the two programs can be used together, including how you can optimize and edit an image created in Fireworks directly from within Dreamweaver.

Finally, in Module 20, "Getting It Out There," the Dreamweaver interface for transferring files from your own computer to the server where they will be accessible on the World Wide Web is the focus. In this module you will learn how Dreamweaver is set up for file transfers, and information important for you to know when it comes time to choose a web-hosting service.

How to Read This Book

Much like taking a class, the modules in this book build on the knowledge you gain as you work through the projects. For the true beginner, the best approach is to work through the modules and projects in order so that you can gain an understanding of the underlying concepts as they are applied to the Web, and how Dreamweaver and Fireworks put theory into practice. For more advanced users, the information in each module can be easily accessed as a reference based on the primary tools and ideas covered in each. If, for instance, you only want to brush up on the new features of the software, you can read only those sections that contain the information you need.

Special Features

As with the other books in the Osborne/McGraw-Hill Beginner's Guide series, this book contains a number of special features that assist your learning. Throughout each module you will find Tips, Notes, and "Ask the Expert" sections that take you beyond simply understanding how the software works. In all of those special inserts, I have tried to anticipate your questions and provide answers for problems that often puzzle beginners. Additionally, "1-Minute Drills" are used to emphasize the important concepts covered in each section of the book, and "Mastery Checks" are included at the end of each module as a way to ensure that you understand the most important elements covered. (The answers for the "Mastery Checks" are found in the appendix at the end of the book.)

Almost all of the modules in this book are supported by free files that you can download from www.osborne.com. These files include not only basic HTML files for use with Dreamweaver, but also templates, graphics, and photographs that support your learning as you move through the book. To access those files simply navigate to the link for this book and download the free files that you will find there. Because the files are in the ZIP format, you will need an unzipping utility such as WinZip for Windows or Stuffit for the Mac. Clear instructions for how files are downloaded and uncompressed are included along with the files themselves.

You can also find these project files, plus on-line resources, frequently asked questions, and a forum for making suggestions on how to improve this book at my own web site—www.dw-fw-beginners.com. If you are a teacher or instructor using this book as a resource, you will also find at this site lesson plans and ideas for using the book in your courses.

A Note for Macintosh Users

As a long-time fan of Apple products and the Macintosh OS, I appreciate how loyal Mac users often feel a little left out by books that seem to be targeted only for the PC world. Although all of the illustrations in this book were captured from a PC, each and every project that was developed was simultaneously tested on a Mac. In fact, many of the graphics and web pages were developed on a Mac and then transferred to a PC.

Significant differences (and there are very few) that were found between the two operating systems are noted in the text. However, so as not to clutter the book unnecessarily with hundreds of "right-click—command-click" notations, it is assumed that Macintosh users know that their computer thinks differently and will be able to make the necessary adjustments as they work through the projects.

Part 1

Dreamweaver 4 and the World Wide Web

Module 1

Fundamentals of the World Wide Web

The Goals of this Module

- Understand basic Internet terms
- Gain an overview of how web pages are built using HTML
- Learn basic HTML tags and attributes
- Investigate how different browsers interpret web pages
- Understand how Dreamweaver 4 generates HTML

It seems like the Internet is completely inescapable these days. Everywhere you turn, you see another advertisement for the latest web site or service or another story about someone making (or losing) millions of dollars on their hot Internet idea. For many people, using the Internet has become as common as using the telephone. In fact, entirely new terms have been coined that today seem completely familiar to most people, such as dot coms, surfing the Net, e-business—the list goes on and on. But how many people know what the Internet is really all about, such as how it works, how web pages are accessed, and how sounds and animations get created and placed so that we can get to them? At its heart, this book is all about how those things happen—from designing web pages, to creating and inserting pictures and graphics, to crafting sophisticated animations that move and react to our commands. By following along with the exercises in this book, you'll soon be creating dynamic web pages with original graphics, like the one shown in Figure 1-1. But to do those things, you first need to know how they work.

Understanding the Web—Basic Internet Terminologies

With the Internet seemingly everywhere, it's hard to believe that the Net as we know it has been around less than ten years. While the basic structure of the Internet was created during the 1960s and 1970s, when scientists who needed a way to share their research created an *inter*connected *net*work of computers, the modern Internet wasn't born until the arrival of the first software program that allowed the average consumer to look at pages that included colors and pictures, and to move to another page by clicking a link with their mouse. A software program with those capabilities is known as a *web browser*.

The first popular graphical web browser was created by a group of graduate students led by Marc Andreessen and Eric Bina at the University of Illinois. Called Mosaic for X, it was first released in 1993. Marc Andreessen went on to start Netscape Corporation, and his revised browser became the cornerstone of our modern online experience. The Netscape browser is still with us, of course, and it's been joined by browser programs created by Microsoft (Internet Explorer) and by other browsers as well.

All browsers have the same basic functions: to read a set of instructions, or code, that directs our computers to display text and pictures, enable us to get files from another computer (*download*), or send information to a computer

Figure 1-1   The exercises in this book will soon have you creating your own
unique web pages for publication to the Web

(*upload*) and receive a response. While that seems pretty simple, in the short
history of the Internet, the capabilities of browsers have expanded many times
over, and today you not only can see a simple picture displayed at the top of a
web page with some text below it, but also can track an airplane in flight, make
reservations for a movie at the cinema, or chat with people all over the world.
Yet even though the Internet has become incredibly sophisticated, the basic
function of every web page you see is controlled by the code that is read by
the browsers on our computers.

What Is HTML?

This basic code for the design of Web pages is called Hypertext Markup Language
(HTML), and it is the foundation of every web page on the Web. The next section
of this module takes a closer look at HTML.

Notice what the code actually does, though. It gives directions to your computer to perform certain actions, such as display text or images, format the page in a particular layout, and insert objects that you can interact with. As a new web designer, this is one of the first lessons that you have to learn. Most of the actual work is done at the user's (or *client's*) computer. Something you'll hear over and over again is that you need to design your pages for the user's, or viewer's, experience, and that includes considering the fact that their computers control how the page is displayed for them.

Your job is to provide pages that neither get bogged down with long download times nor consume so much of the users' computer resources that they leave your page out of frustration. And, of course, you need pages that attract viewers because the content is something they want to see. Thankfully, the technical challenge of designing quick-loading web pages is much easier to address when working with programs like Dreamweaver and Fireworks, because managing and optimizing your pages and files is the primary function of these programs.

Getting Connected

What happens after you log on to your Internet Service Provider (ISP), the company that provides your connection to the Internet? Your computer takes the first action when the browser that you're using transmits a request to a remote computer to show you your initial web page. That remote computer—known as a *server*—is the place where all the files are stored that are necessary for your starting page to display properly. In fact, as you'll see when HTML is discussed later in the chapter, web pages are not like printed pages at all. That is, the images and other information on the page are not one object, like a page in a magazine. Instead, the page contains code that tells the browser to retrieve and display those images, as shown in Figure 1-2. The browser's job is to bring the images all together and display them for you, which is why your pages don't always load all at once, but tend to display the text first and then the images as they are received from the server.

Your home page and every other web page on the Internet have some basic things in common. The page is part of a *web site*—a collection of web pages, files, and links all associated with a particular *domain name*. These domain names are purchased by companies or individuals (such as www.amazon.com, www.yahoo.com, and www.msnbc.com), registered to nonprofit groups (such as www.pbs.org and www.splc.org), or assigned to government agencies or educational institutions (www.whitehouse.gov, www.stetson.edu, and www.firn.edu, for example) as a way to identify them as unique locations on

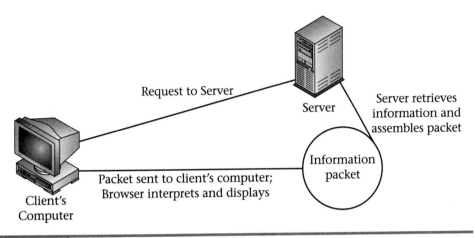

| **Figure 1-2** | Retrieving a web page from the Internet |

the *World Wide Web* (or simply the *Web*), the collection of servers that store the files of the web sites. The most common current domain suffixes (the three-letter code after the dot) are provided in Table 1-1.

Seem confusing? It's really not. Just as you have a unique address for your home, each web site needs a unique address so that it can be found. Depending on your browser, this address may be shown in the Location bar (Netscape) or the Address bar (Internet Explorer). Either way, it means the same thing: it identifies to the server exactly where the files you are requesting can be found. Those addresses are called *universal resource locators (URLs)*.

As you'll see when you start working with Dreamweaver, web site managers (or *webmasters*) have a lot to do with keeping the files and all the supporting

Domain Suffix	**Domain Type**
.com	Commercial, for-profit web site
.org	Nonprofit organization
.gov	Government agency
.net	Internet service provider
.mil	Military
.edu	Educational institution
.k12	Kindergarten through high school

| **Table 1-1** | Common Domain Names on the World Wide Web |

assets of their web pages organized and in proper working order. As a client of a browser program, all you really care about is getting the page to load quickly and properly and getting to the information you want to see.

Do you remember the first time you used the Internet? You probably were fascinated by how easy it was to move from one page to another, all with the click of a mouse. It's no accident that the term "web surfing" was coined as a way to describe the experience of moving effortlessly from page to page to page. What makes all that possible? Again, it's all controlled by the instructions written into the code. One of the things that makes HTML so valuable is its ability to insert *links* (or *hyperlinks*) in each page. In the same way that HTML allows a browser to display images, it can also create instructions to go to another web page or another section of a page when the user clicks their mouse on an image or string of text. Without this ability, web pages would be static, immovable objects—far different from the dynamic and interactive experience of the Web today.

In a nutshell, the Internet is simply (simply!) a huge worldwide interconnected network of computers, all using a common language, that allows users to retrieve information stored on remote computers, and display it on their computers at home, work, or school. This is all done through the magic of a programming language, HTML, that lets web page designers insert images, text, sounds, and other objects into their pages, through the browser programs that read the instructions in the code and display the results on the user's computer. Hmmm. When stated that way, it doesn't seem hard at all, does it? And, as you'll see in the next section, gaining a basic understanding of HTML isn't all that difficult either!

1-Minute Drill

- What is the basic function of a web browser?
- Define the term *web site*.

Getting a Handle on HTML

Just saying the words "programming language" to some people can cause their eyes to glaze over and their senses to go numb. Other people are fascinated by the challenges presented by learning to program computers and by sorting out

---

- The basic function of a web browser is to read a set of instructions, or code, that directs your computer to display text, show you pictures, enable you to get files from another computer (*download*), or send information to a computer (*upload*) and receive a response.
- A web site is a collection of web pages, files, and links all associated with a particular domain name.

1

all the instructions necessary to get a computer to perform the way they want it to. Whether you're a natural programmer or not, however, you need a basic understanding of HTML to go very far as a web designer. Although Dreamweaver (and Fireworks, as you'll see) will certainly do the majority of the programming for you, by gaining an understanding of what's going on under the hood of your web page, you'll have a better chance of tracking down problems and getting them corrected when something isn't working just right. You'll also see as you work with Dreamweaver that you can save yourself a lot of work by going directly to the point on your page where you want to do something. To do that, you need to know about tags.

HTML Tags

You'll start by looking at what a page displayed in its raw HTML state looks like. If you haven't done so yet, download and unzip the files located in module_one.zip at www.osborne.com. After you unzip the files, use your browser to open the file called html_one.htm.

After your browser displays the page, select on View | Page Source (for Netscape), or View Source (for Internet Explorer). You should see something like this:

```
<html>
<head>
<title></title>
</head>
<body>This is a very simple web page.
</body>
</html>
```

while your browser displays this:

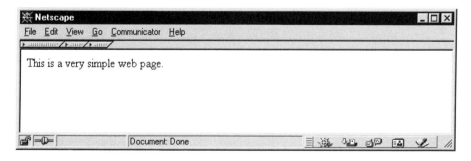

So what's going on here anyway? Why did it take so much code to display one little sentence? And what's with all of those left and right arrow brackets in the code? Let's take a look at that string of code and decipher it.

Hint

You'll notice that the filenames throughout the book use the underscore symbol (_) to separate words. Although modern computer operating systems can easily deal with filenames that have spaces in them, not all servers operate correctly when they come across a space. For that reason, you won't see any spaces in exercise filenames or in files that you'll create.

The first thing to understand about HTML is that it is written in a series of commands known as *tags*. Tags are the commands written by the programmer (or by Dreamweaver or another web authoring program) that tell the browser what to do. Take a look at the tags in the preceding example:

```
<html>
<head>
<title></title>
</head>
<body>This is a very simple web page.
</body>
</html>
```

Notice first of all that all the tags are written as pairs, just as parentheses are always written in pairs (like this). And, just as you need opening and closing parentheses, an opening tag and a closing tag are almost always necessary.

Every web page begins and ends with the <html> tag. This lets the browser know that it must process the page as an HTML or web document instead of, say, a word processor document or an image file. The brackets are there to let the browser know that a tag is enclosed and that certain actions are expected. Finally, notice that the final (closing) </html> tag adds a forward slash inside the left arrow bracket, which lets the browser know that it should stop processing, or close, that tag.

Next, you see the <head> tag and, enclosed within it, the <title> tag. The <head> tag tells the browser that the information inside it goes at the top, or head, of the document, and the <title> tag is where the information about the title of the web page is displayed. In the first example, your browser calls this an "Untitled Document" because no information is enclosed by the <title> tag. Now, open the file called html_two.htm from the exercise files and you'll see that a title has been added to the page. Viewing the source of the page reveals that more information has been added to the HTML in the example page—the words "A Simple Web Page" enclosed by the <title> tags.

```
<html>
<head>
<title>A Simple Web Page</title>
</head>
<body>This is a very simple web page.
</body>
</html>
```

HTML Attributes

Take a look at another example. Open html_three.htm on your browser and look at its source, shown here:

```
<html>
<head>
<title>A Simple Web Page</title>
</head>
<body bgcolor="#CCFFCC">
<div align="center">This is a very simple web page.</div>
</body>
</html>
```

Notice that one new tag, the <div> tag, was added. But something else has been added—another set of instructions inside the left and right bracket arrows that enclose the tags. Did you notice the difference when you first opened the practice file? The page background is now pale green and the text has been centered in the page. If you look at the code, you can probably guess that bg color="CCFFCC" is the code to make the background color that shade of green. And if you look closely at the command inside the <div> tag, you see the added instructions to align="center".

These added instructions are known as *attributes,* and they are used to do things such as change the color of text; change the alignment of text, paragraphs, and images; change the background color; or insert an image in the background of the page. As Wendy Willard describes in her excellent book, *HTML: A Beginner's Guide* (Osborne/McGraw-Hill, 2001), you can think of the tags in a web page as the ice cream in an ice cream sundae, while the attributes are all the toppings. Tags provide structure and organization to your pages while attributes make them tastier!

Take a look at another example. Open html_four.htm in your browser. You can see a number of attributes at work here. The text has been changed quite a bit—different colors have been added, sizes have been changed, and bold and italic styles have been added. Also, a background image has been added to the page, and the final result is as you see in Figure 1-3. The source code reveals that what's really been done is that a number of tags have been changed by inserting attributes within them. The attributes in the source code are underlined so that you can locate them more easily. You'll quickly notice that while the way that HTML works isn't really all that complicated, by the time you look at the code for a complex page, you might have trouble seeing the forest for the trees. Don't worry! Dreamweaver is going to make this all much simpler for you.

```
<html>
<head>
<title>A Simple Web Page</Title>
</head>
<body background="grayparchment.gif">
<div align="center">
<p><font color="#0000FF" size="7">This</font><font color="#0000FF"
size="5">is a <font color="#FF0000">very</font> <b>simple</b> <i>Web</i>
<font size="7">page</font>.</font> </p>
<p><img src="images/simpleimage.gif" width="299" height="122"> </p>
<P><a href="http://www.osborne.com">Visit Osborne Publishing.</a></p>
</div>
</body>
</html>
```

What do you notice about the way the attributes are written? If you look closely, you'll see that they all have a few things in common:

- Attributes are always inside the tag (between the opening and closing tags) that they modify

- The command for the attribute (`color` means we want to change the color, for instance) comes before an equal sign. Every attribute needs that equal sign!

- The value of the attribute comes after the equal sign and contains the information you want applied.

You also see two attributes that control the images displayed in your page. The first is `background`, and the second is `src`. One very important note about images: Your code has to tell the browser not only *what* the image is—its name and size—but also *where* the image is.

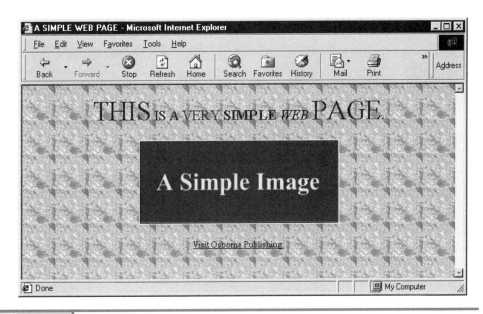

Figure 1-3   The results of the HTML code in html_four

Hint

A quick note about colors. On the preceding example web page, the word "This" is blue. Why does the attribute for that word list it as "#0000FF"? Couldn't you just type **blue** instead? Actually, you could, and you'd get the same color. But what if you wanted a grayish-green blue color? To get more-specific colors, you need more-specific instructions, so when that first consumer browser was developed by Netscape, a way had to be developed to display a variety of colors—all on different computers that might have different settings. For that reason, a list of 216 "Web safe" colors was developed, written in a type of code called *hexadecimal*. This code uses letters and numbers to specify exactly which colors are to be displayed by your browser. Color is discussed in more detail in Module 4.

Notice that the background attribute is different from the src attribute. It only lists the name of the file that is used for the background on your page, because the image is in the same folder as the HTML file itself:

```
<body background="grayparchment.gif">
```

Because no other information is provided, the browser assumes that this image can be found in the same location as the HTML file itself.

Now, look at the SRC code:

```
<p><img src="images/simpleimage.gif" width="299" height="122"> </p>
```

Notice that "images/" comes before the filename. In this case, your image is in a different folder (named images) than the source code, and you have to give the browser more specific information on where to find it. As you'll see in the next module, it's very important to plan the layout of your site so that you can easily find and file the pictures and other resources you want to use. Otherwise, you might end up with the dreaded (and unprofessional) broken image link symbol on your otherwise beautiful web page.

The last attribute to discuss is the <a href> combination that you see near the bottom of the sample code. This is the place where you can insert a link into your page. Again, notice how it comes before the words it modifies (Visit Osborne Publishing) and that it is very specific in nature. While it's getting increasingly common for users to just type a few words into the location bar of their browser and zoom off to a web site, when you insert a hyperlink, you need all the information included, including the information that specifies you want your files transported using a process known as Hypertext Transfer Protocol (http://)—the web protocol for linking one page with another.

Hint

The hyperlink in our sample is called an *absolute* link because it is outside the web site you're currently in. Absolute links always require the entire URL. *Relative* links, or those within your own site, can be linked by filename, as you'll see in Module 5.

One other type of tag that hasn't been discussed yet is known as a *metatag*—a specialized tag that is located within the head of pages and that provides hidden information about the page, its author, and its contents. You'll see when working with Dreamweaver that this is one of the ways that you can be sure you get visitors to your web pages, because the information inside your metatags is often what search engines actually search for. Right now, you just need to know that HTML has that capability.

And, of course, HTML has many other capabilities as well, but for right now, understanding how tags and attributes work in combination with each other is all you actually need to know about HTML. Table 1-2 lists the most common tags that you're likely to see when working with Dreamweaver.

Tag	Description
<a href="URL">	Creates a hyperlink to the specified URL
<b>	Bolds text
<blockquote>	Indents text left and right
<body>	Defines the visible portion of the web page
 	Creates a line break
<font >	Describes the font (text style) to be used
<form>	Creates a form
<frame>	Defines a single part of a framed web page
<frameset>	Defines a set of frames in a web page
<h1>	The largest headline-styled text
<h6>	The smallest headline-styled text
<head>	Defines information and instructions that do not appear on the page itself
<html>	Defines the file as an HTML document
<hr>	Inserts a horizontal line (rule)
<I>	Creates italic text
<img>	Inserts an image
<ol>	Creates a numbered (ordered) list
<p>	Formats a block of text as a separate paragraph
<table>	Creates a table
<td>	Defines table divisions—separate cells in a table
<th>	Creates a header for a table
<title>	Describes the text to be displayed in the browser title bar
<tr>	Defines table rows
Attributes	**Description**
<body background="imagename">	Sets the image to be used as a page background
<body bgcolor=?>	Sets the page background color
<body text=?>	Sets text color in the body of a page
<div align=?>	Used to format blocks of text
<font color=?>	Sets the color of text
<font size=?>	Sets the size of text
<table border=?>	Sets the width of the border around a table
<table width=# or %>	Sets the width of a table as an absolute number of pixels or as a percentage of the page
<tr align=?>	Sets alignment of individual cells

Table 1-2   Basic HTML Tags and Attributes

1-Minute Drill

● Describe the function of HTML tags.

● Describe the function of HTML attributes.

● What two items of information must be included when inserting an image in a web page?

The Present and Future of HTML

The development of the Internet has happened in an amazingly short period of time. Along with this rapid development, an incredibly competitive marketplace has developed in which those who develop the latest and greatest Internet capabilities for their browsers can quickly overtake and dominate their competitors. The problem is that one browser may not display code written for another flavor of browser, and visa versa. HTML standards quickly became an issue of great concern to developers worldwide as growing differences in browser technologies indicated that entire web sites soon would need to be developed for each browser platform.

The World Wide Web Consortium (W3C, at www.w3c.org) was formed as a means of addressing these growing problems. The W3C is the organization responsible for ensuring that a common set of HTML standards is developed and maintained, and that the capabilities of those standards are widely available to webmasters.

So, with a common set of standards, developers should have no problems at all, right? Unfortunately, that isn't the case.

Remember that the work of displaying your pages is done at the viewer's computer and by the browser they have installed. Currently, all browsers handle the HTML standards developed by the W3C through version 2—but, as of this writing, the W3C has developed standards through version 4.01! Furthermore, neither Netscape Navigator nor Internet Explorer, even in their latest versions, supports all the tags in HTML 4.01, or they interpret the code differently. This can cause web authors and developers real headaches as they try to construct pages that will display properly no matter what type of browser is being used. As you'll see in Module 2, the result of all this is that you need to have a very good understanding of who will be viewing your pages, what kind of browser they are likely to have, and how this impacts the features you want to make available through your code.

● HTML tags are the commands written by the programmer that tell the browser what to do.
● HTML attributes allow authors to change the color of text; change the alignment of text, paragraphs, and images; change the background color; and insert an image in the background of the page.
● Images must be identified by both filename and file location.

As a sophisticated web authoring tool, Dreamweaver 4 includes ways to address browser compatibility. These compatibility problems are discussed throughout this book, and you'll quickly come to appreciate the variety of ways in which Dreamweaver enables you to test your project.

Hint

To check for browser compatibility, you need to install at least the two most common browser programs—Netscape Navigator and Internet Explorer. They can be downloaded at www.netscape.com and www.microsoft.com, respectively.

What You See Is What You Get

After you understand the basics of what HTML does and how it interacts with your browser, it won't be nearly as intimidating. In fact, in the early days of the Internet, almost all web pages were created by hand—that is, raw code was written in its HTML text form. Many of these early pioneers taught themselves how to do their coding by carefully studying the code they saw on web pages and emulating (okay, sometimes copying) it. To this day, plenty of hard-core HTML junkies won't build their web pages any other way.

For the rest of us, those who see a huge page with streams of hard-to-follow commands and quickly feel overwhelmed, Dreamweaver offers the ability to design pages in a much friendlier environment, one that enables you to actually see what's going to be on your page as you work. Dreamweaver enables you to design in an almost real-time environment, and is the best software available for those who want to work in this what you see is what you get (WYSIWYG) mode. With Dreamweaver, you can apply elements to your pages, change the text size and style, insert images, and control the overall look of your pages without ever looking at HTML at all.

In addition, Dreamweaver provides clean, standards-driven, code that can easily be modified in its raw code directly within the program. Version 4 has even added the capability of viewing two simultaneous windows, displaying the design version of the page in one window, while the code itself is displayed (and automatically updated) in its pure form, as shown in Figure 1-4. Dreamweaver calls this "round-trip" HTML because page authors can switch seamlessly between a code view and a design view without worrying about the program creating code that is not compatible with current standards. This may not seem important to you right now, but at some point in the process of becoming an accomplished web author and site developer, you're going to want to have access to options that are more easily created and modified in "raw" HTML.

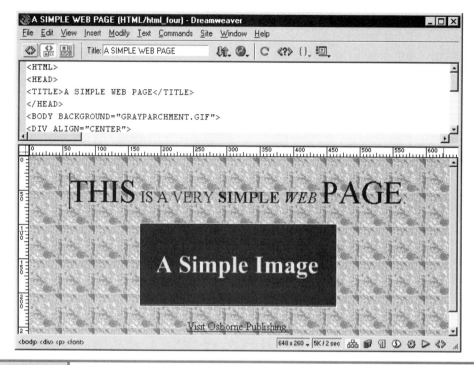

```
A SIMPLE WEB PAGE (HTML/html_four) - Dreamweaver                    _□×
File  Edit  View  Insert  Modify  Text  Commands  Site  Window  Help
◇ ◇ ⬚    Title: A SIMPLE WEB PAGE        ↕ ◉   C  ‹?›  {}  ▦
<HTML>
<HEAD>
<TITLE>A SIMPLE WEB PAGE</TITLE>
</HEAD>
<BODY BACKGROUND="GRAYPARCHMENT.GIF">
<DIV ALIGN="CENTER">
```

THIS IS A VERY SIMPLE *WEB* PAGE.

A Simple Image

Visit Osborne Publishing

`<body> <div> <p> <font>`   `648 x 260 ▾` `5K / 2 sec`

Figure 1-4   Dreamweaver's code view and design view of html_four.htm

For the new author, or even someone who has previously done their entire HTML coding by hand, Dreamweaver also provides some other useful coding help:

● Automatically corrects overlapping and redundant tags and attributes

● Highlights incorrect code and code that is not supported by current standards

● Includes a comprehensive reference for HTML, JavaScript, and cascading style sheets (CSS)

1-Minute Drill

● What organization maintains and establishes standards for HTML?

● Describe how browser compatibility issues can impact web design.

● The World Wide Web Consortium maintains and establishes the HTML standards.
● Tags and attributes can be read and interpreted (or not read at all) by different browsers or even different versions of the same browser.

Project 1-1: Viewing Source Code

Many web authors got their start in web design by doing something very simple—they looked at the code contained in other web pages through the View command in their browser. You can also learn a great deal about HTML and how tags and attributes are employed by examining the source code of web pages.

You'll start by looking at one of the world's most popular sites, Yahoo! (www.yahoo.com). Yahoo! is an example of an *Internet directory*—specially constructed web pages filled with links to other sites listed by category. You can almost think of it as Yellow Pages for the Web. This section looks at both the page itself and the underlying code.

Step-by-Step

1. Open Yahoo! in your browser and you'll see a very tightly organized page with a huge number of hyperlinks, shown in Figure 1-5.

2. Choose View | Page Source (Netscape) or Source (Internet Explorer), and you'll see the HTML code for that page, as shown in Figure 1-6.

3. Now identify some of the tags you see:

- What tag do you find most often on this page?
- What is the page title?
- Does the page use tables to lay out its content? What tells the browser to develop the tables?
- Do you see any tags you don't recognize?

Note

Yahoo! uses a number of special HTML tags called cascading style sheets. These special formatting tags will be discussed in Module 8.

4. Next, visit a few of the following web sites:
 www.osborne.com
 www.nbci.com
 www.microsoft.com
 www.apple.com
 www.zdnet.com
On each of the sites, do the following:

  a. Locate the code for an image that is on the page. What is the name of the image? Is the image in the same folder as the main page? If it's in another folder, can you identify the name of the folder that holds it?

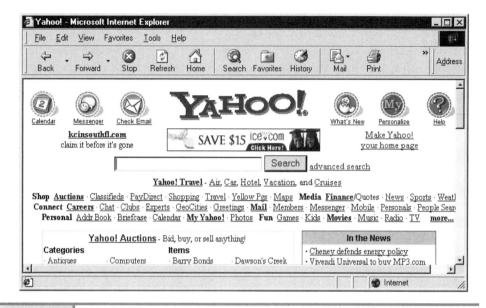

Figure 1-5 Yahoo! is one of the world's most visited web sites

    b. Try and locate special text attributes on the page. Do you find instances of the bold or italic tags? How about tags for text color?

    c. Notice how tables are used in the construction of the page. Can you identify the attributes that define the table and its contents?

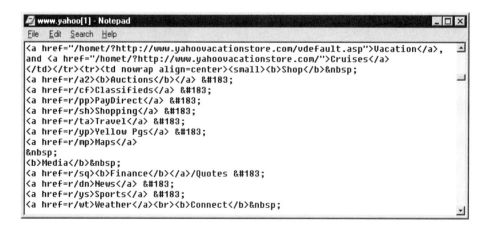

Figure 1-6 Viewing the code for the Yahoo! home page

d. Look for tags and attributes listed on these pages that haven't been discussed yet. Can you tell what they do?

e. Look for a tag that is formatted like this: <!--some text in here-->. What do you think the purpose is of this kind of tag?

f. Look at the exact same web site using both Internet Explorer and Netscape Navigator. Do you see any difference in how the two browsers display the page you're viewing?

What to Take Away

Understanding HTML and how web pages are created is not an overwhelming chore. Just like with any craft, designing web pages requires patience and lots of practice. If you're willing to put the time into learning the software, and then practice your skills using the projects in this book, you'll find that within a very short time, you will be confidently building web pages and assembling them into well-defined web sites. It's going to be a lot of fun—and you'll get started in the next chapter by looking at web site planning and how you use Dreamweaver to build your site from the ground up.

Mastery Check

1. What is the term to describe a web page's address on the Internet?

2. Every web page begins and ends with what tag?

3. What is the function of this tag: <a href="http://www.osborne.com">?

4. What is the term used by Dreamweaver to describe its standards-based HTML code?

5. What is the difference between a relative link and an absolute link?

Module 2

Planning and Organizing Your Web Site

The Goals of this Module

- Identify the audience for your web site
- Plan site content for your audience
- Create a site plan
- Create a site structure
- Understand the importance of good site management
- Understand and use site management features in Dreamweaver

Module 1 described how the Internet works and introduced some of the basic terms that you'll be seeing throughout this book. It also noted that designing good web pages is a craft that takes patience, planning, and lots of practice to make everything work the way you want.

If you think a little about some of the craftspeople that you may have seen at work you'll realize that advanced planning is a big part of their success. Let's face it, you wouldn't want to buy a house from a contractor who told you that he'd just "wing it" when it came to planning and building your new home. Or, imagine how you'd feel if the builder only wanted to talk about all the cool new tools he has in his truck and how he is going to put those tools to work for you. And yet, you've probably seen web sites that take both of those approaches. It's evident when the designer has decided to wing it when we find pages or sites that are poorly organized and have no logical flow to them. You've seen what happens when the focus is on the tools and technology instead of the content if you've ever been to a site that has practically every possible Java applet and JavaScript effect, and lots of fancy animations and sounds, but no real content.

A successful web site has many of the same attributes as a well constructed home. Just as a home-builder needs to be thoroughly familiar with the house plans before the first shovel of dirt is ever turned over, you will need a plan for your site before you begin building it. If you don't plan for who you want to reach, what kind of experience they'll find at your site, and how your site will be put together, more than likely, you'll have, at best, a site that is not as successful as you want it to be, and, at worst, an unmanageable mess.

Luckily, Dreamweaver makes the chore of managing your site much easier and provides powerful tools for you to make the inevitable additions and revisions easier as your site grows and changes. Without a solid foundation and good planning, though, even the best software won't be able to overcome poor decisions made at the outset of your project. Your first chore, then, is to come up with a rock-solid plan for your site.

Planning Your Site from the Ground Up

Probably the most useful tool at your disposal at this point in your site creation is a simple piece of paper and something to write with. You need to give some serious thought to exactly what it is you want to create before you ever make your first HTML document. Taking notes and making early sketches of what you want to accomplish is an important element of your early site design.

2

Identify the Target Audience

As I just noted, every good craftsperson develops a plan before they start building something. If they're building homes, they research the market and decide which type of home to build. Are simple suburban ranch style homes in demand in their area or are people more interested in nice big colonial style homes? Even if the builder's personal preference is to build huge mansions or gleaming ultra-modern homes in chrome and steel, if those homes aren't selling then the builder won't have a very long career. Likewise, you need to look at your target audience before you start laying down that first line of code if you want to develop a successful web site.

Understanding your target audience has far-reaching implications. Imagine if only one style of web pages was allowed on the Internet and the style happened to be based on a page developed for people who enjoy making quilts. Now, making quilts is a fine hobby, but if your passion happens to be hardcore skateboarding, you'll probably be turned off by a web site that features a style that holds no appeal for you. Your first goal in designing your page, then, is to answer these two questions:

- Who exactly do you want to attract to your site?

- What do you want them to find when they get there?

The answers to those two questions determine not only the style of your pages but also the organization. Deciding up front who you want to reach enables you to focus your efforts on designing pages for them, and keeps you from wandering off on tangents that have nothing to do with your primary goals. Designing pages that have appropriate content for your audience ensures that those people will come back to your site.

Primary goal? Yes, you do need a goal for your site. You not only need to understand who you're writing for, but also have to know what you want your audience to do when they find you. Using the quilting site again as an example, if you were designing a site for quilting enthusiasts to send in pictures of their favorite quilts, it would be much different than a site designed to sell quilting supplies to the same people. The target audience is the same, but the goal of the site is very different. Knowing what the viewer will do at your site is an extremely important element of site planning.

Consider a few examples of how well-organized sites can be developed. First, imagine that a local homebuilder in your area has decided that she wants to expand her advertising reach by building a web site to feature examples of work her company has done and to give potential customers information on how to contact her about projects they're considering. Table 2-1 shows a simple planning guide that will help you focus on the most important things you need to know about developing your site.

Tip

You can find a blank copy of this planning guide (planning_guide.pdf) in the Module 2 files at www.osborne.com.

That all seems pretty simple, right? You first decide who it is you want to develop your site for, and then begin planning how you will reach them. You can probably see some of the implications for this site based on your initial planning, and others are discussed as you move through this module.

The next example is a site that will be designed for a local skateboarding retailer. The people who own RadSkateboarding, Inc. want to expand their offerings to the public. They not only want to provide information about their retail store, but also want to be able to sell supplies, clothing, and all things

Task	Conclusion
Define Your Audience	
Describe your target audience.	Home owners in the geographic area served by All Thumbs Construction.
How proficient is your target audience at using the Internet?	Varies from novice to expert users.
What kind of computer and browser will your target audience use?	Varies. Viewers may use computers at home or work to do research, so plan for a wide variety of systems.
Will the audience's age, gender, education, income, or location affect the site design? If so, describe how.	Homeowners are adults. Gender and education have no impact on site design. The site is for a local company.
Define Your Goals	
How will your audience find your site?	From Internet searches and links on local city-information sites.
What services will you offer at your site?	Information Company phone number and contact names Types of services offered References Project portfolio
What will make your site different from others that serve the same audience?	Web site is for a specific company—All Thumbs Construction.

Table 2-1   Planning Guide for All Thumbs Construction

associated with radical skateboarding on their web site. For this site, your planning guide (shown in Table 2-2) looks much different.

Task	Conclusion
Define Your Audience	
Describe your target audience.	Skateboarding enthusiasts.
How proficient is your audience at using the Internet?	Probably quite proficient. Most skateboarders are young males who also are likely to have lots of experience on the Web.
What kind of computer and browser will your audience use?	You can safely assume that most members of your audience have newer computers, have all the current plug-ins installed, or are willing to upgrade to see all of your content.
Will the audience's age, gender, education, income, or location affect the site design? If so, describe how.	Skateboarders tend to be young males between the ages of 10 and 25 and may be located worldwide. Your site will need to have the latest technology available to satisfy your audience.
Define Your Goals	
How will your audience find your site?	From Internet searches, through referrals from fellow skateboarders, and through advertising in skateboarding magazines.
What services will you offer at your site?	Types of services offered: INFORMATION 　　Magazine-style feature articles 　　Product reviews 　　Buyer's guides 　　How-to section for skateboard tricks 　　News about skateboard competitions SALES 　　New products 　　Replacement parts 　　Clothing 　　Videos INTERACTION 　　Chat room 　　Message boards 　　"Ask the Expert" section
What will make your site different from others that serve the same audience?	Feature articles by some of the sport's leading authorities. Provide a style that matches the enthusiasm of the audience. Build on the client's long history in retail skateboarding.

Table 2-2   Planning Guide for RadSkateboarding.com

Hint

One good way to get a feel for your potential audience is to create fictional viewers, in different categories, who might visit your site. You can even give them names like "Betty Beginner," "Irving Intermediate," and "Paula Powersurfer." Then think about how the experience and expectations for Betty, Irving, and Paula will impact your site and page design.

A different audience with a different set of goals for the site produces some very different results from your first example, doesn't it? Take a look at Table 2-3 for one more example.

The final example is a site for the Chamber of Commerce of the fictional town of Poinciana Beach, Florida. (You'll be visiting Poinciana Beach repeatedly throughout this book, because you'll be using this site as a common example in all of your projects.)

Three different audiences dictate three very different web sites. You can see that knowing your target audience and knowing what you want them to do once they find you on the Internet has a profound impact on how your site is constructed.

Task	Conclusion
Define Your Audience	
Describe your target audience.	People interested in visiting or moving to Poinciana Beach. Businesses interested in more information about the business climate of Poinciana Beach. Current Chamber of Commerce members who wish to use the site for advertising.
How proficient is your audience at using the Internet?	Varies widely.
What kind of computer and browser will your audience use?	Varies widely.
Will the audience's age, gender, education, income, or location affect the site design? If so, describe how.	Expect a wide range of visitors to the site, although most will be adults.
Define Your Goals	
How will your audience find your site?	From Internet searches and links in local city guides.

Table 2-3 Planning Guide for Poinciana Beach Chamber of Commerce Web Site

Task	Conclusion

What services will you offer at your site?	Types of services offered:
	INFORMATION FOR VISITORS
	    Recreation
	    Entertainment
	    Shopping
	    Weather and climate
	INFORMATION FOR RESIDENTS
	    Government
	    Schools
	    Housing
	INFORMATION FOR BUSINESSES
	    Business climate
	    Business regulations
	    Local economics
	    Community Events
	    Chamber of Commerce members

What will make your site different from others that serve the same audience?	Designed specifically for those who want to visit, live, or do business in Poinciana Beach, Florida.

Table 2-3   Planning Guide for Poinciana Beach Chamber of Commerce Web Site *(continued)*

Hint

Researching what's available on the Internet can give you some great ideas for planning your site. Look at other sites that appeal to the same target audience. Can you tell right away who the site is designed for? Is there an easy-to-follow structure? Can you navigate easily? Do they include topics similar to those you intend to include? Do they leave anything out? Do they include things that aren't necessary?

Planning Site Content

In this section, you'll do a little more planning and focus in on the content of your pages, as well as the overall site structure. You will be more successful in designing your pages such that viewers will be attracted to them (and return in the future) if you can answer these questions:

- Who is your audience?
  - What would cause your audience to want to find and visit your web site?
  - What kinds of content will you provide that will bring your audience back or bring in new viewers?

- What is the age, gender, and location of your audience?
  - Are you designing for a general audience or do you have a tightly focused group in terms of age and gender?
  - If your audience is generally the same, how can you target content that they will find appealing?
- How experienced is your audience at using the Internet?
  - Should your content be simple and straightforward or can you experiment with newer technologies?
  - Should your site navigation be kept simple or are your viewers experienced enough to search for information within your site?
- What kind of computer is your audience likely to have?
  - Will the audience have the latest browsers and all the plug-ins needed to view your content?
  - Will the audience use other means of accessing your site (such as WebTV, AOL browser, text-only browsers)?
  - Will your audience be viewing from only one platform (for example, Windows, Macintosh, or Linux) or will the platform vary?

Hint

I always like to think of my audience as my clients. Not only is that technically correct, as you'll see in the discussion of client-side server programs such as JavaScript, but it also serves as a reminder that web pages and web sites are designed for the viewer, not the programmer.

1-Minute Drill

- What two questions do you need to answer at the outset of planning your site?
- How does the audience's experience in using the Internet influence site and page design?

Creating a Site Map

Good site structure is important not only because it will make your job as a developer easier, but also because it's absolutely essential to the proper operation

---

- Who exactly do you want to attract to your site? What do you want them to find when they get there?
- Inexperienced users appreciate a simple-to-follow site and page structure. More experienced users can be expected to have the latest browsers installed and will expect to find more advanced features on your site.

Ask the Expert

Question: I just want to build web pages. Is all this planning really necessary?

Answer: Building real web sites does require planning. You can certainly dive right in and build some simple pages if you want to. (I recommend Netscape Composer if all you want to do is get the "feel" of putting a page together.) If you want to build a web *site*, though, you need more powerful tools, such as Dreamweaver, and you absolutely must have a plan in mind before you start. I understand that it's much more fun to start building pages immediately and leave all the drudgery of planning the site until later. But I've also learned from my mistakes, and you can believe me when I say that your life as a web site developer will be much easier if you start with a good plan. Going back later and "fixing" the structure of your site or even the layout of your pages can be a time-consuming and frustrating experience. Better to get it right from the start!

of your site and pages. Module 1 explained that the HTML code for a graphic includes both the filename and the file location. You have to know where your files are at all times so that you can properly link to them and so that they'll load correctly when viewed live on the Internet. As previously noted, Dreamweaver has some great tools to make this easier for you, but you still need to define the basic structure of your site before you move on.

Returning to the Poinciana Beach example, here are the services that you want to offer at the site (and a few that have been added):

Information for Visitors

- Recreation
- Entertainment
- Shopping
- Weather and climate

Information for Residents

- Government
- Schools

- Housing
- Churches

Information for Businesses

- Business climate
- Regulations
- Local economics
- Community events
- Community calendar
- Chamber of Commerce calendar
- Chamber membership
- Membership listing
- How to join the Chamber

If you were to map this out graphically and show the folders where the web pages for each topic area are located, it would look similar to Figure 2-1.

The more elaborate your planned site is, the more difficult site mapping becomes. Using sticky notes is a great way to plan your site structure, because you can simply move the notes around on a page until you get the structure you want.

Another great tool for planning is an inexpensive program called Inspiration (www.inspiration.com). Inspiration lets you enter text in an outline format, and then creates the graphic map for you. You can even drag and drop different elements around on the screen and have your outline updated automatically.

Understanding Paths and Site Structure

The term *path* refers to the precise location of a file on a computer—whether that file is located on your computer at home, work, or school, or on a server somewhere. Understanding this term is very important, because knowing the path to a file is a crucial element of site layout. Remember that your HTML code has to describe both the *what* of the file (its name) and the *where* (its location and the path to get to it). Understanding these requirements when naming files is another good reason to develop a solid plan for your site before you write any code.

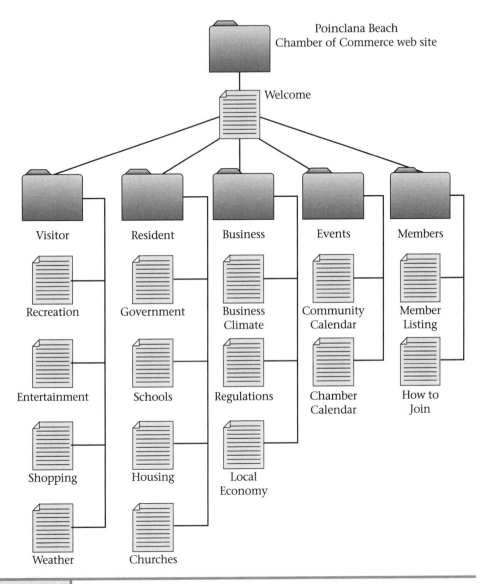

Poinclana Beach
Chamber of Commerce web site

Welcome

Visitor | Resident | Business | Events | Members

Recreation | Government | Business Climate | Community Calendar | Member Listing

Entertainment | Schools | Regulations | Chamber Calendar | How to Join

Shopping | Housing | Local Economy

Weather | Churches

Figure 2-1 The initial diagram for the Poinciana Beach Chamber of Commerce web site

An important element to discuss at this point is how computers respond to your folder names and filenames. If you've been using computers for very long, you likely remember the days when filenames were very restrictive. If, for instance, you wrote a story about a cat, you'd have to give the file a name with no more than eight characters before the dot, such as catstory.txt, and then hope that you could remember what you named the file when you wanted to find it later. Macintosh users, and now Windows users, have gotten used to longer names with few restrictions. Today, you could name your file "the calico cat in the tree.txt," for instance, and your computer would have no problem finding and reading the file.

Web servers are not so forgiving. At this point, you're a long way from posting your site to a server. However, you need to know that servers generally run either a Unix or Windows NT operating system, and without some forethought, your pages may fail to load correctly if the filenames you choose are not supported by the server software. If you think this sounds like another example where advanced planning eliminates problems later on, you're right! I've seen examples where my students have created wonderful, elaborate web pages with great-looking graphics that work perfectly on their computer, but once the files are loaded on the server, nothing seems to work right. After much digging and head scratching, we finally found the culprit—incorrectly named files and folders. You can avoid that by following some simple rules:

Folder Names

- Folder names should be kept as short as possible, and having no more than eight characters is a good rule to follow.

- Folder names should contain only letters or numbers. Spaces are not allowed.

- Folder names cannot contain special characters except the underline or hyphen symbols.

Filenames

- The filename for the first page in any web site is (almost) always index.htm.

- Filenames can be as long as necessary (up to 64 characters), but spaces should be avoided.

- In place of spaces, use the underscore or dash symbol.

- Only the underscore and dash characters are permitted. No other special characters may be used.

- Never start a filename with a number.

Hint

Although you can use both upper- and lowercase letters in your file and folder names, it's best to stick with all lowercase letters. This is another way to avoid unforeseen problems later on, such as the failure by some older versions of web browsers to properly read your files.

With those points in mind, you now can clean up your site map for Poinciana Beach and put the files and folders into their proper format, as shown in Figure 2-2.

In addition to changing the file and folder names, some additional folders in which to store your images have been added to the site. These subfolders will be located in the main folder for each section of your site, making it easier to find those files and properly link to them.

Of course, this style and format is not the only way that your site can be organized. Remember that site structure and organization are dependent first and foremost on the target audience and the goals for the site. Project 2-1 will give you an opportunity to think about some different kinds of sites you might potentially develop and let you map them out on your own.

1-Minute Drill

- What two items of information are required for a graphic file to be displayed properly in a web page?
- What two special characters are permitted when naming files?
- Why should spaces in filenames be avoided?

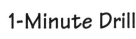

Project 2-1: Defining a Web Site from the Ground Up

In this section, you've taken a look at several different web sites and read how both the structure and content should be tailored for your intended audience. You've also seen that with a good understanding of what your site's goals are, you can create a structure for your site before you've ever written the first line of HTML code. You're going to put that information to use now as you map out an imaginary web site.

- Both the filename and the path to the file location must be included for a graphic file to be displayed properly in a web page.
- The underline and dash symbols are permitted in filenames.
- Spaces in filenames may cause errors when the file is posted to a server.

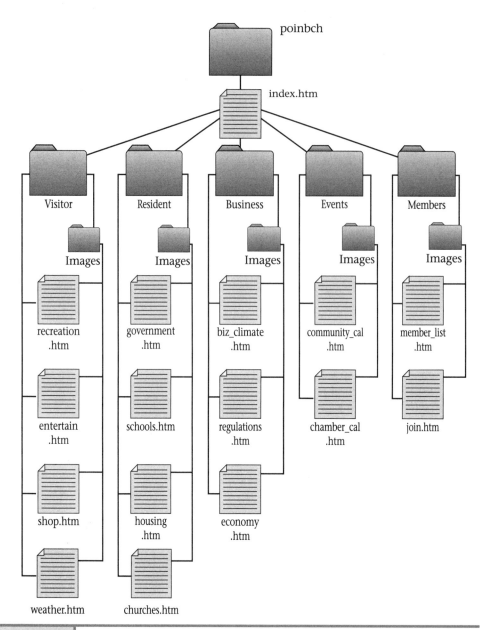

Figure 2-2 Revised web site map for Poinciana Beach Chamber of Commerce

Creating a personal web site can be lots of fun, but to get a feel for what professional site developers go through, you need to approach this project from the standpoint of someone developing a site for a business or nonprofit group. Choose a group from the following list or, if you already have a project in mind, use the site that you ultimately hope to develop.

Suggested Sites to Develop:

- A local nonprofit or civic group that you are familiar with

- Your school or one of your children's schools

- A local service company such as an air conditioning, plumbing, or electrical contractor

- A company that provides products or services for one of your hobbies

- A company that you invent that will provide a completely new service

Step-by-Step

1. Before you can fill out the planning guide for your site, you need to gather information and do research. If this is a real group that you hope to work with, spend some time talking to members of the organization so you can get a feel for what they hope to accomplish by publishing their site to the Web. Do they have any specific goals in mind that will affect how the site is organized or how the content is developed?

2. Research what is included on the pages of sites similar to the one you're developing. Be sure to visit a number of web sites so that you can get a comprehensive look at the types of information provided, the way the sites are organized, and common features.

3. Print a copy of planning_guide.pdf from the resources at www.osborne.com for this book. Work through the questions contained in the Planning Guide and fill in the results that you get from your study of the intended audience and goals for your site.

4. Draw your initial site diagram. Don't worry about filenames at this point—just focus on how your site will break up into its different components and how you'll link from your main page to those components. Use Figure 2-1 as a guide.

Adjust your site map so that folder and filenames are correct, and include subfolders where necessary. Use Figure 2-2 as a guide for your final site map.

Planning for your site may not be the most interesting part of web design. It is an essential element, though, and one that you'll come to appreciate after your site grows to hundreds or even thousands of files! By focusing at the beginning on exactly what you want to say and who you want to say it to, you create a much more structured and easy-to-manage web site.

You'll also find that to get the maximum value out of the projects and exercises in the rest of this book, developing this initial site should be something that you commit some time and thought to. You'll be returning repeatedly to this initial site as you work through the modules. The better your work is here, the better you'll be able to understand succeeding projects, and the more you'll ultimately learn!

How Dreamweaver Handles Site Management

As mentioned throughout the first part of this module, Dreamweaver puts some great tools at your disposal that make the process of managing the files on your site much easier. In fact, as you first start using Dreamweaver, you may feel that the program places an unnecessary importance on the idea of file and site management. Don't be tempted to get around the site management features, though. They are an integral part of the job that Dreamweaver does in making the chore of managing your web site easier. This section starts by looking at how Dreamweaver helps you to define your site and how those site management features can be used to their full advantage.

Getting to the Root of Your Web Site

To begin any project in Dreamweaver, you must first define the folder on your computer that will be known as the *root folder*. This is the primary storage location for all the files associated with the web site you are building, and all other folders are subservient to that main folder. Think of the root folder as the roots on a tree, the central location from which the trunk and all the branches stem, and you'll understand the root folder's function.

If you use your folders and files from the example in Figure 2-2, your root folder and the structure of the folders in it look like Figure 2-3.

Notice that, even at this early stage, you've designated a file to be the main page for your site—index.htm. Dreamweaver not only needs to know the root folder of the site itself, it also needs a file labeled index.htm in order for some of the advanced site management features to be available. This doesn't mean that you have to build that page first; it just means you'll need to at least create a blank document with the filename index.htm or Dreamweaver will continue to remind you that this file needs to exist.

2

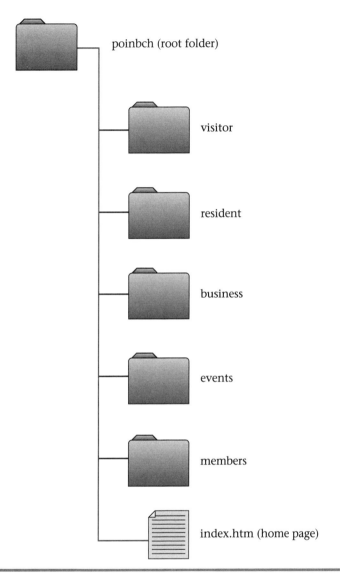

Figure 2-3 The initial structure for the Poinciana Beach Chamber of Commerce web site

Hint

Dreamweaver makes no distinctions between a web site that is stored on your own computer and one that is already loaded on a server and live on the Internet. Any collection of HTML documents and all of their supporting files is considered a web site.

Project 2-2: Defining Sites in Dreamweaver

In this section, you're going to work through the process of creating a site structure for your Poinciana Beach web site. At the end of this section, you'll understand how to designate a root folder, how to add subfolders, and how the site structure can be viewed and modified using Dreamweaver's site management features.

Step-by-Step

1. Dreamweaver handles most of the work of helping you to create and define your site, but it cannot create the root folder. To do this, find a convenient spot on your hard drive and create a new folder called poinbch.

Hint

I like to keep sample and exercise files on my desktop. Creating new folders is easier this way, and it's a simple job to get back to something I'm working on.

2. Open Dreamweaver and press the F8 key to open the Site window. (If this is the first time you've used Dreamweaver, you may get a message that says the root folder is not defined. Don't worry. Just click OK.)

3. In the Site window, select Define Sites in the Site drop-down list box to open the Site Definition dialog box. (If you've already used Dreamweaver, simply select New.)

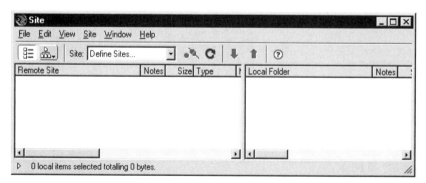

4. In the Site Definition dialog box, give Dreamweaver some basic information so that you can get started. Be sure that the category Local Info is selected, as shown in Figure 2-4.

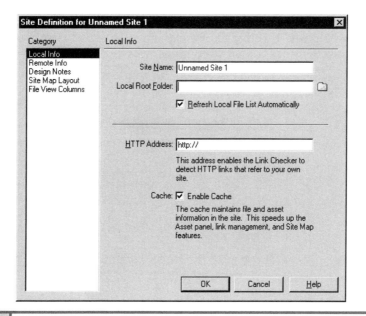

2

Figure 2-4   The Site Definition dialog box for a new web site

Note

In addition to defining your site locally, this is the dialog box that you'll return to in Module 20 when you're ready to upload your files to a server.

5. Give your site a name. Consider this your project name for this site. Since it isn't something that will be posted on the Internet, you can name it as you like. Select inside the Site Name box and type **Poinciana Beach CofC**.

6. To associate the name of the site you're creating to the root folder where it will reside, you need to let Dreamweaver know the location of that all-important folder. Click the small folder icon to the right of the Local Root Folder box and you'll be able to browse to the poinbch folder that you created in step 1. Double-click the poinbch folder and then choose Select. When you're finished, the name of the folder on your hard drive, as well as its path, will be displayed in the Local Root Folder box of the main Site window.

7. Be sure that the two check boxes in the Site Definition dialog box (Refresh Local File List Automatically and Enable Cache) are checked. This allows Dreamweaver to automate some of the site management tasks you're facing, and makes your life that much easier. Click OK to let Dreamweaver know that you're finished defining this first site.

8. You may receive a notification at this point that says "The initial cache site will now be created. This scans the files in your site and starts tracking links as you save them." Click OK to continue.

9. Dreamweaver now displays the Define Sites dialog box. Click Done, because you're not going to be working on any other sites at this time.

Hint

Now that you've defined your first site in Dreamweaver, the preceding Define Sites dialog box is the one you'll see every time you want to make a change to a site or add a new one. If you want to maintain a folder so that you have a place to try out new skills or just play around with sample files, you can create a folder called Practice and then define a new site called Practice Files. Gaining access to the Define Sites dialog box is as simple as choosing Define Sites from the main Site window (as you did in step 3) and choosing the name of the site you want to work on.

You can consider the preceding steps to be basic housekeeping for your web site. As you become more accustomed to using Dreamweaver, you'll find yourself returning to this site definition process again and again to add, edit, and even delete sites that you've created.

Project 2-3: Creating a Site Structure

Your next task is to duplicate the folder structure for your web site that you mapped out in the first section of this module. Dreamweaver lets you create new folders and files directly within the main Site window, which enables you to work much more efficiently. Review the site structure you defined earlier in Figure 2-2. You'll next work step by step to create that identical structure using Dreamweaver.

2

Step-by-Step

1. In the main site window, you see that the Poinciana Beach CofC web site consists of only one folder—the root folder. Dreamweaver provides the folder name and the path to the folder (your path will probably be different from the example), as well as its type (folder) and the date it was last modified.

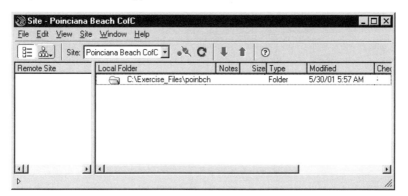

—|Note

Be sure the Site Files button is selected—it's just below the File menu in the menu bar.

2. Add a subfolder to the root folder by right-clicking the folder icon and choosing New Folder, or clicking File | New Folder. An unnamed folder appears, and a line is drawn to indicate that it is a subfolder of the root. Name this new folder Visitor.

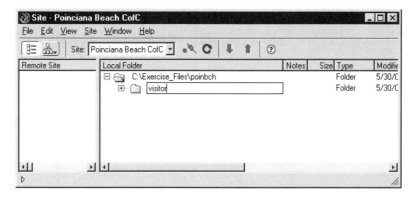

3. To add the other folders for your site, repeat the process outlined in step 2 and create the following folders: Resident, Business, Events, and Members. When you're finished, your budding web site should look like this:

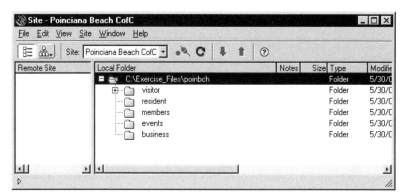

Tip

Clicking the Local Folder bar, just above your root folder, puts your folders in alphabetical order.

4. Your next task is to add the images subfolder to each of the folders you created in step 3. The process is identical to the one outlined in the preceding steps. Right-click the folder you want to add the images subfolder to and then choose New Folder (or select the folder by clicking its icon and then choose File | New Folder). Create a new folder named Images in each of the five folders you just created. When you're finished, the folders on your site will look like this and will be ready for you to start adding files to them.

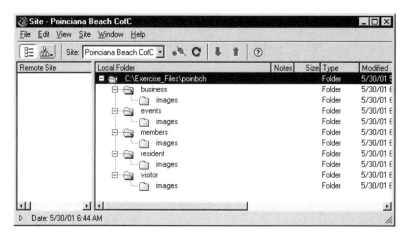

2

Ask the Expert

Question: Do I really need all of those images subfolders?

Answer: The structure of your site is always determined by your site goals and how you intend to reach your target audience. However, as you'll soon see, adding and updating images to your site is something that will be a part of almost any site you build. You've already mapped out 16 web pages for this site, and if each page contains only 4 images, you've committed yourself to having 64 image files for this site alone. Managing all of those images, and other files that will support your site, can quickly become a very big job. Starting out with a good plan for storing and organizing your files will only make your work that much easier when, instead of 64 images, you have hundreds or even thousands of images.

5. Your last task is to create the all-important index file that serves as the main starting point for your site. The process is identical to creating a folder. Right-click the root folder and choose New File (or select the root folder and choose File I New File). By default, Dreamweaver assumes that the file is an HTML file, but to lock in that option, you must type in the correct file extension. Type **index.htm** in the File Name box, and you're done.

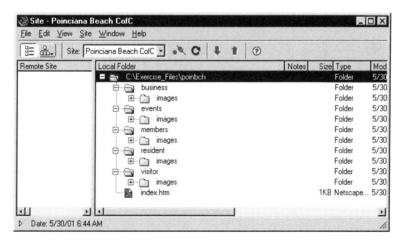

+Note

Always type the full file extension—the three-letter file designation after the "dot"— when naming files. Since Dreamweaver will track all the files that are in your site, providing the file extension as well as the filename ensures that your files will be associated properly.

Congratulations! You have now successfully created all the structure you need for your very first web site.

1-Minute Drill

- What is the name of the folder that you must create on your hard drive before you can define the site?

- How are new folders created in Dreamweaver's Site window?

- Why is adding subfolders to hold images a good idea when planning a new site?

Project 2-4: Creating a New Web Site Structure from Scratch

In Project 2-1, you had the opportunity to research and plan for a new web site of your own. In this project, you'll take that information and build the site structure for your site using Dreamweaver's site management features.

Step-by-Step

1. Review the information you mapped out in Project 2-1. Knowing what you know now about how Dreamweaver defines sites, you should be able to get a clear idea of the structure of your site.

2. Create a new folder on your computer's hard drive, being sure to follow the rules for naming folders discussed in the first part of this module.

3. In Dreamweaver's Site window, click the Site drop-down arrow and select Define Sites.

4. In the Define Sites dialog box, select New to open the Site Definition dialog box.

- You must create the root folder on your hard drive before you can define the site.
- To create a new folder in the Site window, right-click the folder in the Site View window and select New Folder (or choose File | New Folder).
- Creating separate subfolders for images allows for better organization of the site and makes it easier to create the necessary links to the images.

5. Just as you did earlier, give your web site a project name in the Site Name box and click the folder icon next to the Local Root Folder box. Browse to the folder you created in step 2.

6. Click OK and then click Done to return to the main Site window.

7. Review the site structure that you defined for your site in Project 2-1 and add those folders necessary to support your site. Don't forget to add subfolders for your images!

8. Add the index.htm file that every web site needs in the main root folder. Your final site structure should be similar to the one you created for the Poinciana Beach Chamber of Commerce.

You should have an appreciation at this point for how the process of mapping out site structure is done and how you can duplicate that structure for all of your sites. Dreamweaver provides a very easy-to-use interface to get all of this preliminary work done, and, as you'll see as you move through the remainder of your projects, each step along the way is made easier by the software's powerful features.

What to Take Away

By using the advanced layout and site definition features found in Dreamweaver, you have designated the root folder for all of your folders and files, created subfolders to hold the HTML files that you'll create, and even done some advanced planning by creating subfolders to hold your images—a pretty good day's work!

In Module 3, you'll begin looking at how those HTML files will be created using the features found in Dreamweaver's Document window.

✓ Mastery Check

1. What two questions must be answered at the outset of site planning?

2. How might the age of your intended audience affect your site design?

3. Define the term "root folder."

4. Which dialog box in Dreamweaver is used to add, modify, and delete web sites?

5. What is the name of the HTML file that every web site needs?

Module 3

Understanding the Dreamweaver Interface

The Goals of this Module

- Understand the Dreamweaver interface
- Understand the function of the Properties Inspector
- Learn how the Objects panel is used to insert objects into web pages
- Investigate options for changing the work area
- Identify the major components of the menu bar

It may seem strange that you have yet to take a look at how Dreamweaver creates web pages in the previous discussions of the software. Instead, you've spent your time learning Internet fundamentals, gaining an understanding of HTML, and even planning your first web site—all without spending any time actually working on your first web page.

As previously discussed, though, all of this groundwork will go a long way toward making you a better web designer. Now that you have the basics under your belt, you will begin looking at the Dreamweaver interface. This module spends some time acquainting you with the program's interface—the way that Dreamweaver lets you get your work done.

If you have already taken your own self-guided tour of Dreamweaver, you've probably realized that it doesn't look like any other program you've used in the past. In fact, opening Dreamweaver for the first time can be a little intimidating. Instead of seeing familiar interface elements such as toolbars and button icons across the top of the screen, you see that Dreamweaver uses a different approach to putting its tools at your disposal. You don't need to feel intimidated, though—you just need to spend some time with the program to see that these powerful features, and their great variety, require an interface that gives you maximum flexibility in creating the clean HTML that is the hallmark of Dreamweaver. In fact, the designers at Macromedia have done a fabulous job of packaging all the capabilities in a form that is easy to follow, gives the designer a great deal of latitude, and can be modified as your skills in using the program grow. And, as with everything you have done so far, each new element that is introduced has a practical exercise to accompany it, so you'll have plenty of time to get comfortable with using the program as you move along.

The Document Window

If you have not done so already, go ahead and open Dreamweaver. By default, every time you open the program, Dreamweaver opens a new untitled document and returns you to the last site that you were working on. If you're still working from the exercises in Module 2, you can create a new document by choosing File | New Window.

Figure 3-1 shows how the Document window appears the first time you open the program. Some of the major components that you see on the screen are discussed generally next, before you learn the details of each element.

Menu bar   **Properties Inspector**

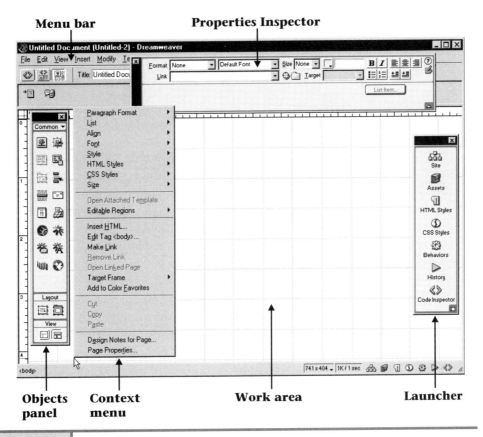

Objects   Context   Work area   Launcher
panel   menu

Figure 3-1   The Dreamweaver Document window

Dreamweaver uses a unique system of floating panels and inspectors that puts an incredible amount of the program's assets right at your fingertips. As pointed out in Figure 3-1, the major components of this unique system are the following:

- **Objects panel**   Used to insert different elements into your page

- **Properties Inspector**   Enables you to view and modify the attributes that have been assigned to different elements of a page

- **Launcher**   Enables you to access other important capabilities through additional panels and inspectors

- **Context menu**   Pops up when you right-click an object in the work area to give you easy access to dozens of commands and options

- **Menu bar**   Contains common commands for working with files, editing, inserting objects, and modifying elements of the document

The preceding tools, along with the work area itself, are the major components of Dreamweaver that you will use most often. Panels and inspectors can easily be moved, resized, hidden, and even modified to meet your own particular work style. Dreamweaver makes it easy for everyone—from the beginner to the most experienced web author—to work in an environment that suits his or her needs.

Try moving the panels around on your screen now. Just place your pointer over the active title bar (in blue) in each panel and then click and drag the panel around your screen. Panels and inspectors can also be closed by clicking the Close button (the × button) in the title bar area. To open a panel, select Window in the menu bar and choose the panel you want to open by name.

Close button

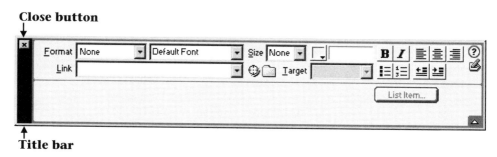

Title bar

For now, you're going to hide all the panels so that you can concentrate on the work area itself and discover some of the key features you need to be familiar with. To hide all panels, choose Window | Hide Panels or View | Hide Panels, which results in a nice clean work area, as shown in Figure 3-2. The tour begins in the upper-left corner of the work area and moves clockwise around the screen.

Toolbar

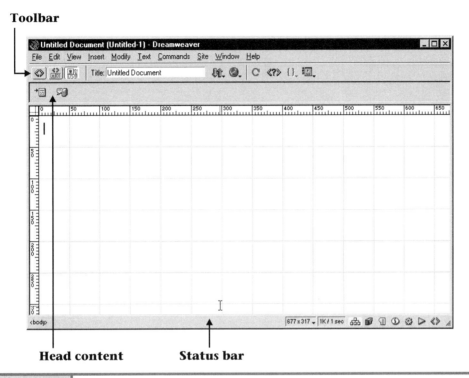

Head content   **Status bar**

Figure 3-2   The Dreamweaver work area

The Head Content Bar

In Module 1, you saw how HTML code always includes a tag called head
(<head>). Dreamweaver uses the Head Content bar as a place for designers to
quickly see what head content has been included in the page. In addition to the
actual title of the page itself, <head> tags can also enclose other specialized
information, such as metatags (used for inserting items such as keywords and
site descriptions) and even automatic coding that is activated when the page is
opened. In a new document such as the one you're looking at, only the title and

a simple metatag that identifies the HTML specifications used in designing the page are inserted; therefore, only the icons representing those two items are shown.

Title information

Metatags

Every time additional head content is inserted in the page, a new icon appears in this area. As with most of the visual aids and panels in Dreamweaver, if having access to the information contained in the head of the document is not important to you, you can easily hide individual items or the entire Head Content bar. Simply select View | Head Content and select or deselect the item to turn that option on or off.

The Toolbar

Dreamweaver provides easy access to a number of common tasks for developers via a series of buttons in the toolbar area just above the Head Content bar.

Code View **Refresh Design View**

Code and Design View **Preview in Browser** **Reference** **View Options**

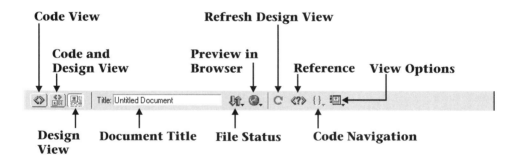

Design View **Document Title** **File Status** **Code Navigation**

You could almost think of this area as an extension of the View commands available from the menu bar, because most of the tools available in this area are used to change the view of your page—without actually changing the content of what is in the page itself. The Code View, Design View, and Code and Design

View buttons on the far left of the toolbar, for instance, change the view of the coding that is generated for the page you're working on. To see just the raw HTML for the page click the Code button. Choosing the Code and Design View button creates a split screen that lets a designer work simultaneously on the source code or the layout versions of the same document. Finally, clicking the Design View button returns you to a full screen layout version of the page.

Tip

Try clicking the three different view buttons. Notice that even in a "blank" document, Dreamweaver has already generated the basic code required for the page to work—just as you saw in Module 1.

The Document Title area is self-explanatory; in your new, untitled document, you see that the title of the page is "Untitled Document." In the Dreamweaver window Document Title is capitalized as a label for the area where the information is entered. Recall that document titles are important because they contain important information needed by the web search engines that many users of the Internet depend on to find information. These search engines often use document titles as a way to find and index sites, so failing to include a title may mean that your page is seen by far fewer people than otherwise would have seen it had you included a title. In addition, history and bookmark files list pages by their title, and a page listed as "Untitled Document" will be meaningless to your audience.

To give this document a title, simply click within the Title window and type **My First Dreamweaver Page**. Click the Code View button and you'll see that the title you just created has been inserted into the HTML for the page.

Clicking the File Status icon opens options for file and site management and gives you some handy shortcuts for posting your new creation to the server on which your site is stored. In addition, you can add notes about the page itself that can be shared with others who might be working on your web site with you. Some of these options are discussed further in Modules 9 and 20.

Recall from previous discussions of HTML that one of the considerations for web developers is that not all browsers have the same capabilities for reading code. You also know that one of the challenges of web page design is that you have no control over which browser the members of your intended audience will be using. Being able to see what your page looks like in a real-world situation— in the actual browser itself—is easily accomplished by clicking the Preview In Browser button.

Clicking the Refresh Design View icon enables you to do the same thing that you may be used to doing when viewing pages online—reload the page while in the Design View.

As you read through Module 1, you may have wondered "How am I ever going to remember all of this information about different tags and attributes and other HTML details?" Clicking the Reference button on the toolbar provides a complete library of information on not only HTML but advanced features of JavaScript and cascading style sheets (CSS) as well. To see the library in action, switch to Code View and select any of the tags or attributes in the page. Click the Reference button, and a very comprehensive description of the HTML element, its use, and how it is formatted appears in a pop-up window.

The Code Navigation button enables designers to run any JavaScript code contained in the program and search for common problems that may require debugging. Although coding JavaScript itself is beyond the scope of this book, you will find out how to add dynamic elements to your pages in the form of rollover buttons and other effects in later modules. Luckily, the JavaScript for these effects is created by Dreamweaver (and Fireworks) for you.

Finally, the View Options button lets you change how different elements of your Document window are viewed. Just as you learned before, you can turn off certain elements, such as the rulers, layout grid, and Head Content bar, by selecting or deselecting them via the Options button.

Note

Both the Refresh Design View and the Code Navigation buttons are grayed out (unavailable) in your blank document. As you add content that is affected by these two buttons, they will become active.

The Status Bar

At the bottom of the screen is the status bar, from which you can access some very important tools as you design your pages. Again, the software developers at Macromedia have done a great job choosing which elements you need quick access to, and have included them in a format that makes them easy to use.

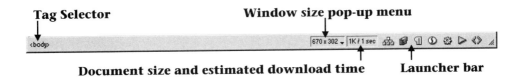

Tag Selector   **Window size pop-up menu**

Document size and estimated download time   **Launcher bar**

On the far left is the Tag Selector. As the name implies, this handy feature enables you to click directly on top of the name of a tag or attribute to view, change, modify, or delete it. By using the Tag Selector, you have code-level control of your document, even while working in the Design view window. While this may not seem essential now, once you have developed a few complicated web pages with elements such as tables nested inside each other, you'll quickly come to appreciate the flexibility and control that you have over your document by selecting a tag directly by name. For now, you see that the only tag that's available is <body>. To try out this feature, go to the Head Content bar and click the Title button and you'll see that <title> appears in bold type in the Tag Selector. Now, switch to Code View and you'll see that the <title> tag and all of its contents are highlighted.

```
<title>My First Dreamweaver Page</title>
```

On the right side of the status bar, you see the window size pop-up menu. Take particular note of the little arrow near the bottom of this option. This expansion arrow is another common feature of the Dreamweaver interface that allows you to access additional settings by clicking it. Doing so now reveals a number of options that enable you to change the size of the Document window.

```
592w
536 x 196  (640 x 480, Default)
600 x 300  (640 x 480, Maximized)
760 x 420  (800 x 600, Maximized)
795 x 470  (832 x 624, Maximized)
955 x 600  (1024 x 768, Maximized)
544 x 378  (WebTV)

Edit Sizes...
```

Why would you change the size of your window anyway? Why not simply maximize the screen so that you have the greatest available workspace to do your designs in?

Again, designing for the Web is always about designing for your intended audience. For instance, as I write this text at home, I'm looking at my trusty 15-inch monitor. At work, though, I use a laptop computer for most of my design work. And when I'm working with my students, we use 17-inch monitors almost exclusively. All of those monitors feature different screen resolutions and have more (or less) actual screen size available. By having the option to change the size of your work area, you can be sure that the size of your page will work with the monitor that a viewer is using when they see it. As Module 2 stated, considering the type of computer system that will be used to view the page is an important part of site and page design. Dreamweaver lets you take that knowledge and apply it here by adjusting the size of the work area to match the size of the monitor that is most likely to be used by your audience. You can also customize the work area dimensions to fit a size not listed as browsers change their interfaces—as has already been done in Internet Explorer 5 for the Mac and Netscape 6.

In addition to designing for particular monitor sizes, you also know that your viewers may use a variety of modems to download your pages—from slower 28.8 Kbps modems to the newer ultrafast broadband connections. As you're working, Dreamweaver keeps you updated regarding the size of your file and the estimated time it will take for the viewer to download it based on a particular connection speed. By default, the connection speed is set to 28.8 Kbps. In a page with only a title and basic code, the file size is 1K and will take one second to download.

This is extremely valuable information, and you'll see as your pages become more complex that Dreamweaver tracks your changes every step of the way and provides you with this little visual reminder of how long it will take for someone to see your fabulous creations.

The final element of the status bar is the Launcher bar on the far right. As demonstrated earlier, one of the panels that's available is known as the Launcher—which enables you to quickly access other tools that you may need when designing your pages, such as the Site window, HTML styles, and others. The Launcher bar duplicates those options here and allows you to quickly access them simply by clicking one of the buttons.

As with most elements of Dreamweaver, the work area is easily customizable based on your own preferences. As you work through the exercises in this book, these options will be described in detail, and as you become more familiar with the program, you're sure to find ways to work more efficiently based on your own style. For now, leave all of these settings as they are (their default settings) as you read about the other elements of the Dreamweaver interface.

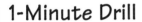

1-Minute Drill

● How is the reference library accessed from the Dreamweaver Document window?

● How can specific tags be selected in a document?

● Why does Dreamweaver provide the option of changing the Document window?

The Properties Inspector

Without a doubt, the one component of Dreamweaver that you will use more than any other is the Properties Inspector. As the name implies, the Properties Inspector provides detailed information about different elements on your pages—text, graphics, and other elements—and lets you change them to meet your design needs. The Properties Inspector provides powerful features in an easy-to-access format, greatly expediting your formatting needs.

The Properties Inspector is context-sensitive, meaning that it changes based on which type of element you've selected in your pages. A few examples follow.

● The reference library is accessed by clicking the Reference button in the toolbar at the top of the screen.
● Tags are selected by choosing the specific tag in the Tag Selector in the lower-left corner of the Document window.
● Dreamweaver provides the option of changing the Document window so that you can approximate the size of your page when viewed in a particular monitor resolution.

Text Properties

To work through this exercise, you need to look at a web page that has some of the elements that can be modified using the Properties Inspector. In Module 1, you looked at the coding in some sample files; you'll use the sample file named html_4.htm here. From the Dreamweaver Document window, choose File | Open and navigate to the location on your hard drive where you stored that file earlier. Open the Properties Inspector by choosing Window | Properties.

Tip

If you haven't downloaded this file, you can find it in the Module 1 resources file for this book at www.osborne.com.

Figure 3-3 shows the Properties Inspector as it appears when the word "This" is selected in your sample file.

Because subsequent modules will give you ample practice in formatting text on a real web page, the intent here is simply to get you acquainted with the formatting options. However, you should take some time to select different text in the sample file so that you get a feel for how the options available change with the context of the item selected. Table 3-1 gives you an overview of the different buttons and their functions when formatting text.

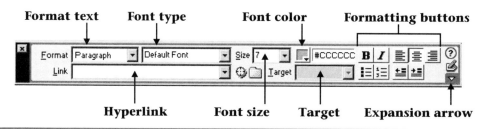

Figure 3-3 Formatting text with the Properties Inspector

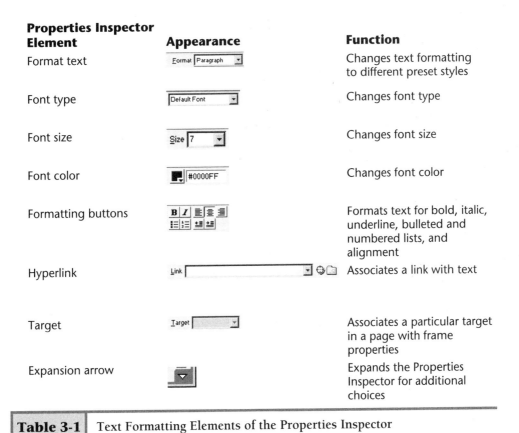

Properties Inspector Element	Appearance	Function
Format text		Changes text formatting to different preset styles
Font type		Changes font type
Font size		Changes font size
Font color		Changes font color
Formatting buttons		Formats text for bold, italic, underline, bulleted and numbered lists, and alignment
Hyperlink		Associates a link with text
Target		Associates a particular target in a page with frame properties
Expansion arrow		Expands the Properties Inspector for additional choices

Table 3-1   Text Formatting Elements of the Properties Inspector

Image Properties

Being able to use the Properties Inspector to change every element present in your web pages makes the chore of formatting, resizing, aligning, and controlling the appearance of those elements extremely easy. Since the Properties Inspector changes based on the element selected, as shown in Figure 3-4 where simpleimage.gif is selected, you can make changes without having your page cluttered with so many panels and palettes that you can't see what you're doing. In Module 6, you will learn more about working with images, but for now, take a look at some of the elements available when an image has been selected.

Image preview   Filename and location   Image alignment

Image dimensions

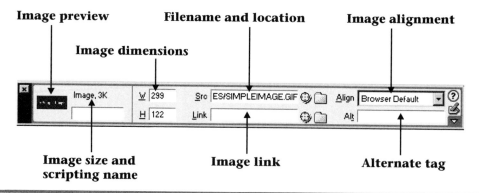

Image size and   Image link   Alternate tag
scripting name

Figure 3-4 Formatting an image with the Properties Inspector

Formatting images can be one of the most challenging parts of page design. Again, Dreamweaver enables you to apply formatting options easily, as summarized in Table 3-2.

Properties Inspector Element	Appearance	Function
Image preview		Presents a thumbnail view of the image.
Image size and scripting name	Image, 3K	Provides image size. A name is provided if the image has a script function, such as a rollover.
Image dimensions	W 299 H 122	Lists the image width and height in pixels.
Filename and location	Src ES/SIMPLEIMAGE.GIF	Lists the filename and its location.
Image alignment	Align Browser Default	Aligns the image to text.
Alternate tag	Alt	Alternate text that displays if the image is not loaded.
Image link	Link	Provides hyperlink information when the image has an imbedded hyperlink.

Table 3-2 Image Formatting Elements of the Properties Inspector

Working with the Properties Inspector will become a natural extension of your overall skills as a page designer as you become more familiar with Dreamweaver. The next section looks at the panel that lets you quickly insert the elements you need to make your pages more interesting and dynamic—the Objects panel.

The Objects Panel

The quantity and variety of objects that can be inserted into a web page can be a little mind-boggling. You may remember from Module 1 that you spent some time looking at source code for a variety of web pages and saw an incredible variety of tags in use. Everything from simple images to tables to multimedia content can potentially be coded into a page. The developers of Dreamweaver were confronted with the task of figuring out how to enable users to insert all of those objects into a web page, without overwhelming the users. Their response to this challenge is the Objects panel, in which they found a way to include 58 different elements into a format that is sensible, easy to understand, and easy to apply.

Figure 3-5 shows the default appearance of the Objects panel—set to display the most common elements used by page designers. If your panel is not already open, choose Window | Objects to display it.

By default, Dreamweaver always displays the objects in the Common category when the panel is opened. However, the choices don't stop there. By clicking the expansion arrow, you see that several other options are available for categories called Characters, Forms, Frames, Head, Invisibles, and Special. The bullet to the left of the Common category indicates that this is the panel currently selected.

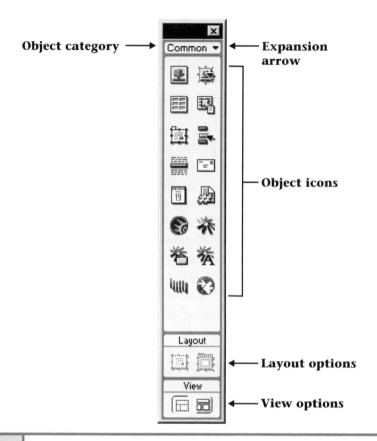

Object category → Common ▼ ← Expansion arrow

Object icons

Layout ← Layout options

View ← View options

Figure 3-5 The Objects panel for common objects

Changing categories is as simple as clicking the expansion arrow and then clicking the category you want to use. Try clicking all the different categories and you'll see that the number of options available is extensive. However, by placing them in different categories, the choices become manageable. Imagine what it would be like if you had to have a panel open for every option; you'll quickly appreciate the logic behind the style that the developers at Macromedia chose.

As with the Properties Inspector, you will be spending a lot of time with the Objects panel as you move through the exercises in this book. For now, you just need to become familiar with the different icons so that you'll be able to work with them easily later on.

Note

Providing a description of all the objects available is beyond the scope of this book. Although the following tables list all 58 objects so that you know what they do, you won't actually be using all 58 objects in your sample exercises.

Common Objects

Table 3-3 lists the elements available in the Common category of the Objects panel.

Common Objects Panel Element	Appearance	Function
Image		Inserts an image
Rollover image		Inserts a rollover image
Table		Inserts a table
Tabular data		Inserts a table that is filled with data from another file, such as a database or spreadsheet
Navigation bar		Inserts a set of images that can be used for navigating a site
Layer		Creates a layer that can be sized by dragging the pointer in the work area
Horizontal rule		Inserts a horizontal (side to side) line
E-mail link		Places a link to open the user's e-mail program and directs mail to the specified address
Date		Inserts the current date
Server-side include		Inserts a reference to a file that will be transmitted by the server when the viewer opens the page
Fireworks HTML		Inserts an HTML file created by Fireworks into the document

Table 3-3   Common Objects in the Objects Panel

3

Common Objects Panel Element	**Appearance**	**Function**
Flash		Inserts a movie file created in Macromedia Flash®
Flash button		Places a prebuilt button, created using Flash, into the document
Flash text		Inserts a Flash text object
Shockwave		Inserts a movie created with Macromedia Shockwave® into the document
Generator		Inserts dynamic elements created using Macromedia Generator

Table 3-3 Common Objects in the Objects Panel (*continued*)

Character Objects

Characters are those special-duty symbols that used to involve a complicated set of instructions to include in an HTML document. Dreamweaver places the most commonly used elements into this category and makes their insertion as easy as clicking the buttons listed in Table 3-4.

Character Objects Panel Element	**Appearance**	**Function**
Line break		Inserts a line break—usually in text
Nonbreaking space		Places an additional space in a document
Copyright		Inserts the copyright symbol
Registered		Inserts the registered trademark symbol
Trademark		Inserts the trademark symbol

Table 3-4 Character Objects in the Objects Panel

Character Objects Panel Element	Appearance	Function
Pound		Inserts the pound currency symbol
Yen		Inserts the yen currency symbol
Euro		Inserts the euro currency symbol
Left quote		Places a curved left quote symbol in the document
Right quote		Places a curved right quote symbol in the document
Em dash		Inserts the em dash (hyphen) symbol
Other		Inserts other special characters by opening a dialog box with additional characters listed

Table 3-4   Character Objects in the Objects Panel (*continued*)

Form Objects

Forms are those elements in web pages that allow the viewer to insert data and submit information. Dreamweaver provides a number of standard form elements that can be inserted into web pages, as summarized in Table 3-5. You should know that inserting these form objects does not actually create the form itself but creates HTML code that defines the form object. In order for the form to work, additional code is required, as you'll learn in Module 10.

Form Objects Panel Element	Appearance	Function
Form		Creates a container to hold another form object
Text field		Inserts a text box in which the user can type information

Table 3-5   Form Objects in the Objects Panel

Form Objects Panel Element	Appearance	Function
Button		Creates a blank button that activates a form action; usually used to create a Submit button
Checkbox		Creates a checkbox-type button so viewers can select multiple options
Radio		Creates a radio-type button that allows the viewer to select an exclusive option
List/menu		Inserts a list or pop-up menu
File field		Creates an option for a viewer to submit an entire file to the server
Image field		Creates code that allows an image to be used as you would use a Submit button
Hidden field		Creates a hidden element that captures data when the viewer submits information, such as the date and time the information is submitted
Jump menu		Creates a pop-up menu of URLs

Table 3-5 Form Objects in the Objects Panel (*continued*)

Frame Objects

Frames are specially designed web pages that have been divided into separate containers to hold multiple web pages. As you'll read in Module 8, which goes into more detail about frames, you can think of a frame as being similar to a plastic food container with dividers to hold different food. Creating framesets involves defining not only the container, but also all the items that are stored in it. Generally, framesets include a main document area where the majority of your content will go, bordered by smaller areas that hold items such as navigation links, advertisements, or basic information that remains the same no matter where a viewer goes in the site. The Frames Objects panel enables you to choose different frame layouts for your pages, as described in Table 3-6. Notice that the

Frame Objects Panel Element	Appearance	Function
Left		Creates a narrow frame on the left and the main document on the right
Right		Creates a narrow frame on the right and the main document on the left
Top		Creates a narrow frame on the top and the main document on the bottom
Bottom		Creates a narrow frame on the bottom and the main document on the top
Left, Top-Left Corner, and Top		Creates a frameset with four panels, with the main document in the lower-right corner
Left and Nested Top		Creates a long narrow frame on the right and on the top and the main document in the lower-right corner
Top and Nested Left		Creates a frame across the top of the window, with a narrow frame on the left and the main document in the lower-right corner
Split		Creates a frameset split into equal quarters

Table 3-6   Frame Objects in the Objects Panel

larger frame areas, on the button icons where the majority of the page content will be stored, are highlighted in blue.

Head Objects

The way that head elements are inserted into a page to provide hidden notes, keywords, descriptions, and automatic formatting options was discussed previously. The Head Objects panel enables you to create and insert these elements at your discretion and put them directly into the <head> tag of your document. Table 3-7 summarizes the buttons available in the Head Objects panel and their functions.

Head Objects Panel Element	Appearance	Function
Meta		Inserts a metatag used for including information about the page's author, copyright information, or keywords
Keywords		Provides a dialog box for inserting keywords into metatags
Description		Provides a metatag for inserting a description of the site
Refresh		Provides a way to automatically reload a page after a certain time; often used when a site changes servers and has a new URL
Base		Provides additional information for site management by associating all pages in a site with a particular URL
Link		Used to automatically link to a file located on the server to extract information; not the same as a hyperlink

Table 3-7 Head Objects in the Objects Panel

Invisible Objects

The Invisibles category includes those elements that are not visible when viewed in a browser but that are useful in page layout and navigation. Dreamweaver inserts a special character to let the page designer know that an invisible element is present when View | Visual Aids | Invisible Elements is selected. This category includes only a few elements, as listed in Table 3-8.

Invisible Objects Panel Element	Appearance	Function
Named Anchor		Used for inserting anchors into the document that can be linked internally; useful for providing a way to jump to the part of a page where the anchor is inserted
Script		Provides the ability to insert JavaScript or VBScript directly into the document
Comment		Allows the page designer to insert comments regarding inserted script or other notes that they do not want to appear when the page is loaded in the browser

Table 3-8 Invisible Objects in the Objects Panel

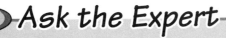

Ask the Expert

Question: Wow, 58 objects! Will I really use all of those elements in my web pages?

Answer: Actually, you can even add new elements to the Objects panel and further extend its functions. The truth is, though, that no single web page ever uses all of those objects, but you'll be surprised at how many you will use. The beauty of the Dreamweaver interface is that when you do need them, all the objects covered in this module are just a few mouse clicks away.

3

Special Objects

Special objects are those elements that provide additional functions to a web page by inserting small programs, or the ability to access a program that extends the capability of the browser itself. Programs that add extra functions to a browser are generally referred to as *plug-ins*. Table 3-9 summarizes the default objects found in the Special category.

Layout and View

You've probably noticed that no matter which category of object you're working in, four buttons appear at the bottom of the Objects panel. These buttons control how the page is viewed as you work, and add the ability to lay out your page with special table elements before you begin adding content. Since subsequent modules cover the process of laying out your pages in some detail, Table 3-10 simply lists the function of each button.

Special Objects Panel Element	Appearance	Function
Applet		Inserts a special function created in the Java programming language
ActiveX		Inserts a special function created in the ActiveX programming language
Plug-in		Inserts directions to access a file requiring a plug-in when using Netscape Navigator

Table 3-9   Special Objects in the Objects Panel

Layout and View Button	Appearance	Function
Draw Layout Cell		Provides the capability of drawing an individual layout cell while in Design view
Draw Layout Table		Provides the capability of drawing a layout table while in Design view
Standard View		Opens the Standard design view
Layout View		Opens a special design view where layout cells and tables can be added to the page

Table 3-10   Layout and View Buttons in the Objects Panel

1-Minute Drill

- What is the function of the Properties Inspector?
- Which category of objects includes images, Flash text, and navigation bars?
- Where are layout and view options found on the Objects panel?

The Launcher and Mini-Launcher

The third major element of the Dreamweaver interface is the Launcher, and its smaller version found in the status bar, the Mini-Launcher. Once again, the software engineers at Macromedia have provided a quick and easy format for gaining access to additional tools that extend the capabilities of the program and allow designers to access powerful tools for managing their site and automating frequently performed tasks. Some of these tasks are repeated elsewhere—in the menu bar and status bar, for instance. Depending on the way that you wish to work, you can access these features in a variety ways. There is no right or wrong way to approach getting the job done—it's up to you to choose the method that suits you. In fact, you can add additional elements to the Launchers if you decide that you want a shortcut to opening a particular panel or inspector. Table 3-11 summarizes the function of each of the buttons in the two Launchers.

- The Properties Inspector provides detailed information about any object found in your document—text, images, or objects.
- The Common category includes images, Flash text, and navigation bars.
- Layout and view options are available at the bottom of every Objects panel, regardless of the category.

Launcher Button	Appearance	Function
Site	Site	Opens the Site window
Assets	Assets	Opens the Assets window where your site assets are organized by type, including images, colors, URLs, and others
HTML Styles	HTML Styles	Accesses HTML styles that apply special formatting to text and paragraphs in your documents
CSS Styles	CSS Styles	Applies a CSS style to text and document formatting; used to apply styles that are automatically updated across the entire site
Behaviors	Behaviors	Opens the Behaviors panel, enabling you to insert interactive elements in a page
History	History	Opens the History panel; used to undo or redo previous steps done in the document
Code Inspector	Code Inspector	Opens the same inspector found in the toolbar; used for debugging script

Table 3-11   Dreamweaver Launcher Buttons

The Menu Bar

Across the top of your Document window is the old familiar menu bar. Even though many of the items found here are duplicated as buttons in the various panels and inspectors available in Dreamweaver, a few are found only here. Those that appear only in the menu bar are discussed next, wrapping up the discussion of the Dreamweaver interface.

Note

Many of the options found in the menu bar are also available via shortcut keys, such as CTRL-C for copy.

The File menu contains the items necessary for working directly on your file, such as Save, Save As, New, and other familiar menu bar commands. Notice that Dreamweaver includes some additional commands that let you work with files created in other programs, such as spreadsheet and database documents.

The commands in the Edit menu also are familiar. Here you find the capability of copying and pasting not only objects but also HTML. Notice at the bottom of the menu the category called Preferences. This item is used for changing the way various panels and inspectors appear in the program. Feel free to open the Preferences dialog box, but you should leave the settings as they are for now, because changing the appearance of an item may lead to confusion when the program's features are discussed later on.

The View menu includes many of the items discussed earlier that enable you to change how items are displayed on the screen. As with most View commands, changing the view of an item does not change what you're working on—only how it appears on your monitor.

After spending so much time reading about how Dreamweaver organizes objects for the Objects panel, you may be surprised to find out that all the same items are available in the Insert menu—only organized a little differently. However, if you feel that using the Objects panel is confusing or difficult, you have the option of completing the same task by clicking the Insert menu and finding the object you want there instead.

In the Modify menu, you see the first items that are available only in the menu bar. These tools, such as the ability to modify table properties automatically and arrange items on your page, extend your capabilities and take some of the guesswork out of completing these tasks. You'll be working with these tools in subsequent modules.

Options for formatting text are contained (surprise!) in the Text menu. Module 5 will detail how text is formatted both from the Properties Inspector and by using this menu.

The tools for automating repetitive tasks and applying consistent color and layout schemes are contained in the Commands menu. These tools not only save you time as you work, but also ensure that you can create a uniform look and feel for your overall site design.

As you know from the discussion in Module 2, managing a web site is an integral part of site design. The Site menu enables you to jump to the Site window and go directly to items that need your attention.

You have already seen how the Window menu is used to display or hide the various panels and inspectors that you need to have access to. In addition to the three primary panels—the Properties Inspector, Objects panel, and Launcher—Dreamweaver provides many other panels that can be activated by choosing them by name here.

Finally, the Help menu (which you may feel you need about now) puts a great set of tools at your disposal to assist you in learning the Dreamweaver program. Not only are the usual help topics available, but Dreamweaver also ships with

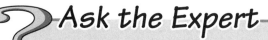

Ask the Expert

Question: Isn't this supposed to be a beginner's guide? I'm feeling a little overwhelmed by all this information.

Answer: I agree that it is a lot of information to absorb. However, remember that the goal of this module is only to acquaint you with the Dreamweaver interface so that working through the rest of the exercises will be easier. Now that you're familiar with Dreamweaver, you can use this module as a reference in the future.

3

a nice tutorial and provides links to live sites on the Web where you can find additional information about Dreamweaver and other Macromedia products.

The Context Menu

Many of the options that you just read about are also available in the context menu—which you open by choosing an item in your page and right-clicking it. You'll get a little practice doing this later in the module in Project 3-1.

1-Minute Drill

● What item in the Launcher is used to open the Site window?

● Which menu item in the menu bar contains commands to Save, Save As, and create new documents?

● What action causes the context menu to appear?

Project 3-1: Using the Objects Panel and the Properties Inspector

As with most computer programs, the best way to become accustomed to using it is to use it! In this exercise, you're going to go step-by-step, alternating between inserting objects with the Objects panel and then looking at how the

---

● Clicking the Site button on the Launcher opens the Site window.
● The File menu contains the Save, Save As, and New commands.
● Right-clicking an object in the document causes the context menu to appear.

Properties Inspector reads the information about the object you've put in your page. This project will give you some practical examples of Dreamweaver's capabilities.

Step-by-Step

1. Choose File | New to create a new untitled document.

2. Although you won't be using this file again, it's a good idea to get in the habit of saving a file with a unique name as soon as it is created. Choose File | Save As and call this one **practice1**. Save it to your desktop or some other easy-to-find location on your hard drive so that you can delete it later.

3. From the Objects panel, be sure that the Common category is selected and then click the Insert Table button. Click OK to accept the default table settings that you see in the Insert Table dialog box.

4. A table with three rows and three columns will appear in your document. Select the table, either by clicking its outside border or by choosing <table> in the Tag Selector. Be sure the Properties Inspector is open by choosing Window | Properties.

5. Notice that the Properties Inspector changes depending on what is selected. With the entire table selected, your page appears as you see in Figure 3-6.

6. Click inside one of the table cells—the small rectangles formed at the intersection of a row and column. What happens to the information in the Properties Inspector? What additional items become available in the Tag Selector?

7. Using the ENTER key to move down in your page, insert the following objects:

- The trademark symbol
- A horizontal rule
- The copyright symbol
- The date

8. Type the following text: **This is my first Dreamweaver page.**

9. Select each item you inserted and look at its properties displayed in the Properties Inspector. How do the properties change based on the object type? What objects have similar properties?

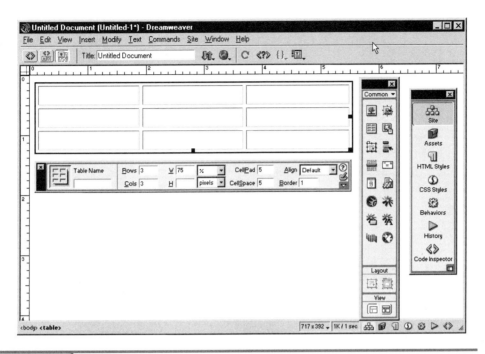

Figure 3-6 Arranging panels and selecting objects is a fundamental skill you will need to successfully use Dreamweaver

10. Acquaint yourself with some of the other objects available in the Objects panel by clicking those buttons. Since many of them need additional information before they can actually be inserted, you may have to choose Cancel in the dialog box that appears after you select them. Don't worry. This is a time to explore the different capabilities of the program.

This project demonstrated that all the capabilities of Dreamweaver are just a few clicks away as you work on your pages. Inserting objects is as simple as choosing a category and inserting the object you wish to use. Inspecting and modifying the objects you select is made simpler by using the Properties Inspector, allowing you to change each element to meet your overall goal of providing your intended audience with an Internet experience that they will find valuable.

What to Take Away

In this module, you've seen that the Dreamweaver interface provides in a neat, compact, and logical format a wide variety of tools for use in page design. By understanding how to use Dreamweaver's primary tools for web design—the Properties Inspector, the Objects panel, the Launcher, and the work area itself—you'll soon be creating dynamic web content of your own. In the next module, you'll learn how to develop an overall page structure and build the framework in which you'll be able to use *all* of Dreamweaver's tools.

☑ Mastery Check

1. What is the primary use of the Properties Inspector?

2. What is the primary use of the Objects panel?

3. What two objects appear in the Head Content bar of a new untitled document?

4. What tool is used to select an HTML tag directly by name?

5. How does Dreamweaver update designers regarding the size and download time of each page?

6. Which item in the Objects panel enables a special design view where layout cells and tables can be added to the page?

Module 4

Layouts and Alignments: Building Your First Web Page

The Goals of this Module

- Understand web page properties
- Learn how files and web pages are named
- Explore the Page Properties dialog box
- Use images for page backgrounds
- Understand design considerations when working with colors
- Learn how page margins are set

The first three modules discussed some of the Internet's basic principles and reviewed some of the primary concepts associated with web site design. You have learned the fundamentals of the Internet and HTML, gained an appreciation for how browsers interpret code, explored how web sites are planned and organized, and familiarized yourself with the Dreamweaver interface and its many different elements. Now, it's finally time to start making your first real web pages. You'll discover how page properties are defined and changed, investigate options for changing text and background colors, and look at ways that your overall goal of providing content that meets the needs of your intended audience can be impacted by designing pages that apply solid design principles.

Creating Your First Web Page

To meet the goals of this module, you need to open Dreamweaver and navigate to the Poinciana Beach Chamber of Commerce web site that you created in Module 2. To do so, open the Site window and look at the Define Sites box. If the correct web site opens (Dreamweaver always opens to the site you were previously working on), then you are all set. If not, review the steps in Module 2 and then select the site that you titled "Poinciana Beach CofC."

Note

In addition to working in the correct site, you also need to download the Module 4 files from the resources section for this book from www.osborne.com. Create a new folder on your computer's desktop called **Exercises** and be sure that the files that you download and unzip are located there so that you can follow along easily with the examples.

Project 4-1: Creating and Saving a New HTML Document

Your Poinciana Beach site currently contains very little—the empty folders that you created in Module 2 and the index.htm file that must reside in every site. You'll now add a new document, give it a name, and begin changing its properties to suit your needs.

Step-by-Step

1. Your first page will contain a greeting message from the chairperson of the Chamber of Commerce. Since this page doesn't fall naturally into any of the categories you defined earlier, locate it in your root folder of the site. To create a new folder, open the Site window and right-click the root folder at the top of your site file structure.

2. At the top of the context menu that pops up, select New File. Selecting this choice creates a new untitled document and places it into your site structure window.

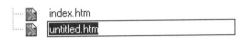

3. Ever helpful, Dreamweaver may now give you a not-so-gentle warning that, for the program to do its job correctly, you need to give this new file a name. Remember that one of the great features of this program is its ability to check your files for missing information. The warning is a valid (if sometimes annoying) one. Click OK to move on, and if you don't think you'll need to be reminded of this every time you create a new document, check the box that says Don't Remind Me Again.

Hint

Another way to create a new file is to select File I New Window. And, while you can *also* create a new file from the Document window, you may prefer to work only from the Site window when you want to add, modify, or delete files from your site. You'll appreciate the ease with which Dreamweaver performs this task, and by using this method, you can be sure that your files are created in the proper folder—helping you to maintain your overall site structure.

4. Before you begin work on this file, go ahead and give it a name. While still in the Site window, double-click the filename and rename this file **greetings.htm**. One of the essential habits to get into when creating any new document, whether it's an HTML file or a graphics file that you create in Fireworks, is to immediately give the file a name. Remember the warning you received? Naming your file right away ensures that you'll be able to preview it properly and that Dreamweaver will be able to track changes to the file and do its job properly.

5. Your new file is now part of your site, as you can see in the Site window.

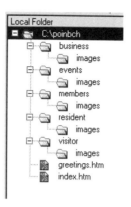

6. To open this new document, simply double-click the icon for the file and you will move immediately to the Document window for your greetings.htm document.

File Naming and Page Titles

In the title bar of the new page created in Project 4-1, Dreamweaver displays the essential information of your page properties—the title of the page, the folder where it is located, and the name of the file itself.

This information serves as a quick reminder of exactly what file you're working on, which becomes helpful when working on multiple files in your site.

Every web page contains both a filename for the document and a page title that describes the page. The following discussion describes the differences between the two.

Module 2 noted that you have to follow some specific rules for file naming that ensure the files will work properly when posted on a server:

● The filename for the first page in any web site is (almost) always index.htm.

● Filenames can be as long as necessary, but spaces should be avoided.

4

- In place of spaces, use the underscore or dash symbol.

- Only the underscore and dash are permitted. No other special characters should be used.

- Never start a filename with a number.

Web page designers need to know the distinction between filenames and page titles. Consider this analogy. If you tell someone you're going to a particular mall, then you've sufficiently described your destination. But, if you want to mail a letter to the manager of that mall, you need to know the street address and ZIP code. Similarly, page titles describe your page, whereas filenames provide computers with the exact information required to find and display the file.

Page titles are descriptive and are displayed in the browser title bar when the viewer looks at the page. In addition, if the viewer chooses to add your page as a bookmark or go back into their browser history file to find your page, the title is what is displayed. If you don't give your page a title, all they'll see is either a blank line or the confusing (and all too common) "Untitled Document" listing.

In version 4 of Dreamweaver, changing the page title is now as simple as selecting the page title in the toolbar and changing it from Untitled Document to what you want. Go to your greetings.htm file and change the title to **Greetings from Poinciana Beach**. Choose File | Save to save your document.

Ask the Expert

Question: I noticed a folder called _Notes when I looked in my root folder. Where did that come from? I didn't create it and it doesn't show up in my Site window.

Answer: Dreamweaver automatically generates some folders as it defines your site structure. This folder provides a place to store information that you may want to make available if you're working collaboratively with others on your site or if you just want to keep notes on your designs. You'll see later that some additional folders will be created for you that contain templates and library items.

Modifying Page Properties

You have now changed one of the essential page properties of your document—the page title. Dreamweaver features a comprehensive Page Properties dialog box for changing the ingredients of your documents. As you'll see in this section, you not only can change the title of your page, but also can specify information about the page's background color, whether you want to use an image as a background, and how the page will display margins, among other elements. This dialog box lets you quickly set many of the basic elements of your page design, and has a big impact on how your finished page will look. To open this dialog box, choose Modify | Page Properties from the menu bar.

---Hint---

Dialog boxes are an important way to provide information required to set the correct parameters of any element you want to add or modify in your pages. Dreamweaver uses many of these dialog boxes as a way to keep the program interface uncluttered while giving you great latitude in choosing the way you want an object to be created or changed.

Figure 4-1 identifies the elements of the Page Properties dialog box that are discussed in this module. Subsequent modules discuss some of the other options available.

At the top of the dialog box, you see the page title that you created in the toolbar earlier. You could just as easily have come directly to this dialog box to change the title, and you may find that to be a more convenient option for you. Either way the title is created, it will be available both here and in the toolbar of the Document window if you need to change it.

Below the title box you see the Background Image box. As the name implies, this is where you can choose to use an image as the background of your page rather than a solid color, as described next.

Project 4-2: Using Images for Page Backgrounds

Having an image in the background of your page is similar to using stationary when you write a letter. Everything else on the page will be on top of the background image. You can create some great effects this way, and many web designers use background images as a way to set off different elements on their page, such as navigation bars.

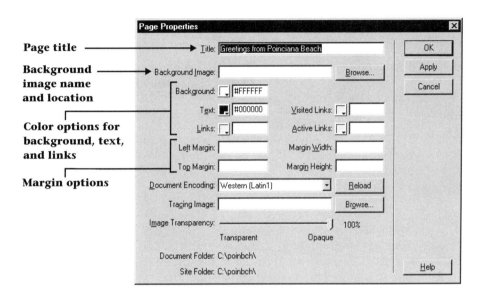

Page title ──────────────→ Title: Greetings from Poinciana Beach

Background ──────→ Background Image:
image name
and location

Color options for
background, text,
and links

Margin options

Figure 4-1 | The Page Properties dialog box

Using background images does require caution, though. The essential rule to understand is that the background image should be used only when it enhances, or improves, the look and feel of your pages. Just like everything else you do, before you decide to use a background image, you must decide if it is something that will appeal to your intended audience and meet the overall goals of your site. Just because you think it looks cool doesn't mean that someone else will. In addition, backgrounds can seriously detract from the viewer's ability to read what is on the page itself. Take a look at the following procedure, which shows how you can use background images to enhance a document.

Step-by-Step

1. Before you can include an image in your background, you need to create a folder in your site to hold it. While you could simply copy the image file into the root folder, continue to practice good site management and create a *new* folder in the root folder of your site. To do so, return to the Site window and right-click the root folder at the top of your site structure. Choose New Folder from the context menu and rename the folder **backgrd**.

2. Return to the Document window for your greetings.htm file. If the Page Properties dialog box is not visible, open it by choosing Modify | Page Properties.

3. The Browse button to the right of the Background Image box (refer to Figure 4-1) lets you go directly to your Exercises folder and choose the background you want to insert.

4. Click Browse and navigate to the Exercises folder you created on your desktop earlier. There you will find several backgrounds to choose from. Select stars.gif from the files listed.

Note

Images for backgrounds must be in GIF or JPEG format. While Internet Explorer supports the BMP format, only viewers using that browser will see the background images.

5. Clicking the Select button will accept this choice, but before you do that, take a look at the information in the Select Image Source dialog box. Dreamweaver has some important information listed here that you will see again, so it is useful to get acquainted with these features. Figure 4-2 highlights some of the most important elements of this dialog box.

6. Notice in the lower-left corner that Dreamweaver gives a quick review of the location the chosen file has relative to the site that you're working on and provides a warning that it is outside your root folder. Also, you're provided with valuable information regarding the size of your file and the amount of time it will add to your estimated download in the Image Preview area.

7. Clicking Select causes the following warning to immediately appear. Click Yes.

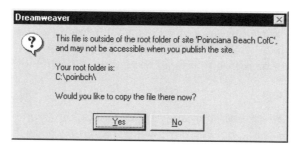

8. While you could have easily gone directly to the hard drive on your computer and copied and pasted the file you wanted into the proper folder in your site, it is much easier, and more efficient, to let Dreamweaver do it for you. Dreamweaver now presents you with the Copy File As dialog box.

Filenames   Folder name   **Image preview with size and download time**

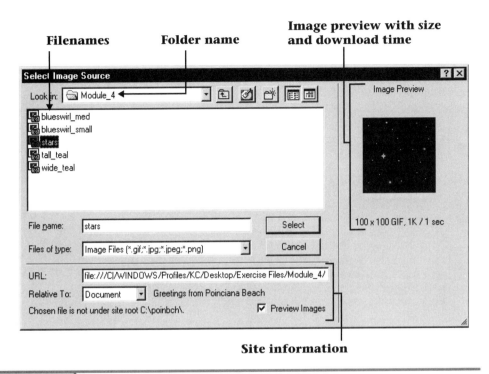

4

Figure 4-2   Dreamweaver's Select Image Source dialog box

Simply navigate to the proper folder (backgrd), open it, and save the file into that folder.

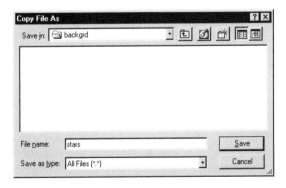

9. Click OK after you are returned to the Page Properties dialog box to accept the new background image. Your new web page now sports a beautiful blue starfield background. Select File | Save to save your page.

10. Images that are inserted in the background of an HTML document are *tiled*—that is, they are pasted together in succession across and down the page, much as tiles are laid on a floor or wall. To see a more dramatic representation of this, return to the document and change the background image to bluswirl_small.gif and then change the background to blueswirl_med.gif. These images are provided as a representation of how tiling is accomplished, but they also point out one other factor when working with backgrounds: the images can become very annoying and make the text and images in the foreground difficult to see. The use of backgrounds is a decision that must be made very carefully.

11. As noted earlier, backgrounds can also be used to mark out areas on a page for special purposes. Change your background to tall_teal.gif and you'll see a document that could have a navigation bar or advertising placed across the top of the page. Changing you background to wide_teal.gif does the same thing, but places the teal-colored area on the left side. Each of these images is simply a small graphics file built (using Fireworks) so that it can take advantage of the tiling feature of background images.

Background images can greatly enhance the overall design and even functionality of your pages. Some design considerations will be discussed when using colors later in this module, but for now, you should congratulate yourself on learning an important skill in designing your first web page.

1-Minute Drill

● How are new files created from the Site window?

● Why should files be given a name immediately after they are created?

● What is the difference between a filename and a page title?

Project 4-3: Changing Page Background Colors

As an alternative to using background images to enhance the design of your pages, HTML also lets you use solid colors in the background. Just as with using background images, though, the decision to use a background color is one that must be made carefully.

● To create a new file, right-click the folder icon where you want the file to reside and then choose New File.

● Naming files immediately not only is a good habit to get into, but it also ensures that Dreamweaver will be able to assist in site and file management as you add content to the file.

● Filenames provide the information required by the computer to find and display a file. Page titles provide descriptions for the viewer of the pages and allow the pages to be more easily found in a bookmark or history file.

Step-by-Step

1. Open the Page Properties dialog box. The background image that you specified earlier can be removed from the properties for this page by choosing the ... ACKSPACE or DELETE key. This does not remove the ... only deletes any reference to it in the HTML for ... deleting the filename, and your page will return ... und.

... he areas for changing colors for the page, text, ...). By default, Dreamweaver always makes the ... age white. Notice also that the hexadecimal code ... is listed next to the small square color button itself.

... ton opens the Color Chooser—determined by the ... ig. This is one of the few times where a panel or ... ffers significantly based on whether you are using a Windows or Macintosh OS. Here you see the Windows version:

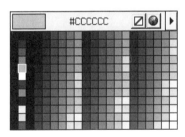

4. The small swatches of color represent the 212 colors that Macromedia has tested and determined to be truly web-safe, meaning the colors will display correctly regardless of the browser or operating system that the viewer is using. Previously, it was assumed that a web-safe palette consisted of 216 colors, but after comprehensive testing, this number was proven to be inaccurate. Dreamweaver only displays 212 colors as a result.

5. The small icon that replaces your pointer is the eyedropper tool. This tool lets you choose not only the colors that you see in the color palette, but also any colors that are already present in your document, or anywhere else on your screen for that matter. This is a very handy feature that you'll soon find

4

yourself having great fun with, and saving considerable time, by using it to capture colors as you work.

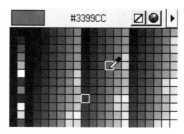

6. Greater color options are available by clicking the small color wheel in the upper-right corner of the Color Chooser window. Since color options are discussed extensively when you begin learning how to use Fireworks, that discussion will be left for later and you'll leave the color options set as they are at this point. You should feel free to experiment with this panel if you choose.

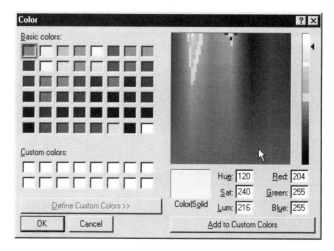

7. Try some different color options for your page by selecting different color cubes and clicking the Apply button when you are returned to the Page Properties box. What colors do you think would be appropriate for a web page? What colors do you think might cause problems?

8. When you're finished experimenting, set the color for your page back to white, click OK to exit the Page Properties dialog box, and save your document.

Changing Text Colors

Changing text colors for an entire page is no different from changing the background color. Again, the process involves selecting the button that represents the color you want to change and then using the Color Chooser to select the color you want to use. Dreamweaver includes options for changing the color of regular text (Text), the color of text that has a hyperlink attached (Links), the color of links that the viewer has already seen (Visited Links), and the color that linked text changes to when the viewer clicks on it (Active Links).

Try this now by typing in a line of text in the work area of the document window—something like **This is my first Dreamweaver document**. Practice changing the color and you will quickly see how efficient this process is.

4

Using Preset Color Schemes

In addition to changing the color of the different text options, Dreamweaver also includes a number of preset color schemes that combine page backgrounds with text options that are easy to read and make good sense from a design perspective.

To access these options, choose Commands | Set Color Scheme. This opens the Set Color Scheme Command dialog box, which lets you choose a basic background color and a variety of options for text and link colors that compliment the background. This is a great time-saver if you're looking for a colorful page design.

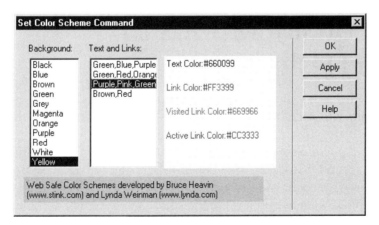

Choose any color scheme that you find appealing, click OK, and then return to the Page Properties dialog box, where you'll find that all the changes have

Ask the Expert

Question: Why would you want to change text colors anyway?

Answer: That is a question that generates great debate in web design circles. Many people are very accustomed to finding hyperlinked text, in particular, presented in the color blue with an underline under the words that are linked. The blue color and the underlined words jump off the page and let the viewer know immediately that if they click those words, they will go to another web page. The default blue underline link is one of the few things about web pages that has become somewhat standard.

For others, though, this standard becomes an unwelcome restriction to their goal of achieving a visually appealing web page, and they prefer to experiment with other options. Which one is correct? Again, it all depends on the audience. If you feel that your audience needs the comfort zone of a familiar interface, then stick with the default colors. If not, then feel free to change them.

been made for you. Imagine if you had to do all of that by coding the HTML line by line.

Color Considerations in Web Design

With so many color options available, it would seem that the Internet would be brimming with pages that feature colorful backgrounds and text that varies based on the particular preferences of the page designers. However, taking a quick tour of major web sites reveals that many of them stick with the basics—white background, black text, and blue links. Visit any of the most popular web sites—www.yahoo.com, www.msnbc.com, www.cnn.com, and even www.macromedia.com—and you'll find pages with conventional color schemes.

Still, tastefully and carefully thought out color schemes can lend visual impact to page design. A perfect example of good color choices applied on the Web is www.americangirl.com, which has a pale-purple background, white text, and pink accents—a perfectly appealing color scheme for a preteen girl.

Applying some basic rules to your use of color will lead to a more viewer-friendly design and a site that presents an environment consistent with your goals:

- *Use color to evoke emotions.* Think about those web sites that you've visited that really grabbed your attention right from the start. What was it about the color scheme that affected you? Was it jarring, soothing, funny, calming, cheerful, mysterious, professional? Colors have the capacity to generate moods in your viewers and should be aligned with the goals of the site.

- *Use a consistent design.* Once you've found a color scheme that meets the goals of your site, stick with it. Many designers develop color swatches for use on their sites so that no guesswork is involved—as you will practice in Project 4-4.

- *Make sure the text and the page background have good contrast.* This applies especially if the site involves much reading. For example, if you were to specify blue text with the stars.gif background that you used earlier, you might be able to decipher the text, but you certainly wouldn't want to read page after page of it.

- *Be careful when using white text.* If you create a page that has a dark background and nicely contrasting white text, it will probably look great on the viewer's monitor. If they decide to print it, though, it will be a different story. Since most browsers do not print background colors, the viewer will get a page full of white text on white paper.

- *Use web-safe colors wherever possible.* With 212 choices in Dreamweaver's color palette, it isn't likely that you'll run out of options. Even if you do go to the trouble of designing a custom color because you want your site to be "just so," the chances are that you're the only person who will ever see that perfect color anyway—unless a viewer who has the exact same computer monitor with the exact same settings on it as yours stumbles across your site.

- *Experiment with different colors.* While many references on color theory are available, most graphic artists come to their final choices of color schemes based on a lot of trial and error. Try different combinations until you find the one that you decide is pleasing and effectively meets your sites needs.

- *Be cautious of "experts."* It seems that anyone who has ever developed even one web site immediately becomes an expert, and many of them believe that only default colors should be used in web design. The ultimate choice is yours or, if you're working for pay, your client's. If you feel that using a textured or colored background provides your page with the impact you desire and meets the goal of reaching your intended audience, then go for it.

- *Test your color schemes before you get too far into your design process.* Once you start creating buttons and supporting graphics that fit your scheme, it can be very difficult to go back and redo all of your work. Seek out the opinion of friends, colleagues, and especially clients before finalizing color choices.

- *Remember that a page that looks great on your monitor won't necessarily look as good on someone else's monitor.* Some monitors display colors with more or less contrast and brightness. A color scheme that looks nice and subtle on your monitor may scream at a viewer on their monitor. Once again, try out your creation on different computers and even different operating systems if possible.

1-Minute Drill

- How many colors are in the web-safe color palette as defined by Macromedia?
- What is the tool called that lets you pick up colors from the color palette or from any other color present on your screen?
- Where are options found that let you set color schemes for a page?

Previewing Pages in a Browser

Before you can move on to testing some of the color choices that you have in designing your pages, you need to be sure that your systems are ready to preview the pages you create in a browser. Being able to jump quickly from Dreamweaver's Design or even Code view to see how your work will be interpreted in a browser is another important tool in your arsenal of tricks. As you create more complicated content, you'll quickly come to appreciate this capability because you know that, although HTML is moving toward some real standardization, you still need to design for the real world, where one browser may display code differently from another.

- The web-safe color palette has 212 colors.
- The eyedropper tool lets you choose colors from the color palette or from your screen.
- Color schemes are set by choosing Commands I Set Color Scheme.

Note

Macromedia has included the latest versions of both browsers on the program CD for Dreamweaver 4 Fireworks 4 Studio. If you don't have both browsers installed, you should install both and use the Edit Browser panel to let Dreamweaver know that you want these browsers available for previewing your work. Many web designers also maintain older versions of both browsers on their computers simply to verify the functionality of their work on the older versions.

Dreamweaver provides three different ways to call up a browser to read your files. You can click the Preview icon in the toolbar.

4

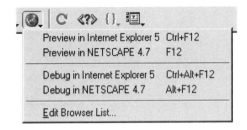

Or you can choose File | Preview In Browser, or simply press the F12 key for your primary browser or CTRL-F12 for your secondary browser.

The primary browser is determined by the system settings for your computer. If you have Netscape set as your default system browser, then Netscape will open and read your file to give you a preview of the page.

Clicking the Preview icon and choosing Edit Browser List gives you the option of changing your primary and alternate choices and also lets you add additional browsers. The Preferences panel can also be reached at any time by choosing Edit | Preferences and then choosing Preview In Browser, as shown in Figure 4-3.

Tip

In the Windows OS, previewing your work in a browser causes a temporary file to be created every time you preview. Many users of Dreamweaver report that after they've been working in the program for an extended time, their computer operates increasingly slower. Some of this problem can be attributed to the system resources used by these temporary files. To avoid this problem, set your Disk Cleanup utility to automatically delete temporary files at system startup, during a time when you know you won't be using your systems, or at regular intervals.

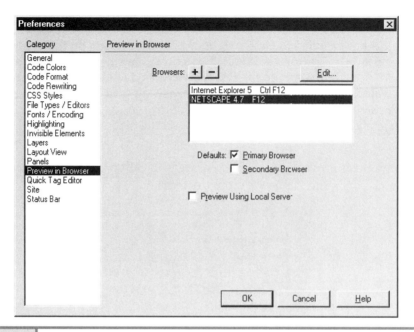

Figure 4-3 The Preferences dialog box provides the opportunity to set a wide range of choices for program options such as browser preferences

Setting Page Margins

Page margins are the final page appearance feature affected by the Page Properties dialog box that this module discusses. As you would expect, page margins are the areas at the top and left side of pages that are left blank when these values are entered. But you may wonder why there are four margin settings for only two areas of the page.

Once again, this is a browser compatibility issue. As indicated in Figure 4-4, Internet Explorer reads the values in the Left Margin and Top Margin entries, while Netscape reads Margin Width for the left side of the page and Margin Height for the top of the page. To be sure that you see consistent results for your margins, always set all four. Dreamweaver does not display the margin settings in the Document window. To see the results of your actions, you must preview the page in a browser.

Margins are set in pixels, which generally are seen at about 10 pixels per inch. In your example, your page margins are set at 5 pixels, or a little less than one-half inch.

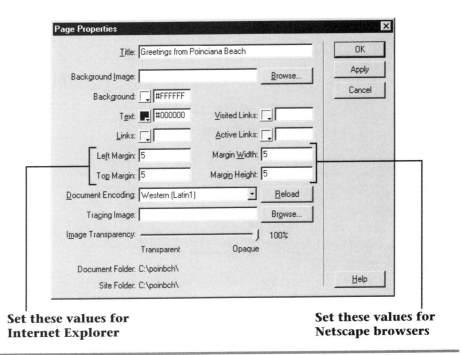

Set these values for
Internet Explorer

Set these values for
Netscape browsers

Figure 4-4 To obtain consistent page margins be sure to set both sets of margin
values in the Page Properties dialog box

Margins give your page a nice clean look because they move all the content
a little way from the edge of the monitor screen. Pages that do not use margins
scrunch the text and images against the edge of the screen, making reading text
more difficult.

Project 4-4: Exploring Page Options and Colors

Now that you've seen how color changes are made throughout an entire web
page, you'll spend some time exploring how making these changes affects the
look and feel of your pages. To do so, be sure that you have downloaded the
exercise files for this module from www.osborne.com. In the Module 4 folder,
you will find two HTML files that you'll be using for this project.

Step-by-Step

1. Open Dreamweaver and navigate to the site folder. You need to create a new site to hold the two HTML files that you'll find in the Module_4 folder.

2. Choose Define Sites from the site definition window and then click New.

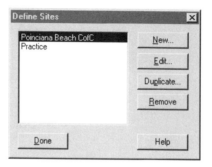

3. Navigate to the Exercise folder that you created earlier and then to the Module_4 folder. Click Select and then click Done to create your new site. When you're finished, the temporary site structure will look like this:

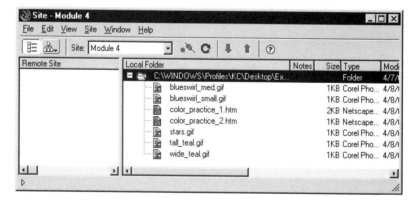

4. The preceeding steps were necessary so that the links that are attached to text in the two HTML files will function properly. Now that you have that groundwork out of the way, you can have some fun.

5. Open color_practice_1.htm from the Site window by double-clicking the icon next to the filename. This is a very simple web page that enables you to see the use of colors and background images in action. Start by looking at some preset color schemes.

6. For your first exercise, you'll make the stars.gif file you saw earlier your new background image for this page. Choose Modify | Page Properties to open the Page Properties dialog box.

7. As you did earlier, use the Browse button to select the stars.gif file to use as your background. Since this time it is in the same site as the page you're working on, you won't see any warnings or need to copy it into your site's root folder. Simply click Select once the filename is highlighted, and then click OK to accept the changes in the Page Properties dialog box. Your beautiful new web page now should look something like Figure 4-5.

8. That really doesn't look that good though, does it? The black regular text and the blue linked text fade into the background image, making all of it difficult to read. To appreciate the difficulty of this problem, press the F12 key to preview your document in your default browser.

9. Luckily, you know how to fix this problem. Change the color of both the text and the linked text so that they stand out from the background. Return to the Page Properties dialog box, but this time click the color button for the page text. Change the color to white. Change the other colors as you please, keeping in mind that they need to contrast with the blue starfield background, as shown in Figure 4-6.

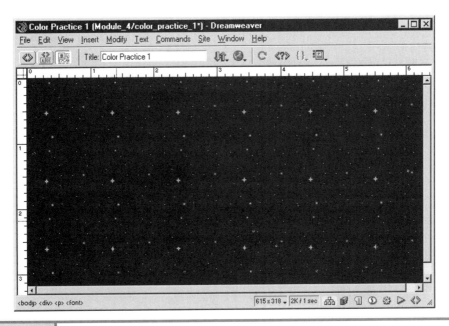

Figure 4-5   A web page with a dark background may make it difficult to read text

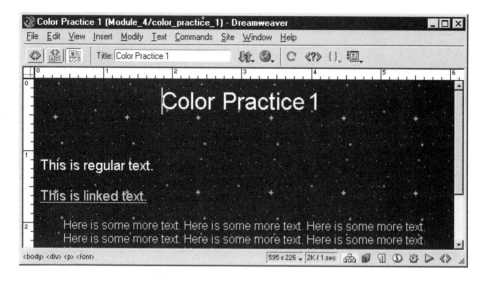

Text colors are changed by accessing the Page Properties dialog box

You can also change the text colors by using the color scheme options. You'll keep your starfield in place but change all the text colors simultaneously.

10. Choose Commands | Set Color Scheme to open the Set Color Scheme Command dialog box. Choose Blue in the Background column and then Green, Yellow, White in the Text And Links column. Click OK and all the color schemes will be changed simultaneously.

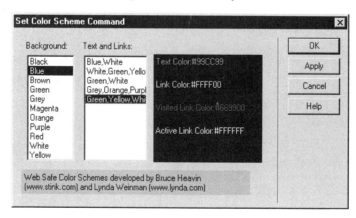

11. Take some time now to experiment with both solid-color backgrounds and backgrounds composed of images. What color combinations make the greatest impact? Which selections that you make are closest to the preset color schemes? Which colors allow you to read the text most easily? Do the pages look the same in the Dreamweaver Document window as they do when seen in a browser? How are they different?

12. Finally, experiment with changing the margins for your page. Don't forget to set all four parameters so that the results will be consistent regardless of the browser being used.

Using colors in web pages for backgrounds and text is just the first step in creating a great experience for the viewers of your site. Color can go a long way toward setting the mood for your site and can be an important factor in reaching your audience. Take some time here to experiment. Try capturing colors from live web pages on the Internet by using the eyedropper tool. As long as you can see the color on your monitor, Dreamweaver will capture the color that you point the tool to.

You can even find great libraries of additional background images on the Web. Just do a simple search for **background image files** in your favorite search engine and copy the ones you like into the Module_4 folder.

What to Take Away

Defining page properties begins with setting the overall look and feel for the page by using (or not using) colors and images in the background of your pages and by choosing the color scheme for page text. Using Dreamweaver's Page Properties dialog box is an easy way to set these parameters, and when combined with the ability to use predetermined color schemes, gives authors a great deal of control over the use of colors in their documents. Margins are also set in this dialog box, and can add greatly to creating a polished look for your work and generating pages that are easier to read.

☑ Mastery Check

1. What special characters are allowed in filenames?

2. What restrictions are placed on the titles of web pages?

3. How are background images in a web page arranged?

4. What does it mean when a color is called "web-safe"?

5. What color consideration is important when creating pages that contain a great deal of text?

6. What are the three methods for activating the Preview In Browser function?

Module 5

The Printed Word: Working with Text

The Goals of this Module

- Understand how text is entered into web pages
- Explore text appearance and alignment
- Use block quotes and lists
- Create hyperlinks to text
- Create e-mail links
- Understand the use of page anchors

The Internet today is a far different creature from what it was in the early days of its inception. When this computer network was first devised, it was used for transmitting raw scientific data and short messages—all in capital letters! But even though the Internet these days is the home to all sorts of animations, graphics, and even music and video files, at its heart, it is still basically a communications medium that depends on text, just as it did at its inception.

This module examines how text is inserted into web pages and how its appearance is controlled using the tools provided in Dreamweaver. By the end of this module, you'll understand how to get your message across not only by typing your message, but also by formatting the look of your finished project to make it more readable and more accessible to your audience.

Understanding Text and Typefaces

You will be working in your Poinciana Beach Chamber of Commerce site again during this module. If you have not done so, make sure that you have saved the exercise files for this module, which you can find at www.osborne.com. Included among these files are some simple text files that will save you a lot of time spent typing.

This module describes the process of manually formatting text. Later, this module discusses how you can make your formatting more consistent by creating HTML styles and cascading style sheets (CSS). Unfortunately, though, each of those methods comes with its own limitations, so manually formatting is still the safest way to get the job done. HTML styles are generally in disfavor because of their tendency to create larger file sizes as a result of the number of tags that are generated to apply this method. And, as of this writing, literally tens of millions of web users still have not upgraded to browsers that are capable of viewing CSS-formatted pages.

Note

Cascading style sheets have been designated as the formatting tool of choice for future versions of web browsers, and the manual formatting methods covered in this module will slowly fade away over time.

Text Terminology

Typography, or the process (some would say art) of using type in a document, has a history dating back to the very invention of the printing press by Johannes Gutenberg in the mid-1400s. Almost continually since that time, type has been revised and modified to meet the needs of printers, publishers, and readers. That trend continues today on the World Wide Web, as newer and more efficient means of producing and displaying text that is easily read and creates an impact through its style are developed and implemented by the producers of browsers and by web designers themselves.

Text styles are known as *fonts* and the term is often used interchangeably with the term *typeface.* Either term simply describes the style of the text. Fonts are divided into two broad categories—*serif* and *sans-serif.* A serif is the little stroke that decorates some letters, as in this example:

5

Times New Roman is a serif font.

A sans-serif font is one that literally is without (sans) the extra decoration, as you see here:

StoneSansl is a sans-serif font.

Additionally, text for the Web is defined in terms of the amount of horizontal space it uses and falls into two categories—*proportional* and *monospaced.*

Proportional text is a font style that uses only the amount of space necessary for each character to display properly. For example, the capital letter W is allowed more space than the lowercase letter i. Proportional fonts are generally preferred because they are easier to read and more characters can be displayed in the same physical space.

Monospaced type, on the other hand, allocates exactly the same amount of space to each character regardless of how wide the character actually is. In this example, you see both categories:

Proportional—Long ago, in a galaxy far, far away.

`Monospaced—Long ago, in a galaxy far, far away.`

By default, most browsers display the proportional font Times or Times New Roman. However, monospaced type, usually Courier, is often used when the author wants to indicate the text has a particular function—such as when computer coding is listed—`like this`.

The choice of font styles has as great an impact on the overall design of a web page and web site as choosing a color scheme. Consistency is the key. If you choose a font such as Times New Roman for your home page, and then switch to a completely different font for another page in the site, your audience may become confused by the change and feel that they have wandered off your site into unknown territory. In addition, since fonts also have an impact on the feel of your page, you must carefully consider your choice of fonts early in the design process. Again, consider your intended audience and the style that will appeal to them the most.

Considerations when Working with Text

Dreamweaver has many of the same attributes of a good word processor. Text can be inserted and aligned, fonts can be set, and the document can be checked for spelling just as if you were using Word or WordPerfect. You read in the last module that text can also be set to display in different colors and different sizes.

However, HTML is not a word processing language, nor was it ever intended to be one, and the effects that Dreamweaver uses are a bit of an illusion. Remember, as you type text and then format, the program is creating HTML tags that are applied to the text you have inserted. And, as always, you must consider the viewers' browsers, because the code ultimately is displayed and read on their screens. Dreamweaver attempts to give you an approximation of how that text will be displayed on their screens, but, as you will learn, even though the software does a good job of creating an environment that mimics a word processor, you have to keep the following in mind:

- *The browser, not the source code, controls text appearance.* HTML was designed to define the structure of a document, whereas the final presentation was always intended to be left to the browser. To use a familiar metaphor, the page author uses HTML as an architect uses paper and drawing tools to design a home. However, it is the home builder who executes the actual construction of the home, just as the final construction of a web page is left up to the browser and the viewer's computer.

- *Fonts that are not installed on the viewer's computer will not be seen when the page is viewed.* Although the browser will search for the font that is specified in the code, if it does not find it, it will revert to the browser's default font. If you design your entire site and all of its pages around the fun and frivolous Jokerman font, for instance, if the viewer doesn't have that font installed on their system, they're likely to see the very business-like Times New Roman font instead.

- *Font sizes are relative, based on the settings on the viewer's computer.* Most people leave the default font settings as they are when they install their browser, but both Netscape and Internet Explorer allow users to change the size of their font to meet their needs. You can see the effect of this yourself by visiting your favorite web site and then choosing View | Increase Font or View | Decrease Font in Netscape or by selecting View | Text Size in Internet Explorer. Try different sizes and you'll quickly see that the viewer is the one who ultimately controls how text will be displayed.

- *Competition produces inconsistencies.* Font sizes on a Macintosh computer display in a size roughly equivalent to sizes in a typed document, whereas Windows operating systems increase the size of text to make it easier to read on a computer monitor. Combine these differences with those found in the browser programs themselves and you have a wide variation in how text is coded and displayed. While both Netscape and Microsoft have committed to moving toward the standards established by the World Wide Web Consortium (W3C) in their latest versions of their respective browsers, both companies are still driven by the need to capture their particular piece of the Internet audience and will likely continue in the near future to offer competing programs that operate differently.

Entering and Formatting Text

Having said all that, the task of creating web pages that convey information in an accessible and attractive format is an achievable goal, as witnessed by the numerous web sites that accomplish this in an exemplary fashion. Part of the reason for the surging popularity of Dreamweaver is its ability to let designers work in an environment that is similar to a word processor while maintaining strict adherence to HTML standards. With the tools at your disposal in the program, you too will be able to publish pages that have visual impact and are properly formatted based on sound design principles.

Entering Text in Dreamweaver

Dreamweaver gives you a number of ways to enter text, the most obvious of which is to simply start typing. But, in addition, text can be copied directly from a word processor program and pasted into the Document window of Dreamweaver. The caution here is that *all* of the text formatting will be lost in the process. This is a handy shortcut, though, especially if you want to use the automatic spell check found in word processors that is absent in Dreamweaver. If you're a ham-fisted typist, this can save lots of time.

Two text files are located in the exercise files at the Osborne web site for this book—index_text.txt and greetings_text.txt. You'll be using both of those files as you move along, simply in the interest of saving time. As you might have guessed, these files contain the text you want to include in the index.htm and greetings.htm files you created earlier. Follow these steps to insert and format text in a document:

1. Open Dreamweaver and navigate to the Poinciana Beach Chamber of Commerce web site that you created earlier. Open the index.htm file by double-clicking the icon next to the filename in the Site window, shown in Figure 5-1.

Note

If you've added anything to the index.htm file in previous modules, you need to clear the document before you begin. Choose Edit | Select All and then Edit | Clear to erase all text and objects from the page.

Ask the Expert

Question: Doesn't Dreamweaver come with a spell check feature?

Answer: Dreamweaver does have a spell check feature, but it is not automatic, as you would find in Word, WordPerfect, or any other modern word processor. The spell check can be accessed by choosing Text | Check Spelling and will search for words that are not included in its built-in dictionary. While this is a feature that you should use just prior to saving any file you've created, you may prefer to be able to type in a regular word processor first, check your spelling as you go, and then paste the resulting text into a web page—especially if you're working on a long document.

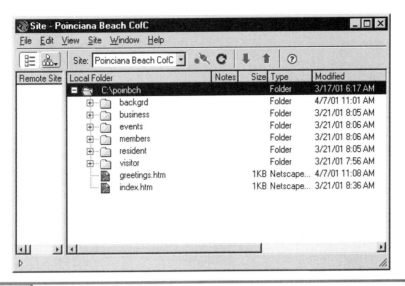

Figure 5-1   Locate index.htm in the site files for the sample web site by using the Site window

2. You will now use the basic copy-and-paste function to capture the text located in the file called index_text.txt. Navigate to the Exercises folder that you created in the last module and then navigate to the Module_5 folder. This file can be opened in any basic word processing program you have installed on your computer. In this example, Microsoft Notepad is being used, but you can just as easily use Word Pad, Word, or Simple Text on a Mac. Once you have the file open, simply copy the text by choosing Edit | Select All followed by Edit | Copy.

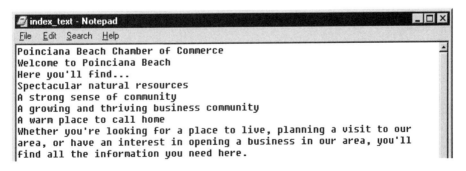

3. Return to your index.htm file and choose Edit | Paste from the Dreamweaver menu bar. All the content you need for your home page for the Poinciana Beach Chamber of Commerce web site now is in place, as shown in Figure 5-2.

Note

The title of your page has not been entered. Erase "Untitled Document" and then copy and paste the text **Poinciana Beach Chamber of Commerce** into the Title box in the Dreamweaver toolbar and your page will be properly titled.

4. Save your document by choosing File | Save.

5. Preview this page in your default browser by pressing the F12 key and looking for the following:

- How are long lines wrapped when you increase or decrease the size of your browser window?

- Where does a break in the text appear to be?

- What font is displayed in your browser?

Dreamweaver has accomplished its task in the exact manner it was intended to achieve—quickly bringing in text that was created elsewhere. In the process, though, all formatting was removed from the text, even the returns created when the ENTER or RETURN key is pressed. You now have to work with one

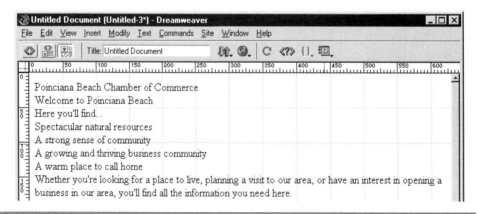

Figure 5-2   The result of pasting text into a Dreamweaver document

unbroken block of text with no formatting whatsoever. To appreciate exactly what has happened, you need to look at the code for this document and the information in the Properties Inspector, as you see in Figure 5-3.

In the source code, you see that the most frequently inserted tag is <br>, indicating that the end of a line of type has been reached and that you wish to drop one line down in your document without changing any of the text formatting. You also can see by examining the Properties Inspector that no formatting is applied to this page at all—the format and font size are set to None and the font is the default font for the system. And although this page is readable, it certainly lacks any visual impact and does little in creating an atmosphere suitable for a Florida resort town. You have a lot of work to do!

5

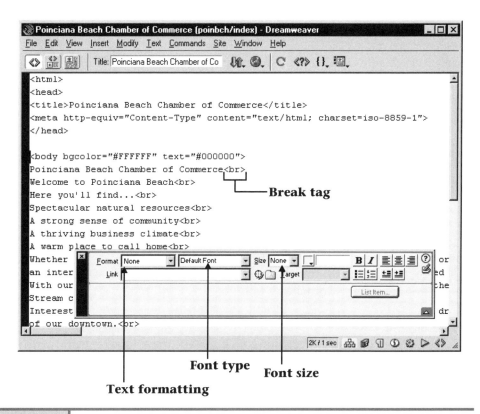

Figure 5-3   Source code and the Properties Inspector for index.htm

Text Formatting

As previously noted, your document currently has no formatting applied to it. As it is, any formatting instructions that you apply to one line of text will actually be applied to the entire block of text. You are missing an essential tag—the paragraph or <p> tag—and to do any formatting, you need to break up your text into distinct paragraphs.

Paragraph Formatting

With your index.htm file open, complete the following steps:

1. Place your cursor at the beginning of the line with the text Welcome To Poinciana Beach and press the ENTER key.

2. Place your cursor at the beginning of the line with the text Here You'll Find... and press the ENTER key.

3. Repeat this process by placing your cursor at the beginning of the following lines of text and pressing the ENTER key.

   - Spectacular natural resources
   - Whether you're looking for a place to live…
   - Poinciana Beach is your place in the sun!
   - Poinciana Beach Chamber of Commerce
   - Contact us via e-mail at info@poincianabeach.org

Viewing the code for this page reveals that the <p> tag now encloses the lines of text where you used the ENTER key to insert the tag, as shown in Figure 5-4. You also see that a blank line now separates the lines of text. This formatting rule for HTML can cause real headaches for page designers, since there is no way to apply formatting to lines of text without inserting the <p> tag, and there is no way to do that without inserting a blank line. Some workarounds for this design problem will be given as you move through this and succeeding modules. Since your goal here is to understand how formatting is done, press on in the knowledge that you can clean up and rearrange your text layout later.

Using Headings

Just as a newspaper uses headlines to introduce a story, and this book uses headings to announce new sections and concepts, headings can also be applied in HTML documents. Six different tags are used to accomplish this task—from <h1> to <h6>, with corresponding size differences as you see in Figure 5-5.

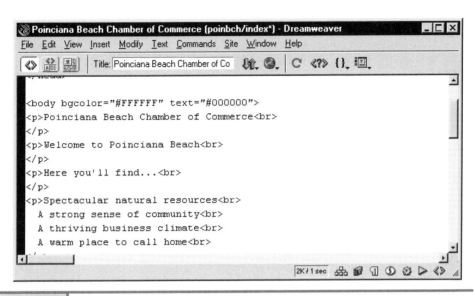

Figure 5-4 Paragraph tags are inserted in text each time you press the ENTER key

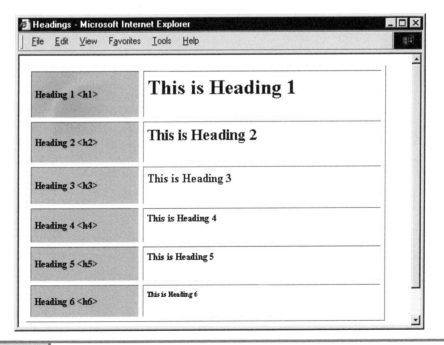

Figure 5-5 Headings tags set pre-determined size and bold styles to text

5

The best way to see how headings are applied to a document is to put them into action. Follow these steps to apply headings to your index.htm file. Be sure that you have the Properties Inspector open by selecting Windows | Properties.

Note

You will be using the Properties Inspector to complete these tasks, but you could also use Text | Paragraph Format, or right-click the text to be formatted and choose the heading from the Paragraph Format selections in the context menu.

1. Place your cursor at the beginning of the text Poinciana Beach Chamber Of Commerce and click the drop-down arrow in the Format options area of the Properties Inspector. Choose Heading 2.

2. Place your cursor at the beginning of the line with the text Welcome To Poinciana Beach and choose Heading 1 from the drop-down selections.

3. Apply Heading 4 to the text Here You'll Find... and to the text at the bottom of the document Poinciana Beach Is Your Place In The Sun!

4. Choose File | Save to save your document.

5. Previewing your work in a browser shows that your text is now bigger and bolder—perfect for setting off important elements of your text that you want to draw attention to, as shown in Figure 5-6.

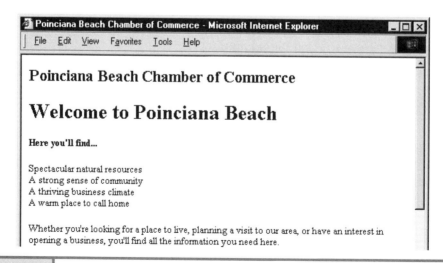

Figure 5-6   Using heading formats can lend impact to text elements of a web page

You have now seen methods for inserting text into an HTML document, preparing the text for formatting by using the <p> tag, and creating headings to set off parts of your text that you want to use for introductions to important portions of your pages. In the next section, you will look at how to change font types and how you can adjust the alignment of text to give your pages a cleaner and more uniform appearance.

1-Minute Drill

- What two terms are used for describing text styles?
- What happens to text formatting when text is copied from a word processor document into an HTML document using Dreamweaver?
- Which heading tag produces the largest text format? Which produces the smallest?

Controlling Text Appearance

The difference between formatting text and changing text appearance may seem to be minor since both formatting and choosing a larger font size, for instance, apparently accomplish the same thing. The primary difference is that formatting generates predetermined appearances, whereas inserting specific tags allows text to be manipulated in a variety of ways. In this section, you will see how font styles, size, and alignment are changed, as well as how to apply layout features such as numbered and bulleted lists and how to align text.

Changing Font Styles

Since you know that the choice of fonts is established in the viewers' browsers, and fonts that are not installed on their computers will not be displayed, how can you be sure that your page will show text other than Times New Roman? Again, Dreamweaver lets you do this in a manner that is entirely consistent with good coding by using font lists as a way to generate code that will have the greatest possibility of displaying your pages as you intended—all without generating any dubious code that may be read in one browser but not another, as some WYSIWYG (what you see is what you get) editors do.

- *Font* and *typeface* are used interchangeably to describe text styles.
- All text formatting is lost when text is copied into an HTML document.
- Heading 1, <h1>, produces the largest format, while Heading 6, <h6>, produces the smallest.

Dreamweaver ships with predefined font lists that have the widest acceptance among computer operating systems and browsers. In addition, you can specify custom font lists that extend the program's capabilities. Of course, as you know, caution is required when choosing fonts that may not be present on the viewer's computer.

Once again, you will be using the Properties Inspector to access the font choices available in Dreamweaver, and, once again, you may choose to access these functions from the menu bar or the context menu instead.

Font lists function by presenting the browser with a list of several fonts that are similar in appearance. For the sake of clarity, choose Text | Fonts so that you can see the complete list. Currently, your text is set at Default, which means whatever the default font that is chosen by the user in their browser preferences will be the font

that is displayed. Looking further down the list, though, you see that three additional styles are available—the serif, sans-serif, and monospaced (mono) styles discussed earlier. Each of the fonts will be displayed, in descending order, as long as the viewer's computer has them installed. If, for instance, you choose to set Arial, Helvetica, sans-serif as the font style for a line of text, the code will instruct the browser to display Arial first. If the Arial font is not installed, then text will display in the Helvetica style. And, if that font isn't present, then a font that is sans-serif will be used. This method gives you the greatest possible control over the appearance of your text while working within the limits of HTML and browser capabilities.

Take a look at your fonts in action now. Unlike the previous method that you used, where you simply placed your cursor at the beginning of the line where you wanted the tag inserted, changing fonts requires you to select the text first, just as you would if you were using a word processor. You can choose individual characters, words, or lines of text and change the font style. You can also choose all the text at once by choosing Edit | Select All.

1. Select the text at the top of your document, Poinciana Beach Chamber Of Commerce, and then open the font selection list in the fonts category of the Properties Inspector. Change the font from Default Font to Arial, Helvetica, sans-serif, as shown in Figure 5-7. Notice that in this font style, your line of text is slightly longer than the default Times New Roman font.

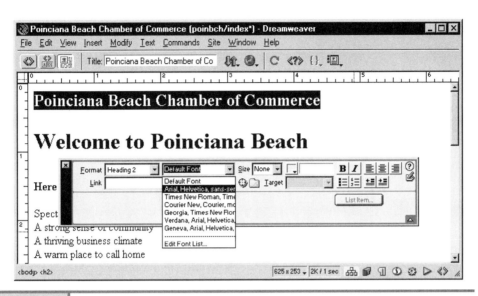

Figure 5-7 Use the Properties Inspector to change font types

2. Working your way down the font list, make the following changes to
the document:

- Set the text Welcome To Poinciana Beach in the Courier New,
  Courier, mono font style

- Apply the Georgia, Times New Roman, Times, serif font to the text
  Here You'll Find...

- Change the font style for the four lines beginning with the word
  Spectacular in the Verdana, Arial, Helvetica, sans-serif style

- Select all the remaining text and change the font style to Geneva,
  Arial, Helvetica, sans-serif style

3. Previewing your restyled text in a browser gives you the best look at how
your work will display. Notice in Figure 5-8 that regardless of the font that
you've chosen, the preformatted size and bold characteristics of your
headings are maintained.

4. Obviously, there are very few instances in which you would mix font
styles as you have here, but you can now see how the different font styles
are displayed. To go back to a more conventional styling for your page,

Figure 5-8 Changing font types does not change text attributes applied with head tags

you only need to choose Edit | Select All and change the font style to Geneva, Arial, Helvetica, sans-serif—chosen for its lighter "feel," which is appropriate for your fictional resort town.

5. Choose File | Save to finish this exercise.

Changing Font Sizes

You now have your font style set in a form that suits your needs. But what if you need to change the size of just a few lines of text without changing other formatting? For this task, you turn again to the Properties Inspector and the font sizing options available there.

Font size is another example of where HTML differs dramatically from word processors in that font sizes are *relative* rather than absolute sizes. This means that the size of fonts is measured relative to the default font size set in the browser. Contrast this with the way that word processors give you choices in text sizes—everything from 8 points all the way to 72 points is possible, depending on the font, and whatever size you specify is the size that will be printed. As Figure 5-9 shows, fonts can be set in terms of either their relative value measured against the baseline size of 3 or in their absolute value from 1 to 7.

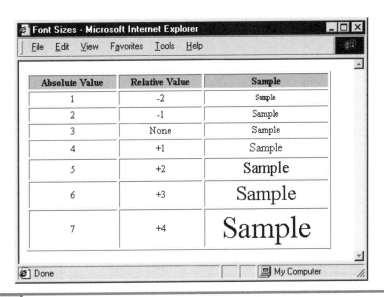

Figure 5-9   This sample lists both relative and absolute fonts sizes

The concept of relative sizes is made even more confusing by the inclusion of options that at first glance seem superfluous—relative values of +5, +6, and +7, and –5, –6, and –7. In most instances, these values will not display any larger than the standard absolute value of 7 or any smaller than the absolute value of 1 *unless* the viewer has changed their default font size to something other than the standard absolute value of 3.

Ask the Expert

Question: Isn't there a way to set point sizes for text just like you would in a word processor?

Answer: Cascading style sheets (CSS) do allow you to set absolute point sizes where HTML tags do not. This is one of the reasons that, in the future, most page and text formatting will be done using CSS.

Confused? Perhaps the best thing to do is to actually see these values placed into action to get a better understanding of how font sizes display after they are applied:

1. Open index.htm. Be sure that the Properties Inspector is open so that you can quickly apply font size options. Once again, these operations can also be completed using the menu bar or the context menu.

2. Select the line of text Spectacular Natural Resources.

3. Notice that the Size box in the top of the Properties Inspector reads None. Change the size to the absolute size of 2 by clicking the arrow to the right of the Size box and selecting 2 from the drop-down list, as shown here:

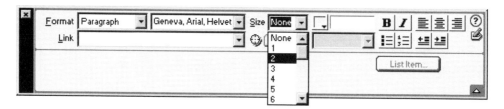

4. Select the line of text A Strong Sense Of Community. Set the size of this text to the relative value of –1.

5. Notice here that the lines of text are identical in size—this demonstrates relative and absolute values at work.

Here you'll find...

Spectacular natural resources
A strong sense of community
A thriving business climate
A warm place to call home

6. Experiment with different sizes of fonts in the two lines that follow, alternating between relative and absolute font values.

7. When you're finished, reset the font size to 3 (or None) and save your document.

Changing Font Colors

You saw earlier how all the text in a document can be changed using the Page Properties dialog box. But what if you want to change just a few lines of text, or even one word? For that operation, the appropriate tool is the color chooser found in the Properties Inspector:

1. Select the line of text at the top of your document—Poinciana Beach Chamber Of Commerce.

2. The Color box is just to the right of the Size drop-down list box in the Properties Inspector, and is identical to the one you saw earlier in the Page Properties dialog box.

3. Clicking this square presents you with the standard Dreamweaver color palette, as shown in Figure 5-10, with the system Color Chooser option, the eyedropper tool, and a small box that lets you return to the default color for the item that is selected.

4. Choose a medium-green color for the text you have selected, as shown in Figure 5-10.

5. Click a blank area of your document and you will see that the text color for the selected text has changed to a nice green color.

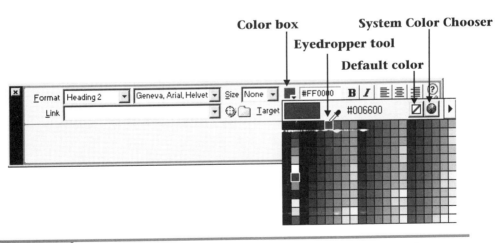

Figure 5-10   Use the Eyedropper tool and the color panel on the standard Dreamweaver color palette to set text color

6. To return the color to its default (black) color that you set in the properties for the page, you have two choices—either undo your previous step by selecting Edit | Undo Font Color (or by pressing CTRL-Z), or return to the Color Chooser and choose the default color box.

7. This is another good time to experiment. Try selecting different lines of text and applying colors to them one by one. When you are all done, choose Edit | Select All and reset the color back to the default black text color. Check your spelling by selecting Text | Check Spelling, and then save your file when you are done.

Caution

Remember that many users of the Internet expect blue text to be a hyperlink. Don't confuse your audience by using a color for normal text that is the same color as links or you'll have them dragging their mouse pointer around the page looking for somewhere to go.

Aligning Text

Aligning text to the left, right, or center of a web page is a fairly simple operation, and one where the commands will seem familiar to anyone who has used a word processing program. The difference for the Web is that the size of the screen can be changed by how the viewer's monitor is set or how the window is sized. Imagine if you could do the same for a printed document.

Having said that, the operation still remains fairly simple, as you'll see as you go through a series of steps with your index.htm file to align your text:

1. Dreamweaver presents you with three buttons, as shown here, on the Properties Inspector that allow you to change basic text alignment to the left, center, or right, respectively.

2. Applying alignment tags to your document is a simple process of placing the cursor anywhere in the line of text you wish to change and clicking the appropriate button.

3. Place your cursor at the beginning of the first line of text in your document, Poinciana Beach Chamber Of Commerce, and change its alignment to center.

4. Do the same for the second line of text: Welcome To Poinciana Beach.

5. Center the address for the Chamber of Commerce found at the bottom of your document. When you are finished, preview your work in your browser, and you'll find that your document looks like Figure 5-11.

6. Try aligning a single line of text within a paragraph. Highlight the text Spectacular Natural Resources and choose right alignment. Notice that all four lines jump to the right, as shown in Figure 5-12. As noted earlier, paragraphs are treated as unified blocks of information, and unless the lines of text have been separated by the <p> tag, you cannot format them differently from other lines of text in the block.

7. Reset the previous paragraph to left alignment and save your document.

Aligning text is a simple operation, but one that can become complicated by the limitations of HTML. You will be looking at ways to work around those limitations a little later.

Figure 5-11 The result of changing text alignment in a Dreamweaver document

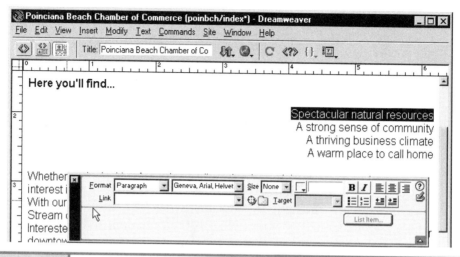

Figure 5-12 Text alignment is applied to blocks of text unless it is separated by a
<p> tag

Using Lists and Indents

The final four buttons that you find on the Properties Inspector are, not
coincidentally, the last four text tools presented in this discussion of formatting
HTML text. Lists are simply either bulleted or numbered blocks of text, which
you are probably familiar with from using a word processor. Indented text is
made possible by the use of the <blockquote> tag—creating text that is set in
from both sides of the page.

Ordered and Unordered Lists

As you know, before you can format a block of text, you must use the <p> tag
to separate it from other text adjacent to it. One peculiarity of pasting text into an
HTML document is that in order to break the lines of text, the break tag (<br>) is
used instead of the <p> tag. As noted before, a break drops text down one line
but does not let you change formatting. Looking at the code for index.htm,
shown in Figure 5-13, reveals that you have a lot of breaks in your page.

To use your list tools, your first task is to remove the breaks and insert a
<p> tag instead. Follow these steps to remove the breaks and apply the list tags
that you want in your page:

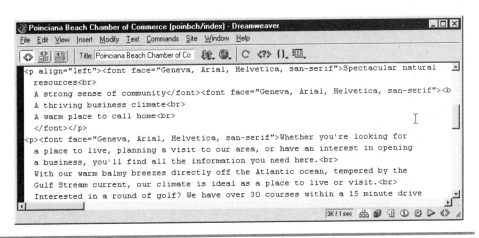

Figure 5-13 Breaks separate lines of text but do not allow for new formatting

1. Identify the text you want to work with in your index.htm file:

   Spectacular natural resources
   A strong sense of community
   A thriving business climate
   A warm place to call home

2. Place your cursor at the beginning of the second line of text and press the BACKSPACE key. The second line of text will jump into the same line with the first line of text—removing the <b> tag.

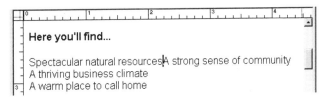

3. Press ENTER to insert the <p> tag, dropping the line of text (and inserting an extra blank line).

4. Repeat this process for the remaining lines in your block of text; when you are finished, your reformatted text will look like the text shown in Figure 5-14.

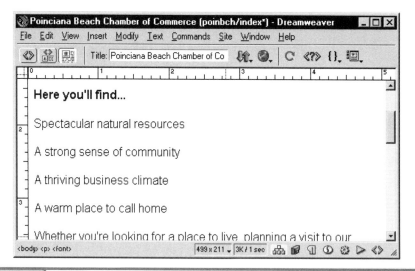

Figure 5-14 Paragraph tags are necessary when you want to change the formatting on a line of text

5. Now that the basic formatting is done, you can use the list buttons on the Properties Inspector to create both ordered (numbered) and unordered (bulleted) lists.

6. Highlight the four lines of text and locate the list buttons on the Properties Inspector.

7. Try each of the buttons and notice the results. Not only is the text numbered or bulleted, but it is also indented and the extra blank lines are gone. Finish this exercise by choosing the unordered list button, so that your text looks similar to Figure 5-15, and then save your file.

8. In addition to the options you have chosen, other choices are available by clicking the expansion arrow in the Properties Inspector and then choosing the List Item button. Bullets, for instance, can be changed from round to square, and numbered lists can be changed to use letters or Roman numerals. Other options are available through CSS properties, as well, where you can even choose a small image to display as your bullets instead of the standard round or square symbols. For now, leave your bullets set to the standard round bullets as you move on to a discussion of indenting text.

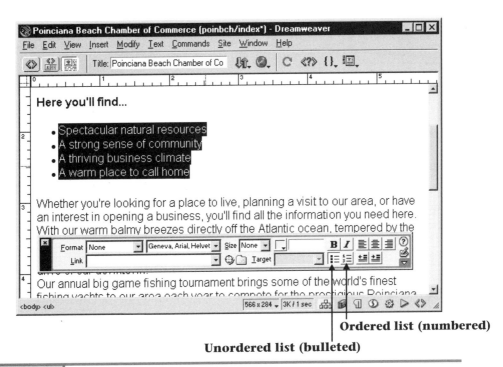

Ordered list (numbered)

Unordered list (bulleted)

Figure 5-15   Ordered and unordered lists are applied with the Properties Inspector

Setting Indents

Indents are a terrific way to increase the *whitespace*—the empty space around text or images in a document—making it easier to read and enhancing the professional appearance of the page. As mentioned before, using the Indent Text and Outdent Text buttons allows you to quickly apply additional margins to the left and right of the document. Follow these steps to see how this is done:

1. Returning to index.htm, you see that the long paragraph below the bulleted text that you just created is currently against the left margin of the page (refer back to Figure 5-15). To move it to the right, you need only use the Indent Text button on the Properties Inspector.

2. Formatting for block text is similar to formatting paragraphs. Simply place your cursor in front of the first line of text in the paragraph and click the Indent Text button. As Figure 5-16 shows, the text is indented both to the left and the right as a result.

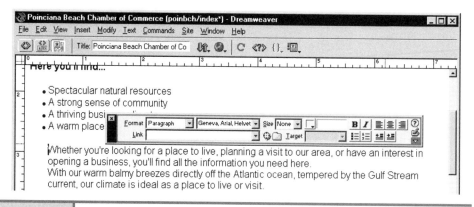

Figure 5-16 The Indent button moves text away from both margins of the page

3. You can experiment now with using both the Indent Text and Outdent Text (shown here) buttons to move the text around. When you are finished, be sure that the text appears as it does in Figure 5-16, aligned with the bulleted text above it, and save your file.

4. Move any additional text that now falls outside the clean lines that you've created in your new page format. Find the text Poinciana Beach Is Your Place In The Sun! and move it to the center of your page by clicking the Center button. Be sure that the Chamber of Commerce address is also centered, along with the e-mail information below it. When you're all done, save your file and preview it in your browser.

1-Minute Drill

● Why is caution required when specifying font types for an HTML document?

● The relative font size of –1 is equivalent to what absolute font size?

● What tag is required to separate lines of text before they can be formatted as a list?

● Only those fonts that are installed on the viewer's computer will display in an HTML document.
● The relative font size of –1 is equal to the absolute font size of 2.
● The paragraph tag (<p>) must separate lines of text before they can be formatted as a list.

Creating Hyperlinks

The previous discussion of HTML noted that the single most important element of this dynamic scripting language is that it enables you to jump from one document to another—whether that page is on your own site or located half way around the world on another server. Hyperlinks make this possible by embedding a tag that is attached to an object on your page—whether its text, an image, or another object—thereby letting your viewers jump to another location with the simple click of their mouse. This section discusses the most common types of links that are used in conjunction with text and how they are inserted in a document.

Absolute and Relative Links

Hyperlinks to other documents on the Web are divided into two broad categories—absolute links and relative links. Recall from the earlier discussion of HTML that an absolute link is to a page outside of your own web site, whereas a relative link is to a page that is related to, or within the same site as, the current page that is displayed. Take a look at both of these types of links in action.

Creating an Absolute Link

Links are attached to an object in a web page. Therefore, creating them is a two-step process: select the item where the link is to be attached, and then specify the address of the document you are linking to.

1. In your index.htm file, you first need to add some additional text that your absolute link will be attached to. Navigate to the very last line in the document (the e-mail information). Place your cursor at the end of that line of text and press ENTER to insert a <p> tag.

2. At the cursor, type **Member of the United States Chamber of Commerce**.

3. Highlight the entire line of text you just typed. Remember that to attach a link, you first have to select the object or text where the link will be assigned.

4. In the Properties Inspector, locate the Link area. For an absolute link, you will be typing the exact address of the URL for the page you want to link to.

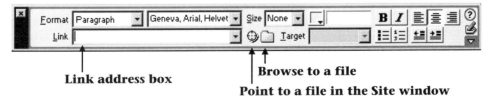

Link address box

Browse to a file

Point to a file in the Site window

5. Type the following URL into the Link box: **http://www.uschamber.org**. Press ENTER to accept the change, and your text changes to the familiar blue underlined link.

Note

The entire URL must be entered, including the protocol (http://), for the link to function correctly.

6. Save your document and then preview it in a browser. You can go online at this point to check whether the link actually works. If you launch from your page to the United States Chamber of Commerce web site when you click the link you just created, then give yourself a pat on the back. If not, go back and check your spelling.

Creating a Relative Link

The next type of link you will create, a relative link, will take you to a page that is within your own web site. Relative links are what you'll be using when you create navigation elements for your pages that allow your audience to drill down to the information on your site that they want to find. Dreamweaver makes this a simple operation by giving you the choice of either browsing to the file you want to link to or dragging a special pointer to a file in your Site window.

Using the Browse To File Feature

In a simple web site like your Chamber of Commerce site, using the Browse To File feature is an easy way to quickly assign a relative link to text or an object.

Ask the Expert

Question: Some URLs can be really long. How can I be sure that I type them in exactly right?

Answer: The best way to capture a URL for use as an absolute link is to open your browser and navigate to the page you want to link to. From there, it's a simple matter of highlighting the URL in the Address or Location box of the browser and copying it by using one of several methods: choose Edit | Copy; right-click and choose Copy; or use the keyboard shortcut CTRL-C. Then, simply return to Dreamweaver and paste the URL into the Link address box.

This method has the added advantage of making sure that the link you are assigning is to a page that is active.

You'll now create a link to the greetings.htm file that you created in the last module:

Note

If you did not complete that exercise, return to the beginning of Module 4 and follow the steps in Project 4-1 for creating a new file in the root folder of the Chamber of Commerce site.

1. Just as in the previous example, the first step in creating a link is to select the text to which you want the link to be attached. In the body of the text of your index.htm file, highlight the text greeting message in the second-to-last sentence.

2. Although you could simply type greetings.htm into the Link box in the Properties Inspector (since this document is in the same folder as index.htm), you'll use the handy shortcut of browsing to the file instead. Again, this is helpful for those of you who are keyboard-challenged and may mistype the filename.

3. Click the folder icon on the Properties Inspector, and Dreamweaver will launch a standard open file dialog box for your operating system, as shown in Figure 5-17, and display the contents of the root folder for the current site. Select greetings.htm and click the Select button.

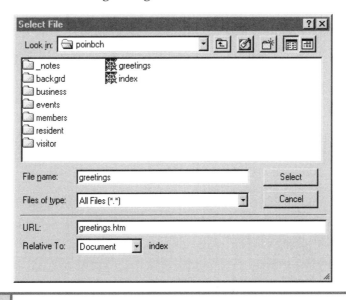

| **Figure 5-17** | Browse to the file you want to link to in the Select File dialog box |

5

Note

Netscape is set as the default browser in Figure 5-17, so you see the Navigator icon next to the filename. You may see the Internet Explorer icon instead if you have that browser set as the default for your system.

4. Returning to the Properties Inspector, you see that Dreamweaver has placed the name of your file into the Link box for the link.

5. Save your file and preview it in a browser. Click the link you just created and you will jump to the greetings.htm file in your site—which is blank at this point.

6. If you had wished, you also could have navigated up or down within your site, or even outside it, simply by opening the folder where the page you wish to link to is found and then selecting the file. Of course, if you try to link to a file that is not within your site root folder, Dreamweaver will remind you that all files need to be located there to function correctly, and give you the opportunity to copy the file properly into the root folder.

Using Dreamweaver's Point To File Feature

Your sample site is pretty simple at this point, and browsing to a file that you want to link to is a straightforward operation. As your site becomes more complicated, though, you might want to consider using the Point To File option instead of the Browse To File function. This is also a good way to create links when you have a page built that needs lots of links associated to files within your own site. In this operation, you will select the text to attach the link to and then drag a pointer from the Properties Inspector directly into the Site window to activate the link:

1. To make this operation viable, make both the Document and Site windows visible on your monitor. Minimize and arrange the two separate windows as shown in Figure 5-18.

2. To remove the link you created previously, highlight the text Greetings Message and then select the filename in the Link box of the Properties Inspector. Backspace to delete the filename, removing the link from the text.

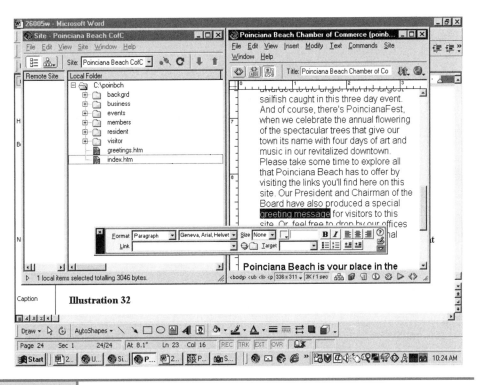

Figure 5-18 Resize the Document and Site windows so both are viewable on your monitor

3. With the text still highlighted, click and hold down the Point To File icon to the left of the folder icon you used previously.

4. Still holding the mouse button down, drag across the screen until the pointer rests on the filename greetings.htm in the Site window, as shown in Figure 5-19.

5. Release the mouse button and the link is (almost magically) created.

6. Save your file.

Creating an E-Mail Link

Adding the ability to contact someone via e-mail is another important capability inherent to HTML. In your next operation, you will attach a link to text that causes the viewer's default e-mail program to open with a window preaddressed

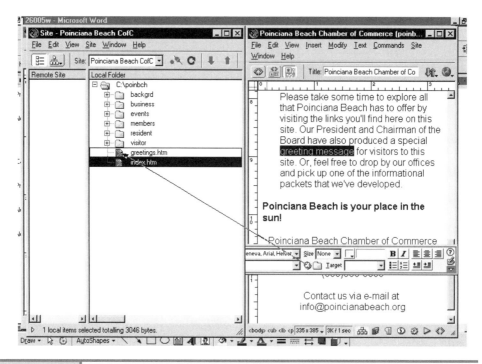

Figure 5-19 Drag the pointer directly into the Site window to create a link with the Point to File feature

to an address you specify. This is a simple operation that uses the Objects panel to insert the link.

1. Find the text Contact Us Via E-Mail At info@poincianabeach.org at the bottom of your index.htm file and highlight it.

Note

It is considered good practice to list the entire e-mail address rather than simply having something like "e-mail us" listed. This gives the viewer the option of copying and pasting the address into a new message window as well as using the link. In addition, if the viewer prints the page, they will be able to use the printed address later to send a message without having to return to the page itself.

2. Open the Objects panel (if it is not already open) by choosing Window | Objects.

3. From the Common category, locate the icon for inserting an e-mail link.

4. Click this icon to open the Insert Email Link dialog box.

5. Since you have already selected the text where you want the link to be attached, you see that line of text in the Text box. You could also have typed in new text at this point and it would have been inserted into the document.

6. To specify the (fictional) address where the e-mail will be sent, type **info@poincianabeach.org** in the E-Mail box. Click OK to accept this change to the document and save your file.

7. Returning to your document, you see that the link that was created now appears in the Properties Inspector. An alternate method for creating this link would have been to type the tag preface **mailto:** directly in the Properties Inspector Link box followed by the e-mail address where you wanted the mail to be delivered.

8. Preview your page in a browser and try out the link. When you click it, the e-mail application associated with your default browser opens a new message form already addressed.

Inserting Page Anchors

The last type of link to discuss is one that creates an internal link that works within a web page itself. These links, called *anchors*, are particularly useful when the document is long, allowing the viewer to jump directly to a specific placeholder in a page or back to the top of the page. While similar to the other links you've created, anchors require two additional steps—creating the anchor itself, which is hidden from the viewer, and then inserting a link to the anchor:

1. Place your cursor at the very top of your index.htm document, just to the left of the first line of text.

2. With the Objects panel open, change the category from Common to Invisibles.

3. The anchor icon shouldn't be too hard to find—it looks like an anchor. Click it and the very simple Insert Named Anchor dialog box will open.

4. Type **top** in the Anchor Name field. Named anchors should always be typed only in lowercase letters. Click OK and you'll be returned to the Document window.

5. The yellow icon that now appears is Dreamweaver's way of letting you know that an invisible element has been inserted into your page. If you don't see this special symbol, choose View | Invisible Elements to have it appear (or to turn it off).

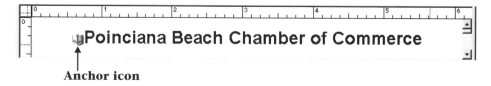

Anchor icon

Note

This is another way that the Properties Inspector can be especially useful—selecting this symbol reveals its name. While that may not seem like such a big deal now, later on when you have a number of these mysterious icons on your page, you will definitely come to appreciate it.

6. At the end of your document, you will now insert a link that will return your viewer to the top of the page when it is selected. To do this, go to the end of the e-mail link you created in the previous step and press the ENTER key, dropping a line and inserting a <p> tag.

7. Type the word **Top** and then highlight it with your mouse.

8. Type a special symbol in the Properties Inspector to link to the anchor you created earlier. The pound sign (#) is used in HTML coding to accomplish this task—followed by the name of the anchor itself.

9. Type **#top** in the Link address box on the Properties Inspector and press the ENTER key to accept the change.

10. Save your file and preview it. If you've completed the steps correctly, you should jump to the top of the page.

11. The Point To File method can also be used to complete this operation, and using it is actually kind of fun. Create and name the anchor and then highlight the text where you want the link to be attached. Then, simply click the Point To File icon and drag your mouse to the anchor icon on your page, as shown in Figure 5-20. Quick and easy!

Figure 5-20 | Use the Point to file feature to drag a link to a named anchor within a page

1-Minute Drill

● What are the two categories of hyperlinks?

● What information is required when creating an absolute link?

● List the three methods for creating a link to a page in your own web site.

Putting It All Together

Creating a readable document and inserting links to other web sites are two of the most fundamental skills required of anyone who wishes to publish their work to the Internet. In this module, you have seen how text can be entered, copied, and formatted, as well as how to apply simple HTML tags to enhance the readability and impact of your pages. The discussion of hyperlinks has shown you how to establish links to a page outside and within your own site, and you have also learned how to create anchors that let you jump quickly from one point in a document to another. All in all, a very solid bit of work that you'll continue next by practicing your newly acquired skills in this module's project.

Project 5-1: Formatting a Web Page

In this project, you will review the steps that you have previously learned—entering text into a web page, applying headings, setting font styles and size, and adding links. At the end of the project, you will have completed the first two documents for your site, complete with text and links.

Step-by-Step

1. In the folder for this module where you previously found your index_text.txt file is another similar file called greetings_text.txt. Open this file in a word processor of your choice.

2. Just as you did previously, select all the text by choosing Edit I Select All and then Edit I Copy.

3. Open the blank document that you created earlier called greetings.htm. To do this, double-click the file icon in the Site window.

● Hyperlinks can be created to a page outside of your web site (absolute) or within it (relative).

● Absolute links require the exact address of the page being linked to, including the protocol—usually http://.

● Relative links can be created by typing the filename in the Link address box, by browsing to the file, or by using the Point To File button.

4. Once again, you'll repeat a previous step by pasting all the text that you copied in step 2 into this blank document. Choose Edit | Paste, and your web page will now be filled with the same type of unformatted text that you saw when you pasted text into your index file, as shown here.

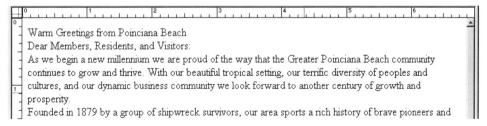

5. Starting at the top of the document, complete the following tasks:

- Press the ENTER key after the first and second lines of text to insert the <p> tag.
- Insert a <p> tag at the end of the last line of text in the body of the letter.
- Insert a <p> tag after the title Chairman Of The Board.
- Insert a <p> tag after the title President.

6. Highlight the text Warm Greetings From Poinciana Beach and apply Heading 2 formatting. Center the text on the page, as shown here.

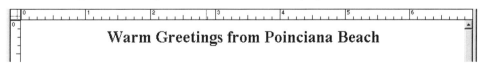

7. Highlight the text Dear Members, Residents, And Visitors: and format it with Heading 4.

8. At the bottom of the page, find and highlight the text Return To Our Home Page and center it in the page.

9. Choose all the text on the page by selecting Edit | Select All and apply the same text style you used in your index file—Geneva, Arial, Helvetica, sans-serif.

10. Align your text and get the nice whitespace around it by using the indent buttons. When you're finished, preview your final product in your browser. If everything has gone well, your final product should be similar to Figure 5-21.

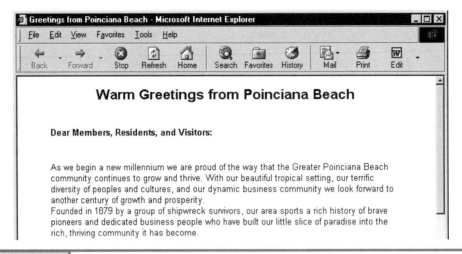

Figure 5-21 The results of applying text formatting to your page

11. Now that you have the physical appearance of your page set, add the links you need to make it functional. The first link is obvious and lets viewers jump back to your home page. Highlight that text at the bottom of your page and either browse to or point to index.htm.

12. Your final link is an e-mail link to be created at the end of this page. Highlight the text e-mail to info@poincianabeach.org and create an e-mail link by using the Objects panel or by typing the required information directly into the Properties Inspector as seen in this illustration.

13. Check your spelling, save your work, and then preview your creation in your browser. Now, you can actually click the links and jump back and forth from one web page to another.

What to Take Away

In Project 5-1 and in the previous exercises of this module, you learned how to format a simple text-based web page, including choosing fonts, applying headings, and even creating your first hyperlinks. Along the way, you've also learned some valuable information about how different tags are created and their specific applications. The two pages you finished in Project 5-1 are your first functional web documents—well designed and interactive. The next module looks at how you can further improve the look and functionality of pages through the use of graphics, pictures, and navigation elements.

5

✓ Mastery Check

1. What font category takes the most space on a page—proportional or monospaced?

2. How do the viewer's browser settings affect the appearance of text?

3. Why are font lists used instead of specifying a single font, as you would in a word processor?

4. Why should the use of a blue font color be avoided?

5. Define a relative link.

6. Define an absolute link.

Module 6

Adding Visual Interest: Working with Images

The Goals of this Module

- Understand the various image formats for the Web
- Insert images using the Objects panel
- Align and size images in a web document
- Create links to images
- Create rollover images
- Use Flash text and buttons
- Preview the capabilities of Fireworks

Looking at your work in the previous module reveals two fully functional web pages that present information in a very straightforward manner—through the use of text. You have seen how text is entered and formatted, copied and pasted, and how links can be inserted to make your pages functional. A few years ago, these pages would have been the norm on the Internet. In many instances, a page that is composed primarily of text is *still* the best choice for getting a message across.

But you also know that the Internet has come a long way since the days of text-based pages. Today, audiences are more sophisticated and the Internet experience has changed to the point that a page without images is nearly as extinct as the dinosaurs. Today's audiences expect a web page to have a little zing to it and, depending on the people you are trying to reach, may demand not only static images but also the kinds of animations and other interactive elements that are rapidly populating many sites. This module is all about the process of adding images and graphics to your documents, and along the way, you'll also see how navigation elements are created and how images can be manipulated so that they look clean and crisp and meet the goals of your site. This module also discusses one of the really exciting features available for the first time in version 4 of Dreamweaver—Flash text and buttons. You'll begin by gaining an understanding of the different kinds of images that are available for use on the Internet, and then see how those images are inserted into your documents with Dreamweaver.

Image File Formats for the Internet

Deciding on the right kind of image to include in a web page goes beyond simply getting the best picture available and sticking it on a page—although making that choice can be a huge chore in itself. You also need to understand which types of files will be displayed properly by the viewers' browsers and the type that is most appropriate for the kind of image you are adding. Two file types dominate the current Internet landscape, but, as always, the Web is constantly changing, so the future will be discussed a bit as you move along here.

Bitmaps, Rasters, and Vectors—Understanding Image Types

Images can be categorized in many ways, but the most common way to think about them is in terms of how they actually work. The first category of graphics is that of *bitmaps*. As the name implies, these types of images are created by creating a map, or grid, and then filling each of the squares created by the grid with bits of color. Bitmaps, also known as *raster* images, are the most common types of images used in all computer programs, and any time you see an image on your computer, especially if it is on the Internet, it more than likely was created by bitmaps.

The other type of image is called a *vector* image. In vector images, mathematical equations are created that describe each point in the image and then further specify the color, size, and other information that makes the image appear. Images that are created in a drawing program such as Macromedia Freehand or Adobe Illustrator are vector images that are most often seen in printed artwork. Here are examples of each:

This image is of the file ball.gif—a bitmapped image.

This image is of the file ball.swf—a vector image.

Notice that in the bitmap image, you can actually start to make out the little boxes that are filled with various shades of gray to give the illusion of shadows and light on the ball. In the vector image, there is a much smoother transition between the colors, and the image appears more natural. When magnified, the difference is even more pronounced.

This is the ball.gif image magnified to 200 percent.

This is ball.swf magnified to 200 percent.

And, by further magnifying a portion of the bitmap ball, you can actually see each individual bit of the image.

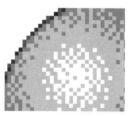

If vectors are so much more efficient at producing realistic pictures, then why aren't they the type of images that you see on your computer screens and on the Internet?

Once again, the problem stems from the competition among the software companies that produce browsers, as well as those that produce the programs that generate vector-based images themselves. Microsoft, Netscape, Adobe, and Macromedia all have a huge financial stake in gaining acceptance for their particular version of vector images. As of this date, there are few standards that have been agreed upon, although both of the latest versions of Netscape and Internet Explorer support the vector-based solution championed by Macromedia through their Shockwave and Flash programs.

Secondly, the two primary bitmapped image formats still do a very good job and are universally accepted—even in the oldest versions of browsers. While Macromedia is changing all of that with its fantastic vector-based program, Flash, at least for the short-term, bitmaps still rule the Internet.

Bitmaps are easy to work with but have limitations inherent to the way computers display the images, so a way had to be devised to get the most out of bitmapped images while maintaining the ability to download quickly. Two bitmap file formats are most widely in use today, and another is on the horizon, having just recently gained support in the latest versions of today's browsers.

Graphics Interchange Format—GIFs

If you happened to be one of the earliest inhabitants of the Internet, then you might have connected using the CompuServe service. CompuServe was one of the first companies to realize the potential of the Web as a place that the average person (as opposed to the scientists who had used it almost exclusively up to that point) might want to visit to access information. Early on, though, CompuServe decided that a purely text-based service would not be acceptable to most people, so it set about to create an image format that would allow for the small file sizes needed to download quickly.

CompuServe's solution was a format known as GIF (pronounced with a hard *g* as in "gift") for graphics interchange format. The GIF format has been the workhorse of the Internet ever since because it allows files to be compressed for transfer without loss of quality. The primary drawback with a GIF file is its limitation to a maximum of 256 colors, and (as you know from previous discussion) the number of colors that look the same regardless of the computer and the browser is actually 212. As a result, GIFs work best when a limited number of colors are needed and there are no fine gradations in hue and tone in the image. The following sketch of a palm tree, then, is best viewed in the GIF format.

GIFs are an excellent choice for posting images on the Web because they can be small in size but still give very good results. Other important reasons for choosing the GIF format include their ability to produce transparent areas that let the rest of the page show through them, and the capacity to create small animated sequences, as you'll see when you begin working with Fireworks.

Joint Photographic Experts Group Format—JPEGs

While CompuServe was the first player on the Web to develop a way to transmit images, the limitations of this format quickly became apparent when photographs were posted instead of simple drawings. With its inability to blend colors effectively and its limitations on the number of colors available, it quickly became apparent that a format other than GIF would be necessary for those instances in which smooth transitions between colors were needed.

The JPEG (pronounced "jay peg") file format was developed as a way to address these problems inherent to GIF files. JPEGs are a great way to post pictures or other images that have subtle differences such as shadows or complex colors. For a photograph of a palm tree in front of a house, the JPEG format is the appropriate choice.

Using the JPEG format has some trade-offs, though, the biggest of which is the fact that, unlike GIF files, JPEGs lose some of their information when they are compressed. And while they do a great job of displaying photographs, they do not compress solid colors very well, do not offer the ability to do animations, and have no way to present transparent regions.

Portable Network Graphic Format—PNGs

The technology that allows GIF files to be compressed is the property of Unisys Corporation, and in the mid-1990s, the company decided that it should really be paid for the work that went into making this file format possible. Early pioneers on the Internet scrambled for a free solution to this dilemma as the specter of having to pay for every image that was posted to the Web loomed on the horizon. Even though the problems associated with the possibility of having to pay a fee for each image on a web page ultimately faded away, the file format that was developed as an alternative to GIF remains today.

The portable network graphics format—or PNG (pronounced "ping")—has many of the same advantages of GIF files but without some of their drawbacks. Images are even smaller than GIFs and can display significantly more colors, all while maintaining GIF's ability to produce transparencies and animations. As you'll see when you work with Fireworks, PNG files can even combine some of the attributes of both bitmap and vector images.

Unfortunately, the PNG file format is another victim of browser compatibility problems. While it is supported in version 4 of most browsers (but not for the Macintosh, for instance), the PNG format has not gained wide acceptance among web designers. Perhaps it's simply a matter of being more familiar with good old GIFs and JPEGs, but for whatever reason, PNG images are still used rarely on the Web.

Shockwave Flash Format—SWFs

While not strictly an image format, the last file type to discuss is essential to an understanding of the capabilities of Dreamweaver 4. In this latest version, Macromedia has added the ability to insert text and small button images created using the vector-based authoring tool Flash.

If you spend any time on the Web at all, you've probably seen many instances of these SWF (pronounced "swif") files without even knowing it. The use of Flash technology and the clean and highly interactive images that it is capable of creating have increased at an exponential rate recently. Even though older browsers do not support the SWF format, the plug-in that makes them viewable is the most downloaded of all of these helper applications for browsers in the world, and many millions of people are viewing SWF files, even if they have yet to upgrade to newer browsers.

As you'll see, using Flash files adds some terrific new features to Dreamweaver and gives you the capability of creating images that can easily be programmed to function as navigation elements on your pages, all while giving you quicker download times than possible with GIF files.

6

Ask the Expert

Question: What is the best way to choose the right format for images and still keep file sizes small?

Answer: Since you're reading this book, it is assumed that you have already made the decision to purchase Fireworks, the companion program that makes creating and optimizing images possible. To be a professional web designer, or to at least make pages that look professional, you will need an image editing program, and in my humble opinion, Fireworks does that better than the competing programs available.

Considerations in the Use of Images

You have seen how image file formats differ, and have learned which type is appropriate for different types of images. Understanding some basic rules for working with images for the Web will ultimately make your pages more attractive and maintain the all-important goal of keeping file sizes to a minimum. Before you begin adding some nifty pictures and drawings to your sample site, review the following guidelines for including images in your pages:

- *Decide on the size of the image before you put it in your page.* Resizing bitmapped images simply does not work well once they are on your page.

- *Maintain your original image files.* Before you convert an image to a different format or play around with its compression settings, be sure to have the full-size image safely stored somewhere on your computer. It doesn't have to be posted to your server, but once an image has been compressed, especially in the JPEG format, you cannot go back and uncompress it.

- *Always keep your images in separate folders.* As discussed in the module on site management, a web site can quickly become huge. Keeping your images in their own "home" makes it easier to get back to them later on.

- *Use logic when naming image files.* Although filenames for images have the same restrictions as the names of HTML files, develop a system early on for how you will name your files based on their use, purpose, or physical description.

- *Exercise caution when using image formats that don't have wide acceptance by browsers.* Know your audience and be sure that including the latest image formats won't become an exercise in frustration because they can't see your work.

● *Test, test, test!* As you've already heard many times before, and will hear many times again, just because they look great on your computer doesn't mean that Aunt Maude in Topeka will see your graphics the same way you do. Test early and often on a variety of browsers and in both the Windows and Macintosh operating systems. There are differences in how images, in particular, display in the two systems.

1-Minute Drill

● How are bitmap images created?
● How are vector images created?
● Which file format is most appropriate for drawings?
● Which file format is most appropriate for photographs?

Using Dreamweaver to Insert Images

Before you can get too far along in the process, it's time again to download the support files for this module from the Osborne.com web site. Copy them into your Exercise folder and you'll be all ready to get started.

Project 6-1: Updating the Site Structure

In addition to grabbing the graphics files, you also need to do a little work on the site itself. One of your goals in this module is to create navigation buttons and elements for your pages, and, as you know, it's pretty difficult to do that without a file to link to. The following exercise runs you through the steps to add pages and new folders to your site in the categories you specified during your site design phase.

● Bitmaps are created by devising a grid and then filling each square of the grid with a color.
● Vector images use mathematical equations to describe the position and color of lines in an image.
● The GIF format is best for drawings.
● The JPEG format is best for photographs.

Step-by-Step

1. Open your site for the Poinciana Beach Chamber of Commerce and go to the Site window. As you see in Figure 6-1, you have only two web pages on your site, but your site structure is in good shape.

2. It's a good practice to have HTML files called index.htm in each of the subfolders for your site. Why? As you know, when a browser finds a file called index, it assumes that this is the main page for that folder. You could call the main file in your business folder business.htm, for instance, but by naming it index.htm instead, you are sure that the main page for that section will open as expected. In addition, many Internet users are used to the practice of "slicing off" the back end of URLs to get to the upper-level sections on the site. Naming your pages properly will let them work backward from a link that might be displayed in a search engine to get to other parts of your site.

Note

While most web hosting services will support this file naming method, you should always check with the service you plan to post your site to in the event it has any special restrictions. AOL, for instance, only allows a single file named index anywhere on your site, regardless of the path and folder structure. In the event that you do need to change filenames, Dreamweaver will automatically update all of your files to ensure you don't have any broken links.

3. Create the new index.htm files in each of your subfolders on the site. With the Site window open, right-click each of the subfolders, choose New File from the context menu, and then name each file **index.htm**.

4. In addition to these new files, you need to create a folder to hold the images that will be shared across the site. To do this, right-click the root folder at the top of the site structure and choose New Folder from the context menu. Name this new folder **common_images**.

5. Add a subfolder in the common_images folder you just created to store your buttons in. For your purposes, buttons are considered to be any graphic file that is used as a navigation element on your site. Even though the samples you'll use don't always look like buttons, they do function that way, and that's what you'll call them. Right-click the common_images folder, add a new folder as you did previously, and name it **buttons**. Figure 6-2 details all the changes that you've made to your site in the preceding steps.

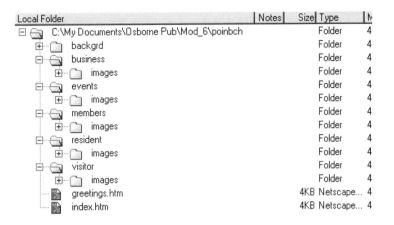

Local Folder	Notes	Size	Type	N
C:\My Documents\Osborne Pub\Mod_6\poinbch			Folder	4
backgrd			Folder	4
business			Folder	4
images			Folder	4
events			Folder	4
images			Folder	4
members			Folder	4
images			Folder	4
resident			Folder	4
images			Folder	4
visitor			Folder	4
images			Folder	4
greetings.htm		4KB	Netscape...	4
index.htm		4KB	Netscape...	4

Figure 6-1   Existing site structure for the Poinciana Beach Chamber of Commerce web site

6

Project 6-2: Adding a Simple Image to a Web Page

Now that you have the groundwork for your site behind you, you can get right into the job of inserting images using Dreamweaver. You'll start by dressing up the main page in your site.

Step-by-Step

1. As always, opening a page from the Site window is a simple process of double-clicking the icon for the file you want to edit. Locate the main index.htm file for the site and open it.

2. Your first task is to change the text heading at the top of your main page to a nice graphic that will reflect the style of your fictional town. Before you can do that, you need to get a good feel for the size of the graphic that you need. Remember, one of the inherent problems with bitmaps is that changing their size often leads to an image with poor quality. Until now, the rulers at the top and bottom of your screens haven't been addressed, but you'll reset them now to measure in pixels rather than in inches so that you can estimate the size of the graphic you need. To reset the ruler, choose View | Rulers | Pixels to change from the standard inches measurement to one that will translate better for measuring graphics.

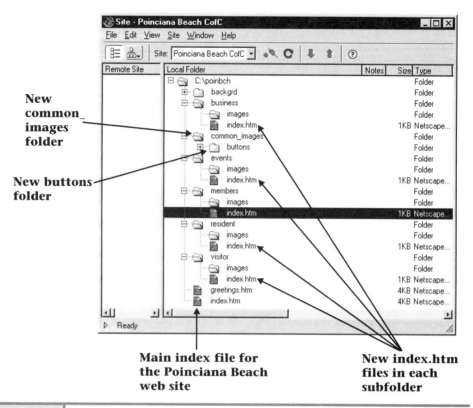

New common_ images folder

New buttons folder

Main index file for the Poinciana Beach web site

New index.htm files in each subfolder

Figure 6-2   Revised site structure for Poinciana Beach Chamber of Commerce

Note

The best way to get a feel for how your final page will look is to sketch it out with pencil and paper. You should always have a good understanding of the overall visual structure of your page before you get too far along in the design process. In the interest of time, you'll bypass that step, but when you are ready to start making your first real pages, you should spend some time sketching your pages by hand *before* you start building them in Dreamweaver.

3. Notice that the cursor position on the page is indicated in the ruler margins with a line. By using this tool, you can place your cursor at the beginning, end, top, and bottom of the Welcome To Poinciana Beach text and approximate the size of the banner you need to replace this text with to be about 450 pixels wide by 30 pixels high.

4. Select that text now and press the BACKSPACE or DELETE key to remove it from the page.

5. Make sure that your Objects panel is open, as you see in Figure 6-3, and locate the Insert Image button in the Common category.

6. Clicking this button opens the standard Select Image Source dialog box for your system—in this case, for Windows 98. Note that, by default, Dreamweaver always opens the root folder for your site, as you see in Figure 6-4, because the file ultimately needs to be there in order for the image to load properly when posted to a server.

7. Browse to the location of your exercise files and locate the file called banner_main.gif in the Module_6 folder, as shown in Figure 6-5. Click Select to insert the image.

8. If this file were in the same root folder as the rest of your files for this site, your image would appear now at the point on your page where your cursor was positioned. In this case, though, banner_main.gif is probably in a

6

Figure 6-3	Locate the Insert Image button on the Objects panel to insert a simple image

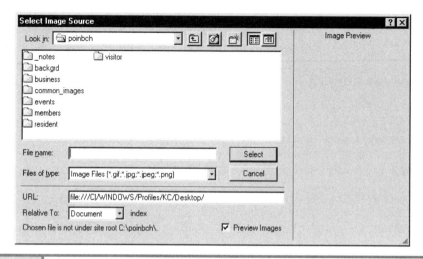

Figure 6-4 The Select Image Source dialog box automatically opens to the root folder of the site

separate folder, and Dreamweaver prompts you to copy the file to the correct location now.

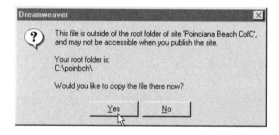

9. To complete the process, browse to your root folder for the site and copy this file into the common_images folder you created earlier.

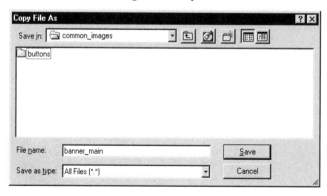

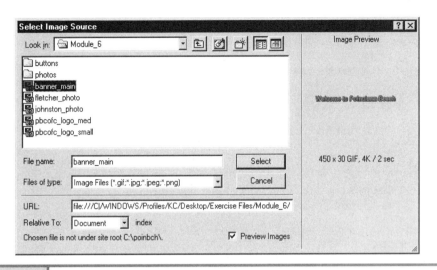

Figure 6-5 Locate files for insertion using the Select Image Source dialog box

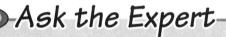

Ask the Expert

Question: That's an awful lot of steps just to get an image into a page! Isn't there an easier way?

Answer: This process is a little artificial because you are being provided the sample files to put into your document. When you begin working with Fireworks or begin building your own sites, image files should be saved directly into the correct folder based on the site structure, eliminating the need for the extra step of copying the files there.

Project 6-3: Resizing and Aligning an Image

Viewing your newly decorated page reveals that your image is in the center of the page, just as the text it replaced was. This section covers the steps necessary to move your image around on the page to meet your needs.

Step-by-Step

1. Whenever an image is inserted into a page, it is selected when it appears. Notice the dark line around your image and the little squares in the corners.

The border lets you know the image is selected, and the little boxes are known as *handles,* which are used to resize the image to fit your needs.

Selection border   **Horizontal resize handle**

Vertical resize handle   **Diagonal resize handle**

2. An image that is selected can be dragged around the screen as you would drag an object in most other programs. Try this now by dragging the image to a new position in your document.

3. Images can also be resized using the handles. Again, give this a try by placing your cursor on top of one of the handles and dragging your mouse up or down, left or right, or diagonally, depending on the handle you choose. Stretch your image way out of shape and you'll quickly see why resizing is discouraged—the image quality degrades the more you change it from its original shape. To put the image back to its original size, right-click it and choose Resize Image from the context menu.

4. Images that are selected can also be deleted by pressing the BACKSPACE or DELETE key. It's no big deal if you do this now; simply reinsert the image by using the Objects panel. Browse to the copy of banner_main.gif that you placed in the common_images folder earlier.

5. When you are finished experimenting, place your image back at the top of the page and be sure that it is in its original size.

6. Your next step is to align the image in your document. Just as with text, images can be set to display either left, right, or centered on your page.

7. Select the banner_main.gif image by clicking it once.

8. The alignment buttons for images appear in the lower portion of the Properties Inspector that becomes visible when you click the expansion arrow. Click the arrow now and note that additional options are available. Some of these options are discussed in a bit, but for now, identify the alignment buttons.

Alignment buttons

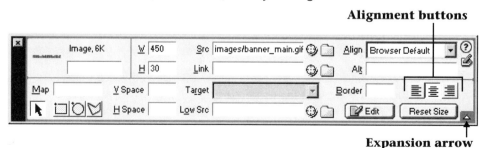

Expansion arrow

You can now move the image to the left, right, or center of the page by using the alignment buttons.

9. Be sure that you have a paragraph tag (<p>) separating the line of text at the top of the page from the image—otherwise, both will be treated as a block of text and everything will be realigned.

10. Try all three positions and then move the image back to the center of the page when you are done.

11. Now that your image is aligned properly, the heading above it seems a bit too large. Reset the text Poinciana Beach Chamber of Commerce to a Heading 4 to make its size appropriate for your new page, and then save your file.

Project 6-4: Discovering Image Properties

6

This project focuses on the Properties Inspector. As noted earlier, this panel changes based on the object that is selected. With the image selected, the Properties Inspector appears as seen here in the expanded view.

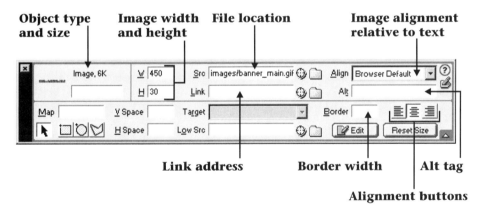

Notice that many of the items in the Properties Inspector are the same as they were when you worked with text properties in the last module. Dreamweaver once again does an excellent job of putting the most important information right at your fingertips with this invaluable tool. Using the Properties Inspector, you can directly manipulate a number of important aspects of your images, as you'll do in the next exercise.

Step-by-Step

1. Your next chore is to insert the logo for the Poinciana Beach Chamber of Commerce. After all, you do want your visitors to know that this site is sponsored by your local chamber, and by using a logo, visitors have a visual reminder that they are on your site no matter which page they visit.

2. Place your cursor at the beginning of the line of text directly below your bulleted items and click the Insert Image button.

3. Navigate to the location on your hard drive where you stored your exercise files and select the file called pbcofc_logo_med.gif. Once again, you will need to copy the file into your site directory, placing it in the common images folder.

   Once you have completed these steps, your logo appears in line with the text where it was inserted, as shown in Figure 6-6.

4. By default, Dreamweaver always sets an image relative to the baseline of the text that adjoins it. (Think of the baseline as a line on a lined sheet of paper where you write something.) Of course, this doesn't look very good, so you'll adjust the alignment here.

5. A number of options are available through a drop-down menu on the right side of the Properties Inspector. Images can be set to align to the top, middle, or center of text, and can be fine-tuned for various settings relative to the baseline. What you're after here, though, is to have the text flow around your image on the right of it, so choose to align the image to the left of the text.

6. One other important feature that you can add to your image now is an <alt> tag. This is a descriptive tag that is hidden in your image that will display if the viewer has set their browser to display in text-only mode. In addition, <alt> tags are responsible for generating those little boxes that appear when you float your mouse over an image. In the Alt box of the Properties Inspector, type **Poinciana Beach Chamber of Commerce**. Press ENTER when you're done typing, and save your file.

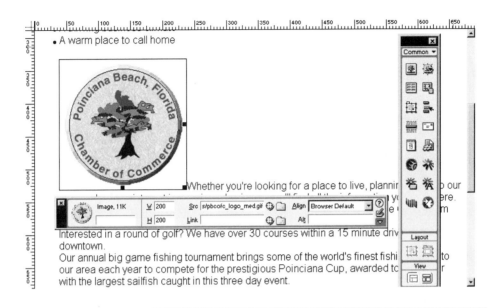

A warm place to call home

Figure 6-6   The image as it appears after it is inserted into the web page

7. Preview your work in your browser and you'll see that things are looking pretty good. In place of your simple text heading at the top of the page, you have a nice colorful welcome greeting and the logo for your organization. Not only that, but notice how your images and text are cleanly aligned, giving your page a nice crisp appearance, as shown in Figure 6-7. If you've been able to accomplish all of these tasks, this is definitely time to shake your own hand, and maybe even take a break!

1-Minute Drill

● What filename should be used for the main page of subsections of a site?

● Why should you have a plan for the size of an image before you insert it into a document?

● What visual clue do you receive that an image has been selected?

- Name the main pages for subsections in a site index.htm so that viewers who come to your site from a search engine can slice off parts of the URL and still have a page open properly.
- Although resizing images is possible in Dreamweaver, the results are often not very good unless the change is small.
- Selected images have a black border around them and resizing handles that appear as small boxes.

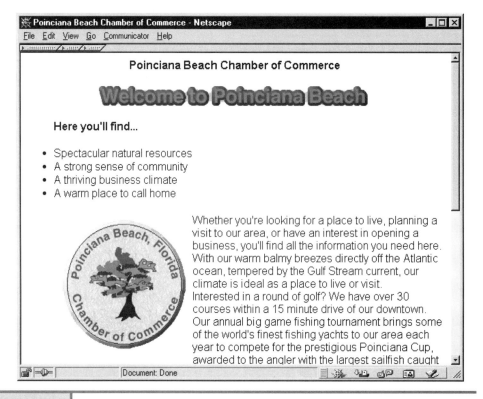

Figure 6-7 Images and proper alignment add a great deal of visual interest to any web page

Images as Navigation Elements

Much in the same way that you can generate HTML code that creates a hyperlink to text, you can accomplish the same task with images. In this section, you'll discover how to create not only a simple linked image, but also a rollover image. When a viewer moves their mouse over a rollover image, the image is exchanged for another. Inserting the images is no different than the tasks you just completed, and Dreamweaver makes the job of creating rollovers almost automatic, so this should be a fun section as you continue to develop your page-building muscles.

Project 6-5: Creating a Navigation Bar with Images

A navigation bar is simply a collection of images that gives a visual reference to your audience that this is the place where they will find links to other areas of your site. Designing functional and accessible navigation bars is an important part of making your pages usable for your viewers.

One important note about using images as navigation elements: As mentioned previously, some people turn off the image capabilities of their browser and will not see your images. Be sure to use the <alt> tag as a way to give these people an optional way to find your links, and create an extra text-only navigation bar. These text-based navigation elements are usually found at the bottom of a page, and you'll include them in the next exercise.

Tip

In the first exercise, you copied your images one by one into your site as you needed them. You'll be working with a number of different files here, so the best method is to use the file management features of your particular operating system to copy and paste all the button files from the Exercise folder directly into the common_images/buttons subfolder. Although you don't have to complete this step, it will save you some time, and you won't see the reminders every time you try to insert an image.

6

Step-by-Step

1. You will begin this exercise by creating a copy of your original index.htm file with a different name so that you can try out some new techniques in the last part of this module. Open index.htm and then choose File | Save As. Rename this file **index_imagelinks.htm**, keeping it in the main root folder for the site. Check the title bar for the page to be sure that you are working in this new file, and not your original file, as shown here:

     Page title   **File location and name**

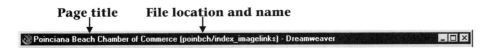

2. The navigation bar for your page will be located at the top of the document. To insert a blank line to contain your images, place your cursor at the beginning of the first line of text in the page and press ENTER. Use the arrow key to place your cursor at the top of the page, and make sure the alignment is set to Center.

3. Insert the first image at the cursor by clicking the Insert Image button on the Objects panel. Navigate to the common_images folder and the subfolder called buttons, as shown in Figure 6-8. Open that folder and select visitors_button1.gif. Click Select to accept this image.

4. Press the RIGHT ARROW key one time to deselect the image and move the cursor to the right.

5. In order, insert the following image files, pressing the RIGHT ARROW key after you insert each file:

a) resident_button1.gif

b) business_button1.gif

c) members_button1.gif

d) events_button1.gif

6. When you are done, your page will have a nice clean navigation bar at the top of the page, as shown in Figure 6-9.

7. Your next step is to type in text that matches the text in your images at the bottom of your page, duplicating your navigation bar in a text-only format. Scroll to the bottom of the page and place your cursor to the right of your anchor link to the top of the page (**Top**). Press ENTER to insert a blank line, and choose center alignment from the Properties Inspector.

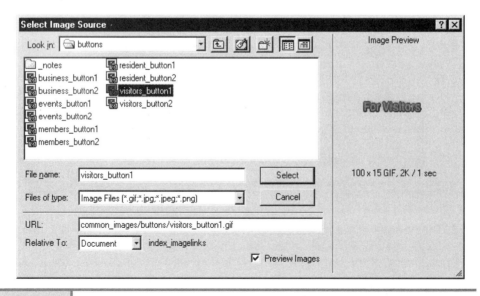

Figure 6-8   Select visitors_button1.gif in the Select Image Source dialog box

Figure 6-9   Images as navigation links can add a pleasant graphical aspect to a web page

6

8. Simply type in the same words that are in your images at the top of the page, and insert a vertical line between them. (The vertical line is made by pressing SHIFT-\ (backslash)—located just above the ENTER key.)

9. When you are done, your text links will appear as shown in Figure 6-10.

10. You're now ready to insert <alt> tags for your images. Follow the guide shown here and insert the <alt> tags for each image using the Properties Inspector:

a) For Visitors—Information for Visitors

b) For Residents—Information for Residents

c) For Businesses—Information for Businesses

d) For Members—Information for Chamber Members

e) Local Events—News about local events

11. With ten files to link to, now is a great time to use the Point To File feature of the Properties Inspector. Recall from the last module that this entails arranging the Site window and the Document window side by side and then dragging a pointer from the link location in the document to the file in the site, as shown in Figure 6-11. It takes a little prep work, but will make short work of this task.

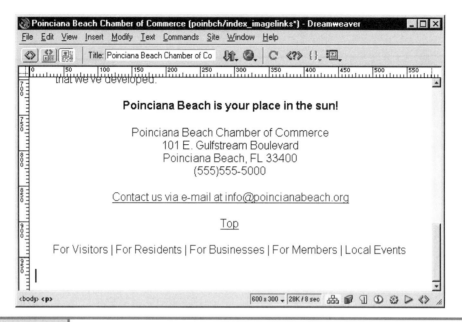

Figure 6-10 Use text as an alternative navigation method for those viewers who use a nongraphical browser or have text-only selected in their graphical browser

12. Link your images and text now to the appropriate index.htm files in their corresponding folders. (Isn't all that work setting up your site structure starting to make sense now?) Select the images, and then the text at the bottom of the page, and create your links. Check your spelling and then save your file when you are finished.

Note

Resizing your windows may cause your images to move out of alignment on the page. You will learn how to control image placement and alignment in the next module.

13. Preview your work in your browser and check your links. If everything was done correctly, you'll be able to use those links to jump to the blank documents you created for each category. Use your Back button on your browser to go back to the main page, and continue checking every link in the page. Fix any broken links and then save, and close, this file.

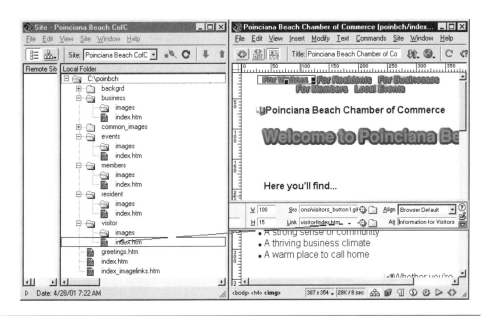

Figure 6-11 Using the Point to File method for creating links can save lots of work when you need to make multiple links

Project 6-6: Working with Rollover Images

Rollover images add an extra level of sophistication to your pages and also help your viewers know that the object they are passing the mouse over leads to something special. As the name implies, rollover images perform a special function when the mouse pointer rolls over them (clever isn't it?).

Rollover images are created by combining HTML with JavaScript code to swap one image for another when the pointer passes over the original image. There's no need to feel intimidated, though. Once again, Dreamweaver is going to do the heavy lifting for you—creating the JavaScript automatically based on a few simple bits of information that you provide.

Step-by-Step

1. Once again, you'll work with a copy of your original index.htm file. Open that document and then select File | Save As from the menu bar. Name the file **index_rollovers.htm**. Check the filename in the title bar to be sure that you're working on the correct document.

2. As you did before, place your cursor at the top of the document and insert a blank line to hold your rollover images.

6

3. The Insert Rollover Image button is just to the left of the Insert Image button on the Objects panel, as shown in Figure 6-12. Clicking this button opens the Insert Rollover Image dialog box, in which you provide Dreamweaver with the information it needs to generate the code to make your rollovers work.

4. In order for the code to be generated, your images need a unique name for each rollover. This name is different from the filename for the images themselves, and is used only in the creation of the JavaScript for the rollover effect. This name should be short but descriptive, and must be composed of letters and numbers only, with no spaces or other characters. Name your first rollover **visitors**.

5. The process of specifying the information needed is pretty straightforward. Browse to the name of the image you want to appear when the page first loads, visitors_button1.gif, and then select visitors_button2.gif as the file to replace it when the rollover occurs.

6. Browse to the index.htm file in the visitors folder as the link you are creating, and you are all done. When you're finished, the dialog box should look like this:

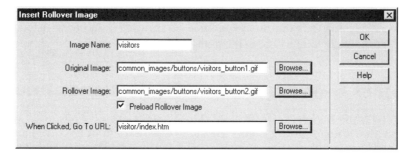

7. To complete the rollover exercise, use the information in Table 6-1 to input data in the four additional rollover dialog boxes.

8. Dreamweaver will display your original images across the top of the page as you insert each one. However, to see the rollover effect, you must preview the page in a browser. Press F12 now to see how your page looks, and notice the simple change in the appearance of the image as the mouse rolls over it. Not hugely dramatic, but the idea is simply to give the viewer a simple clue that this is an active link that will take them to another page. When it comes to rollovers, a good rule to follow is to keep it simple and subtle.

9. Save your work and close this file. Time for another break—you deserve it!

Figure 6-12	Use the Insert Rollover Image button in the Objects panel to begin the process of inserting a rollover image

A Few More Words About Fireworks

All the image files you have used in this module were created over the course of one rainy Sunday afternoon using Fireworks. Working with Fireworks, I was able to quickly and efficiently create logos, text images, and the special effects such as the bevels and glows that you saw in action here. Fireworks makes short work of the process of creating these images, and you saw how those images could be quickly selected and inserted into your web pages. Files were optimized for the

Image Name	Original Image	Rollover Image	When Clicked, Go To URL
residents	resident_button1.gif	resident_button2.gif	resident/index.htm
business	business_button1.gif	business_button2.gif	business/index.htm
members	members_button1.gif	members_button2.gif	members/index.htm
events	events_button1.gif	events_button1.gif	events/index.htm

Table 6-1	Data Entry for index_rollovers.htm

best file size while maintaining quality, and once one set of effects was applied to an image, they were easily duplicated for all the succeeding graphics.

Fireworks also lets you optimize your files directly from within a Dreamweaver Document window, create web photo albums automatically, and generate more complicated rollovers than you worked with here. Dreamweaver and Fireworks continue to develop as two closely integrated software packages, and learning both of them now certainly puts you in a good position as Macromedia continues to refine these programs into the future. As you'll see later in this book, Fireworks is an indispensable tool for optimizing images for the Web.

1-Minute Drill

- What is the function of navigation bars?
- What additional code is generated by Dreamweaver when rollovers are inserted in a page?
- What actions must you take to preview a rollover image?

New for Dreamweaver 4: Flash Text and Buttons

As discussed previously, Flash is the program from Macromedia that is currently gaining a huge following on the Web. With very small file sizes, clean and scalable vector graphics, and the capability of generating sophisticated animation and visual effects through a special coding language all its own, web pages generated in Flash may very well revolutionize the Internet in the near future.

In Dreamweaver 4, Macromedia has included a small portion of the Flash program so that page developers can use some of the program's capabilities directly from within Dreamweaver without actually buying a copy of Flash. This is pretty cool stuff, to say the least, and as you'll see here, the process of generating text and images using Flash has some strong connections to the way that images are placed in a page. While they may not be "images" in the traditional sense of the word, Flash text and buttons do accomplish the same things—adding visual interest to what would otherwise be a very vanilla web experience.

- Navigation bars give viewers a visual reference to the links that are collected in one area of a web page.
- Dreamweaver generates JavaScript code automatically to make rollover images function.
- Rollovers must be previewed in a browser to see the rollover effect.

Project 6-7: Generating and Inserting Flash Text

When you insert Flash objects in a Dreamweaver Document window, you are actually placing a tiny movie into your page. Similar to the way that you inserted rollover images, you'll need to answer some questions in a dialog box, fine-tune your selections, and then sit back and watch as Dreamweaver and Flash work together to create an animation for you. The process can be a lot of fun, and the effects are quite interesting, so get started!

Step-by-Step

1. Once again, you'll open your original index.htm file and rename it. This time, select File | Save As and call the new file **index_flashtext.htm**. As before, check the name in the title bar to be sure you are working on the right file.

2. Since you want to maintain design consistency in your page, replace the Welcome To Poinciana Beach text as you did before with the image file banner_main.gif. You'll actually be using the two primary colors in this image when you create your Flash text. Highlight the text and press the DELETE or BACKSPACE key, and then insert the banner_main.gif file from the common_images folder.

3. Flash text is best used as a linked object. Two unique features that Flash brings to the table are the ability to swap text colors as the mouse rolls over it—just as you did with rollover images—and the ability to be linked to another file or web site. As you did in the previous exercise, insert a blank line at the top of your document to hold the new navigation elements that you'll be adding. Be sure that the cursor is centered on the page.

4. Locate the Insert Flash Text button on the Objects panel and click it to open a dialog box similar to the one you saw when you worked with rollovers.

5. At the top of the Insert Flash Text dialog box is the area for setting font type and size. Since mixing fonts on a web page is almost never a good idea, set the font type to Geneva, Arial, or Helvetica, depending on what fonts are installed on your system. Set the size to **18** in the Size box.

6. Before you choose the two colors for your text, be sure to reposition the dialog box so that your banner_main.gif image is visible, as shown in Figure 6-13.

7. Use the eyedropper tool (which you used in previous work with page colors) to select a color easily and quickly. Click the Color box to choose the color of your text before the mouse rolls over it. Use the eyedropper now to select the darker blue in the bevel around your letters.

6

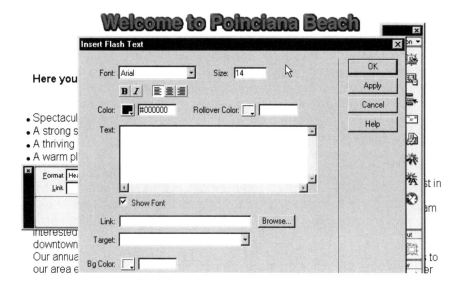

Figure 6-13   Reposition the dialog box so that the banner_main.gif image is viewable

8. The Rollover Color box selects the color to be used when the viewer passes their pointer over the text. Select the lighter blue that makes up the center of the lettering. Notice that you also can enter the colors in the hexadecimal code instead of using the standard color palette, as shown in here:

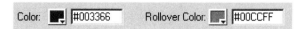

9. Now you're ready to actually insert the text that will function as your link. Type **For Visitors** in the Text box. In order for your text to stand out a little more, click the B button to make the text bold.

10. You're limited to using the Browse button to create your link. This isn't a big deal, since you have already done this before. Browse to the index.htm file in your visitors folder and click the Select button.

11. Set a filename at the bottom of the dialog box that describes this new SWF file that will be created in the same folder that contains this page. If you had an absolute value to enter here, you could specify the exact location for this file on a server, but you'll just accept the default, which places the file in the same folder as the page it is on. Type **visitors.swf** in the Save As box. When you are all finished, your completed dialog box should look the example in Figure 6-14. Click OK to accept your new Flash text.

12. Unlike rollovers, you can actually see the effect created by this new Flash file directly in the Document window. Notice that the Properties Inspector for this new image has a Play button. Click Play and then roll your mouse over the Flash text. Voila! Instant rollover effect! (You need to click Stop if you want to edit or delete the Flash text.)

13. Press the RIGHT ARROW key and continue as you did previously to add the additional text and link it to the proper files. In order, create Flash text for the following:

a) For Residents

b) For Businesses

c) For Members

d) Local Events

14. When you are finished, your new Flash navigation bar will be complete and your text page will have some pretty slick Flash effects. Preview your work in a browser to get a good feel for how it will render when loaded from the Internet, and then save your file.

You've added yet another technique to your bag of tricks here and have seen how you can create text rollovers with Flash. Although the text may look a little crowded in your Dreamweaver Document window, it actually looks better when viewed in a browser. You'll find out how you can use tables to separate and align your Flash text in the next module, so you'll leave these as they are with the understanding that this crowding effect can be fixed later on.

6

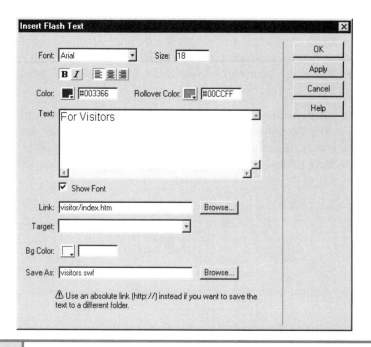

Figure 6-14 The completed Insert Flash Text dialog box for the Visitors link

Project 6-8: Creating and Inserting Flash Buttons

As you'd expect, using Flash to generate buttons for your page is a similar process to the one just covered. In fact, this feature may be the niftiest addition to Dreamweaver 4 and well worth the cost of upgrading to the new version. The buttons that are available can go a long way toward making your site truly unique. This section moves along quickly, but you'll definitely want to spend some time experimenting with this great tool on your own.

Step-by-Step

1. Once again, open index.htm and give it a new name so that you have a working file. Choose File | Save As and name this file **index_flashbuttons.htm**. Insert a blank line at the top of the document and be sure the cursor is centered on the page.

2. Locate Insert Flash Button on the Objects panel and click it to open the Insert Flash Button dialog box.

3. At the top of the dialog box are live samples of the buttons that you are able to create, as shown in Figure 6-15. Scroll down the list to see the different styles and roll your mouse over each one to see the effects themselves. Notice that you can even get additional styles by visiting the Macromedia Exchange web site (by clicking Get More Styles) to download new buttons.

4. After you look at the various buttons available, choose the Diamond Spinner style. The color scheme matches the Poinciana Beach page and it's a good match between the business side of the Chamber of Commerce and the more playful style of the resort town.

5. To create the button, type the **For Visitors** text that you've used before, browse to the index.htm file in the visitors folder to link the button, and change the text to the default Arial font. Name the file **visitors_button.swf** at the bottom of the dialog box. When you're all finished, make sure your settings match those in Figure 6-16 and click OK.

6. Complete the process to create links to your "For Residents" page, "For Businesses" page, "For Members" page, and "Local Events" page. When

6

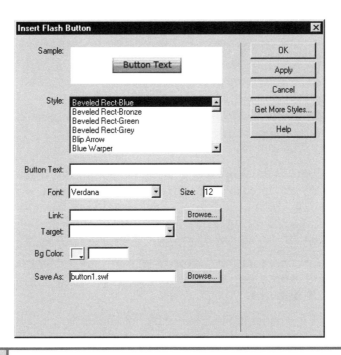

Figure 6-15 | The Insert Flash Button dialog box provides a live preview of the available buttons

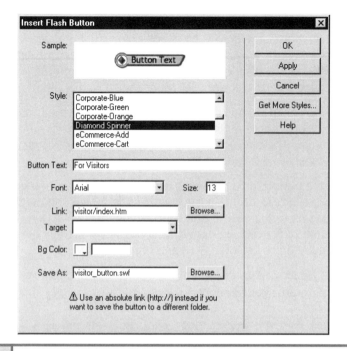

Figure 6-16 Final settings for the first Flash button

you are all done, your document will be sporting some really nifty buttons. Preview the file in your browser to see the full effect in action, as shown in Figure 6-17.

One peculiarity of the process of creating Flash objects is that all files automatically are stored in the root folder for the site, as shown in Figure 6-18. Luckily, you can clean that up fairly easily by creating a new folder for your Flash buttons and dragging all the SWF files there, keeping your site nicely organized and making it easier to use those files again on other pages.

7. Right-click the root folder at the top of your site structure in the Site window and choose New Folder from the context menu. Name the folder **flash_buttons**.

8. You can select a series of files at once by holding down the SHIFT key while clicking the icons. Select all the SWF files and drag them into the new folder you just created.

9. Dreamweaver will ask if you want to update the pages that are affected by this change. Click the Update button each time the Update Files dialog box

Figure 6-17 Flash buttons add a new level of sophistication to page design

Local Folder	Notes	Size	Type	Modified	Ch
⊞ 🗀 members			Folder	4/27/01 6:36 PM	-
⊞ 🗀 resident			Folder	4/27/01 6:36 PM	-
⊞ 🗀 visitor			Folder	4/27/01 6:36 PM	-
business.swf		2KB	Flash Pla...	4/30/01 10:02 PM	-
business_button.swf		7KB	Flash Pla...	4/30/01 10:40 PM	-
events.swf		2KB	Flash Pla...	4/30/01 10:04 PM	-
events_button.swf		7KB	Flash Pla...	4/30/01 10:42 PM	-
greetings.htm		4KB	Netscape...	4/23/01 5:54 PM	-
index.htm		4KB	Netscape...	4/30/01 6:19 PM	-
index_flashbuttons.htm		7KB	Netscape...	4/30/01 10:42 PM	-
index_flashtext.htm		7KB	Netscape...	4/30/01 10:05 PM	-
index_imagelinks.htm		5KB	Netscape...	4/29/01 10:45 PM	-
index_rollovers.htm		7KB	Netscape...	4/29/01 11:31 PM	-
members.swf		2KB	Flash Pla...	4/30/01 10:02 PM	-
members_button.swf		7KB	Flash Pla...	4/30/01 10:41 PM	-
residents.swf		2KB	Flash Pla...	4/30/01 10:02 PM	-
residents_button.swf		7KB	Flash Pla...	4/30/01 10:38 PM	-
visitor_button.swf		7KB	Flash Pla...	4/30/01 10:37 PM	-
visitors.swf		2KB	Flash Pla...	4/30/01 10:02 PM	-

Figure 6-18 Flash buttons are automatically stored in the root folder for the web site

appears, and Dreamweaver will change the link locations and even automatically save the affected files.

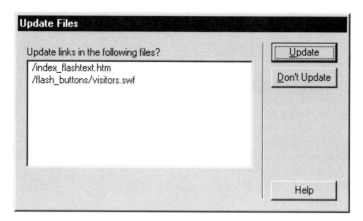

10. When you're done, your more organized site structure will appear as shown in Figure 6-19.

11. Save and close all of your open files. Time for another break!

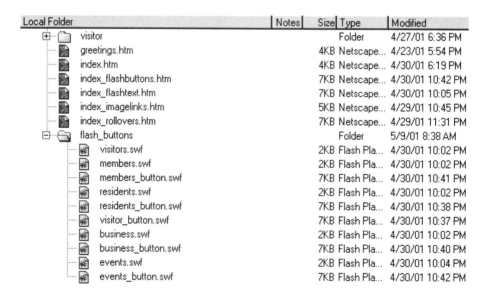

Figure 6-19 The revised site structure after the Flash buttons are repositioned

By building Flash functions into the new Dreamweaver interface, the developers at Macromedia have really given you some great tools to work with. You can use Flash buttons or text to dramatically improve the look and feel and the functionality of your web pages, all while maintaining quick download times.

Having said that, though, you have to remind yourself that not every person will be able to see these great effects if they haven't downloaded the Flash player or have a newer browser installed on their computer. Remember that Aunt Martha in Toledo may not have the technical expertise to install a new browser, much less download and install the Flash player, and if your intended audience includes a large number of these kinds of people, you may ultimately be better off staying with straight image files for creating your navigation elements. That would be a shame, because your visitors would be missing a lot that the Web has to offer, but it is a reality that designing for the Internet often means creating pages that strike a balance between what the latest technology has to offer and what you can expect from your audience.

6

1-Minute Drill

- What tool is used for selecting colors when inserting Flash text?
- How are Flash text and buttons previewed from within the Document window in Dreamweaver?
- Why is caution required when using effects generated by Flash as navigation elements?

Project 6-9: Inserting Images and Navigation Items

Independent Study projects are designed to give you additional practice in the application of the skills and concepts covered in this and succeeding modules. This approach is designed to allow you some flexibility in completing projects in a way that allows your own creative forces to come into play, while letting you master the essential concepts covered in the module.

- The eyedropper tool is used for selecting colors, either from the color palette or from an item on the page itself.
- Flash buttons and text can be previewed by clicking the Play button on the Properties Inspector.
- Caution is required when using Flash effects because some members of the audience may not have the Flash player installed that will let them see the effects.

Independent Study Exercise

Just as you've accomplished in the exercises for this module, you are going to take an existing web page and dress it up by adding images, rollovers, and Flash elements. Your task for this Independent Study project is to take the rather plain greeting page that you worked on in Module 5 and add a variety of visual elements to make it more appealing.

Open greetings.htm and use the File | Save As sequence to create four new files:

- greetings_imagelinks.htm

- greetings_rollovers.htm

- greetings_flashtext.htm

- greetings_flashbuttons.htm.

You've probably figured out that what you're required to do here is duplicate the process of creating pages with different types of image links—standard static images, rollovers, Flash text, and Flash buttons. If you're not sure of the steps to get this done, review Projects 6-2, 6-3, and 6-4 on inserting and modifying images, Projects 6-5 and 6-6 on links and rollovers, and Projects 6-7 and 6-8 on the use of Flash elements.

In addition to creating the links for these pages, experiment with the use of images on your pages by copying them from the exercise files into your site.

- You'll find photographs of the Chamber's Chairman, Mr. Fletcher, and its President, Ms. Johnston. You will also find some pictures from around the fictional town of Poinciana Beach in the folder called photos.

- Try different combinations, different alignments, and different numbers of images on your pages.

- Pay particular attention to the combinations that give your page the best overall look.

- Be sure to use either the medium or small logos that you find on each page.

- Be sure to maintain the original greetings.htm file as it is. You'll need it again in subsequent modules.

What to Take Away

Understanding how images are inserted into a web page is nearly as important as working with text. Sophisticated viewers of the modern Web expect to see pages that have high-quality, fast-loading graphics that stimulate interest and help to navigate the site itself. In this module, you've gone from inserting a few simple images into a page to generating and applying sophisticated animated buttons with the most exciting software available to page designers today. Dreamweaver once again provides the ability to get the job done efficiently and quickly.

In the next module, you'll look at how to manipulate your page design so that you can get as much information into your limited space as possible, all while adhering to some good simple rules of page layout. You need to understand tables and how they perform the task of providing structure to web pages for you to apply these design principles. Soon enough you'll be changing the layout of your pages like a pro.

☑ Mastery Check

1. Which two types of bitmap images are used most often on the Internet?

2. What vector image type is created using Macromedia Flash?

3. Define a navigation bar.

4. What is the function of the <alt> tag?

5. Why should alternative methods of site navigation be included on a page?

6. What computer language is used to generate rollover images?

Module 7

Controlling Page Layout

The Goals of this Module

- Understand principles of page layout
- Understand HTML table properties
- Use Dreamweaver 4's new page layout features
- Employ tracing images in page layout
- Understand table formatting
- Inserting and formatting standard tables

In previous modules, you have seen how to plan for a new web site, develop the site structure, build pages with text and links, and add visual interest by including images on your pages. To do these tasks, you actually don't need Dreamweaver at all—any free web authoring tool, such as Netscape Composer, would easily do the same job. Or, if you were feeling particularly ambitious, you could also hand-code those types of simple pages in a text editor using nothing but HTML. In fact, the only feature that you've used for building web pages that isn't available in a much less expensive program are the Flash buttons that you included at the end of the last module.

To move beyond those simple pages, though, you need a program that can help you manipulate the look and feel of your pages with advanced layout features that will let you divide sections of your pages into discrete blocks of information. Dreamweaver's unique tools allow you to use tables that organize your pages and give you the freedom to move beyond the simple vertical structure of web design that you've used in prior modules.

As a medium that was originally designed for scientists to transfer and share raw data, it should come as no surprise that the use of tables to organize information has been a big part of the Internet since its earliest days. What may be surprising is how tables are actually employed as page layout tools on the modern Web. Whether you realize it or not, tables are everywhere on the Internet today—controlling the alignment of pages, serving as placeholders for images, text, and other objects on web pages, and generally making pages more readable and accessible to viewers—all while remaining hidden from view. Although what you've done up to now certainly qualifies as good basic web design, without tables, you've come about as far as you can in laying out your pages using basic HTML.

In this module, you'll explore how you can use tables to create pages that are designed with an interface that is more usable and accessible to your audience. Dreamweaver 4 has introduced some new tools that makes this process easier to perform, and at the end of this module, you'll understand not only how to employ those tools but also how their use impacts your viewer's experience.

Page Layout Principles

Before discussing how tables will let you align and organize the different elements on your pages, you need to have a good understanding of basic design principles. These ideas are nothing new, and, just like typography, they've been around for as long as there has been movable type.

In many respects, a web page is no different from a printed document, and that certainly is true where these fundamental principles of design are concerned.

What the Web adds is the interactive element that lets viewers flip from one page to another and back again simply by clicking links. A well-designed web page, then, not only looks good, it also has to behave in a way that the viewing audience will find intuitive and easy to use. This combination of design and usability issues makes designing for the Web a challenge beyond just the technical aspects of creating code that functions properly. Dreamweaver does its part by providing the tools to accommodate your designs. As web designers, it is up to you to know and use good design and usability principles.

Alignment

Poor page alignment is perhaps the biggest mistake that new web designers make. Elements of the page that are scattered around without any apparent reason lead to a layout that looks messy and cluttered—failing in the basic mission of drawing the viewer into your site to get a good look at what you have to offer. To avoid this problem, develop good habits early on in the design process and follow some simple rules for page alignment.

- *Choose an alignment for the page and stay with it.* Whatever your ultimate choice in laying out the items on your web pages, stay with a consistent alignment for your pages and maintain it throughout your site.

  The following illustration shows the beginnings of a page alignment scheme, but the heading and some of the other elements break from the pattern by wandering from the strong-left alignment to the center of the page.

<table>
<tr><td></td><td>Poinciana Beach Chamber of Commerce</td></tr>
<tr><td></td><td>Welcome to Poinciana Beach</td></tr>
<tr><td></td><td>Here you'll find...</td></tr>
<tr><td>For Visitors</td><td>• Spectacular natural resources
• A strong sense of community</td></tr>
<tr><td>For Residents</td><td>• A thriving business climate
• A warm place to call home</td></tr>
<tr><td>For Businesses</td><td rowspan="2">Whether you're looking for a place to live, planning a visit to our area, or have an interest in opening a business, you'll find all the information you need here.</td></tr>
<tr><td>For Members</td></tr>
</table>

By contrast, in this illustration, everything on the page has been aligned to the left, including the page heading and all other information. Even the bullets have been removed because they broke from the alignment of the page. The result is a cleaner and more organized page.

- *Maintain both horizontal and vertical alignments.* Recall from the discussion of images in the last module the brief introduction to the baseline—the invisible line that defines the base that images and text rest on. Keeping an eye on the baseline alignment keeps your page elements vertically organized and leads to an easier reading experience for your viewers.

  In this example, you see alignment that ignores the baseline rule, resulting in an unnecessary up and down motion to follow the text with your eyes:

Visitors	Residents	Businesses	Members	Local Events

  Whereas in the next example, the text floats on top of the imaginary line, making it easier to recognize the words as you flow from one cell of the table to another.

Visitors	Residents	Businesses	Members	Local Events

- *Beware of center alignment.* While aligning items to the center of a page or to a section of it does create an invisible line that runs through the middle of your objects, it does not give the impression of strength that aligning to the left or right does. Particularly on pages with a large amount of text, center alignment can make the page look sloppy and unorganized, and make it more difficult to read.

Maintaining a strong page alignment adds emphasis to your pages and presents a more organized and professional appearance. Keeping the same alignment throughout your site creates the impression that some thought and planning has gone into your pages, and serves as a visual reminder to viewers that they are still in your site and haven't clicked their way through into unknown territory.

Repetition and Consistency

Choosing design elements that repeat throughout the entire web site—whether graphics, a color scheme, or even a page layout—helps tie all the elements of your site together, reinforcing the idea that all of the separate pages belong together.

If you think about how much money some companies spend to develop and promote their company logo, you can appreciate how important symbols are to the association between a design and a concept. Consider the Nike "swoop" symbol, McDonald's "golden arches," or even the red and white cursive lettering used by Coca-Cola. Seeing those symbols and color schemes causes you to think of their parent company, but they did not become as familiar as they are without literally being repeated millions and millions (if not billions) of times. For web developers, repetition of a consistent design scheme is even more important, because of the short time available to capture the viewer's attention. With that in mind, here are some basic rules for branding your site:

7

- *Use the same navigation scheme throughout the site.* If you choose to put your navigation bar on the left side of your pages, for instance, keep it there throughout every page on the site. It's difficult enough for viewer's to learn how to navigate in a newly visited site. Don't make it harder by asking them to find your links in a different spot on each page.

- *Use the same color scheme throughout the site.* Consistent color schemes can add greatly to a feeling of unity when they are used throughout a site. (A bit later in the module, a new addition in Dreamweaver 4 is discussed that makes this process a little easier—the Assets panel.)

- *Use the same layout scheme throughout the site.* While the initial design decisions are based on meeting the needs of your intended audience, once you've settled on a page design, stay with it. If you decide on a particular style for your main page, be sure that you maintain a similar style through every succeeding page. Yet another reason to do as much advanced planning as possible.

Contrast

Designing pages with good visual appeal often involves the concept of contrast—changing the formatting or color of particular objects to draw attention to them. This is especially important in web design, because you want your viewer to immediately find and focus on the most important elements of your page—who you are, what you offer, and how to find more information. Using contrasting elements can greatly improve the possibility that this primary goal will be met.

To see this principle in action, take a little Web field trip and visit the following sites:

- www.apple.com
- www.macromedia.com
- www.palm.com
- www.msnbc.com
- www.radioshack.com

What kinds of contrast did you find? Larger pictures that dominated the screen, larger text that divided the text into discrete blocks of information, large areas of one color scheme that let you know that this was the navigation section, or contrasting text colors that made certain items jump out at you? How did the designers of these sites use contrast to let you know what were the most important items on their pages? To assist you in creating a page with good contrast, keep these principles in mind:

- *Decide which elements are most important for your viewer to find and then create a structure that supports your decisions.* Much in the same way that an outline helps organize written text from a main idea to supporting ideas, use contrast to define the structure of your page. The most important element should be bigger, bolder, or in a contrasting color, with less important elements having less contrast.

- *Don't be shy.* If you want that main component to really stand out, then be bold. Don't make text that contains the main idea for a section only one size larger than the supporting text, for instance; make it really stand out by going for a size much larger or in a different color. In order for the principles of contrast to work to your advantage, the differences between elements must be strong.

- *Remove unnecessary items from the page.* You want your viewer to be drawn in by the page design and be able to focus on the essential elements. The use of unnecessary pictures, logos, page counters, or text only clutters the page and makes it difficult for them to find those things that you've decided they need to see.

- *Don't use contrast when you have something you want the viewer to read.* If you have an article that you want the audience to sit and read, then make the text simple and easy to follow. One of the worst things you can do is to insert a link into the first paragraph of an article and then expect the viewer to pass by it as they read your text. More than likely, they will jump to your link, and you can only hope that they will find their way back to finish the article.

Do's and Don'ts of Good Page Design

You have read the various rules to follow for formatting your pages so that they are appealing, usable, and meet your goals by drawing viewers in and then directing them to the information you want them to find. In a few moments, you'll look at how Dreamweaver makes advanced page layouts possible through the use of tables. Before you do, though, take a look at a final few rules for page design that will help you to build pages that are more professional looking and have a more appealing style. Although not all of these rules apply directly to your understanding of Dreamweaver's page layout features, they still are important rules to follow in creating an improved Web experience for your audience.

7

- *Never use all capital letters.* This makes text harder to read and makes your page look like you couldn't be bothered to use the SHIFT key.

- *Check your spelling.* Dreamweaver's spell check feature may not be as sophisticated as what you'll find in a word processing program, but it will help you find obvious errors before they embarrass you.

- *Don't use text colors or images that look like links and buttons unless they are links and buttons.* Don't make your audience drag their mouse pointer around the screen searching for your navigation elements.

- *Beware of italics.* Use italics sparingly—if at all. Italicized text is much harder to read than normal text.

- *Large text and buttons look amateurish.* Large text is fine for small children, but unless your site is designed with that audience in mind, keep the font sizes to a reasonable size. Navigation buttons should be a part of the page, but shouldn't dominate it.

- *Keep similar items together on your page.* Don't introduce a concept in one spot on a page and then ask the viewer to search the rest of your document to find related information. Similar items should be grouped together in close proximity.

- *Control your animations.* Animations can be a great contrasting element on a page, but not if they run continuously. At some point, they just become a distraction, and annoying users is not a good way to build a rapport with them. (You'll learn how to create animations and control their playback with Fireworks in Module 17.)

- *Never require the viewer to scroll sideways.* Good page layout includes designing pages that will fit everyone's screen, regardless of their settings. Having to scroll sideways just to see the right edge of a graphic makes the viewer feel that you've given no thought to your page design—or to them.

- *Plan carefully.* As you'll see in the upcoming exercises, tables give you wide latitude in determining how your finished page will look, but in some respects, this can be both a blessing and a curse. By knowing ahead of time what your pages will look like, you'll have a better chance of using tables to create pages that behave the way you want them to.

1-Minute Drill

- What is the most common mistake made by beginning web page designers?
- What three elements of design should remain consistent throughout an entire web site?
- Whens should contrasting elements not be used in a page?

Layout Tools in Dreamweaver 4

Prior to version 4 of Dreamweaver, web designers were somewhat limited when it came to creating tables that were intended solely for use as a layout tool. This wasn't an insurmountable problem, but by reworking the interface, making additional information available, and improving the way that layout tables can be formatted, Macromedia has reduced the number of workarounds

---

- Poor page alignment is the most common mistake made by new web designers.
- Pages throughout a web site should have consistent navigation elements, color schemes, and page layout designs.
- Contrasting elements should not be used in areas of text that you want the viewer to sit and read.

required in designing properly aligned web pages and greatly improved the way that designers can accomplish advanced layout schemes.

Recall from the discussion of the buttons available on the Objects panel that four objects rest at the bottom of every panel regardless of the category of objects that is selected. As you saw in Module 3, these buttons are your primary tools for changing the way that the view of your Document window is presented.

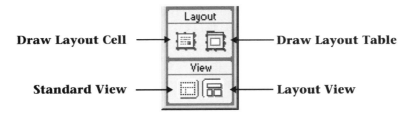

Until now, all of your work has been done in the Standard view of the pages you have created. Prior to Dreamweaver 4, this was the only way to look at a page, and if you're moving up from a previous version, you may feel more comfortable working in that mode. Tables and layers (layers are discussed a little later in the chapter) can still be used as design layout tools in Standard view, and switching from one view to another is easily accomplished by using the buttons on the Objects panel.

7

Ask the Expert

Question: I'm used to using the Standard view from Dreamweaver 2 and 3. Do I need to know the new table layout feature?

Answer: Not taking advantage of the new tools for page design made possible in Dreamweaver 4 is much like insisting on writing every single page on your site in HTML alone. You can certainly get the job done, but it will take more time and be less effective than if you let the software do the grunt work for you. Personally, I'd rather work on the creative side of my page design without getting bogged down in the details of formatting and coding. There's enough work involved in getting the look of the page just right, and if I have a great way to accomplish formatting and coding at my disposal, then I'd much rather spend my time designing and let the software do those tasks.

Understanding Tables

Before you can begin working with Dreamweaver's layout tools, you need to have a basic understanding of tables and their components—rows, columns, and cells. Figure 7-1a shows a basic table with information presented in a standard table layout.

The table itself is the entire body of the object in the illustration—in this case, with an exterior border, although borders are not necessary, and are not used when tables are used for page layout. Tables are composed of a series of rows and columns and their intersecting cells. *Rows* are the horizontal sections of the table that span the table from side to side. In this example, the month of January and its average temperature are in one row. *Columns* are the elements in the table that contain information that is organized vertically, or top to bottom. The months of the year are contained in one column. Finally, *cells* are the rectangular boxes created where a row and a column intersect. The heading for the table, for instance, is in one cell—created by the intersection of one row and one column.

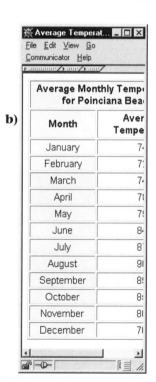

Figure 7-1   a) A standard HTML table and b) an HTML table set with an absolute width

Understanding how tables, rows, and cells are sized and formatted can be one of the really perplexing aspects of working with these objects in HTML, and many web designers become quite frustrated trying to figure out why their carefully constructed page is not displaying properly.

Table size can be set in two ways: either as percentage of the width of the browser window, or as an absolute value based on the number of pixels the table occupies in width and height. The table in Figure 7-1a was set with a percentage value, allowing it to resize as the browser window itself changes. The same table set with an absolute value will appear much differently in a browser window of the same size. Notice in Figure 7-1b how the table now displays only the portion that is visible for the size of the window—no longer stretching the table as the window size changes.

This seems easy enough until you take into account that a hierarchy of values puts the properties of the cell first, followed by the properties of the row or column, and then finally the table properties. While each item can be changed in size, the formatting of the individual cells has the highest priority. This means that cell size will override the table value if the object that is contained in the cell is larger than the space allocated to it by the table properties.

Imagine stuffing a 10-gallon plastic trash bag with 20 gallons of trash. The bag is still a 10-gallon bag, but it will bulge and stretch out of shape to contain the trash that is put in it that exceeds its intended capacity. The same thing can happen when an image or another object that is inserted into a cell is bigger than what the cell is designed to hold. The cell expands to hold the additional size of the image, and stretches the row, column, and table itself to hold all the information. The result is often a very messy table, and if the table is used for page layout, your entire page will be affected.

Formatting these containers that you'll use in your page layouts can often be a trying experience, especially when you are first starting out. As with any new skill, learning to use tables for page design requires two things: patience and practice. You'll get started now so that you get the chance to practice. Patience will be something you'll have to provide on your own!

Project 7-1: Working with Layout Tables

Before you get started, be sure that you've downloaded the exercise files that support this module from www.osborne.com and have stored them in the Exercises folder you created earlier. In this first exercise, you will create an index page that re-creates the one you completed in the last module. Recall how the images that you used as links moved out of alignment when you resized your

7

window. You're going to fix that little problem by employing a table to hold the images.

Step-by-Step

1. If you don't have Dreamweaver open, open it now and navigate to the Poinciana Beach Chamber of Commerce site. Create a new file called **index_topnav.htm** in the root folder for the site and open the document.

2. Find the window size button in the status bar at the bottom of the Design window and set the size of the workspace to reflect what a viewer using a monitor set for a resolution of 640×480 pixels will see when the page is viewed. Remember that one important design consideration is to never make the viewer scroll their window side to side. Figure 7-2 shows how your window should appear after you have it resized.

Tip

Setting the window size lets you get an appreciation for what viewers will see in their browsers, but does not limit the area you can work in. You may want to work at a higher setting, but then switch back to the smaller window size to be sure that everything still fits.

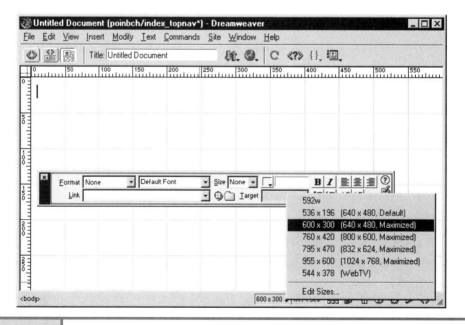

Figure 7-2   The Dreamweaver Document window set for 640×480 resolution

3. Click the Layout View button at the bottom of the Objects panel to switch into that design mode.

Note

The first time you use this option, Dreamweaver will open a Tips window, explaining how to use this feature. To turn off this option, check the box that says, "Don't show me this message again."

4. While in layout view, you can do one of two things: draw a layout table or draw a layout cell (which automatically generates a table as well). Try a table first.

Tip

To have complete control over the layout of the tables you draw, be sure to turn off the option that snaps objects to the grid lines on the screen. Choose View I Grid I Snap To Grid, and be sure that no check mark appears for this option.

 5. Click the Draw Layout Table button on the Objects panel.

6. Notice that the cursor now changes to cross hairs. Move the cursor to the extreme upper-left corner of the Document window and drag it down and across the screen, filling the available space in this window. When you're done, release the mouse button, and your new layout table will appear on the screen, as shown in Figure 7-3. This is only a visual clue for you, the designer. This table would not appear at all if you previewed this page in a browser right now.

7. The Properties Inspector also changes to reflect the new object that is on the page—the layout table. With the Properties Inspector, you can change the way that the table is formatted—from a fixed width, set here at 600 pixels, to a percentage-based table, called Autostretch by Dreamweaver. You'll see some other new features in action that are contained in the Properties Inspector in a few moments. For now, take note of the options available in the Properties Inspector when a table is selected.

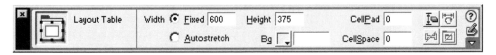

8. At the top of the layout table is an area known as the *column header*, including a small notation of the table's width. Not only is this a handy reference, but, by clicking it, it also enables you to see additional options

7

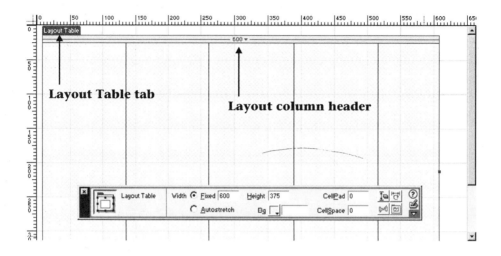

Figure 7-3 A layout table in the Dreamweaver Document window

for changing and formatting your table (for example, Make Column Autostretch, Add Spacer Image, Clear Cell Heights, etc.). Feel free to investigate this option, but do not make any changes to the table's properties at this time.

9. Tables can be drawn inside of each other, but they cannot overlap in width or height. Try this by drawing another table on the far left of the Document window. Make this table 100-pixels wide and extend it to the bottom of the original table. You may find that after you draw the table, you need to enter the precise width in the Properties Inspector.

10. Draw two more tables at the top of the window, each 30-pixels high, to the right of the long table you just created. The background colors in this illustration have been changed so that you can see the size and layout of your new page as it should be when you're done with this exercise.

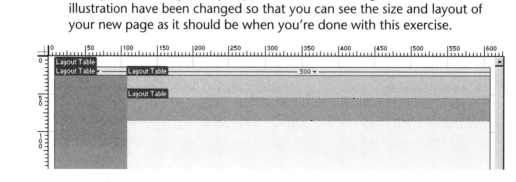

Tip

If you aren't happy with one of the tables you create, choose Edit | Undo Layout Table or press CTRL-Z to go back and try it again.

11. The small tables you have just created are called *nested tables,* because they nest inside a larger "master" table. This type of layout would be helpful if you wanted to set some parts of the page to be a fixed width, such as those that contain and organize graphics. Other tables can still be set to Autostretch so that they fill the viewer's window regardless of the monitor setting. For now, you only need to understand how nested tables are created and some of their possible uses as this project concludes.

12. Save your file now and move on to a project that uses layout cells.

Project 7-2: Working with Layout Cells

Adding layout cells to a document is a process very similar to the way you just inserted layout tables. Even though you have defined some areas of your page with tables, you can't put any content into place until you have cells to hold the information. With layout cells, you can also affect the formatting of smaller areas of your page, changing alignments and the background color of a small portion of the page. Now you are going to add some cells to your page and prepare to insert content into the page.

Step-by-Step

Your goal is to use the top of the page as a navigation bar, and to do that, you need to add some cells in the topmost table to hold the objects that will serve as your navigation bar. By adding cells, you are creating individual containers for each item.

1. On the Objects panel, click the Draw Layout Cell button. Once again, the cursor will turn to cross hairs and you can draw the cell in the position you wish.

2. In the topmost table that you created in Project 7-1, draw a cell that is 100-pixels wide. Notice how the lines snap to the existing borders of the table as your cursor approaches them. Very handy, because previously you would have had to use the arrow keys on the keyboard to nudge the cell into position, often with inconsistent results.

3. Dreamweaver uses a light-blue border as a visual guide to the position of your cells. To select a cell, float your pointer over its border. When the border turns red, click the mouse button, and the cell will be selected. Once selected, the

7

Properties Inspector will change, and you may want to fine-tune the size of the cell to get it to the correct size by entering the width and height.

Tip

Since cells cannot overlap each other, it is best to work from left to right, inserting a cell and then adjusting its width, before placing a new cell next to it.

4. Continue this process until you have a series of five cells that you'll use as a navigation bar across the top of the window.

5. Finish blocking out the page by adding the rest of the cells that will contain the content of this page.

6. In the upper-left corner of the page, add a cell that is 100-pixels wide and 100-pixels high. Fill out this table by drawing another cell below it that extends to the bottom of the table.

7. Place a single cell into the small table that lies just below the navigation bar area and then complete the process by adding another single cell over the raining portion of the page. When you are finished, your page will be blocked out as shown in Figure 7-4. Once again, the cell and table backgrounds have been changed so that you can see their position more easily.

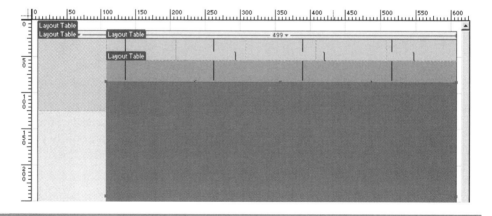

Figure 7-4 The Dreamweaver Document window with layout tables and cells added

Project 7-3: Adding Content to Layout Tables and Cells

In addition to being used as a way to block out sections of a new page, content can also be added directly into the document while in Layout view. This process uses many of the same commands you've used in previous modules, so you should be able to move quickly to add images and text to this page and gain an understanding of some of the considerations you need to make when using Layout mode.

Step-by-Step

1. In the upper-left corner of the page, you want to add the logo for the Chamber of Commerce, as shown in Figure 7-5. Click inside that cell so that the borders of the cell become outlined in blue and the blinking cursor appears. Click the Insert Image button on the Objects panel and browse to the pbcofc_logo_small.gif file in your common_images folder.

2. You'll be using text for the navigation elements at the top of this page. While you could just as easily insert images or Flash objects into these cells, you'll use text for this exercise and in the next module, which looks at cascading style sheets. Moving from left to right, type in the same text you've used before: **For Visitors**, **For Residents**, **For Businesses**, **For Members**, **Local Events**.

3. Change the font style for each to Geneva, Helvetica, Arial, Sans serif and link the text to the index.htm file for each section of your site. When you are finished, your page should appear as shown in Figure 7-6.

7

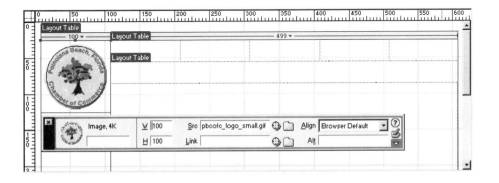

Figure 7-5   The Document window after inserting your first image

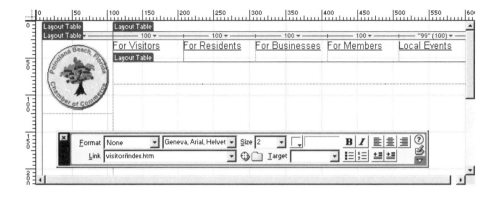

Figure 7-6 Insert text links at the top of the page

4. Your next task is to add some contrast to the page so that your navigation area, and a new navigation section that you will create, are separate from the main content in the page. You'll do that by changing the background color of the cells and tables themselves.

5. Locate the Layout Table tab just above the logo you just inserted, and click it once to select the table and the single cell in it. The table is selected when the cell has square "handles" around it and is outlined in green. Notice also that the Properties Inspector indicates that the Layout Table is the current active selection, as shown in Figure 7-7.

6. On the Properties Inspector, locate the Bg color button (see Figure 7-8) that allows a background color to be specified for the background of the cell itself. Select the button and then use the eyedropper tool to pick up a pale-yellow color from inside the logo.

7. Repeat this process to change the background color of the table where your navigation images are located. Instead of the color in the logo itself, use the background color that was just inserted in the table holding the logo.

8. Preview your completed file in a browser and notice the results that you've achieved. Not exactly right is it? You have a little more work to do in the next section, where you'll see how you can modify and adjust cell and table properties to meet your design goals. For now, check your spelling and save your file.

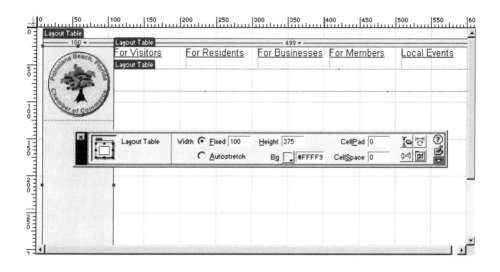

Figure 7-7 The Properties Inspector changes based on the object selected

7

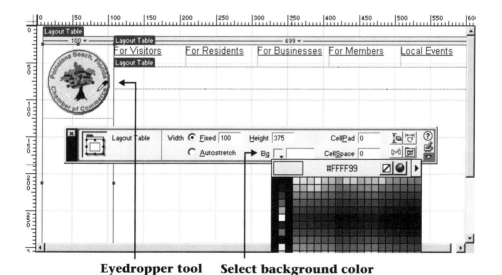

Eyedropper tool   Select background color

Figure 7-8 Use the eyedropper tool to "pick up" a color from an image

Project 7-4: Modifying Layout Cells and Tables

One of the great things about this new layout interface that Dreamweaver 4 introduces is the ability to easily modify the layout tables and cells themselves. Again, prior to this new interface, making changes to a single cell or to a table could be a frustrating experience. You'll use these tools now to finish your index_topnav.htm document and get it into its final form.

When you previewed this page in a browser before, you probably saw a number of problems. The navigation links were squeezed against the top edge of the screen, the yellow bar that holds the buttons seemed to end in midair, and there was a white border around the left and top of the screen that gave the page an unfinished look. You're going to fix all of those little problems now as you wrap up this section.

Step-by-Step

Your first task is to change the alignment of the text that you inserted into the navigation bar at the top of the page.

1. Notice again how the border of a cell changes to a red rectangle when your pointer passes over it. This is a visual clue that clicking the button will select the cell. Float your pointer over the cell that holds the For Visitors text and then click once. The border changes from red to blue and handles appear, letting you know you have successfully selected the cell. (This is very similar to the way that objects are selected in the Fireworks interface.)

2. After the cell is selected, change the vertical spacing (using the Vert list box) to Middle on the Properties Inspector and then select the text itself and set the alignment to the center of the cell.

3. Continue across the row, changing the vertical alignment and centering the text in each cell so that your settings in the Properties Inspector look like this:

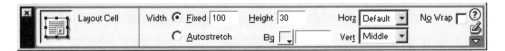

4. Preview your work in a browser and you'll see that the text for your navigation bar is very closely aligned to the top edge of your logo—a nice neat look.

Project 7-5: Using the Autostretch Feature

Your next task is to add some new cells to your table that will appear when those people who have their monitors set to a higher resolution view this document. Remember, you want to make sure that those who have the lowest resolution will view your information correctly, but you also want to avoid neglecting those who have higher monitor settings. Luckily, you have a quick method for correcting this problem—the Autostretch feature.

Step-by-Step

Your goal is to change the layout of the navigation bar area so that the yellow band where your links are located will expand to the right when seen at a higher resolution, but will keep the other items in your page neatly aligned.

1. Select the cell where the Local Events text is located and reduce the width of that cell to 80 pixels by changing its value in the Properties Inspector.

7

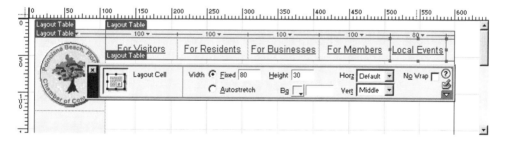

2. Reducing the width of this cell creates a "blank" area in the table where you can now insert a new cell. Draw this cell into place now—allowing it to snap to the right edge of the table that contains it.

3. Getting this small cell selected can be a bit of a challenge, but by moving the adjacent cell to the left temporarily, you should be able to ultimately hit the borders of the cell and bring up the Properties Inspector.

4. You need to change the formatting of this cell so that it will Autostretch across the screen based on the viewer's window size. In the Properties Inspector, click the Autostretch radio button.

5. The first time you use the Autostretch feature, Dreamweaver presents a dialog box that asks how you want it to help with the task of inserting a special spacer image that will be used to fill in the empty spaces created in Autostretch mode. Accept the default settings, as shown in Figure 7-9, and save this new image as **spacer.gif** in the common_images folder.

6. Preview your work in a browser and you'll see that the navigation bar now stretches across the top of the page because of this new cell that has been added. The cells containing text, set with a fixed pixel width, remain neatly in place, regardless of how large or small the browser window becomes.

Tip

If you want to eliminate the white bands that appear at the top and left sides of the page, go to the Page Properties dialog box (select Modify | Page Properties) and set the left and top margins and the margin height and widths to zero. Using tables automatically formats a border on the page, but the border can be removed by resetting these values.

7. Now that your navigation bar is formatted the way you want, you can resize the cells that hold the text into a more appropriate width. Once again, you'll use your mouse and the handles that are displayed when the cells are selected. Select the cells, moving from left to right, and resize them until

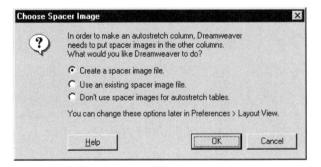

Figure 7-9 Dreamweaver presents several options for creating images to be used as spacers

each line of text is bordered by approximately the same amount of yellow space. As always, you can also set the number of pixels in the Properties Inspector. Notice that as the cells are resized, small gray areas appear, letting you know that there is an unfilled area in the table that contains these cells.

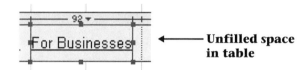

Unfilled space in table

8. Adjust the position of the cells by selecting each and then sliding it to the left until it snaps into place with the adjacent cells. The Autostretch cell at the far right will expand as necessary to fill any unused space.

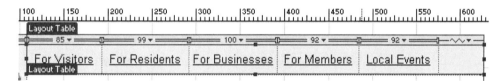

9. The completed design still lacks some of the content that it needs. Adding content is easily accomplished by inserting the image at the top of the page, adding some links on the left side to Chamber of Commerce member web sites, and even copying and pasting the text from your original index page. If you feel that you need to practice these operations, then this is a good time to do so. Otherwise, look at Figure 7-10 or open the index_topnav.htm file in the exercise files for this module to see the final product of all of your hard work.

The user interface that Macromedia has designed for Dreamweaver 4 puts some incredibly easy-to-use new tools at the disposal of web designers. This ability to draw a series of tables and cells that block out your pages makes the entire process of designing properly aligned and formatted pages much easier than it was with the previous, often difficult, methods for page design that were available. Still, you need to look at a few more tricks that you can add to your arsenal of design tools—other methods that you will use to get your pages looking just right.

7

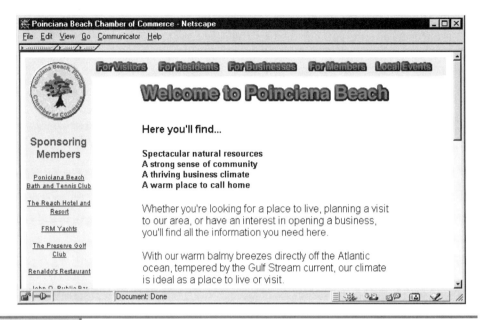

Figure 7-10 | The completed web page created with Autostretch tables and cells

1-Minute Drill

● What is the primary function of layout tables and cells?

● What restrictions are there are on the placement of layout tables and cells?

● What tool is used for precisely setting the pixel width of layout cells?

Page Layout Using Tracing Images

Many people who move from the world of graphic design to that of creating web pages come with a background in the use of illustration software that enables them to design beautiful mock-ups of the pages as they expect to see them in their final form. In fact, many web sites have been developed in the

---

● Layout cells and tables are used primarily for blocking out sections of a web page.
● Layout tables and cells cannot overlap each other in width and height.
● The Properties Inspector is used when the exact width of a cell needs to be applied.

conceptual phase by someone working with either Macromedia Freehand or Adobe Illustrator—drawing exactly what their finished product will look like before they ever wrote the first line of HTML. (All of the images you will use were produced, of course, with Fireworks.) Dreamweaver makes this possible by allowing designers to take a graphic image and then lay out their page on top of the drawing.

Project 7-6: Using Tracing Images in Page Layout

Tracing images can greatly speed the process of moving from concept to reality in the design of web pages. In the next series of exercises, you'll see how pages are created around a graphic image, and especially how layout tables and cells can make this process even easier.

Step-by-Step

1. Right-click the root folder in the Site window and choose New File from the context menu. Name this new file **index_topnav_trace.htm** and open it.

2. In the Exercises folder for Module 7, you will find two GIF files that you will use as tracing images: trace_topnav.gif and trace_sidenav.gif. Use your computer system's copy and paste feature to copy the files into the common_images folder in the site files for Poinciana Beach.

3. Choose Modify | Page Properties for your new document to open the Page Properties dialog box, shown in Figure 7-11. At the bottom of the dialog box, locate the area that applies to tracing images.

4. Click the Browse button and locate the file called trace_topnav.gif that you stored in the common_images folder earlier. Click OK to accept this image, and you'll be returned to the Document window where you will have an image that appears very similar to the web page you created in your last exercise, with the exception that you are using the graphical buttons for your links instead of text. (The black lines have been added to provide a guide for page layout.) Notice that the image is behind the layout grid on the page, though, and if you were to preview this document in a browser, you would find it to be a completely blank document. The tracing image exists only as a guide for the page designer. It does not become a part of the HTML document that you are creating, but instead rests in the background so that you can use it to block out your page. The image transparency can even be set with the slider in the Page Properties dialog box so that it fades further into the background.

7

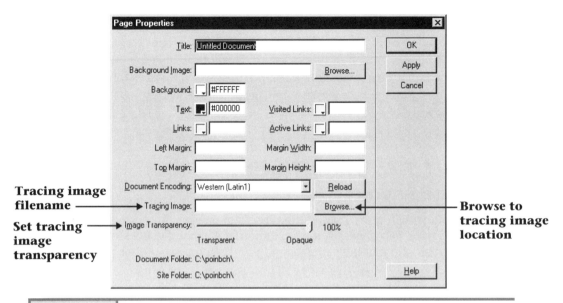

Tracing image filename →

Set tracing image transparency →

← **Browse to tracing image location**

Figure 7-11 | Use the Page Properties dialog box to control tracing images

5. When you first insert the tracing image into the background of your page, it may not be aligned properly to the page. To correct this minor problem, choose View | Tracing Image | Adjust Position to move the graphic into proper alignment, either by using the arrow keys on your keyboard or by setting the value numerically. You will probably find that you need to readjust the position of the image once you begin drawing layout tables and cells. Just repeat the process to nudge it into the proper position as necessary.

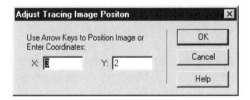

6. To have complete freedom over the positioning of your tables and cells, choose View | Grid | Snap To Grid and be sure that option is *not* checked.

7. Start the layout process by drawing one large table that covers the graphic from top to bottom, and then draw three additional tables inside it—one at the far left for your logo and links section, one at the top for the navigation bar, and a final table at the bottom for the e-mail link. Notice that the tables begin to obscure the tracing image somewhat.

8. To complete the process, use the black lines that are part of the tracing image to draw in the individual cells. As each cell is added, the tracing image will appear more clearly. Be sure that a layout cell covers every area of the page.

9. Set all the cells that are to the far right of the page to Autostretch so that they will fill the screen in monitors that have higher resolutions.

10. You'll add the content and change the formatting for this page in a little while, so for now, simply save your file.

This combination of tracing images and layout tables and cells gives you some remarkable tools for ensuring that your final page design follows good design principles and has a professional appearance. What had previously been an extremely tedious, and often frustrating, chore has been made much simpler with the new user interface of Dreamweaver 4.

Working with Tables in the Standard Layout View

7

Although using Layout view is certainly the best way to block out sections of a page during the design phase, often it is not the best choice for inserting content and making small changes to the properties of the tables and cells themselves. In Standard view, tables and cells can be easily

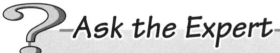

Ask the Expert

Question: Aren't layers also used for page layout? Does Dreamweaver 4 still support this method?

Answer: In Dreamweaver 2 and 3, layers were frequently used as an element for designing page layout. Layers can be created in any size and positioned anywhere on the page, providing they don't overlap each other. One of the problems with using layers in page layout—and there are many—is that they have to be converted back into tables to ensure that viewer's with older browsers can still see them, and they often produce tiny table cells when converted that are nearly impossible to modify and bloat the document's file size. With the new layout tools of Dreamweaver 4, my recommendation to a beginner would be to stay with tables until you develop your skills in the use of layers.

modified, combined, and fine-tuned in ways that are not as easily done while in Layoutview. This section looks at the process of viewing and modifying tables in Standard view of the Document window, as well as inserting and formatting tables into a document.

Project 7-7: Modifying Tables in Standard View

For this first exercise, you need to open the file called table_practice.htm from the exercise files for this module. Since this is just a practice file, you don't need to worry about saving it into the site for Poinciana Beach.

Step-by-Step

1. Click the button at the bottom of the Object panel to switch to Standard view.

2. The page view now switches to the Standard view, and you can clearly make out the table and accompanying cells in this page, designated by dashed lines that show their location and that their borders are set to zero pixels in width.

3. Move your mouse pointer around the screen and take note of how it changes as it encounters different objects in the page. When your pointer passes over the outside edge of the table itself, for instance, it changes to a four-way arrow. Click the mouse button when you see the arrow and the outside border of the table will appear with a heavy black line and the familiar resize handles will appear. Notice also that the <table> tag is in bold in the Tag Selector portion of the toolbar, as shown in Figure 7-12.

4. As always in the Dreamweaver interface, a selected object changes the Properties Inspector to reflect the settings for that item. You see in the Properties Inspector for this table that there are three rows and six columns, that the border and all the spacing values are set to zero, and that only the default values for formatting are applied. Notice also that the table can have a background color applied, which you learned to do previously, and that an image can be placed in the background as well.

5. Selecting and modifying individual cells is accomplished just as easily. Roll your pointer across and around the cell boundaries. The double-headed arrow allows you to resize the individual cell, while the dark single arrow allows you to select the individual cell.

6. One of the easiest ways to select items in a table, particularly after you've inserted content, is to click directly on top of the tag for the table or cell in the Tag Selector. Practice this selection method by moving your cursor around

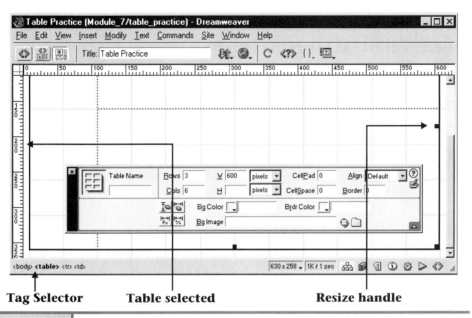

Tag Selector   **Table selected**   **Resize handle**

Figure 7-12   The Dreamweaver Document window in Standard view

the screen and then selecting the tags that appear in the Tag Selector. Notice that when a cell is selected, it is bordered by a darker border that makes it appear to pop out from the page. Remember that the following HTML tags apply to these objects:

<table>	Selects the entire table
<tr>	Selects a table row
<td>	Selects a table division—an individual cell

7. When you are finished experimenting with this document, you can ignore the changes or save it for further practice on your own. Move on now to your last exercise in working with tables.

Modifying tables and individual cells in both Standard and Layout views does require a bit of practice. As noted earlier, modifying a cell automatically changes the properties of the table that contains it, as well as any adjacent cells and tables. In the beginning, you should move slowly when modifying cells, and, as always, plan ahead so that later modifications can be kept to a minimum.

Project 7-8: Inserting and Formatting a Table

In this next exercise, you will be inserting a table that contains a calendar for your Chamber of Commerce home page and then modifying its properties using the tools available in Dreamweaver.

Step-by-Step

1. Open the file that you used during the discussion of tracing images—index_topnav_trace.htm. Be sure that you are in Standard view. Change the transparency setting of the tracing image to around 40% by selecting Modify I Page Properties and adjusting the slider at the bottom.

2. Locate the area on the page that you blocked out for a calendar previously and click inside the cell. Since you want the table to be centered in the cell, go ahead and set the alignment to Center on the Properties Inspector.

3. Click the Insert Table button on the Objects panel.

4. Set the values in the Insert Table dialog box as you see in Figure 7-13. Cell Padding and Cell Spacing insert extra pixels into each cell and are not appropriate for the small table you are creating. Be sure those values are set to 0.

5. Your next step is to apply some automatic formatting to the table. Select the table and then choose Commands I Format Table to open a listing of available table styles, as shown in Figure 7-14. Choose Simple3 from the list of styles and leave the other options set in their default values. Click OK to accept the formatting.

6. To combine the cells in the top row of the column to hold the name of the month, place your cursor in the rightmost cell and then click and drag across

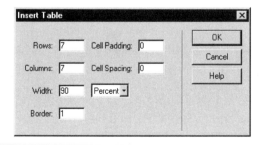

Figure 7-13 The Insert Table dialog box contains settings for designing a table manually

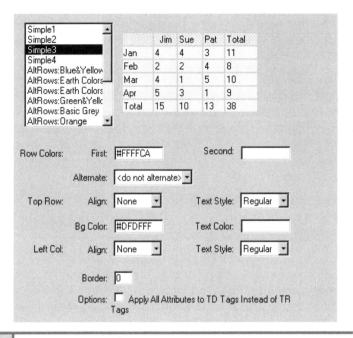

Figure 7-14   The Format Table dialog box can be used to customize preformatted tables

the row, or select the <tr> tag in the Tag Selector. You will know that your row is selected when each cell is outlined with a black line.

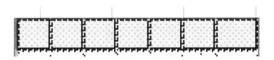

7. The Merge Cells and Split Cells buttons on the Properties Inspector allow you to change the divisions in a cell—either to merge them or to split them. Merge these cells now and type the name of the month.

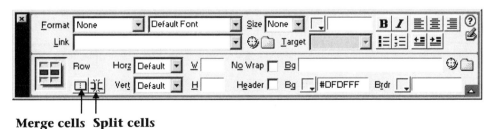

Merge cells Split cells

8. To complete the calendar, type the name of the month you want to display in the top row, followed by letters denoting the days of the week, and finally the dates themselves.

9. You may need to adjust the properties of the table as you insert content—especially if you change the size of the text either up or down. One quick way to get all the cells the same width is to select the cells you want to change by using your mouse, and then set a relative width value that equals the width of the table (100%) divided by the number of columns (7). In this case, the cells were set to 15%, but you may need to change your setting based on the font type and size you use.

10. As with everything else, the separate days, even if they are only one number, can be linked to another page. In this case, you would probably link them to the index file located in your Events folder.

11. When you preview your work in your browser, you will notice that any cells that do not contain content do not display properly in the browser window—another peculiarity of HTML. To fix this problem, you can type a single period into the cell and then change its color to be the same as the background color, or insert the spacer.gif image that you stored earlier in the common_images folder.

12. Preview your work again and then save your file when you are satisfied with the results.

1-Minute Drill

● What is the primary function of tracing images?

● How does the Tag Selector assist in formatting an element of a page?

● How are predefined styles applied to tables?

Project 7-9: Practicing with Page Layouts

Developing page design and layout skills requires a good deal of practice, and in this project, you will continue building those skills by completing one page

---

● Tracing images are used to create tables and cells that will contain content by employing an image file created in an illustration program such as Fireworks or Freehand.
● The Tag Selector is useful in that it allows the designer to select individual elements on a page more easily than is possible with a mouse.
● Predefined styles are set by choosing Commands I Format Table and then choosing the style that is appropriate for your design.

that you began earlier, and by building another page with an entirely new style. Remember that these examples are only here to give you practice on the process of blocking out pages in Dreamweaver and then inserting the content into your pages. At some point, you will make your own decisions on what you think looks best and meets the needs of your audience, and your final designs may be radically different from the examples you see here. Experimentation is highly encouraged as you work through this project, and if you feel that your own layout scheme is a better plan for you to follow, by all means do your own thing.

Independent Study projects are designed to give you additional practice in the application of the skills and concepts covered in this and succeeding modules. This approach is designed to allow you some flexibility in completing projects in a way that allows your own creative forces to come into play, while letting you master the essential concepts covered in the module.

Independent Study Exercise

1. Open the file index_topnav.htm that you worked on earlier in this module and complete the process of inserting text and images. A duplicate copy of this file exists in the exercise files for this module, and you should look at the last-minute refinements that were made to the page to improve its alignment. What further improvements can you make? Would the page look better with graphical buttons replacing the text used? Does this page contain good contrast? Is your eye naturally drawn to one element first, and then to the objects that are second and third in importance?

2. Create a new document using the trace_topnav.gif image, located in the Exercises folder for this module. Using that file as a tracing image, build your new page using layout tables and cells and then insert the content that would complete this page. What problems do you encounter during the layout process? Which working style suits you the best—Layout view or Standard view? How can switching between the two modes enable you more easily to modify the tables, cells, and content for this page?

What to Take Away

Advanced layout of web pages is a skill that requires a great deal of practice and patience. Dreamweaver 4 adds some new layout features that provide designers not only incredible latitude in planning and executing their page designs, but also the ability to format the results so that they employ good design principles. This module discussed those principles and then demonstrated how they are put into action in a real-world setting. The addition of layout tables and cells, working in conjunction with tracing images, enables you to design the types of pages that help you to meet your overall goal—designing pages that are appealing and easy to use by your audience.

The next module continues the discussion of the advanced layout features available in Dreamweaver, by teaching you how to use frames and cascading style sheets to further define and enhance the Web experience for your viewers.

Mastery Check

1. How are tables and cells most commonly used in modern web pages?

2. What four elements of design must every web designer keep in mind when laying out their web pages and web sites?

3. Where are the buttons located that allow a quick change from Layout to Standard view in a Dreamweaver document?

4. Why would a designer choose to set a table or cell to Autostretch?

5. When should a cell not be set to Autostretch?

6. What dialog box controls the functioning of tracing images?

Module 8

Advanced Page Design: Frames and Cascading Style Sheets

The Goals of this Module

- Understand the use of frames in page design
- Explore the appropriate use of frames
- Use the frame layout features of Dreamweaver
- Understand the use of cascading style sheets
- Design custom cascading style sheets
- Employ cascading style sheets in a web page

Always keep in mind while creating web pages that you are generating code that is interpreted and displayed by a browser. HTML and the supporting scripting languages that extend its capabilities are very different from the types of documents that you may have created on a computer before. A former advertising campaign for the State of Florida once contained the line "The Rules Are Different Here"—and that certainly is true of HTML, and especially true of the two topics covered in this module.

Frames and cascading style sheets (CSS) require a good understanding of the rules for their use because of the way that they are employed in the underlying code of the document. As such, their use can be a bit daunting to a new designer. In your previous design work, you have been ably assisted by the tools that Dreamweaver contains that enable you to work without giving much thought to HTML. You have been able to insert text, images, links, and tables, all while allowing Dreamweaver to do the chore of generating the necessary code for you. Although Dreamweaver certainly makes the job of creating frames and the custom coding of cascading style sheets simpler than what would be possible if you were coding by hand, using these two design features does require a deeper understanding of the rules for their use than you have needed for other features.

Understanding the Use of Frames in Page Design

Figure 8-1 shows a typical web page that has been designed with frames. The page is broken into two separate areas, with a navigation element on the left and a larger section that holds the main content for the page. Scrolling down the main section of the page allows you to see all the content in that portion of the window, while keeping the other pane fixed in place. In fact, it wasn't that long ago that few people who considered themselves "serious" web designers would have posted a site to the Internet that wasn't formatted with frames. This design scheme was considered at the time to be the future of the Web, allowing designers to block out different sections of their pages based on their intended use. Designers also appreciated the way that using frames allowed them to design one navigation scheme and easily and consistently employ it in all the pages throughout the site—significantly cutting down on their workload.

Users of the Internet had a much different take on the use of frames, however, and many quickly decided that they didn't like frames at all. Frames make it difficult to easily bookmark a single page within a site, make printing a hit-or-miss proposition, and often chop the page into rectangular sections, which violates some of the basic design principles discussed in the last module. Designers also discovered

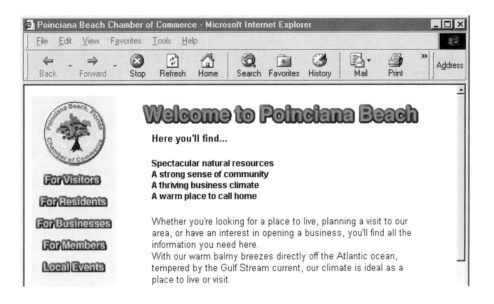

Figure 8-1	This page uses frames to create two separate sections of the document, for navigation and for main content

that search engines often refused to document pages deep within a site, and because of that and other technical difficulties in the use of frames—and the love-it or hate-it relationship that many members of the Internet audience developed toward them—their use has been diminishing of late.

The decision to use frames goes back to the previous discussion of site development—and the most fundamental question of all: how does their use impact the experience of your intended audience and meet the goals of the site? Using frames in site and page design is a decision that has to be made carefully after weighing both the pros and cons of their use.

The Case for Frames

Even though the use of frames carries an inherent risk, many designers feel that there are enough advantages to their use that working around the problems associated with frames is worth the effort. Some of the advantages to the use of frames include the following:

- *Frames allow page designers to develop a single navigation scheme and then repeat it throughout the site.* As stated before, consistency in site navigation is an important fundamental of page design, and frames can assist greatly in developing an easy-to-follow scheme for the audience.

- *Frames can reduce the amount of work required for the designer by allowing certain elements to be repeated throughout the site—without having to redesign them each time.* Imagine a web site with hundreds or even thousands of individual pages that each requires a navigation bar, and you can appreciate how being able to design that element only a single time and then reuse it as necessary is an attractive option.

- *Frames make the chore of updating content easier for the page designer.* On a site where many pages need frequent changes, having to modify just a single part of the document at a time can be a big advantage.

- *Frames often load more quickly than a page designed in a "standard" layout scheme.* Since only a portion of a page has to be reloaded when the viewer clicks a link, frame pages give the impression that they load more quickly.

- *Frames can keep viewers within your site—even when they link to an absolute URL outside of your site.* Frames can be designed in such a way that a page outside of yours can still be loaded into your window, effectively keeping the viewer under your control.

The Case Against Frames

With the advantages previously listed in mind, why not use frames for all your pages? While the disadvantages to using frames may not overwhelm you, they are significant enough that you should give them equal consideration before you dive into designing your entire site with frames. Some of the problems with frames include:

- *Frames are not effective tools for page layout.* Much of the disdain for frames stems from their misuse for page layout—leading to blocky, inelegant designs that are hard for the viewer to decipher, and simply don't look good. Frames are fine when used for defining certain parts of the page based on their function, but not when they are used as a design element.

- *Pages with multiple scroll bars can be confusing to the viewer.* If you've seen a page that asks the viewer to scroll left in one frame and then down in another, you can appreciate how difficult it is to determine what is required to get to the information you want. Besides, having a scroll bar in the middle of a page chops up the page and just looks ugly.

- *Frames cause printing problems.* Although the most current versions of browsers have alleviated this problem, viewers with older browsers often find themselves printing a copy of the navigation bar for a page when they only wanted to print an article that was on the main portion of the page. Very frustrating!

- *Frames cause problems with bookmarking.* Because of technical issues involved with how files are named, viewers often have problems bookmarking more than one page for your site.

- *Frames cause problems with search engines.* Again, because of the way that files are named, search engines often have difficulty indexing more than one page in the entire site.

The use of frames in site and page design is a decision that has to be made after considering the preceding factors and how they will impact your intended audience. If after careful deliberation you feel that frames are the best way to meet the goals of your site, then by all means use them. There are many fine examples of thoughtfully employed page design using frames. One site that you should have already visited by now is www.macromedia.com, where the navigation bar is in one frame at the top of the page, the content is in the center, and a search box (and advertising) are contained in a bottom frame. If, like the site designers at Macromedia, you have considered both the pros and cons of using frames and have decided that they suit your needs, then you're ready for this module's exercises in their creation.

1-Minute Drill

- What is the primary function of a frame?
- What are frames not appropriate for?
- How can frames be used to make web pages more consistent?

Designing Web Pages with Frames

During my travels around the Internet while researching lessons for my students I have seen the principles of frame layout compared to everything from TV dinners,

---

- Frames are used to separate a web page into sections based on their function—such as navigation, search, and advertising.
- Frames should not be used as a page layout tool.
- Frames are useful for making pages more consistent when certain areas, such as navigation elements, are used throughout the entire site.

picnic baskets, and even aquariums. Perhaps the reason that so many writers search for an appropriate metaphor for frames is that frames are a bit difficult to understand.

Web pages that are created with frames are actually a collection of pages—all displaying simultaneously in the browser window. At the top of the frame structure is the frameset itself, an HTML document that defines the layout of the page and holds the other documents in place, similar to the way a picnic basket holds all the goodies for your day at the park. Held in place within the frameset are the supporting documents—the goodies themselves—which are separate HTML files all their own. A web page with two frames, for example, actually consists of three documents: the frameset and the two documents that are displayed within it, as you see in Figure 8-2.

Because of the way that framed pages are created and displayed, you need to follow a very strict set of rules in naming the files and posting them to a site. Dreamweaver assists in this operation by allowing you to save all the frames in the page at once, thereby eliminating at least one opportunity to go wrong in dealing with these complicated objects.

Project 8-1: Creating Your First Frameset

You now are going to create your first series of pages, which will familiarize you with the Dreamweaver interface when dealing with frames. For these exercises, it's best that you follow the steps exactly as they are outlined, because failure to get everything just right will result in pages that don't display properly. You'll have an opportunity for exploration later on, after you have the rules under your belt.

Be sure that you have downloaded the exercise files that support this module from www.osborne.com, and have saved them into the Exercises folder on your hard drive.

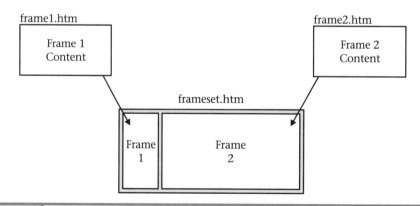

Figure 8-2 Pages built with frames consist of the frameset and the supporting documents

Step-by-Step

1. Create a new document in the root folder of your Poinciana Beach web site. For this exercise, *do not* give the file a name yet—simply open it and leave the filename as the default untitled.htm that Dreamweaver assigns to it.

2. Recall from the discussion of the Dreamweaver interface that a number of preset frame arrangements are already specified in the Objects panel. Change the category in the Objects panel from Common to Frames by clicking the expansion arrow in the upper-right corner.

3. Notice that in each button of the Frames panel, one frame is highlighted in blue, indicating that this is the area where the main content of the page will be contained. Choose the button in the upper-left corner and create a frameset with a navigation bar on the left and the main content in a larger window on the right. By selecting this option you have chosen to create three HTML documents; or to use the example described earlier, you now have the picnic basket and room for two items to go into the basket.

4. The page that displays in the main document window of Dreamweaver is the frameset document, but without the separate pages that will fill the left and right frames (the goodies that go into the basket), nothing will display in this page as it is constructed now. You need the additional content contained in the other two pages to make this page work.

5. You first need to be familiar with the new working environment of a framed page before you add any content. When you clicked the button in the Objects panel to create the structure of this new frameset, Dreamweaver opened a new window—the Frames panel. If this new panel does not appear, choose Window | Frames to display it. The only purpose of this panel is to give you a reminder of which area of the page you are currently working on—the frameset or one of the supporting documents contained in it—and to let you switch from working in one frame to another.

8

6. Click in the center of each pane of the Frames panel now and notice how a dotted line appears in the accompanying section of the main Document window. Click the outer border of the Frames panel and the entire frameset will be selected. Very handy, since moving between frames and the main frameset can be a little tricky when working in the Document window. And, since you are working on three pages simultaneously, it's critical to know which one you are working in at any given time.

7. Your other visual clue as to which item is selected is your old friend the Properties Inspector. As each frame is selected, the Properties Inspector changes to reflect the settings for the frame or frameset. As you select different frames using the Frames panel, note how the Properties Inspector changes to reflect the position of the selected frame.

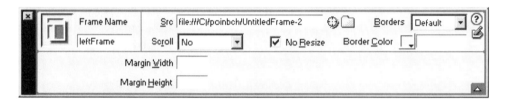

8. Leave these files open as you continue in this module.

Project 8-2: Modifying and Saving Frames

Understanding the way that Dreamweaver presents information while working in frames is the first step toward successfully designing pages in this challenging environment. Your next steps involve modifying the pages themselves (keep thinking pages, plural, when working with frames) and inserting content as you would normally do.

Step-by-Step

1. Similar to tables, the divider between the two frames in the example can be modified either by using the mouse pointer, after it changes to a double arrow, or by entering a value for the frameset divider directly in the Properties Inspector. Remember that changing the divider means that you are working in the frameset—not in the left frame. Modify the width of the left frame by changing the divider in the frameset to a value of 130 pixels.

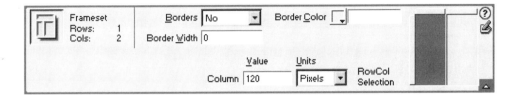

2. Laying out both of the frames in this page could be done in the same way that you used in the last module—either with standard or layout tables. In the interest of time, though, simply open the two files in the Exercises folder and paste their content into the correct frame. Open left_content.htm and select all the cells in the layout table, as you did in Module 7, and then select Edit | Copy to copy the table and cells onto your computer's clipboard. Return to your untitled.htm document and select inside the left frame, or select the frame with the Frames panel, and choose Edit | Paste to put the table and cells into place. Repeat this step to place the contents of right_content.htm into the right frame.

3. You now have your three HTML documents nearly ready for saving. Insert the small logo and the buttons from the common_images folder into the cells in the left frame. Use the eyedropper tool to set the background color to the pale-yellow color in the middle of the logo. Insert the banner_main.gif file into the top cell in the right frame. Finally, find the file called right_text.htm in your Exercises folder and copy and paste the text in that file into the bottom cell in the right frame of your untitled documents.

4. A scroll bar will appear in the right frame and you will be able to scroll up and down in this window while the left frame remains static. When you are finished adjusting the vertical alignments of the images in the pages your finished product should look something like what you see in Figure 8-3.

5. Select the frameset document and give the page the title **Poinciana Beach Chamber of Commerce** by typing the text into the Title box of the document. Remember that if a viewer were to bookmark this page, the title in the frameset is what would appear in their Bookmark (or Favorites) listings. The title of the frameset is also what appears in the title bar of their browser.

6. You're now ready to save your documents. As you'll see, this process is a little different from saving a normal file, since you'll be saving the three documents that make up this page simultaneously. Select File | Save All Frames.

7. Dreamweaver automatically presents three separate Save File dialog boxes that you need to save your three documents. However, it is very important that you pay close attention to the dark hash marks that appear around the

Figure 8-3 The completed page design with left and right frames

border of each frame as you are about to save them. This is your visual clue as to which portion of the page is actually being saved—and the only clue you will get.

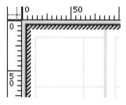

8. In the Save As dialog box, save the first document as **index_frameset.htm**, the left frame as **left_nav.htm**, and the large frame as **right_welcome.htm**. Check those hash marks before you click the Save button to be sure that the file you are saving is named the way you want. Frames and the frameset that contains them must always be saved in the same folder.

9. Move slowly and carefully so that each frame is saved correctly. In general, it is a good idea to include the position of the file and a clue as to its function in the filename.

10. Once you have established the name of the individual files, you should always continue saving pages designed in frames using the File | Save All Frames procedure. This ensures that the frames are saved in the proper relationship to each other and that you don't inadvertently save the file with a name that will cause the structure to fail.

Congratulations. If you preview your work in a browser and the page displays correctly, you have completed a very complicated task in an exemplary manner.

Project 8-3: Linking Files in Frames

One of the great advantages of using frames is the ability to reduce the amount of work necessary to develop and publish an entire web site. With the three documents that you created in the previous exercise, you are well on the way to having the entire web site for the Poinciana Beach Chamber of Commerce completely finished. With frames, and their ability to link to and display a new document within the same browser window, you can significantly speed up the process of site design.

You may recall from the previous discussion of image rollovers that, at times, a file needs a special name associated with it for the code to be generated that will let it function. This use of a name for the coding to function can sometimes lead to confusion, especially since the name is different from both the name of the file itself and the page titles that you have worked with before. Naming in frames involves the concept of establishing targets for the file to load into, and in this exercise, you will see this concept in action.

Step-by-Step

1. Open index_frameset.htm from the Site window. When the frameset is loaded, the supporting documents—left_nav.htm and right_welcome .htm—will also be loaded into it.

2. Your first task is to name the two frames so that they can be properly targeted when you establish the links on the two pages. To do this, open the Frames panel (if it is not open already) by selecting Window | Frames. Click inside the left frame to open the Properties Inspector for the left frame.

3. In the upper-left corner of the Properties Inspector, find the Frame Name box. By default, this frame is called leftFrame. Change the name to **navFrame** by typing directly into the Frame Name box.

8

4. Name the frame for the main content of the page (the frame on the right) in the same manner. Select the frame using the Frames panel and rename this frame **contentFrame**.

Note

These frames could have been left with their default names and would still work properly. You are renaming them here primarily for instructional purposes. It is important to name your frames in a way that makes their use easy to decipher.

5. You can now link and target the images in the navigation bar, as you have previously done. Your first link will be created on the logo, giving your viewers a way to find their way back to the main page of the site. You may have noticed that many web pages feature this design: the logo in the upper-left corner includes a link to the home page. You could also create and insert an image that would return the user to the home page of the site.

6. Select the logo in the left frame and browse to the file you created earlier—right_welcome.htm. Even though that page is currently loaded in the frameset, you have to remember that this frameset will be used to load all the pages in the site, so creating a link back to the home page is still a necessity.

7. The area for specifying the target for this link to load into is in the expanded portion of the Properties Inspector. Click the expansion arrow to gain access to the additional areas of the Properties Inspector and locate the Target drop-down list box. Click the drop-down arrow to expand the box, and choose contentFrame from the selections. Specifying the target ensures that the content will display in the larger frame on the right. Failure to change the target for this link would cause the content of the right frame to attempt to replace the content of the left frame—a very messy situation.

8. Four additional presets are available for targeting links in frames. The two that are most commonly used are _blank and _parent. The _blank preset creates a new browser window, without frames, to display the content— useful if you want to avoid the potential problems caused when viewers wish to print a document. Creating a link that says something like **Printer Friendly Page** and then using the _blank target allows the viewer to open a new window without frames, and then print the document. Using the _parent target automatically loads the linked file into the larger parent frameset of the page—in this case, index_frameset.htm. Using the _parent target would create the same effect as what you have created by specifying the right frame.

9. As you have done before, link the images that you are using as navigation elements to the index.htm files that reside in their respective folders. Remember that for each and every link you create, you must also specify the correct target.

10. The third type of target that you will need to use is located within the frame where the new page is to load. In this case, the correct target is _self, specifying that the new file will open in the same window where the link currently sits. Find the text greetings message at the bottom of the right frame and set the target to _self. This text should be linked to the greetings .htm document that you worked on earlier.

11. Select File | Save All Frames to complete this exercise.

If you were to proceed with the development of the site in Project 8-3, you would have one very important design consideration to keep in mind: the document that loads in the right frame must be designed to fit into that area (which in this case is an area no wider than 470 pixels), to fit neatly into the 600-pixel maximum width of monitors set to the lowest display settings.

You can also appreciate now why bookmarks and search engines are problematic for pages designed with frames. After all, the entire web site that you just developed would appear to have only one single page—the frameset document that is displayed in the browser window and the supporting files that are linked within it. For example, if you wanted to allow the viewers of this site to bookmark the Local Events page so that they could come back for frequent updates, that page would need to be developed outside the frame structure of the frameset.

Dreamweaver has additional tools available for designers who choose frames as their navigation scheme for their site. For instance, for viewers using very old versions of browsers, you can insert special coding that displays a message to these viewers that states the page contains frames and that they can click an alternate link to see a page (which you would have to create) designed without frames.

Using frames for site development can give designers a quick and easy way to develop and implement their site design based on frames that define the function of the separate parts of the browser window. However, frames have their pitfalls, and any decision about their use must be made with those drawbacks in mind. Using frames also requires a good working knowledge of the rather strict rules for file naming and saving, as well as for targeting links properly. If you have been able to complete the exercises in this section, then you are well on your way to being able to design with frames.

8

1-Minute Drill

● How many documents would be open if you were working on a page with three separate frames?

● Why do links require targets when using frames?

● How does the use of frames affect bookmarks and search engines?

Modifying Pages with Cascading Style Sheets

To many web designers, cascading style sheets (CSS) are considered a true godsend because of the ease and flexibility they provide in formatting their work. The ability to quickly define a series of instructions for formatting text, for instance, and then applying it to every page on a web site gives designers a terrifically flexible tool for making broad changes to the look and feel of their creations. And, since CSS has been designated as the tool of choice for formatting pages in the future—replacing some HTML tags that are in current use—learning how to define and apply these specialized lists of rules for content presentation will be a must for anyone working on web pages in years to come.

The impetus for changing the formatting structure of web pages comes from the organization that oversees Web standards—the World Wide Web Consortium (W3C). You may remember from a previous module that the HTML coding language was never intended to be a vehicle for controlling page appearance—and now that you've seen some of the manipulation that is required to get it to function that way, you have a better understanding of how hard it can be to get your page to display the way you intend. The W3C has developed a series of standards built around CSS to replace the formatting gyrations that web designers have to go through now to get their pages to look the way they want. In the future, many HTML attributes that you have used will fade away, to be replaced by CSS and the greater control it affords.

● Four—the frameset and the three supporting files that load into it.

● Targets tell the browser where to load the link—by name or by a location relative to the position of the linked object.

● Since the frameset is the file that is named, and other pages within the site are loaded into it, only the main page appears in bookmark files and when indexed by search engines.

Ask the Expert

Question: Where can I find more information about browser support for Cascading Style Sheets?

Answer: One of the best references for the challenges presented by browser support for CSS can be found online at www.webreview.com. Visit the section on style sheets and look for the Master Compatibility Chart for a handy reference on the latest news from the CSS vs. browser battleground.

At the present time, though, support for CSS by browsers is spotty, and, as always, the fiercely competitive companies that produce browsers keep putting their own twists on CSS in an effort to gain an edge over the competition. As of this writing, Internet Explorer 5.5 does a fairly good job of supporting CSS, while the latest version of Netscape, Netscape 6, is also said to have excellent support of CSS styles. However, since many people will not upgrade their browsers in the near future, the CSS styles covered in this section are only those that are widely supported by current browsers—versions 4.0 and higher of both. Better support of CSS and the ease it will give web designers in formatting their pages is still off in the distance somewhere.

Note

The term *cascading* in cascading style sheets refers to the way that different styles are applied based on their position in a hierarchy established by the W3C. It is possible, for instance, to have conflicting styles assigned to the same page simultaneously —with page-specific properties and site-wide styles applied at the same time. By anticipating this problem, and establishing the rules that specify which style is applied and in which order, the W3C made the use of style sheets much less troublesome.

Project 8-4: Defining Styles for HTML Tags

The simplest form of CSS is known as an *internal style,* because it applies only to the formatting of one page at a time. It is internal to that page, unlike some of the styles that can be specified that will affect an entire web site. In the first example, you will see how an internal style sheet is applied to change the standard formatting available in basic HTML.

Step-by-Step

1. From the Exercises folder for this module, locate the council_tags.htm file in the css_pages subfolder. Open the document, choose File I Save As, and place the file in your root folder for the Poinciana Beach web site.

2. Take a look at the formatting properties for the text in this page by selecting them and then checking the information in the Properties Inspector. The heading for the page is formatted with the <h2> tag (Heading 2), the subheadings have an <h3> tag applied (Heading 3), and the names of the city council members are formatted as <h4> (Heading 4). Your goal is to redefine those tags in this document—in effect redefining the tags themselves.

3. Open the CSS Styles panel by selecting Window I CSS Styles. Currently, no styles are defined for the site, so the frame panel displays None in the styles list. Since the formatting you are going to apply will affect only the tags you specify, this setting will remain the same throughout this exercise.

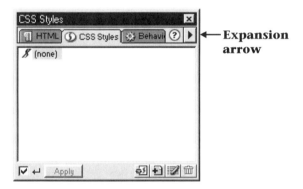

4. Click the expansion arrow in the upper-right corner to access options for this panel. You are going to make a new set of rules for this page, so choose New Style from the pop-up menu.

Note

The lower-left corner of the CSS Styles panel has three buttons that let you create a new style, edit an existing style, and link an existing style to a document. You may find these buttons easier to use than the expansion arrow method.

5. Click the drop-down list box to see the number of HTML tags that are available to redefine with CSS. If you're feeling ambitious, then check my counting—I found 40 separate tags that can be defined in new ways. The ones you are after are the <h2>, <h3>, and <h4> tags, and you want to apply this new definition to this page only. Be sure that the New Style dialog box appears as you see here for the <h3> tag, and then click OK.

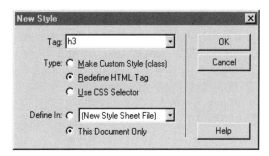

6. Now for the fun stuff. CSS gives you control over the appearance of a wide variety of tags in your document. You only want to change the appearance of the text here, but feel free to have a look at the other categories. Remember that even though Dreamweaver supports the W3C specifications on CSS styles, most browsers will not display many of the options that you can apply here. Still, it is a peek into the future when you see that pages someday will be as easy to format as is formatting a document in a word processor. When you are finished experimenting, your final settings should appear as shown in Figure 8-4.

8

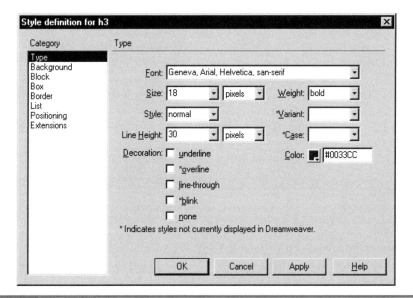

Figure 8-4   Styles can be specified for a range of HTML tags

7. The different settings for various styles are fairly self-explanatory. Fonts can be specified, text can be made bold, and the color can be changed. One very useful setting that gives terrific control over the appearance of text is the Line Height setting. Try changing this selection for the different tags in the document and notice the results. Remember that HTML is very limited in how you can set line spacing—either text is together on one line or a blank line separates it, and that's about it. Setting the Line Height value gives you the opportunity to nudge your text apart and give it a more uniform appearance. Feel free to experiment, but when you are done refer to Figure 8-4 for the correct settings needed for this project.

8. Not happy with the results of your style? Click the expansion arrow on the CSS Styles panel and choose Edit Style Sheet.

9. Find the tag you formatted, <h3>, select it (or one of the other available tags), and then choose Edit. You will go back to the same dialog box you used previously, in which you can change this style to suit your needs, or just experiment with the results of various settings. (You can see my final interpretation by opening council_tags2.htm from the Exercises folder.)

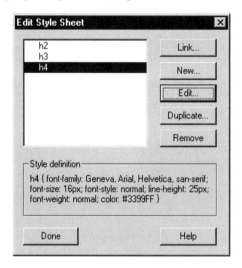

10. You have now defined your first set of styles. Even though this set applies only to this page, you still have a good feel for how powerful CSS can be in page design. To see the coding that Dreamweaver just generated, press the F10 key to view the underlying code, where you will find all the style instructions contained within the <head> tag for this page, as shown in Figure 8-5.

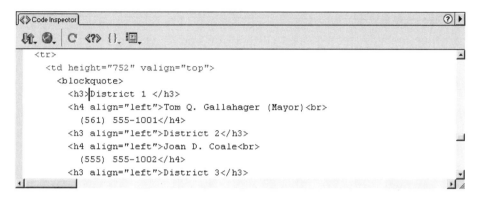

Figure 8-5   Dreamweaver automatically generates the necessary code and places it in the <head> tag of the document

Tip

To make this page viewable in an older browser that does not support CSS, you can let Dreamweaver reformat the basic HTML tags automatically to apply many of the changes you just made. Choose File | Convert | 3.0 Browser Compatible. In the Convert to 3.0 Browser Compatible dialog box that appears, choose CSS Styles to HTML Markup and then click OK. Dreamweaver does the rest!

11. You will be revisiting this page a little later, so save your document with the formatting you chose, and move on to the next category of CSS styles.

Project 8-5: Defining a Custom Class Style

The previous exercise looked at how new formatting rules can be applied to a specific HTML tag (in this case a <heading> tag). In this exercise, you will see how you can apply a style to a range of text, a paragraph, or another element in your page. This type of style formatting is useful if you want to automate the formatting for a particular text entry, without having to redefine the tag to do so. If you want to keep the standard heading tags as they are, for instance, creating a custom class as you will do next would let you have a shortcut for formatting particular items, while still keeping the standard HTML tags available for your use. If that sounds a little confusing, a practical example is provided here.

Step-by-Step

1. Open the file named council_custom.htm from the exercise files for this module. Notice that limited formatting is applied to this page.

2. Custom classes are only applied to items that are selected on the page. Highlight the District 1 text in the document. Alternatively, you could select a tag with the Tag Selector if, for instance, you want to change all text that is formatted with the paragraph (<p>) tag. The key to remember is that custom CSS styles are only applied to objects that are selected.

3. To create a custom class of CSS styles for this document, open the CSS Styles frame and use the expansion arrow to access the options. Choose New Style as you did in the previous exercise.

4. Give the new style a name, as shown here, and select the This Document Only radio button. (Styles that can be applied throughout the site are discussed in a few moments.) Feel free to experiment with the style settings for this document, or set them as you see here.

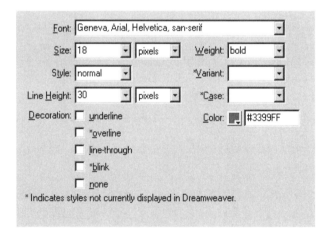

Note

Custom style names always begin with a period and must begin with a letter. If you don't insert the period, Dreamweaver will do it for you automatically.

5. Notice that the name for this style appears now in the CSS Styles panel when you return to this document. To apply the style to other elements on the page, first highlight the text and then simply select the heading style by

clicking it. Any selected text will automatically be reformatted to the settings you have specified for this style. Styles can be removed by selecting the object and then clicking None in the CSS Styles panel.

1-Minute Drill

● What organization establishes and maintains the formatting standards for CSS?

● What is the primary technical difficulty in using CSS styles in web design?

● How can CSS styles be converted by Dreamweaver to function in older browsers?

Project 8-6: Formatting with Selectors—Removing Link Underlines

8

Many web developers, especially those who have a background in graphic design, are troubled by the underlining that HTML automatically applies to links. As a result, many of them use CSS styles to redefine the links on their site to a format that is more aesthetically pleasing. On the other hand, doing so removes an important visual clue to the viewer as to the location of the links on the page. Reformatting links is easy, but it should not be done without thinking about the impact it will have on your audience. Having said that, read on to see how the style is applied. The final decision of whether to use this trick is up to you.

In this exercise, you will be redefining a series of tags based on commands that you will define using a CSS selector. The operations are very similar to changing HTML tags, but by creating a series of instructions that can be applied to any page in the document, you greatly improve your ability to work quickly and efficiently.

● The World Wide Web Consortium (W3C) is the controlling authority for CSS specifications.
● Support for CSS styles is highly inconsistent between different versions of browsers, and even among browsers for different computer platforms.
● Dreamweaver will convert CSS styles to HTML formatting when File I Convert I 3.0 Browser Compatible is selected.

Step-by-Step

1. Open the file called council_selectors.htm from the Exercises folder for this module. Choose File | Save As to place the file in the root folder of the Poinciana Beach web site.

2. Once again, you will define a new style for this document alone. For this exercise, you want to use the Use CSS Selector setting in the New Style dialog box, and then choose from the preformatted selectors that Dreamweaver supplies—those that apply to links.

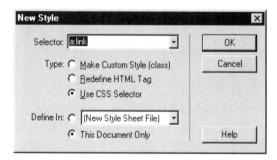

Note

Once you are more familiar with Dreamweaver and CSS, you may want to explore the possibilities for setting styles based on a combination of tags. For instance, if you want every heading that is contained within a table cell to appear a certain way, you could manually enter the tag and attribute combination here and apply a style setting to them that would only apply when that combination appears.

3. To format the links for this page, first set the a:link properties, which change the way that a link appears when the page first loads into the viewer's browser. In a moment, you will change the other styles, as well, to set the appearance of a link when a viewer rolls their mouse over that link (a:hover), when a viewer clicks the link (a:active), and after someone has visited the page associated with the link (a:visited).

4. Set the properties for this new style as you see here. Note the small boxes in the Decoration area. Checking None removes the underline for the links, and this is the only way that you can remove the underline.

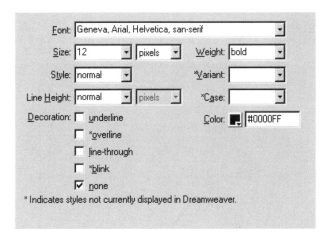

5. Returning to your document, however, you see that those lines are still there. Any guess as to why? Perhaps it's to remind you that links are assigned to the text, or perhaps it's because the designers of the program know that not every browser will display this style properly. Regardless, this no-underline style applies only when the page is previewed in a browser. Try viewing the page in a browser now, and see what kind of results you get. If possible, preview your work in both Internet Explorer and Netscape Navigator to see how the two browsers react differently to this new style.

6. The next style you will apply is the a:hover style, which defines the appearance of the links when the viewer places their mouse pointer over them. You could simply repeat the previous steps, but Dreamweaver gives you a handy shortcut, and you'll use that method instead.

7. From the CSS Styles panel, click the expansion arrow and select Edit Styles. Click the a:link selector that appears in the dialog box and note the Duplicate button that becomes available.

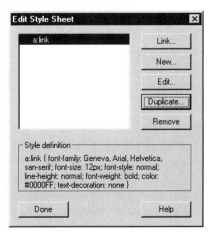

8

8. Click the Duplicate button, and specify in the Duplicate Style dialog box that the a:hover style is where you want the a:link settings to be duplicated.

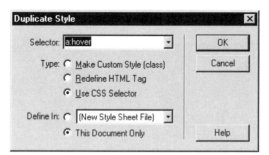

9. This lets you change just one element of the style without having to specify everything else from memory. Highlight a:hover from the listing of available selectors and then click the Edit button. Change the color to a lighter shade of blue than the original setting for a:link, and then click OK. Click Done to exit from the style editor. Preview your masterpiece in your browser to see the effect. Just a word of warning. This style will look great in Internet Explorer, but may not appear at all in Netscape.

10. Continuing with this same method will allow you to change the other two settings for links as well. When you are finished, you should have style settings for all four categories of links (a:active, a:hover, a:link, a:visited). Editing the settings for the links is a simple matter of choosing the link selector in the Edit Style Sheet dialog box and clicking the Edit button to return to the editor. This is another great time to experiment.

Note

Since this document was copied into a different root folder, the links will not operate correctly. If you are feeling ambitious, you can relink the text to a valid file in the site, or you can simply click the Back button on your browser to go back to this page.

11. Be sure to save this file when you are finished, and then move on to your final exercises with CSS styles.

Project 8-7: Creating and Using External CSS Style Sheets

To this point, every style you have created has been an internal style—specific to the document in which it was created. Wouldn't it be great if you could create styles and then make them available to all the pages in your site, or even export the styles you've created into a central location where you could call on them again and again? Luckily, this type of CSS style, called an *external CSS style sheet,* is easily created and is then available through the tools that Dreamweaver provides.

Step-by-Step

1. Before you can specify a style sheet, you need to create a location within your site to store the text file that will be created. Continue to practice good site management by making a new folder in which to store these instructions. As you've done before, right-click the root folder for the site and choose New Folder. Name this new folder **Styles**. The revised site structure appears in Figure 8-6.

2. Open the file that you used in the last exercise, council_selectors.htm, by double-clicking its file icon in the Site window. You will create a new style in this page and then save it to the Styles folder you just created.

3. From the CSS Styles panel, click the expansion arrow and select New Style.

4. Remember that you are not creating a document-specific style at this point, so the settings for your initial New Style dialog box will be a little different from those you saw when working with internal style sheets in Project 8-6. Name this new style sheet **blueheading** and be sure that the Define In box is set to New Style Sheet File.

8

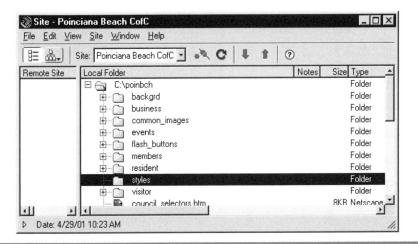

Figure 8-6 The revised site structure adds a Styles folder for maintaining style specifications

5. Rather than going directly to the style editor, you first have to save the file to the Styles folder. Name the file **blueheading** and be sure to place it in the correct subfolder, Styles, as shown in Figure 8-7.

6. Once this new style sheet has been assigned a name, you will be taken to the style editor, where you can set the values as you prefer. Since this style will be applied to text as a heading, set the font size to at least 16, the line height to 30, and make sure the color is specified as a shade of blue. Click OK when you are finished and you will be returned to the document.

7. Your new style has been linked to this document and is now available from the CSS Styles panel. To apply the style, simply select the text that you want to format and then click the name of the style in the CSS Styles panel. Save your work when you are finished.

8. Now that you have this style available, you can attach it to any document in your site. Simply choose Text | CSS Styles and apply the blueheading style to a page where you wish to employ it.

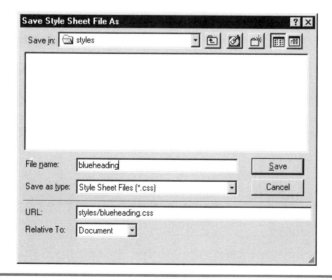

Figure 8-7 Style sheet files should be saved in their own separate subfolders

Linking, Importing, and Additional CSS Features

Cascading style sheets have significant capabilities beyond those demonstrated in the rather simple exercises that you have performed in this section. One of the most important features is the ability to establish a style and then use it throughout your site by way of two options: importing and linking.

Importing a CSS style brings the specifications into the document and then imbeds them into the coding for the particular page. Not a bad idea, except that adding code to the page causes the file size to grow, and the unfortunate result of growing file sizes is slower downloads. Still, if you wish to use only once a particular style that you've created, and the file size is relatively small, then importing the style could be a viable option.

The preferred method for reusing CSS styles is to establish a link to the file where the styles are defined. If you choose this method, it is important that the file be posted to your server so that the document will properly retrieve the information it needs to format the page as you specify. Besides the advantages previously mentioned, if you choose to edit the style that is posted on your site, the changes will automatically take effect when the page is loaded. Importing the styles directly into a document will not have this feature, and each and every file will need its individual styles edited in order for changes to take effect.

To either import or link to a CSS style sheet, select Edit from the CSS Styles panel (either by clicking the Edit button or by using the expansion arrow). When the Edit Style Sheet dialog box appears, click the Link button, which will take you to the Link External Style Sheet dialog box. In this dialog box, select either the Link or Import radio button. Browse to the location of your style's file (aren't you glad it's in a separate folder?), choose the style by name, and then click OK. Your style is now either available in the current document (Import) or throughout your entire site (Link).

8

This section has barely scratched the surface of all the things that CSS styles can do for you. In addition to formatting the appearance of text, CSS can be used to position text (left, center, or right), to tile images in the background of the document in new ways, to place a variety of borders around different objects, and to do many of the things that you would expect to be able to do in a word processor or desktop publishing program. The rub, of course, is that not all of these things will actually display in your browser, even if you have the latest and greatest program available. In time, however, the Web and the documents that populate it will transform from their heavy dependence on HTML tricks and formatting work-arounds to a place where page design will be accomplished by CSS, with HTML operating in the background to provide the structure for data delivery.

1-Minute Drill

● Redefining HTML tags and using CSS selectors are both examples of what type of CSS style?

● What is the primary advantage of using the linking method to access CSS styles site-wide?

● How can CSS styles be used to align text?

Project 8-8: Choosing an Advanced Layout Scheme

Recall from Module 2 that the site design process is one in which many of the informed decisions about the ultimate style and layout of a site are determined. From defining the potential audience, to determining the type of navigation scheme, to ultimately choosing a page and site style, the process of site design is one that is paramount in developing a good Web experience for the audience. Since that time, you have learned how to insert text and images, how to apply page layouts, and, in this module, how to make more sophisticated designs with frames and CSS. While you certainly should spend some time practicing the application of the skills covered in this module, this is also a good time to revisit the questions asked in Module 2 to see if your answers would be different based on the experience you have gained up to this point. In particular, answer the following questions and compare them to the answers you developed in the project at the end of Module 2:

● *Who is your audience?*
  What would cause them to want to find and visit your web site?
  What kinds of content will you provide that will bring them back or bring in new viewers?

● Redefining HTML tags and using selectors are both internal CSS styles.
● The linking method enables you to modify a style sheet and then have the changes applied automatically when the page is loaded by the viewer.
● Text can be aligned left, right, and center using CSS styles.

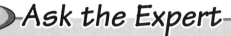

Ask the Expert

Question: If cascading style sheets are so hard to use, why should I even bother?

Answer: Much like making a soufflé, the first time you sit down to work through the process of defining CSS styles, things may fall flat. Your results may look drastically different in different browsers, you may get lost in the midst of defining a style and have to throw the whole thing away, and you may ultimately find yourself very frustrated by the process. Because of the terrific control that cascading style sheets give you over the look of your pages, and because they will ultimately replace formatting tricks such as using tables for page alignment, CSS styles are an important part of learning the art of web design. My suspicion is that further versions of Dreamweaver will make defining and using CSS styles easier and more intuitive.

   Stick with it, and ultimately you will be rewarded by pages that not only look better, but also are easier to build because of the work you have put into defining styles for your site. And sometime in the future, you will be able to tell your grandchildren that you were one of the first people to use the formatting language that they take for granted when they use the Internet. Perhaps you can even share stories of the days when web pages had to be created in this dinosaur of a programming language called HTML—and that you had to walk 12 miles through the snow to get to your computer!

8

- *What is the age, gender, and location of your audience?*
  Are you designing for a general audience or do you have a tightly focused group in terms of age and gender?
  If your audience is generally the same, how can you target content that it will find appealing?

- *How experienced is your audience at using the Internet?*
  Should your content be simple and straightforward, or can you experiment with newer technologies?
  Should your site navigation be kept simple or are your viewers experienced enough to search for information within your site?

- *What kind of computer(s) are your site's viewers likely to have?*
  Will they have the latest browsers and all the plug-ins they need to view your content?

Will they use other means of accessing your site (WebTV, AOL browser, text-only browsers)?
Will they be viewing from only one platform (Windows, Macintosh, Linux) or will there be variation?

Having to answer these questions early in the design process—before you had much information on the different options available for page design and layout—may have seemed like a difficult exercise. However, even if your initial answers were sketchy, with what you know now, you can make more informed decisions about how the look and function of your site and its pages can affect the audience's experience.

What to Take Away

Both frames and CSS present challenges to the new web designer because they are not as easy to employ as the types of work you have performed previously. Both have their place in gaining an understanding of the capabilities of Dreamweaver, and using them is a decision that you need to make after you have had time to get comfortable with their creation and the rather strict rules that must be followed to take advantage of these two advanced page design features.

This module has served as an overview to two complicated topics and is intended to give you a good feel for how page design can be altered by the use of frames and CSS. In the next module, you will discover how to make the work of designing your pages a little easier by using tools that let you duplicate work that you have already done. Templates, libraries, and the new Assets panel all provide you with ways to automate many design tasks, and give you even more flexibility in the ultimate look and style of your sites.

✓ *Mastery Check*

1. How does the use of frames reduce the workload on web site designers?

2. What factors led to frames falling out of favor with Internet users?

3. How many documents are open when you work on a page with two separate frames?

4. What command should always be used when saving frames?

5. Why were the formatting standards of CSS developed?

6. Why has the use of CSS styles failed to gain wide acceptance by web designers up to this point?

8

Module 9

Automating Your Work: Tools for Consistent Content

The Goals of this Module

- Explore Dreamweaver's tools for automatic formatting of content
- Understand the features of the Assets panel
- Designate and use library items
- Design and employ page templates
- Understand the use of Behaviors
- Use Behaviors for automated tasks
- Understand extensions and the Extension Manager

As you move beyond the basics of simple page design and your site becomes dependent on more complicated objects, more challenging issues arise for the designer, and having the ability to capture and re-create the work that you have done becomes more and more essential. After all, if you've struggled and worked to get a page design just right, so that the page follows good design principles and has an attractive, easy-to-follow user interface, and you have (finally!) worked out all the kinks so that the page displays properly in different browsers, it certainly would be frustrating if you then had to do it all over again for the *second* page of your site.

Dreamweaver has a number of tools available for the automatic insertion and control of the text and objects in your site, and in version 4, these tools have been made easier to access through the inclusion of a new tool: the Assets panel. In this module, you'll look not only at the Assets panel but also at other ways that designers can use the tools included in the software to speed the work on their site, and to apply a level of consistency to their content that improves the viewer's experience.

This module also introduces a new concept, *behaviors,* a combination of a viewer action followed by an event generated through the use of prebuilt JavaScript code that is part of the Dreamweaver program. Although any number of actions can be generated by the robust capabilities of behaviors, to stay with the theme of this module, only those behaviors that assist the designer in presenting a more consistent experience for the user are discussed here.

Exploring the Assets Panel

Prior to version 4 of Dreamweaver, the tools for automating content were contained in separate panels, which made their use a little more complicated because different panels had to be opened based on the tasks the designer wished to perform. In the new layout, all the commonly used tools are conveniently located in one panel, making them easier to access and use.

In addition to this organizational change to the interface, Dreamweaver now automatically searches for the different assets available for the site, and keeps a running list available for you as you work. This section looks at this great new feature in action by surveying the assets for the Poinciana Beach Chamber of Commerce web site.

Note

Be sure that you have copied the files from www.osborne.com for this module into the Exercises folder you created earlier.

The Assets panel is a site-wide tool. It surveys all the resources available throughout the site, and is not dependent on the page in which it is currently being viewed. Open the page titled index_assets.htm from the Exercises folder for this module and then choose File | Save As and save it into the root folder for the Poinciana Beach web site. This is an important step, since having the page located in the site where your assets are found ensures that you will be able to take advantage of all the tools at your disposal. If you try to work on this file directly from your Exercises folder, then only the assets that are located in that location will be surveyed.

To view the Assets panel, choose Window | Assets. The first time you open the Assets panel, Dreamweaver will let you know that it is loading a listing of site assets. This process will take a minute or so, after which you will see the panel as pictured in Figure 9-1.

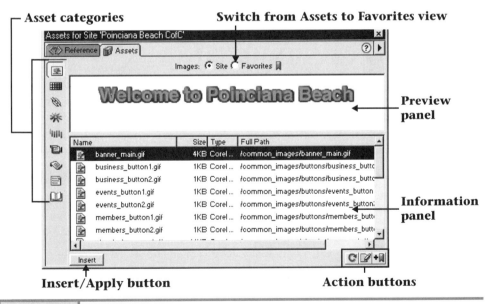

Figure 9-1   Assets panel for the Poinciana Beach Chamber of Commerce web site

9

Note

Since I have my system set to use Corel Photo House to view GIF and JPEG images, those file types are listed as Corel images here. Your file types may display differently based on your system settings.

Arrayed down the left side of the panel is a series of buttons that, when clicked, display the various asset categories for the site. By default, Dreamweaver always displays the Images category first. The icons for the various categories should look familiar, since they are similar to those found in the Objects panel and throughout the Dreamweaver interface, but for clarity, their functions are summarized in Table 9-1.

Name	Appearance	Function
Images		Lists images in GIF, JPEG, or PNG formats by name, size, and path
Colors		Lists all colors used in the site with color swatches and hexadecimal values
URLs		Lists both internal and external links applied in the site
Flash		Lists all Flash (SWF) movie files
Shockwave		Lists files created in Macromedia Shockwave format
Movies		Lists movies in QuickTime or MPEG format
Scripts		Lists JavaScript and VBScript files that are independent of HTML documents
Templates		Lists the templates created and stored in the site
Library items		Lists library items created and stored in the site

Table 9-1 Categories of the Dreamweaver 4 Assets Panel

Along the bottom of the Assets panel is another series of buttons that perform certain actions based on the category of objects selected. For instance, when the Images category is selected, images can be inserted using the Insert button. The same button becomes the Apply button when either the Colors or the URLs category is selected. You'll see some of these buttons in action here, and others are described later in the book when discussing the way that Fireworks and Dreamweaver work hand-in-hand.

Project 9-1: Inserting Objects from the Assets Panel

The Assets panel has a number of great features that allow you to speed up common tasks for controlling page appearance and function. In this exercise, you'll look at how to use the Assets panel to insert images and assign colors to a simple web page.

Step-by-Step

1. Open index_assets.htm and make sure that the copy you are working with is the one that you saved earlier into the Poinciana Beach web site. As always, the best way to open a file is from the Site window for the site you are working on.

2. Your first task is to insert the banner at the top of the page. With the Images category for assets selected, a thumbnail for this asset will be shown in the preview panel, and the name will appear in the information panel. Since images are shown in alphabetical order, the filename for this file, banner_main.gif, should be at the top of the list, as shown in Figure 9-2.

Tip

Files can be reordered by clicking the Name button just above the filenames in the information panel.

3. If you're a click-and-drag kind of person, you'll appreciate the way that Dreamweaver lets you select an image either by its filename or by its thumbnail image and then drag the image directly to the insertion point in the document. To try this method, move your insertion point to the right of the anchor symbol at the top of the document and simply drag either the thumbnail or the filename directly from the Assets panel onto the page.

9

Figure 9-2   Image assets for the Poinciana Beach web site

4. To apply a color asset, select a line of text in the document and then open the Colors category in the Assets panel. Once again, a color can be applied by dragging the little color swatch directly from the Assets panel onto the selected text. Select the four lines of text that are grouped at the top of the page and apply the blue color (#0000ff) that is found in the Assets panel.

5. If you prefer to work using an insert-and-apply method, the button in the lower-left corner of the Assets panel is for you. To try this method, place your insertion point in the extreme upper-left corner of the page and locate the file named pbcofc_logo_small.gif in the Images category. Click the Insert button and this image will be placed on your page.

6. The Insert button becomes the Apply button when the asset selected is one that is appropriate for that action—such as assets in the Colors and URLs categories. Try this now by selecting the text at the very bottom of the page that urges your viewer to download the Flash player. In the URLs assets for the site, locate the URL for Macromedia's download site. Highlight the text and then click the Apply button to create the link on this line of text.

7. Notice that you did not insert the URL. If that option had been chosen, the entire text of the URL would have been inserted. While the link would have functioned, your viewers would have had little clue as to what they were linking to.

8. Since you will not use this page again, feel free to experiment with the other site assets on this page. Try the different methods for inserting and applying assets. Can you see how having access to all of your site's assets in one convenient location could greatly improve your workflow—and add a consistent look to all your pages?

Note

For those of you who like the right-click method, you can also select Apply or Insert from the context menu that appears when you right-click the asset name.

Most of the tools available in the Assets panel are very easy to use; simply select the asset and then apply it to a selected item or insert the object. The two major exceptions are the library and template items. While not difficult to use, these two functions do require some advanced planning and a little more work to get them ready for use. The next section explains how this is accomplished.

1-Minute Drill

● What is the function of the Assets panel?

● Why should you pay close attention to the location of your site when accessing the Assets panel?

● What three methods are available for inserting or applying an asset?

Automated Formatting with Libraries and Templates

As Dreamweaver has grown from its initial versions, the developers at Macromedia have continued to refine and improve the appearance and function of the interface. That certainly is true of Dreamweaver 4; not only have additional capabilities been added, but the tools themselves have been refined and reorganized to make them easier to use. Two of the most important changes have been the

---

● The Assets panel tracks and lists all the assets available in a web site in predefined categories such as Colors, Images, Templates, and Library.

● The Assets panel lists assets according to the site in which the file is located, not for the page itself.

● Assets can be dragged from the Assets panel onto the page, can be inserted or applied using the Insert/Apply button, or can be placed in the page by right-clicking the object in the Assets panel.

addition of the Assets panel, and the way the templates and libraries have been modified to make them easier to design, employ, and update.

Project 9-2: Creating and Modifying Library Items

Library items are single elements that are inserted into a web page from a central storage location—a special folder within the site that Dreamweaver creates—and that can then be accessed and changed when needed. This enables you to update the element automatically throughout the site by simply changing the library item itself, and then letting Dreamweaver do the work of finding every instance of the library item and making the changes as necessary. If you had to do the same job manually, it would mean opening each individual page, making the changes, and then saving the document—an exceptionally tedious task in even a moderate-sized web site.

To see a library item in action, jump right into the next exercise, in which you apply a site-wide element composed of text-based links that will rest at the bottom of every page within the site. This gives you an alternative method of site navigation for those people who may turn off their browser's image-viewing capabilities.

Step-by-Step

1. From the Exercises folder for this module, locate and open the file called index_library.htm. You'll note that this page uses rollover images for site navigation at the top of the page, which necessitates an alternative site-navigation scheme.

2. At the bottom of the page is a series of text-based links that you want to make into new library items. Click and drag completely across all the links to select them.

For Visitors | For Residents | For Businesses | For Members | Local Events

Note

Only objects that are contained within the <body> tags of the document can be selected and made into library items. This means that internal CSS styles, some JavaScript code, and other items contained in the <head> of the page cannot be placed in the library.

3. As usual, there are several ways to convert these links into library elements. The easiest, since you have the Assets panel open already, is to click the button (shown here) in the lower-right corner that creates a new library item. If you don't see this option, be sure that the Library category is selected by clicking the library icon in the categories listing on the left.

4. Once you have selected the option to make a selected object a library item, you will be returned to the Assets panel, where you will find that Dreamweaver has automatically generated a file for this item. To replace the default Untitled name that is applied, simply type over the name. Type **textlinks** and be sure this item is set as you see in Figure 9-3. Notice also that a preview of the completed library item is displayed in the upper portion of the Assets panel.

Tip

If things don't work out as planned, a library item can be deleted from the site assets by clicking the trashcan icon in the lower-right corner of the Assets panel.

5. Dreamweaver performed several tasks when that new item was created for your use. In addition to formatting the file, it also automatically created a new folder in the root folder of your web site called, simply, Library. Check the Site window to see this new folder for the site.

9

6. To use your new item, you can insert the object into a page by using the same methods as discussed before—drag it from the Assets panel, use the Insert button, or right-click and choose Insert.

7. The beauty of working with Library items is the ease with which a page can be updated. To do this, you will open the library item, modify it, and then let Dreamweaver update your pages automatically. Be sure that the textlinks library item is selected in the Assets panel, and then click the Edit button in the bottom-right corner.

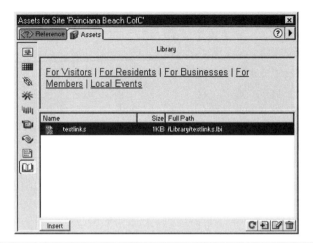

Figure 9-3 The Assets panel as it appears for the textlinks library item

8. Dreamweaver opens a new Document window and displays the object that is contained in the Library. As a visual cue that this page is different from a regular Document window, the background appears in gray, as shown in Figure 9-4. At the beginning of the line of text, add the word **Home** and link it to the index.htm file for the site.

9. When you are done with your addition, choose File I Save. Since the whole point of using library items is their ability to automatically apply changes as

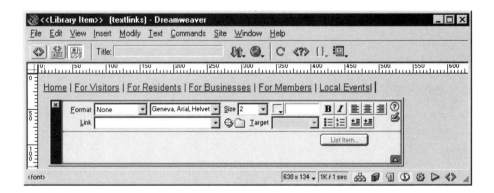

Figure 9-4 The Edit Library Item Document window

they are made, Dreamweaver asks if you wish to update the pages in the site that use this item. Click Update, and the work of revising the textlinks item will be done without opening another file.

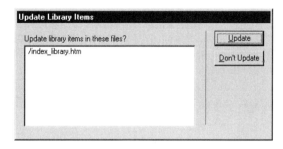

10. You may run into an instance where one library item is something you've created that you have applied to a number of sites, such as the logo for your web design company, and you need those sites to be changed as well. Or, if you've recently added some new pages, you may not have updated the internal log that contains information about which pages use your library items. In any case, either choose to update all the files that use the textlinks item in the current site, or choose a new site from the drop-down list box to update a different site. Click Start to have a site updated, as shown in Figure 9-5, or limit Dreamweaver's search to the current site. Once this operation is complete, your pages will be automatically updated to reflect the modifications you've made to your library element.

9

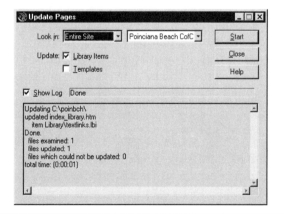

| **Figure 9-5** | Dreamweaver's Update Pages dialog box |

11. Experiment on this page with other objects that can be turned into library items. When you are finished, close this page. You will not be using it for any further exercises.

The major advantage to using library items is their ability to be modified and then have those changes ripple throughout the entire site as Dreamweaver automatically applies them. This can be a great timesaver for those objects that you may need to modify from time to time.

Working with Templates

You have seen how library items can be used to insert individual items into a web page, but what about those times when you need to do more—to design a complete set of repeatable designs that can be duplicated throughout the site, and that can drastically reduce the amount of work necessary for creating content? If you read the heading for this section, then you probably know already that what you need here are templates.

The ability to design a template and then use it over and over again has some obvious advantages, not least of which is the consistency that it gives you throughout the site. In addition, if you are working on a collaborative project, using templates lets one person or team design the final layout of the page, which then can be made accessible to others who are responsible for adding content.

Template pages are essentially web pages in which certain portions of the page have been designated as nonchangeable, while other portions are blank—waiting for the addition of content to complete the page design. These blank areas are usually laid out in advance in terms of their size and position on the page, but otherwise they are considered to be editable by the designer. Just as with library items, Dreamweaver automatically generates a new folder in the site where templates are stored so that they can be accessed and modified as necessary.

Project 9-3: Creating a New Template

Once again, the process for creating templates is not a difficult one. With a little practice and some time developing your own, you should have no trouble getting your first templates ready for use. The key thing to remember, as with any web page, is to test your templates thoroughly before you decide to make site-wide changes based on their design. First take a look at how templates are created.

Step-by-Step

1. Templates can be created in one of two ways: by starting with a completely blank page and then designing the template from scratch, or by converting an existing page into a template. To make a new template, you simply set the asset category to Templates on the Assets panel and click the New Template button.

Note

Templates and frames are generally incompatible. While you can make a portion of a frame-based page into a template, the world of frames and templates are usually kept far apart. Both are methods for creating consistency in page layout and design, but because of the different ways that they approach the same task, the two are not commonly mixed.

2. In the interest of time, a page has been generated that you will modify into a template for your site. This is a real-world example, though, because in practice you would probably build a standard HTML page and test it for both function and design considerations before you decided to turn it into a template. The page is called index_template.htm and is located in the Exercises folder for this module. Open the file and then choose File | Save As to place it into the root folder for the Poinciana Beach web site.

3. Note that this page doesn't contain much information—just a navigation bar across the top, a little logo in the corner, and some table cells that are currently blank. Those blank cells are the key to this template, though, because they are the regions you want to be able to change while keeping everything else on the page fixed.

4. Now that this page is open, your first task is to convert it into a template. Simply select File | Save As Template.

Tip

A page that is being converted into a template is only saved in this manner the first time it is changed from a standard page to a template. Use File | Save to save subsequent changes to the template as they are made.

9

5. The Save As Template dialog box provides some basic information about the site, and lets you assign a name to the template for site management purposes. After all, your template wouldn't be of much use to you if you couldn't get back to it later. Name this template **basic** by typing the new name in the Save As box, as shown in Figure 9-6. Click Save to rename and save your new template.

6. Several operations take place under the hood of Dreamweaver when the Save button is clicked. Just as with library items, a new folder is automatically generated in the root folder of your site, called Templates. In addition, you are returned to your original page, where the heading in the title bar of the document has automatically changed to let you know that the page you are working on is a template. The file extension for this new file, now called basic, is .dwt, for Dreamweaver template.

7. When a template is first created, only one small element of the page is unlocked and available for changes—the page title. Your task, then, is to define the editable areas of the page where you will be allowed to insert the content you desire. If this seems a little restrictive, remember the whole idea is to lock some areas of the page so that they remain the same while allowing some areas to be changed as needed—for the single or potentially thousands of pages that will be built around this template.

8. To add one of these magical blank areas to this template, place your cursor in the empty cell directly below the text "Please visit our Sponsors" and choose Modify | Templates | New Editable Region. In the dialog box that appears, Dreamweaver will prompt you to provide a name for the region, which should be something easily identifiable not only by you, but also by

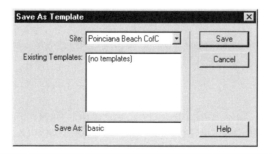

Figure 9-6   The Save As Template dialog box

others who may be working with you on your site. For your first area, enter
sponsor_links in the Name text box.

9. Click OK and you are returned to the Document window for the template,
where you find a nice visual cue that the cell where your insertion point was
located has been converted from a locked area to an editable region,
indicated by the name of the region in a tab and some lovely blue
highlighting around the cell itself.

10. Inserting content in this area now is as easy as anything else you've done to
this point—since it is editable, you have complete control over this section of
the page, with some limitations. For instance, you cannot change the overall
size of the table cell since it is contained within a table that is locked.

11. To complete the definition of the editable areas of this template, create
two new regions as you did previously. Convert the cell directly below the
navigation bar to a region called **header**, and the large area of the page to a
region called **body**. Be sure to save your template when you are finished by
selecting File I Save. Your completed template should appear as shown in
Figure 9-7 when you are finished.

   Creating a template is just the first step in the process of automating the
work for your site. In the next exercise, you will see how to employ that
template in a way that lets you quickly build an entire set of pages based on
this simple design.

Project 9-4: Designing with Templates

Now that your template is ready for use, the process of adding content to your
site becomes much easier. Instead of building each page from scratch, you can
now concentrate on the content you want to add to those pages, and use the
layout of the template as a tool for constraining your page into a format that
will be consistent throughout all of your pages. While the example used here
isn't exactly the snazziest page design you're likely to see, it serves the basic
function that you require by holding those elements that you want to include
throughout your site.

9

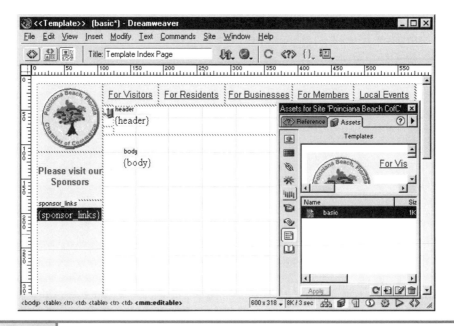

Figure 9-7 The completed basic template for the Poinciana Beach web site

Note

You'll be returning to this basic template later as you begin building new content and graphics for the page with Fireworks.

Step-by-Step

1. There are several ways to begin a new document with a template applied to it. You can start a new blank document and drag the template preview or the template name from the Assets panel directly onto the page, for instance. The recommended method, though, is to choose File | New From Template. Do this now and select your only existing template, basic, by selecting the template name and clicking Select. Notice the box that sets an option to automatically update this page if the template is changed.

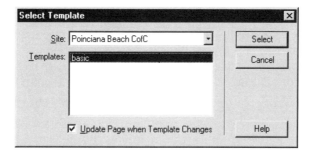

2. The process of adding content to this page is very simple. Click inside the name of the editable region that is contained by the curly brackets and go to work! This area is set as a placeholder for the cell that is editable. Once you begin adding content, you should be sure to remove the curly brackets and the text they contain or it will appear on your page.

3. From the Exercises folder for this module, locate the simple text file called sponsors_text.txt. Open this file using a simple text editor on your computer (such as WordPad or SimpleText) and copy and paste the text into the sponsor_links editable area for this first page. As noted back in Module 5, copying text removes all formatting that was previously applied. To get this area into shape, you could format the fonts based on your site design with HTML or CSS formatting, and create links to the fictional businesses that are listed here. Since this area is editable, you have complete control over the appearance of the content.

4. You may have noticed as you moved your cursor around the Document window that the small universal "no" symbol (⊘) appears in certain areas. Dreamweaver uses this symbol as a reminder that the area is not available for editing.

9

5. You now have all the tools you need to finish an important task—completing the index pages for the subfolders you created throughout the site. To do this, create new pages from the basic template, and then add content as you see fit. If you wish to add text, you can type it in the body section of the template yourself, or you can choose the generic_text.txt file from the Exercises folder for this module and use the copy and paste function to put the exciting prose that you'll find there into your documents.

6. When you are done with each document, choose File | Save As, navigate to the subfolder for each document, and save the file there. When Dreamweaver asks if you want to replace the existing documents, choose Yes.

Updating pages that are created from a template couldn't be an easier task. Suppose that, due to growth on your site, you need to add additional links to the navigation bar on all of your pages. Without templates, you would have to open and modify each individual page. However, since the core of the pages is built with a template, you could simply open the template from the Templates folder on your site, make your changes, and then choose Modify | Templates | Update Pages, and all the pages that are linked to the template would be modified automatically.

Templates are important tools for any site designer to be familiar with because of the consistency they lend to the overall site design, and because of their ease of use and their inherent ability to make automatic modifications site-wide.

In addition to the three primary tools for creating consistent content covered in this section—the Assets panel, library items, and templates—Dreamweaver also includes a History panel, which lets you track and duplicate changes that you make to individual documents, and a sophisticated Find and Replace feature, which automatically looks for particular text or objects and then makes changes that you specify. Although those features aren't covered here, you are encouraged to delve into the Dreamweaver Help files for descriptions of how they work. Both are highly intuitive and provide you with additional tools that make working with your documents easier and move you that much closer to providing the types of well-designed web sites that are the hallmark of professional design.

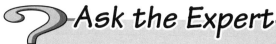

Ask the Expert

Question: How do I use the Favorites feature of the Assets panel?

Answer: The Favorites feature lets you place a copy of any asset on the site into a special folder that you can then further organize by adding subfolders. The advantage here is with a site that contains hundreds or even thousands of assets. By keeping the assets that are most commonly used in their own special holding area, you won't have to search through long listings of images, for instance, to find the one that you need. To designate any item as a Favorite, simply right-click its description (or use the expansion arrow) and select Add To Favorites. Dreamweaver will place a copy of the asset in the same category in the Favorites panel in which the asset was created. A great feature for large web sites.

1-Minute Drill

- How is a library item used?
- What is the function of a template?
- How are pages that use templates updated?

Controlling Content Presentation with Behaviors

9

Now that you know how to create web pages that contain consistent design features, you are still faced with the fundamental problem that all web designers must overcome—what to do about browser compatibility. As discussed for both Flash buttons and cascading style sheets, if you build an entire site around

---

- Library items are singular elements of a web page that are useful as a way to provide automatic updates of common objects that need to be revised periodically.
- Templates are used to lay out a basic web page design, maintaining certain areas as unchangeable, while allowing additions and revisions to other areas.
- Templates may be updated by editing the template and saving the document, and then allowing Dreamweaver to automatically update all pages that use the template. Alternately, choose Modify | Templates | Update Pages.

those objects, a person with an older browser or without the proper plug-in may never see them. Your choice in using those features, and others, may be limited by what type of browser Aunt Tillie in Tupelo has installed on her browser. Luckily, Dreamweaver includes tools for those situations in a new panel, called Behaviors.

Behaviors is the term that Dreamweaver uses to describe a set of interactions between the viewer and the web page. First, the viewer does something, called an *event,* which may be as simple as loading the page or as complicated as dragging a special layer of the web page across their screen. In any case, once this event takes place, pages built with Dreamweaver have the capability to trigger an action based on the event. This combination of event followed by action is created through the magic of JavaScript, and dramatically extends the capabilities of a simple page built in HTML in such profound ways that an entirely new term is applied to it: *Dynamic Hypertext Markup Language (DHTML).*

Note

Technically, a page is said to be written in DHTML only if it contains the regular vanilla HTML combined with both behaviors created by JavaScript and elements designed with CSS.

Behaviors are an extremely powerful set of tools that can dramatically change a web page from a simple document into an interactive powerhouse that interacts with viewers in ways that no other medium of communication can. Consider, for instance, that behaviors can change the appearance of an image as the user passes their mouse over it (as you saw when you worked with rollover buttons), but can also be set to load a predetermined series of images and run an interactive slide show instead. In addition to affecting images, Dreamweaver comes with built-in behaviors to play sounds, change to a new URL, open a new browser window, display a pop-up message, and even have different portions of the page load at different times, among many others. Behaviors are one of the most complicated design elements available, and fully understanding the different ways that they can be utilized in the creation of dynamic web pages goes far beyond the scope of this book.

The main focus of this module has been on creating a consistent experience for your viewers, and thus you will concentrate on the behaviors that support that goal— automatically checking the viewer's browser version for the presence or absence of a plug-in. In the process, you will gain a basic understanding of behaviors and the way that Dreamweaver allows you to define them.

Project 9-5: Using Behaviors to Check Browser Versions

Throughout the course of this book, many instances have been noted in which certain elements of web design are restricted by the browser type and version that a viewer might have installed on their computer. Cascading style sheets, in particular, are problematic because while they present fantastic opportunities for controlling the appearance of a web page, their lack of support in older browsers means that viewers who have not upgraded may have an entirely different experience than what you intended. To alleviate this problem, you will use a Dreamweaver behavior to automatically detect the viewer's browser version, and, if they are using an older browser, redirect them to special pages built without CSS. While this sounds complicated, by combining the easy way that Dreamweaver allows you to define behaviors with a template created for the purpose of building these alternative pages, the process moves along more quickly than you might think.

Step-by-Step

1. You need to copy two templates from the Exercises folder for this module into the Templates folder for the Poinciana Beach web site: basic_with_css.dwt and basic_no_css.dwt.

2. Create a new document from the basic_with_css template by choosing File | New From Template and then clicking it in the Select Template dialog box.

3. Save this new document as **css_test.htm** and place it in the root folder of your site.

4. Follow the same steps to create a new document using the basic_no_css template. Save this file as **no_css_test.htm** in the root folder as well.

5. The document css_test.htm appears with the text in the navigation bar at the top formatted with a CSS style that removes the underline, bolds the text, and changes the rollover colors to ones that match the color scheme of the site. If possible, preview this page in both Internet Explorer and Netscape Navigator. While they look great in Microsoft's browser, Netscape does not support this CSS feature. Viewers who use the Netscape browser will probably deduce that the text at the top of the page contains links, but by using a behavior, you can direct them to another page where these links will be more evident.

9

Note

Netscape version 6 is said to have excellent support for CSS styles, but as of this writing, the browser is still going through some final revisions, and is not available in a bug-free version.

6. Since you need to modify the template, and not the page, you have to return to the source document to apply your behavior. Reopen the document that this new page is linked to—basic_with_css.dwt—from the Templates folder.

7. To open the Behaviors panel, choose Window | Behaviors. You'll now see how easy it is to apply the behavior to this template and then update your page.

8. Behaviors are another example of a feature that must follow specific rules in order to function correctly. In this case, it is important to remember that behaviors must be attached to a particular HTML tag, and that they cannot be attached to text within the document. In many cases, behaviors are linked to an image, a link, or the body of the document itself. Select the <body> tag in the Tag Selector as a quick shortcut to get this done.

9. Your next step is to specify which behaviors you want to work with. Just as with most aspects of web design, the browser determines the availability of features. Dreamweaver lets you choose the options you want to use by letting you specify the browser type you are targeting. Obviously, the older the browser, the less behaviors you will find available, but using this lower standard will also result in more members of the audience having access to the actions you are specifying. To set this option, click the plus sign in the Behaviors panel, and choose Show Events For | 3.0 And Later Browsers.

10. The behavior you will add, by way of the menu that appears when you click the plus sign in the Behaviors panel, is the Check Browser option. Select this now and you will be presented with the Check Browser dialog box, shown in Figure 9-8.

11. In effect, by providing information in this dialog box, you are supplying Dreamweaver with the source for the JavaScript code that it will generate to make this behavior function properly. In this box, you are telling Dreamweaver to write code that checks for a version of Netscape that is version 3.0 or older, and, if it finds it, to redirect the user to an alternate URL. If the browser is not 3.0 or older, then another URL can be used instead.

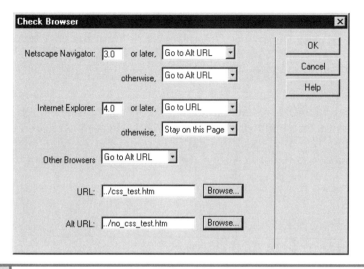

Figure 9-8   The Check Browser dialog box is used to set options for the Dreamweaver behavior

—|Note —

If you have any experience in computer programming, you will recognize these settings as if...then expressions. If one statement is found to be true, then a certain procedure is followed. If it is not true, then another selection is made.

9

12. Notice that the specifications for Internet Explorer are slightly different because of the better support it provides for the CSS styles you are using on this page. You may also have noticed that Internet Explorer supports more JavaScript behaviors than does Netscape—a grand irony since Netscape actually invented this coding language!

13. The Browse buttons are used to find the files you want to use as your alternate pages if a particular browser version is found. These files are set as relative paths, so they will hold up when they are posted to the server.

14. Click OK after you have set your behavior. Returning to the Document window for your template, you see that the behavior has been added to the Behavior panel.

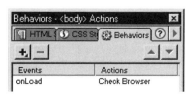

15. Save this template file, and when prompted to update the pages on the site that use it, click OK to have Dreamweaver perform the dirty work for you. Save all your files—your work here is done. Creating alternate content for the site now becomes a simple matter of creating new pages from the templates you just modified.

Congratulations! You have now really stepped into the deep end of web programming. By having your web page automatically check the viewer's browser and then send them to a custom-designed page, you have taken another huge leap toward creating the kind of consistent content that any developer would be proud of.

Ask the Expert

Question: Where can I find more information about browsers and the types of support they have for different features?

Answer: The Web, not surprisingly, is the best place to find information about browsers and their capabilities—and limitations. Four sites in particular are useful for finding information about web browsers:

Webreview.com	www.webreview.com
Webmonkey.com	hotwired.lycos.com/webmonkey
ZDNet Developer	www.zdnet.com/developer
W3C.org	www.w3.org

In addition to these web sites, don't forget that Macromedia's site (www.macromedia.com) is jam-packed not only with information about its latest products, but also support for developers working with all of its software. In particular, I find the TechNotes section of Macromedia's site to be indispensable when I have a problem I can't answer for one of my students. Of all the different types of software I have used over the years, and all the different companies that have sold their products to me, Macromedia's support for users after the purchase is far and away the best I have ever seen.

Project 9-6: Using Behaviors to Check for Plug-Ins

In the last exercise, you saw how a behavior could be used to redirect a viewer to a page built with content that is appropriate for the type of browser they are using. Pretty sophisticated stuff, but, as noted, this behavior merely scratches the surface of what this combination of events and actions can do for you.

If you were to build a web page that made heavy use of Macromedia's Flash program to add sophisticated content and animation, but still wanted to have your site accessible to the widest audience possible, a different type of behavior would be necessary.

Is this absolutely essential? No, it is not, and as always, you have to take into consideration the goals of your site and the audience you are trying to reach. If your site was called something like www.thecoolestflashanimations.com, you probably wouldn't care whether Aunt Teresa in Terre Haute were able to see it. Your audience would be other Flash aficionados like yourself, and they would have the Flash plug-in installed, or would be willing (and able) to download and install it, or would upgrade to the latest browser version. If, on the other hand, your site was something like www.anintroductiontousingcomputers.com, you might need to design for a wider audience. If you make that decision, and still wish to use the advanced features that Flash affords, having a way to develop alternative pages with and without Flash would become very important. Dreamweaver makes this possible by automatically checking for a plug-in and redirecting visitors to your site accordingly. This exercise shows you how that is done.

9

Step-by-Step

1. Once again, you need to open two templates located in the Exercises folder for this module: basic_with_flash.dwt and basic_no_flash.dwt. Save these files to the Templates folder of the Poinciana Beach web site.

2. As before, your first step is to create two new documents based on these templates. Create a document (choose File | New From Template) from basic_with_flash.dwt template and name it **flash_test.htm**. Create a new file from the basic_no_flash.dwt template and call it **no_flash_test.htm**.

Tip

I like to use the word "test" or "practice" in any filename for a document that I create for the purposes of trying out a new procedure. This makes it easier to go back and delete it later after I am finished practicing.

3. Once these documents are created and saved with their new names, you can close them. You will let Dreamweaver automatically update these pages after you add a behavior to the template itself.

4. Return to the basic_with_flash.dwt template file, and, as you did previously, use the Tag Selector to select the <body> tag for this page. Remember, behaviors must be attached to HTML tags, and since you want this behavior to be triggered by the action of loading the page, the <body> tag is the appropriate place to attach it.

5. Click the plus sign in the Behaviors panel and choose Check Plugin.

Note

The term *plug-ins* was originally coined to describe these helper programs that extended the capabilities of Netscape Navigator. Microsoft uses the term ActiveX to refer to similar applications that work with Internet Explorer. The next module talks more about plug-ins and their use.

6. This behavior is much simpler than the one you used in the previous exercise, because you only need to answer a simple yes or no question. If the viewer has the browser, they go to one URL, which can be left blank to keep them on the current page. If the viewer doesn't have the browser, they are taken to an alternative URL, in this case your no_flash_test.htm document, as shown in Figure 9-9. Note that on the page designed for users without the Flash player installed, a link to Macromedia's download page is provided.

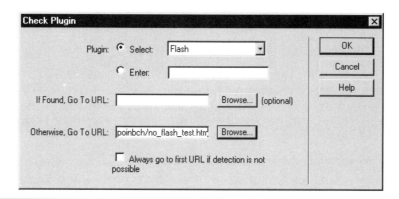

Figure 9-9 Alternate URLs are set in the Check Plugin dialog box

7. Apply the behavior and save your page. When you are finished automatically updating the pages that were created with this template, you will have one index page that includes Flash buttons, and another index page to which viewer's who don't have Flash installed will be redirected without their knowledge. Save and close all open files, and update as prompted by Dreamweaver. And you thought this was going to be hard!

Behaviors add amazing sophistication to your documents in ways that you have only just begun to discover. By completing simple dialog boxes, Dreamweaver builds the underlying code for you to pull off some awesome new tricks for making your site even more interactive, useful, and downright cool than you would have been able to do if you were restricted to simple HTML documents. Although behaviors aren't discussed in much more detail, the next module talks about JavaScript and other ways that the use of this coding language can extend the capabilities of your pages and sites.

1-Minute Drill

- Define the term *behavior*.

- What computer language is used to create behaviors?

- What consideration about browsers must be kept in mind when using behaviors?

Project 9-7: Practicing with Templates and Behaviors

9

As you have moved through the exercises in this book, you may have asked, "Why do I keep hanging on to these practice files that I create?" Well, the moment of truth has finally arrived.

Now that you know how easy it is to create templates and build new pages around them, those practice files that are resting in the root folder of your Poinciana Beach web site give you some great assets for refining the site. During this exercise, your task is to take another look at the practice files that you created in past modules, find one (or two) that appeals to you, and convert it

---

- The term *behavior* refers to the combination of an *event* (input from the viewer or the browser) followed by an *action* (operations created by JavaScript code).
- JavaScript is used to add additional functions beyond the capabilities of HTML.
- Browser support for Dreamweaver behaviors varies widely, and should always be taken into consideration when choosing to employ this feature.

into a template. Remember to open the document and then choose File | Save As Template to turn a standard HTML document into a template.

Try the different navigation schemes that you created previously, with different navigation bars and different images or text as the links. This is your opportunity to experiment with the power of templates and libraries, and you should spend a fair amount of time on this self-guided project.

You should also take the time to create an entirely new template by selecting File | New Template. Try out some different navigation schemes by using layout tables to define editable and locked regions for your new template.

Remember to give the new files that you create a descriptive name that lets you know what template or scheme they are built around. Have fun with this project, and with the creative freedom that Dreamweaver provides through its template and library features.

What to Take Away

The design team at Macromedia has taken great strides in Dreamweaver 4 toward making this highly sophisticated software program even more accessible to everyone. With the addition of the Assets panel, the design team has made it possible to easily track all the elements that you employ in your site in one handy location for your use and reuse.

The changes to the way that Dreamweaver handles behaviors is also a big improvement, and makes the creation of JavaScript code for advanced features something that even those of you who know nothing about JavaScript are able to pull off. The net result of the improvements in these two areas is your ability to quickly and easily design pages that are marked by a high level of consistency. Using libraries, templates, and behaviors designed to actually check the viewer's browser settings allows you to design for as wide an audience as you desire, all while using the latest and greatest web design tools.

✓Mastery Check

1. What Dreamweaver feature lists all the assets of a web site, such as colors, URLs, and templates?

2. How does Dreamweaver handle the management of library items and templates that are created?

3. What two methods can be used for creating a template?

4. What is the file extension for a Dreamweaver template?

5. What behavior is used to check for a particular version of a browser that a viewer has installed on their computer?

6. What object on a web page must behaviors be attached to?

9

Module 10

Forms and Functions: Interactivity in Web Design

The Goals of this Module

- Understand how client-side and server-side programming is accomplished
- Use JavaScript to extend the capabilities of your site
- Understand the function of form objects
- Use Dreamweaver's Insert Form features
- Employ the Macromedia Extension Manager and use Dreamweaver extensions
- Define and understand plug-ins and objects
- Insert embedded and linked plug-in files

As a communications medium, the Internet has developed at an unprecedented rate. In just a few short years, this new dynamic method of sharing information between people has witnessed explosive growth, to the point where it is now possible to share ideas with others around the world with just the simple click of a mouse.

Much of this capability is dependant on the ability to provide information to the owners of a web site by completing special forms found on their web pages, and then receive a reply. Other types of information exchange can be more one-sided, with the web developer generating and displaying a particular message, but one that is still tailored for the individual viewer. Still other interactions take place by using rich multimedia files to enhance and expand the capabilities of the site.

In this module, you will be introduced to some of the concepts and tools that make this two-way communication possible. While the pages that have been developed to this point have contained some elements of interactivity, in the upcoming exercises, you will learn how to employ some new tools for creating interactive experiences for your users, and gain a good, solid foundation for making these interactions possible with Dreamweaver.

Exploring Interactive Technologies

Several special computer languages exist that work with HTML in ways that make it possible to extend the capabilities of the basic language that is used for presenting information on the World Wide Web. Remember that HTML was originally developed as a way for scientists and engineers to communicate information between themselves with little thought regarding how that information looked. As long as it was easy to read and capable of being analyzed, then basic HTML met their needs by allowing them to share information with their colleagues.

As the Web became more of a commercial and communications medium, though, the need to be able to provide two-way communication and to extend the capabilities of the basic coding language became extremely important. After all, isn't it much better if you can visit a web site advertising a company's products and ask for more information or, better yet, place an order? Beyond that simple interaction, what if the owners of the company wanted to allow viewers to search for a particular product by name or catalog number before they placed their order? Or to check whether an item was in stock? More advanced capabilities were certainly necessary, and in an amazingly short period of time, those functions became so commonplace that today it is surprising to find any larger commercial web site that doesn't use these technologies. Even on smaller sites, today's user of the Web expects to find the kinds of interactive possibilities shown in Figure 10-1.

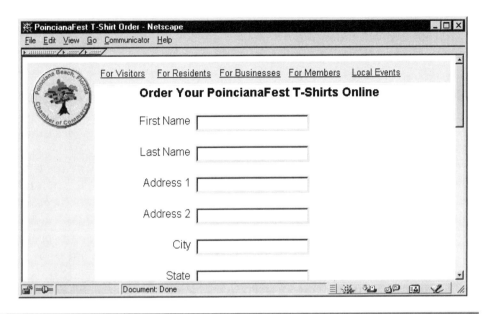

Figure 10-1   Ordering products online has become a common use of the Web

Understanding the way that these computer languages operate is beyond the scope of this book. However, as you move through the exercises that introduce how Dreamweaver provides the tools for interactivity, you will receive some exposure to new terms and concepts. Don't panic! While you need a basic understanding of the concepts of computer programming to make these interactions function, Dreamweaver's usual thoughtful interface and comprehensive set of tools for the designer make this part of web development as painless as possible.

In general, interactive web technologies are described in terms of where the actual processing takes place—either on the viewer's computer or on the server where the web pages are stored. A program that operates on the viewer's computer is said to be a *client-side program* and includes such technologies as JavaScript and Java, while one that operates on the server, such as programs making use of the Common Gateway Interface (CGI), for instance, is called a *server-side program*. You don't need to know how to program in these languages to have a successful web site, because between the capabilities of Dreamweaver and the huge reservoir of free resources available on the Internet, anyone can (somewhat) easily develop interactive elements for their pages.

10

Note

A third category, which depends on "helper" applications that extend the browser's capabilities, is commonly referred to as a *plug-in.*

Notice that all-important "somewhat" qualifier above, though. Providing full functionality for many interactive elements can be a frustrating and laborious process, and the more interactive you want your site to be, the more necessary it will become to understand how the coding is done that enables these elements, or to hire someone who does. In fact, in the world of web development, the types of interactions that create a fully functioning web site are often broken into two distinct categories—front end and back end—where the designers of the visual portion of the site concentrate on how things look and function for the viewer (the front end) and an entirely separate group of designers works on the back end, creating the coding that links the viewer to the capabilities of interactive technologies.

This module looks at all three categories of interactive technologies: client side, server side, and plug-ins. And as you move along, you'll be introduced to some new tools that Dreamweaver provides. You'll get started by looking at client-side interactivity.

Project 10-1: Creating an E-Mail Form with JavaScript

You have already seen JavaScript in action in several exercises completed through the course of this book. Up to this point, Dreamweaver has handled the task of generating the code required for inserting rollovers and behaviors—all actions made possible through the use of this special Internet-specific coding language. In the next project, though, you'll get down and dirty with the code to create an interactive form that contains special fill-in-the-blank boxes, known as fields, that will allow a viewer to provide information and send the data to a specified address that they select. This is a good example of the types of challenges presented when you decide that you want to go beyond the features that are already built into the Dreamweaver interface and start adding some special functions of your own.

The JavaScript code you will be using was captured from the Web at one of the best libraries for prebuilt code available—ZDNet Developer (www.zdnet.com/

developer). Maintained by the publisher of many popular computing magazines, ZDNet is known for its clear and easy-to-use instructions for both the beginning and advanced developer alike. In addition to ZDNet, there are any number of other web sites where you can find libraries that contain pretested and verified JavaScript, as well as tutorials, and additional information on other languages and applications that can be used to extend the capabilities of your site.

Caution

Be sure that any code you download is from a reputable developer or web site and that it has been tested and verified both to function correctly and to be free of any malicious code that may breach the security of your site. A devious hacker can easily hide code within the body of their "free" script in such a way that sensitive information about your site can be transmitted to them. Limiting your search for code and scripts to only those sites that are maintained by well-known and reputable companies can help you avoid tragic results later on.

Most free scripts, as code written in JavaScript is commonly referred to, that you'll find on the Internet will contain instructions on how the code needs to be modified and inserted into your document. Even so, the process of searching through the code for those items that require modification can often be a little mysterious to the beginner. Go slowly when you start out, as you'll do here, and stay with scripts that are easy to follow, well written, and contain clear instructions. How do you know which scripts meet those requirements? Unfortunately, a lot of trial and error is involved, so plan on spending some time working with the code and be prepared for a certain number of failures. In time, though, you will be able to find those special features that you want to include and relatively easily modify them for your own needs.

10

Note

Be sure that you have downloaded the exercise files for this module from www.osborne.com and saved them to your Exercises folder.

Step-by-Step

1. Before beginning the actual construction of your script-enabled page, you need a new folder in the site files to hold scripts used when working with JavaScript. To create this folder, right-click the root folder for the site, and choose New Folder. Name this folder **scripts**. Your revised (and ever-growing) site structure should now appear as you see here.

2. Locate the file called mailer.txt in the exercise files for this module and copy it into this new folder. Once you have the file in place, right-click its icon and choose Edit in Dreamweaver to open it in Dreamweaver's Code view window, shown in Figure 10-2.

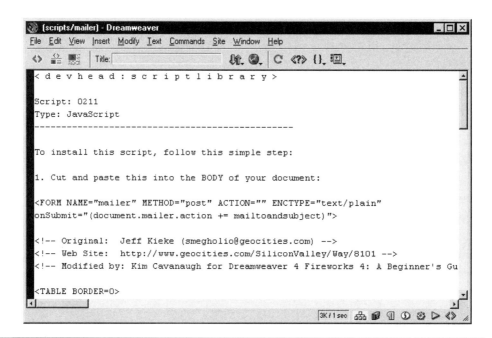

Figure 10-2 | Dreamweaver will open text files in a special code view window so they can be edited

3. Take a moment to scroll up and down in this new window. Notice that this particular script combines some HTML elements with those of JavaScript to create a series of fields that are available for a visitor to insert data and mail the page off to the selected recipient.

4. At the top of the document you will see the instructions for inserting this script. Following the instructions, and some comment tags about the author of this script, find the line that begins

```
<FORM NAME="mailer"
```

and highlight all of the code that follows it, up to and including this final tag:

```
</SCRIPT>
```

5. Choose File | Edit | Copy to place a copy of the text on your computer's clipboard. You will use this copied text momentarily.

Tip

The instructions for this script are relatively easy to follow. Some JavaScript will require you to place some of the code within the document's <head> tag as well. This is another reason to confine your search for scripts to those sites that have easy-to-follow instructions.

6. To see this script in action, create a new HTML file in your root folder and call it **mailer.htm**, and then open the new document.

7. In most cases, the easiest way to place the script that was copied earlier is to go directly into the source code for the document and paste it directly into the location specified by the author of the code. In this case, the code needs to be placed inside the two <body> tags for the document.

10

Note

Dreamweaver allows scripts to be attached to specific tags within the document by using the Invisibles category in the Objects panel to insert script. Since this method is not appropriate for this example, it will be up to you to explore this option.

8. Switch from Design view to Code view by clicking that button on the toolbar.

9. Even though this document is still essentially blank, it contains the basic tags required to give it structure. The trick here is to put your cursor right in front of the closing body tag for this document—</body>.

10. To paste the script that was copied earlier, simply choose Edit I Paste, and the script will be placed into the underlying code for this document. Your completed Code view of this document should appear as shown in Figure 10-3.

11. Return to Design view for this document. Notice that a number of elements were included in the JavaScript that was added to the page, including all the titles and the form objects that are available for a viewer to input data.

12. As shown in Figure 10-4, this page looks pretty good as it is. Obviously, some elements of the code were put in by the author as placeholders, which you would need to replace before you could use this script.

13. Revising the code at this point involves finding those elements in the script that were placed there as examples and modifying them. For instance, if you wanted to enable the e-mail functions of this form and attach them to a real address, you would need to change the e-mail values that are part of the script. Since this script is written in a combination of JavaScript and HTML, you can do that directly in Dreamweaver.

14. Place the cursor inside the first form object at the top of the page—the box where person1@aol.com is located.

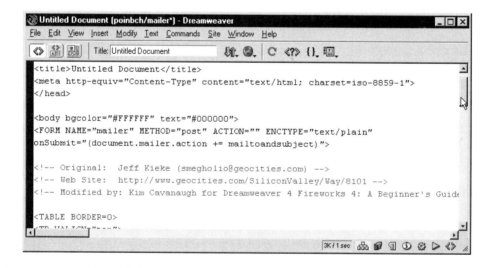

Figure 10-3 Working in Code view allows you to paste scripts directly into the correct position in a document

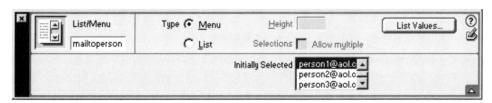

Figure 10-4   The mailer.htm document as seen in Netscape

15. With the Properties Inspector open, notice that this object has unique properties that can be adjusted directly in Dreamweaver, including the values of the mailing addresses in this box. Click the List Values button to be taken to the List Values dialog box, in which you can change these properties.

10

16. In the List Values dialog box, changing the label changes what the viewer will see in their browser, while modifying the value is used to select a new e-mail address to replace the bogus one used as an example by the author.

Dreamweaver makes this pretty easy, and you'll see later on how to make other changes to these objects as well.

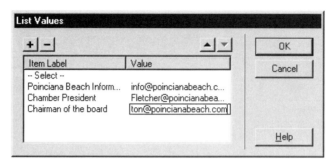

17. One final change to make, and this time you go back to the source code by switching to Code view. If you tried sending a message from your browser, you probably saw the warning message that the file was for demonstration purposes only. Changing this message involves digging around in the code to find the source and then modifying it to something more appropriate, such as "Thank you for writing." Alternately, you could erase the code that relates to this action by eliminating this entire line:

```
onClick="alert('Button inactive. Demo only.')
```

18. The line of text has been highlighted here for clarity. This is a good example of how you will need to be able to examine and modify source code to work with a script that is downloaded from the Web.

```
:"Send Message" onClick="alert('Button inactive. Demo only.')">
:t"></TD>
```

19. It is important that, until you are more familiar with using JavaScript, you save as much of the original code as possible. Always leave the original document that you downloaded as it is and make your changes directly in any new document that you create. If things go wrong (as they inevitably will), you can delete the document and start over again. If you make changes to the original source, you may have to download a new copy to get back to your starting place.

20. Experiment with this file and the ways that it can be changed. Save your work when you are finished.

This exercise has given you a good introduction to how you can incorporate JavaScript into a document that you create in Dreamweaver. However, you should note that this method for gathering and sending e-mail is not without its problems. For instance, the person who sends you e-mail has no way of knowing whether their request for information has been received, and you have no way of knowing whether you are receiving mail consistently. In addition, you probably noticed the following security warning that your browser automatically generated when the form was submitted. Some viewers might find this message alarming and decide not to send information in this unsecure manner as a result.

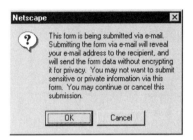

The preferred method, then, is to use another type of programming, to which you'll be introduced in the next project.

In summary, working with JavaScript is a skill that you may or may not feel you need to develop. Just as with the early pioneers of the Web, much of what you need to learn can be obtained by studying the scripts that are contained in other's pages or through online tutorials. The choice is ultimately yours. If you feel that adding the advanced features that are possible through the client-side scripting available with JavaScript and Java is necessary to meet the goals of your site, then you need to study both reference materials and the actual work of web designers that you can see by reading the source code in their pages.

10

1-Minute Drill

- What things should you look for when downloading JavaScript?

- How is JavaScript inserted into a web page?

- How must JavaScript that is downloaded be modified before it is put into use?

- When downloading JavaScript, be sure that the site where the script is found is a reputable one and that the script comes with instructions on how it should be included in your document.
- Switching to Code view in Dreamweaver and pasting the script directly into the document is the easiest way to insert JavaScript.
- Scripts available for download often include "dummy" locations and filenames that must be changed to reflect the actual names of those on your site.

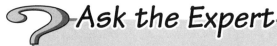

Ask the Expert

Question: What's the difference between JavaScript and Java?

Answer: JavaScript is the coding language developed by Netscape Corporation that extends the capabilities of standard HTML by adding coding into the document itself that allows for some of the advanced features you have seen, such as image rollovers and automatic browser checks.

Java is a programming language created by Sun Microsystems that develops a miniature computer application, called an *applet,* that resides on the server and is installed into a page based on how the commands to call up the Java applet are written into the document. The main advantage to using Java applets is that they are completely cross-platform and cross-browser compatible and avoid many of the compatibility issues inherent with JavaScript. Java applets can be designed for advanced features such as stock tickers, chat rooms, and some interesting visual effects.

Designing a Web Page with Forms

In the previous example, you saw how a combination of JavaScript and HTML created a page that included form objects that enabled viewers to insert data and choose from options to transmit data. Whereas the functionality of the page was provided through the use of JavaScript, the structure was created in HTML. In this exercise, you will see how Dreamweaver handles the task of enabling forms within a page. As noted before, the actual functions that would be associated with these forms are something that you would need to provide either in JavaScript or in an alternative set of instructions created in one of the many programming languages available for these specific tasks.

The most common way to process information received from a viewer is to use one of the programming languages that generate code accessible through a protocol known as the Common Gateway Interchange, or CGI. CGI scripts can be written in a variety of programming languages, the most common of which is Perl. Beyond the challenges of creating the code, or downloading and modifying free code available online, are other requirements based on the type of language that operates on the server itself. When you're finally ready to take the big leap and make the form pages that you create in Dreamweaver fully operational, you will need to discuss the particular requirements with the managers of your web hosting service. Not all services allow the use of CGI scripts, and those who do have particular requirements that you need to meet before you can post the script to their server. Again, the use of CGI scripts is beyond the scope of this book, and this next exercise is designed to acquaint you with the first half of the process—designing the HTML documents that collect data from your viewers.

Tip

An excellent tutorial on CGI scripts can be found at hoohoo.ncsa.uiuc.edu/cgi.

Project 10-2: Creating a Form

In this exercise, you will build a web page that includes some of the form objects that can be inserted and formatted with Dreamweaver. In many ways, these objects are similar to other items that you have inserted into your pages in the past, such as images, but because of the inherent requirements created by the scripts that will process the forms, additional steps are required for the page to function properly.

Step-by-Step

1. Rather than create an entirely new web page for this project, while in the Site window for the Poinciana Beach web site, choose File | New From Template and locate one of the templates that was created in the last module. The samples here will use the basic_with_flash.dwt template. Save the new file as **shirtorder.htm**. Change the title of the page to **PoincianaFest T-Shirt Order**.

2. In the header section for this page, type **Order Your 2001 PoincianaFest T-Shirts Here**, and format the text as Heading 2. Select the "body" label in the body section of this page and delete the text. Be sure that your cursor remains in the body area of the page when you get to step 5.

3. With that bit of housekeeping behind you, it's time to insert the forms for this page. Locate the Forms category in the Objects panel and switch to that view.

10

Table 10-1 provides a summary of the appearance and function of the different form objects you will find in the Objects panel.

Form Object Element	Appearance	Function
Insert Form		Enables forms for a web page by inserting the <form> tag. All form objects must be located within boundaries created by this tag.
Insert Text Field		Creates a fill-in-the-blank box in which viewers can type data.
Insert Button		Inserts a Submit or Reset button in the page.
Insert CheckBox		Inserts a Checkbox object that lets a viewer choose from a range of options, such as "Check All that Apply."
Insert Radio Button		Inserts a radio button that lets the viewer choose only a single option, such as "What is your gender?"
Insert List/Menu		Inserts a List object or Menu drop-down box that allows users to choose from a range of selections.
Insert File Field		Inserts a File Field object that allows the viewer to locate a file on their computer with a Browse button and then send the file to the server.
Insert Image Field		Image Field objects are required when an image is used in place of the standard HTML-based Submit and Reset buttons.
Insert Hidden Field		Provides a storage location for information that is needed to process a form, but is not visible to the user.
Insert Jump Menu		Inserts a Jump Menu that allows viewers to choose relative (on your site) or absolute (outside your site) web pages to jump to.

Table 10-1 Form Objects in Dreamweaver

4. With any form-enabled page, the first task is to insert the <form> tag that is required so that the form objects can be processed by the supporting script. Choose the Insert Form button from the Objects panel to enable form processing for this page. Notice that two red, dashed lines are inserted into the page and that your cursor is contained within these lines, as shown here:

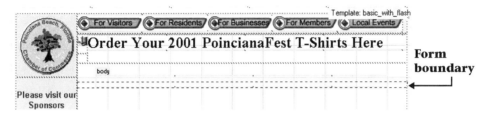

5. While form objects can be inserted as you would with any other object, such as an image, it is best to plan ahead for the structure of your page and use a table to hold in place the objects and the labels they will require. For this page, choose Insert I Table to open the Insert Table dialog box, shown next, and set the parameters as you see here. (Note that you will need to be in Standard view to use the Insert Table option. You could also complete this action by switching to the Common category in the Objects panel and selecting the Insert Table button there.)

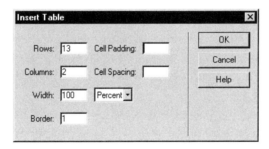

Tip

Leave your border value set at 1 so that the borders of the separate cells are viewable while designing form pages. This property can be reset to 0 after you've finished laying out the page, but leaving the borders visible during the design process can help you in formatting and positioning the different objects while you work.

6. Notice in Figure 10-5 that the red, dashed lines expand to enclose the entire table. It is very important to make sure that your <form> tags completely

Red, dashed lines indicate the area of the page formatted for forms.

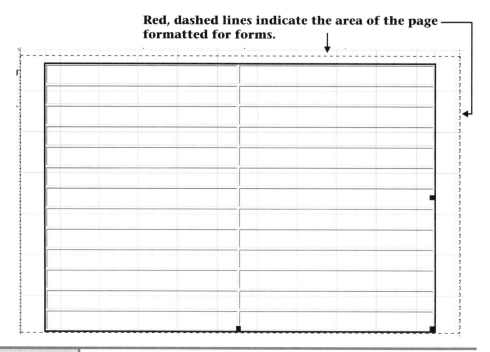

Figure 10-5 Areas of the page that will contain form objects must always be contained by <form> tags, indicated by the red, dashed lines

enclose the area of the page that will contain form objects, because they simply will not function properly unless this bit of HTML housekeeping is tended to.

7. The cells on the left side of this table will contain all the labels for the different form objects that will be used. To label these cells, refer to Figure 10-6, and complete the data entry for this portion of the page.

8. Use your mouse to highlight all the cells on the left side of the table and select right-align from the Properties Inspector. Once all the text is aligned to the right, move the divider between the two columns to the left so that the cells are large enough to contain the text, but don't have any additional space. You may also want to combine the two topmost cells into one by using the join cells option on the Properties Inspector, as shown in Figure 10-7.

9. The Insert Text Field button will be used to provide areas for the viewer to insert data for their name, address, city, and ZIP code. Insert those five

Please complete this order form and click on the Submit button at the bottom of the page.	
Name	
Address 1	
Address 2	
City	
State (choose)	
Zip of Postal Code	
Please choose your size	
Small	
Medium	
Large	
Extra-Large	

Figure 10-6 Type in labels for this page as shown here

Please complete this order form and click on the Submit button at the bottom of the page.	
Name	
Address 1	
Address 2	
City	
State (choose)	
Zip of Postal Code	
Please choose your size	
Small	
Medium	
Large	
Extra-Large	

10

Figure 10-7 Realign and join the table cells for an improved appearance

objects now in their respective cells, accepting the default length of approximately 24 characters that Dreamweaver provides by default.

10. To make these separate fields readable to the script that will be used to process each item, they must contain a unique name. Providing a name and formatting the length of the individual cells is done by accessing the Properties Inspector for each individual form object and then setting it accordingly, as shown in Figure 10-8. Field names must correspond exactly to a field name in the script you are using, and cannot contain spaces. Appropriate names for these five objects might be name, address1, address2, city, and zip.

Tip

Experimentation is always encouraged, but you may find that changing to a different option, such as changing the character width to a large number, or to a multiline box, will drastically affect the size of your table cells. Remember that a cell value always overrides a table value. Going back to your original dimensions requires that you first reset the cell value, and then change the table value.

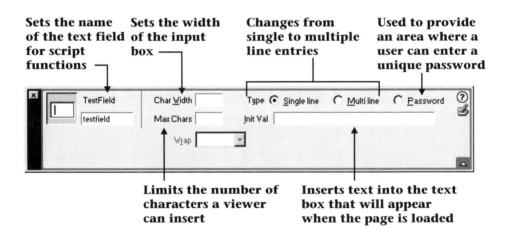

Sets the name of the text field for script functions — Sets the width of the input box — Changes from single to multiple line entries — Used to provide an area where a user can enter a unique password

Limits the number of characters a viewer can insert — Inserts text into the text box that will appear when the page is loaded

Figure 10-8   The Properties Inspector for Text Field objects is used to set multiple properties for the object

11. The next task is to insert a List/Menu form object that will enable viewers to choose their state. Again, this is a two-step process: insert the form object, and then use the Properties Inspector to modify the object to meet the needs of your form and the requirements of the scripting program that will collect the data at the server.

12. In the cell next to the State label, insert a List/Menu form object.

13. Dreamweaver combines the List and Menu options into one button, but the two have some significant differences. Lists allow viewers to select multiple options from a list that they can scroll through. Menus are used when you want to allow the viewer to select a single option from a list that appears when they click a down arrow next to the box. This is the option used here, because obviously people can have only one state for their address.

14. Check the Properties Inspector for this object to see the different values that can be entered, as shown in Figure 10-9.

15. The List Values button in the upper-right corner of the Properties Inspector is used to set the variables that are available to the viewer. You may remember the appearance of this dialog box from the last module, in which new JavaScript functions were added when Behaviors were used in a page. The process is similar here, since you will click the plus sign to add a label that will appear for the viewer, and then type a value that will be read by your script. (If nothing is entered in the Value column, the script will read the data in the

10

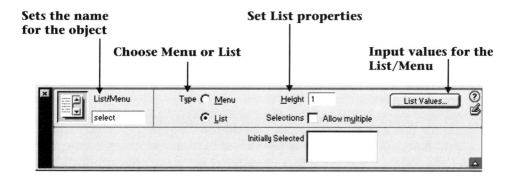

Figure 10-9 | The Properties Inspector for List/Menu objects is used to set multiple properties for the object

Label column.) Try this now by entering a few state abbreviations—or enter all 50 if you have extra time on your hands. You will need to preview the page in your browser to see this object in action.

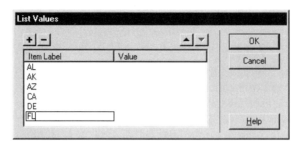

16. The next series of form objects required for this page are the radio buttons that will be added to the cells to the right of their respective labels—Small, Medium, Large, and Extra-Large. Again, after inserting the buttons, it is important to give each an individual label that conforms to the structure of the CGI scripting for this form. This will allow the script to associate the input for a small shirt, for example, with the "small" label that you apply during the design of the form. Complete this section of the form by inserting the four radio buttons and labeling each. Remember that spaces are not allowed in form object labels.

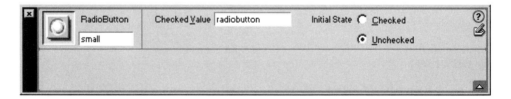

17. The final objects to insert in this practice form page are two buttons that will be placed at the bottom of the document—one to submit the information and one that allows the viewer to reset the form and start over. Were this a "live" form, you would need to have a way to continue processing the form by allowing for credit card orders. If allowing visitors to order products is a goal of your site, this is another example in which your first stop would need to be with the company that will host your site, as it often is able to provide assistance in enabling secure credit card processing.

18. Place your cursor in the bottom cell of the form. Choose Insert Button from the Objects panel and note the change to the Properties Inspector as seen in Figure 10-10.

**Label for
scripting**   **Sets the name of the
button for the viewer**   **Change from submit
to reset value**

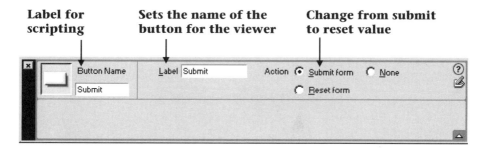

Options for buttons are enabled by using the Properties Inspector

19. Form buttons actually have two labels and this can be a little confusing. On
the left is the label that is read by the processing script, while the label on
the right defines the text that appears on the button itself. Accept the
defaults for the Submit button that you just inserted, and then insert a
second button. Name this button **reset**, change the text label to **Start
Over**, and set the action setting to Reset.

Note

To use a custom graphic with the same capabilities that these basic HTML buttons
possess, you would need to design a graphic and then choose the Insert Image
Field icon in the Objects panel. Using this option allows you to use any graphic as
a Submit or Reset button.

10

20. If this were really the end of this process, you might say to yourself, "Gee,
that wasn't much different from inserting other objects. All I have to
remember is that all the objects have to be inside <form> tags and that each
object needs a unique name that will be read by the script." You would be
about half right, but, as noted, this form still needs to be linked to the script
that is stored on the server that will allow the information to be collected,
processed, saved, and presented back to you in a recognizable form. For this
last step to happen, the <form> tags need some modifications so that the
data is sent to the server properly.

21. The easiest way to select the <form> tag is to locate the tag by name in the Tag Selector at the bottom of the Document window. Selecting this tag will highlight all of the page that is contained within this tag, and change the options available in the Properties Inspector.

<blockquote> <mm:editable> **<form>**

22. There are two methods for sending data to the server—GET and POST—and they operate very differently. The GET method is useful for sending one single data object to the server, such as a search for a keyword. POST is used for multiple data submissions, and is the preferred method for sending data to a CGI script for processing. Set the method for this page to POST.

23. In addition to specifying the method for transmitting data back to the server, you must also provide the location of the script by its URL in the box labeled Action. In the following example, the form for this page has been directed to a special directory that almost all CGI-enabled forms will use—cgi-bin—and to the specific script that will process the order.

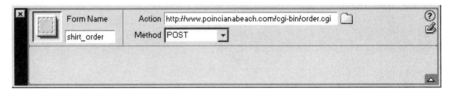

24. This page is now fully enabled to take advantage of the incredible information processing powers of the Web. Save this file and take a well-deserved break. If you'd like to see the final version of this page and compare your results, open the shirt_order.htm document you'll find in the Exercises folder for Module 10.

Of course, much work still needs to be done, including the crucial step of linking the file to a real CGI script to process data, but by completing this rather lenghty project, you have come a long way toward understanding how Dreamweaver handles the HTML portion of designing form-enabled web pages. Many options are available in addition to those discussed here, but you now have a solid understanding of how form objects are inserted into a page and modified so that they are ready for linking to a CGI script.

Form objects open an incredibly rich world of interactive capabilities between yourself and your audience. Using these tools comes with a bit of a cost though. You must either invest the time and energy into learning how to modify or write the scripts necessary for their application yourself, or pay to have it done for you. You should also discuss your needs with potential server hosting companies when you're ready to post your site to the Web. Many hosts will provide free or low-cost CGI scripts to you as part of their service, and will even assist you in the process of establishing form-based services for your site. As the old saying goes, "You get what you pay for," and while a low-cost (or free) hosting service may seem like a bargain, it may be worth paying a little more if a more costly host provider includes scripting services you need to meet the goals of your site.

1-Minute Drill

- What is the name of the protocol that is used for processing most forms on the Web?
- What tag must be present on any web page that employs forms?
- What is the preferred method for sending information from a form to a server?

Working with Dreamweaver Extensions

Programming computer code that enables advanced interactions can be a truly daunting task. As if learning how to use the Dreamweaver program itself weren't challenging enough at times, creating interactions that go beyond the capabilities of Dreamweaver may seem nearly impossible. However, Macromedia now has an elegant and easy-to-use feature included as part of Dreamweaver 4—the Extensions Manager—that takes much of the hard work out of advanced interactions and makes them as easy as selecting an item from the Objects panel.

As of this writing, over 400 advanced functions are located at the Macromedia Exchange—www.macromedia.com/exchange/dreamweaver/—where the files that will allow you to program advanced features can be downloaded. This is a terrific asset that allows you to search for a specific function that you would like to add

10

- The Common Gateway Interchange (CGI) is the protocol that allows the processing of most forms used on the Web.
- Any web page that includes a form object must include the <form> tag.
- The preferred method for sending data from a viewer to a server is the Post method.

to your site and read reviews of how well it performs. Macromedia also gives its "stamp of approval" to many of the extensions so that you know they have been thoroughly tested and conform to current coding standards. Macromedia also provides easy-to-understand instructions for installing the extensions. Figure 10-11 shows one of the pages that displays search results for extensions that allow advanced interactions with a viewer's browser.

Project 10-3: Adding Search Capabilities to a Web Site

One of the most useful items that any web site can include is the ability for the viewer to search the site for specific keywords and then jump to the page that the internal search engine finds. This can save your viewer lots of time. It also could cause a great deal of work for the people who would have to catalog and maintain the database necessary for a search engine to function properly, were it not for the capabilities that a simple extension to Dreamweaver affords. Seeing how easily this is accomplished will give you a real appreciation for some of the powerful capabilities that extensions can bring to your site.

Step-by-Step

1. The first step in using extensions is to locate the file you want to use on the Macromedia Exchange web site. For this exercise, you will be using the AtomZ extension, which enables you to add a free search engine provided by AtomZ.com. This extension can be found by visiting Macromedia's site, or by going to www.osborne.com, which includes both the Macintosh and Windows versions as part of the exercise files for this module.

2. If you choose to download the extension, it is recommended that you accept the default location for the file to be saved to—a folder called Downloaded Extensions, located in the Macromedia folder on your computer system.

3. The Extension Manager is actually a separate application that you will find in the Macromedia program folder that also contains Dreamweaver. Locate and open the Extension Manager in the folder, and you will see the Macromedia Extension Manager, shown in Figure 10-12.

Note

This is one of the few places where a user of a Macintosh operating system will see a difference in the Dreamweaver interface. Surprisingly, the Windows version is more graphical than the Mac version, and the Mac version requires that commands be executed from the File menu.

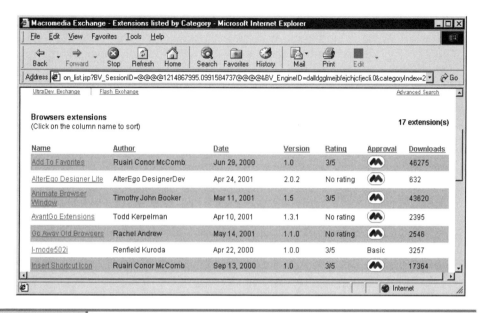

Figure 10-12   Macromedia's Exchange for Dreamweaver includes the ability to search for extensions by name or category

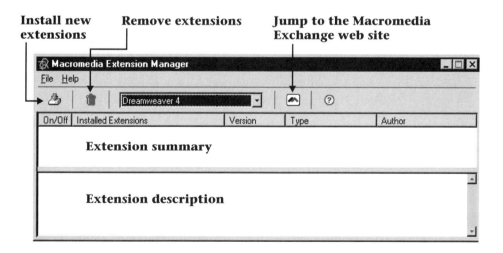

Figure 10-11   The Macromedia Extension Manager allows you to manage extensions for Dreamweaver, Dreamweaver UltraDev, and Macromedia Flash programs

4. To use the extension that you downloaded, it must first be installed into the Extension Manager and made available in Dreamweaver. Do this by clicking the Install New Extension button and navigating to the location on your hard drive where you stored the extension, usually the Downloaded Extensions folder.

5. Many of the extensions you will find include licensing agreements that cover their use. Accept the license agreement that you are presented with, and Dreamweaver will display a message that the extension has been successfully installed.

6. Quite a few services are available on the Web that provide free search capabilities for small to medium-size sites, and provide the same service on a sliding scale as sites become progressively larger. AtomZ is unique in that it provides an extension for Dreamweaver that inserts the form that provides the search capability. To take advantage of AtomZ's service, though, you need to provide your e-mail address and other information about your site, including its URL. If you don't have your site posted to the Web yet, simply use a dummy URL during the sign-up process. You can return later and modify your information when you go live with your site and have a real URL to enter.

7. Complete the sign-on process and follow the prompts that are included to activate your AtomZ account. You need both e-mail and an Internet connection to complete this step.

8. Once your AtomZ account is active and the extension has been installed, you're ready to return to Dreamweaver and begin work on a new page.

9. Choose File | New From Template and navigate to one of the DWT template files stored on your site. For this example, the template basic.dwt is used. Once your new file is open, save it as **index_search.htm** and change the page title to **Index Page with Search**.

10. Open the Objects panel and click the expansion arrow to change the category. Notice that the Extension Manager has added a new AtomZ category to your list of available options.

11. Select that option, and the Objects panel will display the AtomZ icon in the usual button format.

12. To insert a text field and a Search button, you need only locate the position on your page where you want this feature to be inserted. Remember, since this page is based on a template, you first have to choose Modify | Templates | Detach From Template if you want to use a part of the page that is currently locked by the template.

13. Insert the AtomZ search feature just below the logo on the left side of the page. Change the text that currently encourages viewers to visit the site's sponsors to **Search our Site** and insert the AtomZ object directly below this new line of text. Since some of the information in this object is hidden, you need to preview the document in a browser to see the full effect of this new feature. You can also open the index_search.htm file in the Exercises folder for this module and compare your work to the sample provided.

Search our Site

Search

14. Congratulations! In just a short period of time, you have added a very sophisticated feature to your site through the magic of Dreamweaver extensions—all without having to do any of the programming that would have been required to build a search feature into the site by hand.

Dreamweaver extensions and the Extension Manager provide powerful tools for modifying and extending the capabilities of your site well beyond the basics of HTML and JavaScript that would normally only be available to web developers with large staffs of programmers slaving away at the chore of creating sophisticated interactive capabilities. With a few clicks of the mouse and a basic understanding of how the coding works and how extensions are applied in the Dreamweaver interface, you can build your own chat rooms, provide web-based e-mail services, automate formatting tasks, provide a guest book, and employ other advanced features on your site without having to keep a team of programmers supplied with late night pizza deliveries. This is truly powerful stuff and, if the goals of your site warrant the time it will take to discover all the possibilities that extensions afford, something that you will definitely want to explore further.

10

1-Minute Drill

● What are extensions used for?

● What program allows you to install, delete, and find Dreamweaver extensions?

● Extensions add increased functionality to Dreamweaver by packaging the computer code necessary for advanced operations into a package that is accessible from the Objects panel.
● The Extension Manager allows you to access the different Dreamweaver extensions and install, add, or delete them.

Adding Multimedia Elements: Linking and Embedding

The final interactive elements covered in this module fall into a broad category of files that require a special helper application, called a plug-in, which extends the capabilities of the viewer's browser.

In the early days of the Web, plug-ins were a rather annoying part of most users' experience on the Web, because almost any file that wasn't created in HTML made it necessary for the viewer to download and install a plug-in to view the content. While modern browsers have reduced the number of software installations required for a varied Internet experience, many of the types of files discussed here do require plug-ins, and, as such, you should consider your audience's ability to find, download, and install the software a determining factor on whether or not these kinds of files are included on your site.

Note

In addition to plug-ins, another brand-name helper application is the ActiveX control application created by Microsoft. ActiveX controls can be formatted in ways that far exceed the capabilities of most plug-ins, but, just to keep things nicely confused, they are also often used in the same way that plug-ins are used.

Having said that, using files associated with a plug-in can make your site a richer, more interesting place to visit if used wisely. Perhaps the biggest note of caution here is the same one that you've heard over and over throughout this book—be sure that the inclusion of the multimedia element that you are considering has a valid reason for existence as it relates to the goals of your site. It may be just my personal prejudice, but I find the use of automatically loading music that plays when I visit a web site one of the most annoying practices on the Web, and is the reason why my sound is almost always turned off when I use the Internet. On the other hand, if music, sounds, or video plays a large role in meeting the needs of attracting viewers to your site, then by all means include those types of files.

In no particular order, the most popular plug-ins available on the Internet today include the Adobe Acrobat Reader, Macromedia's Flash and Shockwave players, Apple's QuickTime movie and sound software, and the RealAudio's RealPlayer sound and video player. Each of these programs has its own unique capabilities and its own requirements for how the files that are read by the plug-in are created and stored on your site. The following project takes a look at how different types of multimedia content can be added to your site, as an introduction to working with plug-ins.

Note

The document that will be created in the following project will be for demonstration purposes only. There is no need to save this file unless you wish to refer to it later.

Project 10-4: Inserting Plug-In Files

Files that require plug-ins can be included in a web page in either of two ways: by creating a link that the viewer clicks to open a page with the plug-in, or by automatically loading a file that is embedded into the code of the page. This final exercise enables you to try both methods as well as learn how sounds, text, and other multimedia elements can be added to a page.

Step-by-Step

1. Create a new file by right-clicking the root folder for the Poinciana beach web site and choosing File | New File. Name this file **plugin_practice.htm**. Open the document by double-clicking its icon in the Site window.

2. One of the most popular applications sweeping the Web currently is the Flash program developed by Macromedia. You have already seen how to create Flash buttons and text in a previous module, but may have been wondering how you can reuse those elements in other pages. To insert a Flash file, with the file extension of .swf, you need to access the Common category of the Objects panel and find the Insert Flash File icon you see here.

3. Clicking this button will allow you to insert any Flash file stored on your site in the SWF format. For this exercise, browse to the flash_buttons folder in your site files, choose one of the buttons you created in Module 6, and insert it into your document. These objects are considered to be *embedded* in the page, since they do not require any interaction from the viewer. The browser reads the presence of a file requiring a plug-in, activates the plug-in (if it is present on the viewer's computer), and reads and displays the file.

10

4. Another type of file that can be embedded is a sound file. Sound files come in a variety of formats and, once again, the ability to play these files is dependent on the plug-ins installed on the user's computer. Windows Media Player, Apple QuickTime, and RealPlayer are the three most prominent plug-ins that can play audio files, and which one will read the file you embed will depend on how your viewer has set their preferences for handling these types of files.

5. To insert an automatically loading sound file, change the Object panel to the Special category and select the Insert Plug-in icon.

6. Navigate to the Exercises folder for this module and choose one of the looping sound files found there—loop1.wav or loop2.wav. If this were a real web site and you were going to store sound files on your site, you would want to create a new folder to store them in (as you have done with other assets for the site). As it is, you can either ignore Dreamweaver's warning about copying the file into your root folder or choose to do so. Either way, when you preview this file in a browser, the sound file you have chosen should automatically open.

7. Notice that a small icon appears in your browser, which is generated by the sound plug-in that you have installed on your system. To keep your page design uncluttered, this type of embedded file should be placed in an out-of-the-way location on the page. Once you are done with this step, be sure to select and delete this embedded sound file.

8. Sound files can also be *linked,* rather than embedded. With a linked file, instead of linking to another web page or an absolute URL outside your site, you create the link to a file on your site that the browser then finds and opens. Type in a simple line of text on your practice page, something like **Listen to this cool music**.

9. Just as you have done in the past when creating links, select the text and then click the folder icon in the Properties Inspector. Navigate to one of the music loops in the Exercises folder for this module and select it. Once again, you will be prompted to save the file into the root folder of the site. Whether or not to complete this step is your choice.

10. Preview your file in a browser and click the music link. Momentarily, the plug-in that is associated with the file type used will open and play the sound. In this case, Apple QuickTime is the default plug-in for the file, so the QuickTime play bar is shown as the music plays. On your system, and on the system of your potential viewers, the plug-in may be different.

11. In addition to sound files, you can also insert movies as a linked file. Return to your practice file and type in a new line of text: **Watch a cool movie**. Just as before, highlight the new text and click the folder icon on the Properties Inspector. The movie file is located in your Exercises folder for this module and is called cool_movie.mov. Select the file, choose whether or not to copy it into your root folder, and then preview the document in your browser. You should see a "cinematic masterpiece"—like the one shown here—created with Flash and converted to the QuickTime format.

12. Sounds and movies are great, but what if you need a way to convey printed documents across the Web in a way that ensures that everyone who sees them will see, and be able to print, the same thing? For this type of task, the tool of choice is Adobe Acrobat, a text and image conversion program that lets you take any printed document and change it to a format that is read by the Adobe Acrobat Reader. Acrobat Reader is one of the most popular programs on the Web, because it is completely free of the compatibility and formatting problems inherent in HTML.

10

Note

If you don't have the Acrobat Reader installed on your system, you can download a copy for free from www.adobe.com. The program that allows you to *create* a PDF (Portable Document Format) file, however, has to be purchased from Adobe.

13. To create a link to an Acrobat document, repeat the steps previously outlined for linking to sounds and movies. Type in a line of text—**Read this cool story**—and locate the file called story.pdf in the Exercises folder. Once again, preview the page in your browser and click the link. Assuming you have the Acrobat Reader installed, the program will open and display the file.

14. You can try experimenting further with this sample file as you wish. For now, this concludes this project and you can save or discard this practice file.

While these examples provide just a glimpse of the capabilities of linking to and embedding files that are read by plug-ins, you now have a good understanding of how both operations are handled by Dreamweaver. Multimedia files can add a great deal of interest and functionality to your site, but their use should be considered carefully. Since plug-ins may require a level of expertise that your viewers do not possess, always consider your audience before using plug-ins.

1-Minute Drill

● What two methods can be used for placing an audio file into a web page?

● What is the function of a plug-in?

Ask the Expert

Question: Where can I get more information about file types and the plug-ins that read them?

Answer: To stay current on the use of plug-ins and the files associated with them, visit the Plug-In Plaza at Browserwatch (browserwatch.internet.com/plug-in/plug-in-mm.html) or try Netscape's plug-in page (home.netscape.com/plugins/). It is important to have an understanding of how different plug-ins respond in different versions of browsers and on different operating systems, especially if you plan to use file types that are new or not widely supported.

● Audio files can be embedded in or linked to a web page.
● A plug-in is a helper application that extends the capability of a browser by handling file types that the browser cannot handle.

What to Take Away

In this module, you have seen some very sophisticated operations at work that give you the capability of taking your site to new levels of interactivity with your clients. With client-side programming—such as JavaScript—you saw how the type of code that is embedded into the HTML of a document uses the viewer's computer to generate automatic messages, check browsers, and even format and send an e-mail form.

With regard to server-side programming—such as CGI—you received an introduction to how Dreamweaver enables a page to be designed with forms and how the parameters are set in preparation for the final coding that makes this advanced type of interaction possible.

Finally, you have also received an introduction to how files that require a helper application—called a plug-in—can also be inserted into documents, either as a link or as an automatically opening embedded object.

Taken together, these three technologies can extend the capabilities of your site in new and dynamic ways, opening a two-way communication channel between yourself and (hopefully) the many people who will be visiting your web site.

☑ *Mastery Check*

1. What are the two types of information processing that are employed in the use of forms and scripts?

2. Why is the use of JavaScript for sending e-mail information discouraged?

3. What symbol does Dreamweaver use to indicate the presence of a <form> tag?

4. Why do form objects in a web page require their own unique name?

5. How are new extensions for Dreamweaver found?

6. What is the Adobe Acrobat program used for?

Part 2

Graphics Creation
and Optimization
with Fireworks 4

Module 11

An Introduction to Fireworks 4

The Goals of this Module

- Understand Fireworks' unique capabilities as applied to web design
- Review vector and bitmap image types
- Explore the Fireworks interface
- Understand the functions of Fireworks tools
- Preview Fireworks panels

In the previous modules of this book, you have been taken through a whirlwind tour of HTML and the Dreamweaver interface. Let's face it—working with HTML and Dreamweaver, even as thoughtfully as the program has been designed, is a very challenging task. Between the inconsistencies of browsers, lack of support for all available coding features, the unpredictability of using tables and cells, and the often maddening way that pages have to be designed and redesigned when an element changes, working on a web page can often be a real pain.

You'll be glad to know that for the second part of this book, you'll have the opportunity to do something that is just flat-out fun—work with the best tool available for creating graphics for the Web, Fireworks 4. No more difficult concepts to grasp, no more exploration of obscure code, and no more worries about what will and won't work on a web page. Fireworks makes working with graphics simple, intuitive, and, compared to working with HTML, really easy. Still, the features that come with Fireworks will allow you to create some exceptionally sophisticated effects, and while you will need some time to become comfortable with the Fireworks interface, once you've had the chance to work through the projects found in the last half of this book, you'll find yourself feeling incredibly comfortable doing the kinds of image creation and manipulations that you may never have thought possible. Fireworks is a terrific tool, and you'll get started right away by reviewing the two types of graphics formats that Fireworks uses to complete its work, which will be followed by a look at the Fireworks interface.

Vectors and Bitmaps: A Review

In Module 6, you were introduced to the two types of formats that are used to create computer graphics—vectors and bitmaps. Fireworks was the first program on the market (and remains the best) to seamlessly provide the ability to work in both formats, often within the same document. This means that whenever you wish to create a new document and use the drawing capabilities of a vector image, you will be able to draw and transform objects freely. Meanwhile, if you need to work on a bitmapped image, such as a photograph, you will find that switching to a mode that allows you to work in that manner is as easy as clicking a button and using a different set of tools. You'll quickly come to appreciate this ability to work in both graphics worlds and the way that Fireworks accomplishes these tasks.

Vectors and Paths

You may recall from the discussion of images in Module 6 that a vector image is one that is created by a series of mathematical equations that describe the location and color of the object on the canvas. Vector-based images can very easily be modified, moved, combined, and manipulated in ways that are not possible with bitmaps. The majority of your work in Fireworks will be accomplished using vectors because of the ease with which images can be created and changed to suit your needs.

The equations that you create when working with a vector-based image are known as *paths*. In effect, a path is just like a path through the woods—there is a starting and ending point, and along the way the path can have different characteristics, such as being straight or curved, providing a bench to sit on, or featuring a scenic overlook. Vector images create paths in the same way. A starting point is defined, followed by points along the path that can have different characteristics such as varying line thickness, different colors, or even a combination of paths that join objects in new ways. Figure 11-1 shows a vector image with a common path type—a line—that has been modified in five different ways.

Bitmaps

Bitmap images, also called raster images, create graphics by describing a grid and then filling each square in the graphic with a single color. You know these squares as pixels—the same pixels that are used by computer monitors to display information. In Figure 11-2, you see a portion of the same five lines originally created with vectors, but now converted to a bitmap image and magnified. The individual pixels are easy to see in this magnification.

Fireworks allows you to work in either a vector or bitmap mode, and in the latter, you are actually modifying the pixels themselves, and not the lines and curves that are described in a vector image. You may also remember that bitmap images are dependent on the resolution of the monitor that is used to view them, and that changing a bitmap image, especially enlarging it, will often lead to ragged edges and poor quality.

11

Fireworks' Native File Format—PNG

Files that you create in Fireworks use the Portable Network Graphics format—PNG (pronounced "ping")—but in this case, the format is different

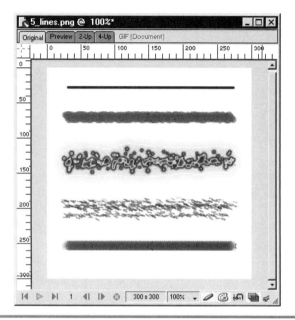

Figure 11-1 Vectors allow for the application of a wide range of styles and effects even when the original path is the same

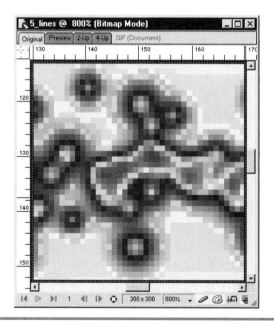

Figure 11-2 Bitmap images use color-filled squares, called pixels, to define an image

Ask the Expert

Question: Why should bitmaps be used at all then?

Answer: It's true that the majority of original work you create in Fireworks will be done in vector editing mode, but there will be those times when you need to work in bitmap mode. Working with images that come as part of a clipart gallery, with images that you capture with a scanner, or with photographs needs to be done in bitmap mode, to work directly with the pixels themselves. In addition, you will almost always export your original Fireworks files to a more web-friendly GIF or JPEG format that is suitable for use on the Web. You can return to Module 6 for a more complete discussion of the types of image files that are used in web pages.

from the PNG files that you learned about in Module 6. While ordinary PNG files can be read by most web browsers, the PNG files that you create when using Fireworks are not suitable for use on a web page because of the extra information that Fireworks creates and tracks as you work on an image document. As you'll learn, Fireworks maintains a library of styles and effects for each object that you create in image documents, and the information that is stored along with the image itself can create large file sizes that would lead to long download times if they were inserted on a web page. For example, the image in Figure 11-1 is over 70KB in size, while the optimized GIF file in Figure 11-2 is only 14KB. Optimizing and exporting Fireworks files from their native PNG format to a more web-friendly version that still maintains the visual quality of the original is something that you will become quite accustomed to.

11

Tip

Create and maintain a folder on your web site for your original Fireworks files and always keep those original images there. Since Fireworks PNG files can become quite large, you may not even want to post those files to your server, but instead only post those that are optimized and in use on your web pages. Keeping the originals in a separate location gives you the option of saving storage space on the server by keeping your working files on your local computer, and allows you to more easily locate the originals if you need to make revisions.

1-Minute Drill

- How are vector images created?
- How are bitmap images created?
- What is the native file format for Fireworks files?

Exploring the Fireworks Interface

In version 4 of Fireworks, the software designers at Macromedia have taken another huge step toward creating an interface that more closely aligns the different programs available in their product line. Just as in Dreamweaver, Fireworks uses a series of floating panels that can be moved, modified, and opened or closed, as they are needed. In the same way that you (hopefully) became accustomed to using Dreamweaver's Properties Inspector, Objects panel, and Assets panel, Fireworks uses a series of panels that allow you to apply, select, and draw objects on a canvas, apply special effects, optimize your image, and perform advanced operations such as creating animations. Figure 11-3 displays the Fireworks work area and its separate components.

The first time you open Fireworks, you may feel a little intimidated, especially if all of the separate panels are open. There are an almost dizzying array of different panels, settings, and effects that can be applied. The key thing to remember is that, just as in Dreamweaver, you don't need to use every panel, and you don't even need to have them open until there is a particular operation you need to perform.

Tip

Since you'll be looking at the panels and inspectors as part of the projects in upcoming modules, you should click the Close button in the upper-right corner of each of the panels on the right side of your screen to hide them. This gives you plenty of room on your screen without the distraction of all of those open windows.

- Vector images are created by a series of mathematical equations that describe the location and color of the object on the canvas.
- Bitmap images create graphics by describing a grid and then filling each square in the graphic with a single color.
- Files that you create in Fireworks use the Portable Network Graphics (PNG) format, but include additional information beyond that found in a standard PNG image.

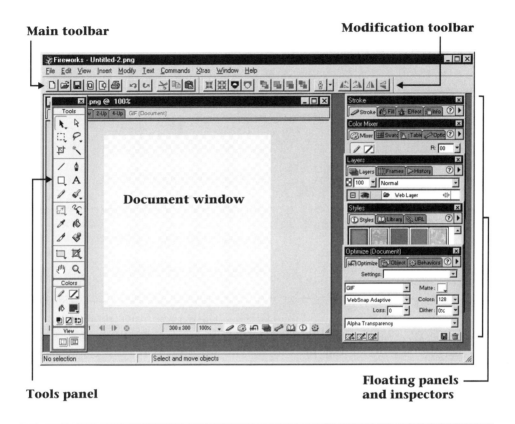

Main toolbar

Modification toolbar

Document window

Tools panel

Floating panels
and inspectors

Figure 11-3 | Fireworks uses the same floating panel interface as other
Macromedia products

Also note that Fireworks has no Document window present when you first
open the program. Your first step, then, is to choose File | New so that you can
follow along with the descriptions of the different features that will be summarized
here. Accept the default settings for this first file and click OK, or use the settings
shown in Figure 11-4.

11

The Tools Panel

As in any drawing program, the tools that are used to create different objects on
a canvas are at the heart of the software. Fireworks uses a floating panel with an

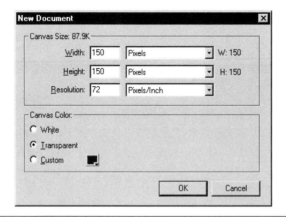

Figure 11-4 The New Document dialog box contains settings such as canvas size and color

arrangement of tools that you may find unusual at first. To save screen real estate, many of the primary tools have additional functions that are accessed by a flyout menu, represented by a small triangle to the right of the tool icon. To access the flyout menu, simply click the triangle and hold on top of the primary icon until the additional tools appear.

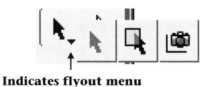

Indicates flyout menu

Otherwise, if you have used any type of drawing or painting program in the past, you will recognize many of the icons that are located in the Tools panel. Figure 11-5 shows the Tools panel and the names of the primary tools that are found there.

Notice that the icons have been grouped into different categories and are separated by a gray line that divides the Tools panel. You'll find this feature helpful as you start working with the program and as you follow this discussion of how the different tools are put into action.

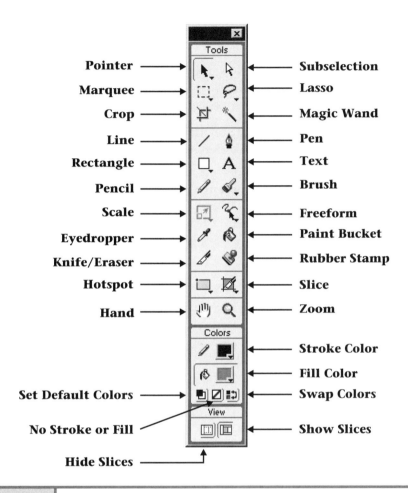

Pointer	Subselection
Marquee	Lasso
Crop	Magic Wand
Line	Pen
Rectangle	Text
Pencil	Brush
Scale	Freeform
Eyedropper	Paint Bucket
Knife/Eraser	Rubber Stamp
Hotspot	Slice
Hand	Zoom
	Stroke Color
	Fill Color
Set Default Colors	Swap Colors
No Stroke or Fill	Show Slices
Hide Slices	

Figure 11-5   Fireworks' Tools panel and icons

11

Selection Tools

At the top of the panel are the six icons that represent selection tools, used for choosing an object on your canvas so it can be modified, copied, deleted, or moved. In addition to the three primary icons that are represented by default, three of these objects also have flyouts that will lead you to additional tools.

Note

As you read through this section, feel free to try the tools in the blank document you created earlier. You can also find a Fireworks PNG file for practicing in vector mode (5_lines.png) and a GIF file for practicing in bitmap mode (5_lines.gif) in the exercise files for this module at www.osborne.com.

Table 11-1 provides a summary of the primary tools available in the selection group. Those tools marked with an asterisk are available through flyouts.

Selection Tool	Appearance	Function
Pointer		Selects an entire object on the canvas so that it can be modified or moved.
Select Behind*		Selects an object that is behind another object on the canvas.
Export Area*		Chooses an area of an image for export to GIF or JPEG format.
Subselection		Allows the selection of individual points along a vector path and selection of an individual item within a group.
Marquee		Selects a rectangular area in a bitmap image.
Oval Marquee*		Selects an oval area in a bitmap image.
Lasso		Selects an irregular area in a bitmap image.
Polygon Lasso*		Selects an irregular area in a bitmap image with straight lines.
Crop		Selects a portion of an image that will remain when the remainder of the image is cropped (deleted) in vector mode.
Magic Wand		Automatically selects an area of a bitmap image based on similar color properties.

Table 11-1 Selection Tools in the Fireworks Tools Panel

Drawing Tools
Below the selection group is the drawing group, which consists of the primary tools for drawing objects on your canvas and for adding text.

Once again, flyouts (marked by an asterisk) provide additional tools for two of these objects. Table 11-2 summarizes the appearance and functions of the tools in the drawing group.

Editing Tools
Tools that enable you to modify a selected object are grouped below the drawing tools.

Drawing Tool	Appearance	Function
Line		Draws a straight line between two points.
Pen		Draws a series of points and connects the points with a line.
Rectangle		Draws a rectangle with a filled center.
Rounded Rectangle*		Draws a rectangle with rounded corners.
Oval*		Draws a round object.
Polygon*		Draws a polygon or star based on options set for the tool.
Pencil		Draws a freeform line that is 1 pixel wide by default.
Paintbrush		Draws a freeform line with attributes that can be changed in the Stroke panel.
Redraw path*		Reshapes vector paths drawn with the Brush tool.

11

Table 11-2   Drawing Tools in the Fireworks Tools Panel

Table 11-3 summarizes these tools that are used for making modifications to objects or entire images. Notice that the two topmost icons include flyouts, listed here with asterisks.

Editing Tool	Appearance	Function
Scale		Makes an object or a portion of an image larger or smaller, rotates it.
Skew*		Stretches or shrinks an object along a plane.
Distort*		Distorts an object by dragging handles in different ways.
Freeform		Reshapes paths in an image by pushing or pulling them.
Reshape Area*		Reshapes a selected area within an image.
Path Scrubber*		Changes characteristics of paths drawn with a pressure option.
Eyedropper		"Grabs" color from anywhere on the screen.
Paint Bucket		Fills an object with the color currently selected in the Fill Color option.
Knife		Slices a path into two or more paths while in vector mode. The tool icon changes automatically when the work mode is changed.
Eraser		Removes pixels when in bitmap mode. The tool icon changes automatically when the work mode is changed.
Rubber Stamp		Duplicates one area of an image onto another area.

Table 11-3   Editing Tools in the Fireworks Tools Panel

Hotspot and Slice Tools

Below the drawing tool group is a set of tools specifically designed for web-related tasks—hotspots and slices.

Hotspots are areas of an image that can have a URL assigned to them for use as a link in a web page. An image that contains hotspots is known as an *image map*. While the hotspot itself is invisible to the viewer of the web page, Fireworks applies a special overlay that allows you to track and modify its location. Slices are used to divide a large object into multiple smaller objects that assist in creating faster downloads when inserted into a web page. These tools are summarized in Table 11-4. Both have flyout options indicated by an asterisk.

 ## Panning and Zooming Tools

The next group of tools is used for changing how you view the image you are working with.

While they are not used for adding or changing anything in the document, you'll find these tools, summarized in Table 11-5, to be handy features when you need to change how you look at an object on your canvas.

 ## Color Tools

As you would expect, Fireworks has a huge number of options available for adjusting the color and color properties of images. Still, the controls that access the color options are neatly arranged into a nice tight area of the Tools panel.

Hotspot/Slice Tool	Appearance	Function
Hotspot		Draws a rectangular hotspot on an image.
Circular Hotspot*		Draws a circular hotspot on an image.
Polygon Hotspot*		Draws an irregularly shaped hotspot on an image.
Rectangle Slice		Divides an image into rectangular slices.
Polygon Slice*		Divides an image into irregular slices.

11

Table 11-4   Hotspot and Slice Tools in the Fireworks Tools Panel

Panning and Zooming Tool	Appearance	Function
Pan		"Grabs" an image and move the canvas around within the Document window.
Zoom		Changes the magnification of an image either larger or smaller.

Table 11-5 Panning and Zooming Tools in the Fireworks Tools Panel

The most commonly used items are easily accessed from the color group on the Tools panel, summarized here in Table 11-6.

Rather than use flyout arrows, additional color options are accessed by clicking an expansion arrow that leads to dialog boxes that are identical to those found in Dreamweaver. With these options, you can choose from the standard palette of web-safe colors that is presented by default, or open your system Color Chooser and use a custom color that you specify. Of course, you now know that custom colors that are not web-safe may not display properly when seen on the Web, so some caution is necessary when making choices that are not listed in the web-safe palette of colors.

Color Tools	Appearance	Function
Stroke Color		Sets the colors of lines and curves (paths).
Fill Color		Sets the interior color of closed vector shapes.
Set Default Colors		Returns stroke and fill colors to their default settings, set by choosing Edit | Preferences.
No Stroke or Fill		Turns off the color in a selected stroke or fill.
Swap Colors		Swaps the color settings for stroke and fill objects.

Table 11-6 Color Tools in the Fireworks Tools Panel

You'll also undoubtedly recognize your old friend the Eyedropper tool. Just as with Dreamweaver, the Eyedropper tool can be used to grab any color found on your screen and use that selection as a fill or stroke color. You'll also recognize the expansion arrow in the color selection box that leads to other options. Again, these options mirror those seen previously when working with colors in Dreamweaver.

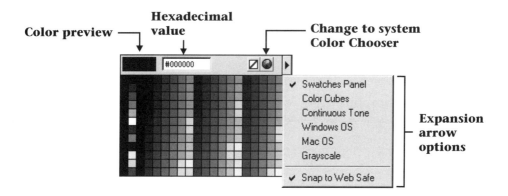

Hide and Show Slices

The final two buttons on the Tools panel are used to hide or show the overlays that Fireworks creates when hotspots or slices are created in a document. There's nothing magical here. Choose the

Ask the Expert

Question: I've used Photoshop (or Freehand, or CorelDraw, or Illustrator) in the past, and Fireworks doesn't seem to have as many drawing options available. Why is that?

Answer: Macromedia never set out to create the most sophisticated drawing and image manipulation tool possible when Fireworks was designed. Remember that Fireworks has one mission—to produce the best (and smallest) images possible for use on the Web. While other programs may have more sophisticated features available, Fireworks excels at the task it was designed to do—create and optimize graphics for use in web pages. Meanwhile, if you're more comfortable working in other drawing and painting programs, Fireworks makes it easy to import those graphics and then optimize them for the Web.

11

button on the left to hide the markers or choose the button on the right to view them. Enough said.

While the possible options available on the Tools panel may seem a bit daunting, not every tool is something that you will use in everyday practice. The cleanly organized interface is something that you'll come to appreciate, though, and with practice, you will quickly find yourself confidently reaching for just the right tool when you need to get a particular job done.

1-Minute Drill

- What tool is used for selecting objects in a document?
- How does Fireworks make it possible to access additional tools that are grouped together with a particular icon?
- What is a hotspot?

The Document Window

The Document window contains the canvas on which all work is performed in Fireworks, plus some specialized options along the bottom of the window that allow you to jump to the modification panels and change the magnification of the image. The Document window is fairly intuitive, and in Fireworks 4, it bears a striking resemblance to the Document window of Dreamweaver. Since you will be spending time modifying documents, canvas size, and canvas colors in succeeding modules, Figure 11-6 serves as an overview of the different components of the Document window.

Two components of the Document window bear emphasis at this point. Notice in Figure 11-6 that a hatched line (blue and black onscreen) borders the image and that a circle (red) with an X appears in the bottom of the window. This is your visual clue that this image is a bitmap and that Fireworks is editing in that mode.

You'll also notice a series of tabs across the top of the document that allow you to see different previews of how an exported document would appear when optimized and converted to a JPEG or GIF file. You will learn about using these features in Module 16.

- The Pointer (selection) tool is used to select a single object on the canvas.
- Fireworks uses flyout arrows to indicate the presence of additional tools available behind the icon on the Tools panel. Clicking the flyout arrow makes the additional tools accessible.
- A hotspot is an area of an image that can have a URL assigned to it for use as a link in a web page.

Preview tabs

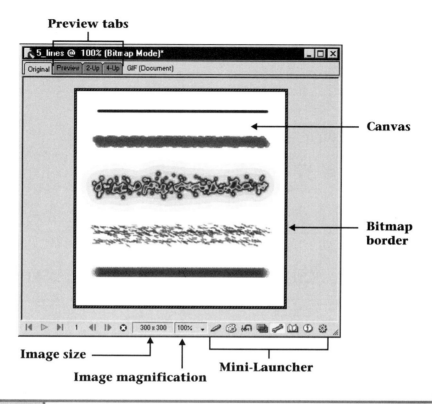

Canvas

Bitmap border

Image size

Image magnification

Mini-Launcher

Figure 11-6 The Document window contains options for changing magnification and for launching modification panels

Additional Options

You have now been introduced to the two most frequently used components of the Fireworks work environment—the Tools panel and the Document window. The great majority of your tasks will be accomplished while working between these two areas of the Fireworks interface, but, as you'd expect, a significant number of additional options are available.

The Menu Bar

Like almost every other computer application, Fireworks includes the usual menu bar across the top of your screen, with the usual array of tools—Print, Save, Save As, Copy, Cut, and Paste. Rather than go into a detailed description

11

of the commands and options available in the menu bar, you will have the opportunity to employ those tools in upcoming exercises. A whole host of additional options are available through the menu bar that relate to Fireworks' primary mission of creating graphics for the Web, and by completing hands-on projects, you'll quickly become comfortable with these tools.

Main and Modification Toolbars (Windows Only)

In the Windows OS version of Fireworks, two toolbars are available directly below the menu bar—the Main toolbar and the Modification toolbar. The Macintosh version does not include these features. If these toolbars are not visible in your program, choose Window | Toolbars to display or hide these features.

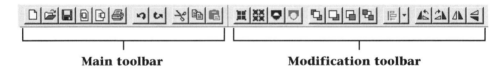

Main toolbar   **Modification toolbar**

In the Main toolbar, you will find buttons common to most programs available in a Windows program—Open, New, Save, Print, and Undo functions can all be found in this area. On the Modification toolbar, you'll find options that are useful when working with a variety of objects on your canvas, including options to combine (group) and arrange objects in a variety of ways.

Context Menu

As with Dreamweaver, additional options can be accessed by right-clicking (CONTROL-clicking with a Macintosh) a selected option in the Document window. Many of these features mirror those found on the menu bar, and include commands to magnify, hide, arrange, animate, and convert objects on the canvas.

Whether you choose to access the commands available from the menu bar, from one of the toolbars, or from the context menu will ultimately be based on your preferred method for working. As you work through the exercises in upcoming modules, the different choices available will be detailed as you move along.

1-Minute Drill

- What is the name of the work area in the Document window?
- What is the function of the tabs across the top of the Document window?
- How is the context menu accessed?

What to Take Away

Fireworks is the first image creation application built from the ground up with the goal of preparing and optimizing graphics for the Web. With an impressive array of tools for creating and manipulating images and then exporting them to web-safe graphics formats, Fireworks makes it possible to create sophisticated images, all while keeping in mind the simple fact that every image needs to be as small as possible to keep download times to a minimum.

In addition to the basic drawing and optimizing tools you have been introduced to in this module, Fireworks also provides the capability to create HTML documents and images enhanced with JavaScript capabilities, as well as tools for authoring web-specific images such as animations, buttons, and drop-down menus.

As you move through the projects included in upcoming modules, you will be introduced to many of these advanced features as well as all of the tools you will need to be a confident user of the program. Fireworks makes the life of a web designer easier by making it possible to create and optimize graphics, animations, image maps, and other images that can make your web pages more useful and interesting for your viewers. Combine its ease-of-use with the excellent integration Fireworks has with Dreamweaver, and you'll quickly come to appreciate why the program has become one of the favorites of web developers everywhere.

11

- The work area in the Document window is known as the canvas.
- The tabs across the top of the Document window allow you to see different previews of how an exported document would appear when optimized and converted to a JPEG or GIF file.
- The context menu is accessed by right-clicking (CONTROL-clicking with a Macintosh) a selected object in the document window.

✓ Mastery Check

1. What is the primary function of Fireworks?

2. Why are files created in Fireworks exported to another image format?

3. How are the different tools in the Tools panel organized?

4. Why should caution be exercised when selecting colors from your system Color Chooser options?

5. What is the purpose of "slicing" an image?

Module 12

Working with Bitmap Images

The Goals of this Module

- Create a new Fireworks document
- Explore bitmap selection tools
- Import bitmap images into a document
- Understand the use of marquee and magic wand tools
- Modify image and canvas sizes
- Explore options for edge controls with bitmap images
- Use bitmap painting tools

Fireworks is one of the few programs that allows you to switch seamlessly between the bitmap world of GIF and JPEG images commonly used for the Web and the world of vector-based drawing. This ability gives you the ultimate in flexibility. When you need to work with a photograph, scanned image, or clipart file, Fireworks allows you to select sections of the image and work directly with the bitmaps that compose it. And when you need to add text, create your own drawing, or even build buttons with JavaScript rollovers, then it's time to crank up the drawing tools and get to work. In either mode, Fireworks provides the tools to get the job done.

In this module, you will learn how to work with bitmap images—how to select areas of an image, crop an image, combine images together, and import graphics from another format. All of these tasks are ones that will become a regular part of your graphics repertoire, and they serve as a good introduction to the capabilities of Fireworks. Of course, before you can get to work, you need a document to work with, and so your first project will explore the options available when creating and modifying a Fireworks document.

Project 12-1: Creating and Modifying Fireworks Documents

Fireworks has a number of options available for the creation of a new document right from the start of the process, as well as many ways that the work area—called the canvas—can be modified once a project is underway. In this first exercise, you will go through the steps of creating a new Fireworks document, see how the canvas and image can be modified, and pick up some valuable tips along the way.

Note

Be sure that you have downloaded the exercise files for this module from www.osborne.com and stored them in your Exercises folder.

Step-by-Step

1. As noted in the previous module, Fireworks does not automatically open a document when the program first starts. Choose File | New to go to the New Document dialog box, shown in Figure 12-1.

2. This dialog box has three purposes: to set the size of the document in width and height, to set the resolution of the document, and to establish the color

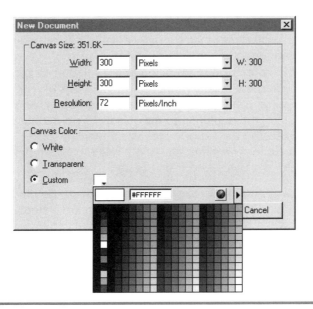

Figure 12-1 The New Document dialog box is displayed every time a new
Fireworks file is created

of the canvas itself. The subsequent steps look at how these options are
adjusted and the effect the settings can have.

3. Width and height aren't too hard, are they? By default, Fireworks presents
this information in pixels, and since you have carefully planned your web
page (right?), you know the exact size in pixels of any graphic you need for
one of your pages before you design it. For this first document, set the width
and height of this new file to the settings you see in Figure 12-1.

4. You may find that you get so accustomed to using Fireworks that you want
to create a document for print rather than the Web. In that case, you could
set the width and height in inches or centimeters, rather than pixels, to conform
to a specific paper size. To do so, simply click the drop-down arrow next to
the unit of measurement and highlight the option you want. Be sure to change
the unit first, and then set the value; otherwise, you may get some highly
unusual results.

5. To use a predetermined size suitable for a web page, you can even choose
Commands | Panel Layout Sets to access three canvas sizes that match the
three most common monitor resolution settings (1024×768, 1280×1024,
800×600). For this project, though, keep your settings set to those shown
in Figure 12-1.

12

6. Once you have determined the size, the next step is to choose the resolution of the image in pixels per inch (ppi). By default, this setting is 72 ppi, a suitable setting for an image that is to be displayed on a computer screen, since almost all monitors are restricted to a resolution no higher than 96 ppi, with 72 ppi being the most common. Why pack lots of extra pixels into an image, increasing its file size, if your viewers won't be able to see them anyway? Keeping the resolution to the default 72 ppi setting can go a long way toward keeping the exported file size down. Of course, if you were creating a document for print, you might need to experiment with this setting, but for the Web, 72 ppi is just fine.

7. The final setting determines the canvas color. Again, nothing too tricky here, except the option to make the canvas transparent. To create a transparent background when the file is ultimately exported to a GIF or JPEG format, you will need to begin with a transparent background at the beginning or change to a transparent background later on. Your other options are to use white, or use the Color Chooser, as shown earlier in Figure 12-1, to pick a custom color. For this project, set your canvas color to white.

8. That's it for settings for now. Click OK and save the file as **flower_practice**, accepting the default file type—Fireworks PNG.

Tip

Create a subfolder in your Exercises folder for each module, and you'll be able to more easily go back and review your work later on.

9. Resize your window so that you have some gray area around the canvas, as shown in Figure 12-2. This "negative area" around the canvas is a tool in itself. Use it when you want to drag images off the canvas so they can be rearranged. Also, whenever you have an object selected on the canvas, a handy way to unselect it is to click in the negative area of the Document window.

10. You open a file in Fireworks in the same way you open any other document—choose File | Open. In this case, the file you want to open is called rose_1.jpg, and you'll find it in the Exercises folder for this module.

Note

Whenever a file is opened in Fireworks, it is automatically converted to a Fireworks PNG format. If you were to save the file now, the correct format would be the native PNG format for Fireworks. To convert it back to a JPEG or GIF format, you would export the file, as you'll learn to do in Module 16.

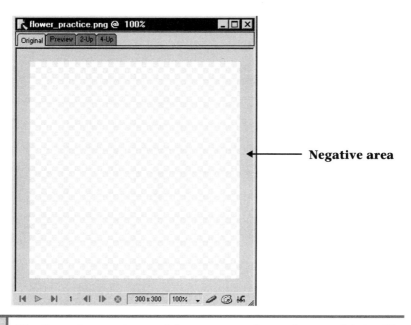

Negative area

Figure 12-2   The "negative area" around the canvas can be used as a tool in itself

11. Typically, a new document that is opened will overlay any documents in the work area. To see some of the available options in working with your files, slide the image of the rose to the right so that it is viewable side by side with flower_practice.png, as shown in Figure 12-3.

12. There are a few differences in the appearance of the two files. Notice in Figure 12-3 that the JPEG image of the rose has a blue and black striped border around the document, and a Stop button in red at the bottom of the screen. The striped border around the image lets you know that you are in bitmap mode, while clicking the Stop button allows you to switch back to vector mode.

13. To return to bitmap mode, double-click the image, or choose one of the bitmap editing tools available from the Tools panel.

14. In the next operation, you will create a copy of the original rose image on the adjacent canvas by dragging the rose from one canvas to the other. Simply drag the rose from the original image, and Fireworks will generate a copy of the image and place it onto your practice canvas when you release the mouse button. It doesn't get any easier that that! When you are finished,

12

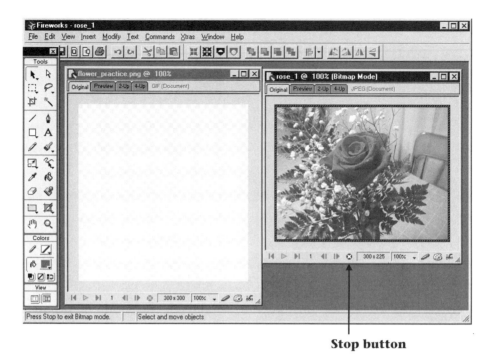

Stop button

Figure 12-3   Arrange the separate windows in the Fireworks work area so both files can be worked on simultaneously

you should have two identical copies of the original image side by side, as shown in Figure 12-4.

15. You can see in Figure 12-4 that the canvas in the practice file is a little too large. Fireworks has a great way to deal with this—choose Modify | Trim Canvas to have Fireworks cut the canvas size down to the smallest possible dimension.

16. Canvases and images can be modified once they are open by choosing other options available in the Modify menu—Image Size, Canvas Size, and Canvas Color. Start by choosing Modify | Image Size at the top of the Modify menu to open the Modify Image dialog box, shown in Figure 12-5.

17. Notice that the Constrain Proportions check box is checked and that lock proportions icons appear next to the Pixel Dimensions and Print Size listings. This ensures that any change that is made to the image will keep the dimensions set to their original proportions, eliminating the distortion to the image that would occur if this option were not selected. Try changing the dimensions of

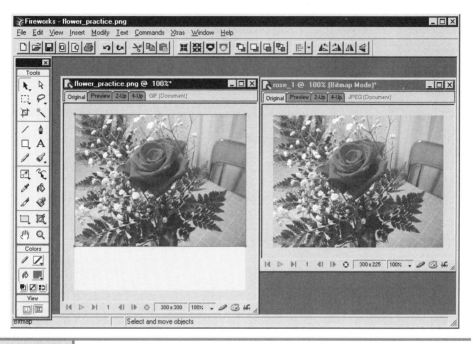

Figure 12-4 Fireworks makes it extremely easy to copy images from one document to another

the image to 200 pixels wide with the proportions constrained, and then to 150 pixels wide with that option turned off. You'll then see how these settings affect the image. Click the Undo button twice (or choose Edit | Undo) to return the image to its original dimensions.

18. When the image size is changed, the entire image changes. But what if you want to have a smaller canvas but keep the image of the rose as it is? For this operation, you could change the canvas size. Try this now by selecting Modify | Canvas size and setting the dimensions as you see here. Click OK when you are finished.

12

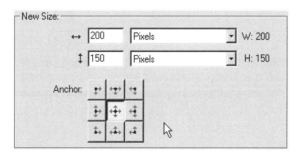

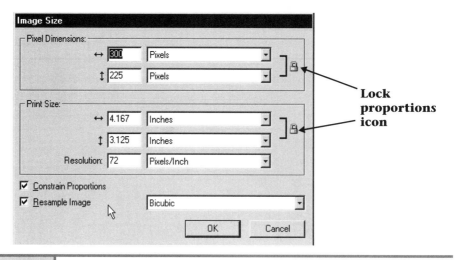

Lock
proportions
icon

Figure 12-5 | The Modify Image dialog box

19. Fireworks trims the canvas size and leaves an image that has only the blossom from the rose on the canvas.

20. Finally, canvas color is changed by selecting Modify | Canvas Color and setting the color you'd like to use. For this exercise, leave the canvas transparent. You'll return to this option in a little while, but for now, you can see that the interface for choosing colors is the same one used elsewhere in Dreamweaver and Fireworks.

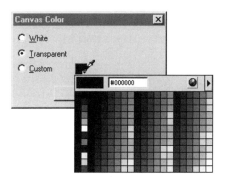

21. One last task—saving this file. Leave the filename as it is, click the Save button (or choose File | Save), and take a break.

As you'd expect with a top-notch graphics program, Fireworks gives you ultimate control over the creation of image files and the canvases on which they are created. Modifying and changing canvas and image sizes is equally easy, and Fireworks makes these tasks intuitive and simple to achieve.

1-Minute Drill

● What is the file format that is native to Fireworks?

● What is the standard resolution setting used when creating images for the Web?

● What visual aids does Fireworks provide to let you know you are working in bitmap editing mode?

Project 12-2: Modifying Bitmap Images

You have now seen two ways that an image can be transformed: by changing the canvas size or by changing the image size itself. So far so good, but for this next project, your task becomes a little more difficult—and a lot more satisfying. Using the bitmap selection tools available in the Tools panel, the rose in your practice file will take on a life of its own as you crop the image to exclude the

12

● The PNG format is native to Fireworks, but generally produces file sizes larger than standard PNG files because additional information is stored along with the image itself.

● For the Web, images are usually set at 72 pixels per inch (ppi).

● When in bitmap editing mode, a blue and black border is created around the canvas, and the Stop button at the bottom of the Document window turns red.

areas of the image that are unneeded and then modify the image in other ways as well. This is fun, so go ahead and get started.

Step-by-Step

1. Working in bitmap mode requires that a portion of the image first be selected. Unlike vectors, as you'll learn in the next module, you can't simply use the Pointer tool to select an object on the canvas. You must first define the bitmapped area that you want to work with and then perform your operations. Luckily, there are some great tools available at the top of the Tools panel to help in this process.

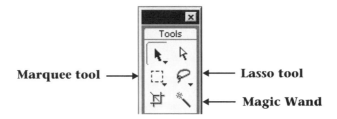

Marquee tool ——→ ←—— **Lasso tool**

←—— **Magic Wand**

Note

Be sure that you have open the practice file you created in the last project—flower_practice.png.

2. The first tool you'll try is the Marquee tool, and it's the simplest to use. This tool will create either a rectangular or oval selection area on the image based on the option you choose. Try an oval marquee first, drawing an oval marquee around the rose blossom as you see here. Once an area is selected, you will see the "marching ants" dashed line that dances around your selection.

Tip

Hold down the SHIFT key while dragging any oval tool in the Tools panel and you will draw a circle with equal height and width rather than an ellipse.

3. Now that part of the image is selected, you can create a new document that will only include the oval cutout of the rose. Fireworks has a slick method for getting this done. To see it in action, choose Edit | Copy to copy the selected area onto your computer's clipboard. As the image is copied, Fireworks will automatically record the exact canvas size that is necessary to hold this image.

4. To create a new image document to hold the rose blossom, choose File | New and notice that the canvas size has already been set. Accept the default canvas size and click OK. Pasting the copy of the rose you created earlier is a simple matter of choosing Edit | Paste (or right-clicking the canvas and choosing Edit | Paste from the context menu) and placing the copy onto the new canvas. Your finished product should appear as you see here.

5. To delete an object on the canvas, use the Pointer tool to select the entire image of the rose by clicking it, and then press the DELETE key. You can also try moving the image around the canvas by using the Pointer tool. Notice how it will snap into place as you near the edge of the canvas. When you're finished, you can save this document or close it without saving the changes.

6. Use the rectangle Marquee tool and repeat the process covered in steps 3 and 4 to select, copy, and then paste the rose blossom into a new document.

7. Marquee tools are great when you want to select a portion of a bitmap image in a rectangular or circular shape. To capture an irregularly shaped area, the tools to use are the two Lasso tools for selecting regular or polygon shaped areas of the document.

8. Return to the original copy of the rose_1.jpg file and select the regular Lasso tool.

9. With the regular Lasso tool selected, you can draw a freehand selection area around an object. Try it now by drawing around the outside edges of the rose blossom. Be sure that you close the circle you are drawing by returning to the starting point and overlapping the selection lines. When you are finished, release the mouse button to stop selecting areas of the image. As you've done

12

previously, copy the selection and paste it into a new document that you create. Your finished project should appear as you see here.

10. The Polygon Lasso tool is also used to select areas of an image, but rather than dragging the mouse to draw a circle, the Polygon Lasso tool is used by clicking the mouse button to define a series of points, which allows Fireworks to draw selection lines between the points. Just as with the regular Lasso tool, be sure to end your selection area as close to the starting point as possible. In this illustration, you see an example of how the Polygon Lasso tool might be used to create an unusual selection area.

11. Next up in your bag of tricks is one of the most interesting tools available—the Magic Wand. As the name implies, what it does can seem a little magical at times because the effects that can be created by using this tool are often very interesting. Essentially, the Magic Wand is able to discern areas of an image based on their colors, and then selects those with similar colors automatically.

12. Deselect any previously selected regions of the rose_1.jpg image you have been working on. Remember, to deselect all regions of an image, you need only click the Stop button at the bottom of the Document window. Using any of the bitmap tools with the image will then automatically take you back to bitmap editing mode.

13. Choose the Magic Wand tool and place your cursor on top of the rose blossom in the image. Click once and notice how the tool selects an irregular area that corresponds to the color of the area of the flower the tool is over when clicked. The image is magnified here for clarity.

14. Hold down the SHIFT key and select another area of the flower. The original selection remains while the new selection area is added. As long as you hold down the SHIFT key, you can move around the flower selecting multiple areas of the image. Try this now by selecting as much of the rose as possible. The result of this selection area when pasted into a new document would appear as you see here.

15. Changing the tolerance for color selections will allow a larger area of the image to be selected. To increase the tolerance of the color settings for the Magic Wand tool, you will need to access the Options panel for the Magic Wand. This panel is opened by double-clicking the magic wand icon in the Tools panel, or by choosing Window | Options. Set the tolerance for the tool to a value of 60 by moving the sliding bar up or by typing in 60 in the Tolerance box of the Options panel.

12

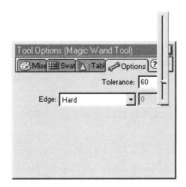

16. Return to the picture of the rose and try the Magic Wand again. Notice how a much larger portion of the image is selected when the color tolerance is changed. Once again, hold down the SHIFT key while making your selections to add selected regions of the rose. Once the object is pasted into a new document, the difference becomes even more noticeable.

Tip

You can drag a selected object directly from the source canvas onto a new canvas by using the pointer tool. While the original selection remains in place, a copy of the selected area will be pasted onto the other canvas.

---

17. Try changing the color of the canvas now by choosing Modify | Canvas Color and seeing what kinds of effects you can create just by changing the background color of the canvas that contains the rose blossom. By using the Eyedropper tool and selecting one of the colors on the rose itself, you can achieve a nice effect like the one shown here. If you wish, you can save this file or continue practicing on your own.

1-Minute Drill

● What is the first step necessary when working with objects in a bitmap format?

● What key is held down when you want to create a circle when using an oval tool?

● What panel is accessed to change the tolerance when using the Magic Wand tool?

Project 12-3: Controlling Edges in Bitmap Selections

Beyond simply selecting a region of a bitmap image for the purposes of copying the selection onto another document, Fireworks' tools also give you the opportunity to carefully control the output of the selection and create special effects as well. By using the Tool Options panel for the selection tool, you can control the appearance of the selected area by compensating for some of a bitmap format's limitations and by using an option called feathering. You'll see these options in action in this next exercise.

Step-by-Step

1. You have already seen the Options panel in action in your last project where you used it to change the Tolerance setting when using the Magic Wand tool, and you may have noticed the Edge option in the same panel. The key feature to remember when using tool options is that they must be set before the tool is put into use.

2. With the original copy of rose_1.jpg open in Fireworks, first choose the Oval Marquee tool by double-clicking its icon in the Tools panel. The Option panel for this tool should appear once the icon is double-clicked. You may

---

● When working with bitmap images, a region of the image must first be selected before it can be modified.

● Holding the SHIFT key down while using any oval tool will create a circle with equal width and height.

● The Options panel for the Magic Wand tool is used when you want to adjust the tolerance setting for the tool.

also open the panel by choosing Window I Options. By default, the settings for either of the marquee tools will appear as you see here.

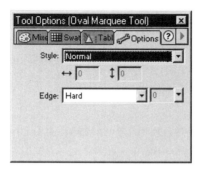

3. Create a new document and set the canvas size to approximately 150×120 pixels and set the canvas color to white. As you did in the previous project, select an oval area of the original image and copy it onto the new canvas. If you were to magnify this image to 400 percent, you could clearly see the jagged edge created when the Edge setting is left at its default Hard option. In technical terms, edges like this are said to be suffering from the "jaggies."

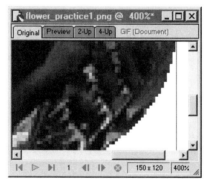

4. Try changing the Edge option to Anti-Alias—a setting that will reduce the jaggies by softening the edge of the selected area. Remember to set the option and then create a new selection with the Marquee tool before you paste the selection onto a blank canvas. Once again, magnified to 400 percent, you can now see that the edge is softer when the Anti-Alias setting is used.

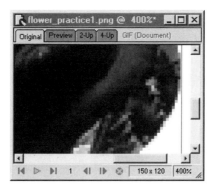

5. The final option for an edge setting is Feather. With the Feather option set, Fireworks will create a transition around the edges of the selection based on a width that you specify in the Options panel. By default, the Feather setting is set to 10 pixels in width.

6. Try this option now by once again selecting the Marquee tool, changing the edge option to Feather, selecting an oval area around the rose blossom, and then pasting the selection onto a blank canvas. The effect is really nice, and quite easy to achieve.

7. Feathering edges can create some terrific results, and hopefully you can see some of the creative possibilities immediately.

8. While feathered edges work best with the marquee tools, they can also be employed with both the lasso tools and the Magic Wand as well. However, setting a feathered edge will limit the area that you will be able to select, so using this option with lassos and the Magic Wand will take a little practice. For example, using the Polygon Lasso tool with feathered edges will round the edges of each selection area. However, you should quickly be able to create

12

interesting images with those tools in a short period of time, as seen here. When you are finished, you may want to save this document for later practice.

?Ask the Expert

Question: Anti-aliased images seem to look much better than those created with a hard edge. Should I use anti-aliasing all the time? Why does Fireworks set a hard edge as a default?

Answer: The big issue with anti-aliasing relates to file sizes. Every time an image is anti-aliased (or when feathered edges are created), extra pixels are added around the outside edges of the bitmap to smooth things out. Of course, as pixels and colors are added, the file size grows larger, and since part of Fireworks' mission is to keep file sizes as small as possible, a hard edge is the default setting. My personal preference is to always anti-alias edges and then work with the image to optimize its size in other ways, as you'll learn to do in Module 16.

Project 12-4: Painting with Bitmaps

Selecting and copying portions of a bitmap image certainly allows for some great ways to control and modify the appearance of an image, but Fireworks' capabilities also include the option of painting new bitmaps onto the canvas by adding lines, shapes, or brushstrokes to the image. In addition, areas of an image can also be "erased" by painting pixels onto the image that match the color of the canvas. Those tools will be covered in this next exercise.

Step-by-Step

1. Once again, start by creating a new document to practice with in this project. Make the canvas size 150×120 pixels and set the canvas color to white. Select an oval portion of the rose blossom and paste a copy of your selection onto the new document. Once your rose is in place, double-click the canvas to change to bitmap editing mode. You should see the blue and black border around the canvas and the active Stop button when you have switched editing modes.

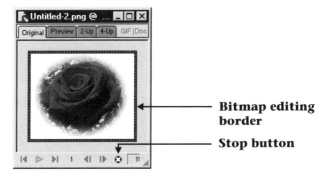

Bitmap editing border

Stop button

2. It is important to be sure that you are in bitmap editing mode before you proceed, because the appearance and function of the tools in the Tools panel will change based on whether you are editing with bitmaps or vectors. With your new document in bitmap editing mode, the Tools panel will appear as you see in Figure 12-6 (the tools you will use for this exercise are labeled).

3. The first tool to try is the Line tool. There's nothing mysterious about this tool—it simply paints a line of colored pixels onto the canvas, based on the color settings chosen at the bottom of the Tools panel. Set the Line Color to red and draw a box around your image by clicking and dragging the tool to create four individual lines.

12

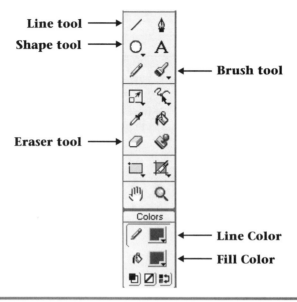

Line tool →

Shape tool →

Brush tool ←

Eraser tool →

Line Color ←

Fill Color ←

| **Figure 12-6** | The Tools panel when in bitmap editing mode |

Tip

Hold down the SHIFT key while dragging the Line tool across the image to create a straight horizontal line. Hold the SHIFT key down while dragging up or down to create a straight vertical line.

4. Once bitmaps are painted onto an image, they are fixed in place as part of the bitmap object, and cannot be selected with the Pointer tool, as you would be able to do with a vector object. To remove these lines, or to correct lines that you don't like, you will have to choose Edit | Undo or use the Undo button on the toolbar at the top of the Fireworks window.

Undo button

5. Shapes are added to a bitmap image in the same way, except that with bitmap shapes, both a line and a fill are created. Choose the Rectangle tool and draw a small box at the bottom of the image, as you see next.

6. The line and fill colors of shapes are set by using the color options at the bottom of the Tools panel. As with tool options, these colors are set before you begin using the tool. However, in the case of fill colors, the color can be changed once the object is on the canvas, by using the Paint Bucket tool. Try this now by selecting a new fill color, selecting the paint bucket icon from the Tools panel, and then clicking inside the rectangle that you created in the previous step.

Tip

If you want to create a box with no fill color, use the No Color option (the rectangle with a red slash) before you draw the object. Once a fill color is applied to a bitmap image, you cannot change it back to a transparent fill with the Paint Bucket tool.

7. Brush strokes are a great way to create interesting effects with a bitmap image because of the many ways that the tool can be modified with the Stroke panel. In Figure 12-7, the Paintbrush tool was used to create a textured border around the rose by using the stroke set to a charcoal effect, as you see in the Stroke panel. To practice with the Stroke panel, open it by choosing Window | Stroke. Try some of the different options available for setting the effects for the Paintbrush tool. You'll be returning to a more detailed discussion of the Stroke panel in succeeding modules, so don't worry if you don't understand all the different options available.

8. You have probably noticed that Fireworks limits the areas you can paint to the original oval selection that was copied onto your practice canvas. Remember that any time you are working with a bitmap image, what you are actually doing is adding or changing colors to the grid that is created. Since the grid was only created in an oval shape, only that area can be painted. Anything painted outside the oval selection area will be trimmed away when the mouse button is released.

9. The final painting tool to use here is the Eraser, and while it may seem that an eraser would be a tool for taking things away, in bitmap mode, you are actually adding colors that you specify in the Options panel. Even though the concept may seem a little unusual, using the tool is not. Simply select the

12

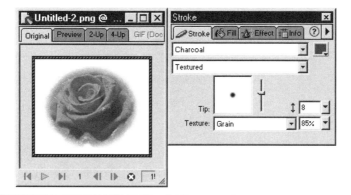

Figure 12-7 | The Stroke panel can be used to modify the effects created with the Paintbrush tool while editing in bitmap mode

eraser icon and scrub away at your image. Try changing the size of the eraser and setting the different options for edges and colors that you find in the Options panel, as shown in Figure 12-8. Here's another great tool that can be used to create some super special effects once you become accustomed to its capabilities.

10. This is a great time to experiment with the different painting tools available. For instance, try using the Magic Wand to select a portion of the rose petals in your sample file, and then use the Paint Bucket tool to change the color of the flower itself. Or try adding a box to hold a caption for the picture. How about using the Eraser tool to further soften the edges of the rose so that only the outermost edges of the flower are showing? The possibilities are almost limitless, and the tools that Fireworks provides give you an incredible amount of freedom in creating your final masterpiece.

1-Minute Drill

● How does anti-aliasing affect the edge of a bitmap?

● How are line and fill colors changed?

● How does the Eraser tool create the effect of erasing part of an image?

● Anti-aliasing makes the edges of bitmaps appear smoother by adding additional pixels and modifying the colors along the edge so they blend more smoothly.

● Line and fill colors can be changed by using the color settings at the bottom of the Tools panel. Fill colors can be modified by using the Paint Bucket tool.

● The eraser works by painting an area of new pixels onto the canvas. If this is set to be transparent or if the color is the same as the canvas, the replacement colors will appear to erase a part of an image.

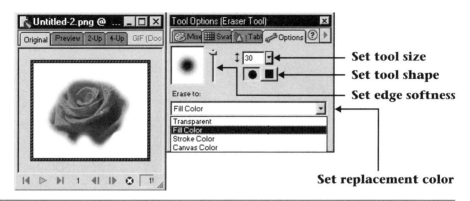

Figure 12-8 The Options panel for the Eraser tool includes options for setting tool size, edge softness, tool shape, and replacement colors

Project 12-5: Combining Selection and Painting Tools

You have now seen some of the capabilities that Fireworks' bitmap tools provide. From selecting different regions of a photograph, to changing edge selections, to drawing new objects onto a canvas, the tools that Fireworks provides allow you to really get your creative juices flowing. In this final project for this module, your task is to use all of those tools in combination to create a virtual postcard for your fictional town of Poinciana Beach. This postcard is something that you would want to allow visitors to e-mail to their friends, for instance, or that you could even use as a navigation element for a web page by using it as an image map. Whatever its use, the first task is to create a collage of images for the postcard itself.

Step-by-Step

1. Start by creating a new document with dimensions of 400 pixels wide by 250 pixels high with the canvas color set to white. Name the file **postcard.png**, accepting the Fireworks file format default.

2. Figure 12-9 shows how your completed project should appear when you are done. Notice that this postcard is simply a series of images that have been cropped in different ways and placed on the canvas.

3. To create your own postcard, find the following JPEG and GIF images in the Exercises folder for this module: boat_1.jpg, cityhall_1.jpg, beach_1.jpg,

12

Figure 12-9 Create a virtual postcard by cropping photographs and arranging them on a canvas

golfers_1.jpg, hotel_1.jpg, poinciana_1.jpg, and curvedtext.gif. These are the source files for your postcard.

4. Decide which of the images you want to use on your postcard after you've taken a look at the photos that are available. Crop each of the photos and paste a copy onto the new canvas. The final image you should use is the curvedtext.gif file, allowing it to lie over the top of the photo collage.

5. The original photographs that were cropped and resized for the images you used above are also located in the Exercises folder, with names such as boat_2.jpg, cityhall_2.jpg, and so on. Try opening these files, changing the size of the image that will fit on your new canvas, and cropping them in different ways.

6. When you are finished with this exercise, you should have created at least two original postcards from the photographs supplied, and gained some valuable skills along the way.

What to Take Away

The bitmap editing tools provided in Fireworks give you outstanding control over the appearance of the types of images that might be captured in a photograph, from a clipart collection, from the Web, or from a scanned image. You have seen how to use Fireworks' tools to select, copy, and resize an image, as well as how to paint new pixels onto a bitmap image through the use of the Shape, Brush, and Line tools, as well as others. Fireworks allows you to create entirely new versions of these types of images, and allows you to manipulate images in a bitmap format in ways that you will come to appreciate more and more as you become comfortable with the program.

☑ *Mastery Check*

1. What three setting are determined when a new Fireworks file is created?

2. What is the purpose of having a negative area around the edges of a canvas in a Fireworks Document window?

3. What options are available for edge settings when using bitmap selection tools?

4. How can bitmap lines, shapes, or brush strokes be removed from a bitmap image?

5. Which bitmap painting tool provides the greatest flexibility for adding colored lines and shapes to an image?

12

Module 13

Creating and Modifying Objects with Fireworks Panels

Goals of this Module

- Explore Fireworks' vector drawing tools
- Select and modify vector objects
- Explore Stroke and Fill options
- Arrange objects on a canvas
- Scale, skew, and rotate objects
- Use the Subselection tool to transform paths
- Understand and use Fireworks Live Effects
- Apply special effects to bitmap objects

In Module 12, you learned how to work with images that were captured from a source outside of Fireworks—JPEG and GIF images that require their own special set of tools for modifications and insertion into Fireworks documents.

The tools for creating original artwork in Fireworks are organized similarly to those you used when working with bitmaps. The primary difference is that with Fireworks' vector-based drawing tools, you can create entirely new objects for use in your web site—greatly increasing your ability to provide fresh and original content on your site.

The primary drawing tools are located on the Tools panel, as shown in Figure 13-1, but to extend the capabilities of these basic drawing tools, you will need to become much more familiar with the use of the panels and inspectors

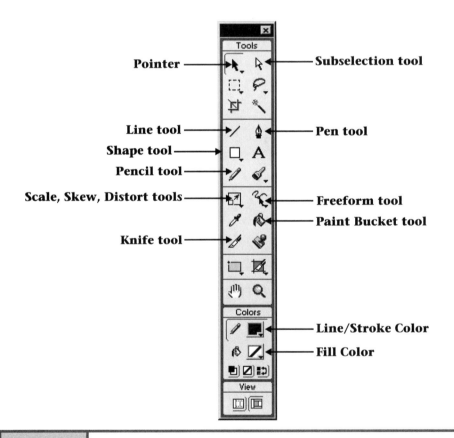

Figure 13-1 Fireworks vector drawing tools provide the opportunity to create original artwork that can then be modified using panels and inspector

that allow for the modification of the images you create. While panels and inspectors were covered briefly in the previous module, you'll get an opportunity here to work with these powerful modification tools to create some truly awesome effects with your artwork. Again, while there are other drawing programs that give you even greater creative control over vector-based drawings—such as Macromedia Freehand and Adobe Illustrator—the real strength of Fireworks is its ability to work so well with images that will ultimately be used on a web page and to seamlessly combine the vector and bitmap worlds of computer graphics.

Project 13-1: Using Vector Drawing Tools

In this project, you will have the opportunity to work with the basic drawing tools that Fireworks provides—tools to create lines and basic shapes such as rectangles, ellipses, and polygons. However, even though these shapes may seem to only include the most basic of objects, Fireworks' capacity for taking a basic shape and then modifying it in different ways can ultimately lead to some truly original works of art. Even if you're not artistically inclined, the ease with which shapes and lines can be combined makes the creation of new images for use in a web page something that even the most graphically challenged designer will be capable of accomplishing.

Note

Be sure that you have downloaded the exercise files for this module from www.osborne.com.

Step-by-Step

1. To begin this project, create a new Fireworks document by choosing File | New. In the New Document dialog box, make the size of the canvas 300 pixels wide by 300 pixels high and set the canvas color to white. Save the file as **line_practice.png**, accepting the Fireworks PNG format as the file type. Also, be sure to expand the Document window so that some negative area is visible around the canvas.

2. Working with lines and paths requires that stroke options be applied through the use of the Stroke panel. Open the Stroke panel by choosing Window | Stroke, and be sure that your settings appear as you see here. If they do not, simply use the drop-down arrows and sliders as you did in Module 12 to adjust the settings.

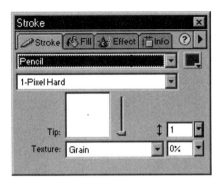

3. The first type of vector shape you will work with is the line—the simplest type of vector path, since it consists of only three primary elements—a beginning point, an ending point, and the line that is created mathematically when the points are joined together. Use the Line tool to draw a simple horizontal line on the canvas, approximately two inches long.

The line will appear in a light-blue color with the two end points represented by small squares. This is Fireworks' way of letting you know that this line is selected. Any time you draw a new object on the canvas with a vector tool, the object remains selected until you tell Fireworks that you no longer wish to work with the object, by deselecting it.

4. To deselect the line, switch your tool selection to the Pointer tool and click anywhere in the negative area around your canvas. The line will now appear simply as a line—1 pixel wide with a pencil-like appearance and with the color you set in the line color options at the bottom of the Tools panel.

5. To reselect the line, pass the Pointer tool over it. Notice that as the Pointer tool comes into contact with the line, the selection points appear and the line changes to a red color. Fireworks is letting you know that if you click your mouse button once, this is the object that will be selected. Click your mouse now, and the line is selected and, once again, changes to a light-blue color.

6. Turn to the Stroke panel for a look at how lines can be modified by the many options packed into this single panel. Make sure that the line is selected and try some of the different settings available for stroke options. Figure 13-2 summarizes the available options for the Stroke panel.

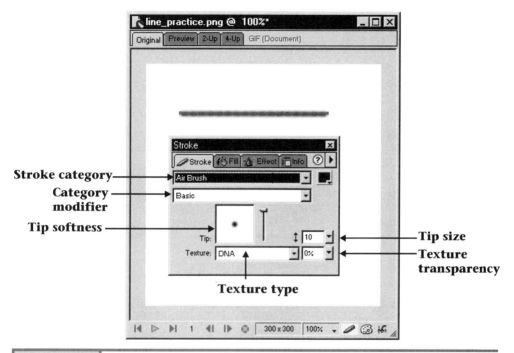

Figure 13-2   The Stroke panel offers numerous options for changing line styles
and strokes

7. At the top of the panel, locate the stroke category options. Everything
from a basic no-nonsense line to a style called "unnatural" is available.
Below the stroke type area are additional options that can be set based on
the selected category. "Oil," for instance, allows five different modifiers to
be applied to an oil stroke. With each category, the options in the category
modifier change. Textures can also be applied to strokes. Simply select a
desired texture and then adjust the transparency slider up or down to see
more or less of the texture through the stroke. It's all lots of fun, and you
can easily spend hours playing with the multitude of settings available
for lines here.

8. Additional drawing tools available for creating lines are the Pencil and
Paintbrush tools, which allow you to draw in a more freehand manner, and
the Pen tool, which allows you to create curved sections of lines. Since using
the Pencil and Paintbrush tools is very easy to pick up on your own, those
two will be left for you to tackle as independent study items.

13

Tip

One interesting feature of the Paintbrush tool that you should explore is its ability to record the speed of a stroke. Try drawing lines slowly and then quickly to see the difference.

9. The Pen tool, on the other hand, requires a little explanation and practice. While this tool provides an incredible amount of flexibility, especially when creating curves, learning to master it requires a fair amount of practice.

10. The Pen tool can create straight lines simply by clicking to define a single point, clicking again and allowing Fireworks to complete the path between the two points, and then adding additional points.

11. The real power of using the Pen tool comes in its ability to create and modify special mathematical paths called Bezier curves. For a quick demonstration of how the Pen tool creates curves, simply select the tool and drag a line onto the canvas. What appears is a set of control handles that modify the curve that you are beginning to create.

12. Move the control point to the middle of the canvas and release the mouse button. Fireworks will draw a curved line based on the location of your original starting point. Continue around the canvas, seeing how each of the two different mouse actions—clicking and dragging and simply clicking the mouse button—affects the line that is created. Watch for the appearance of control handles that allow you to modify curved sections, and try different methods for creating Bezier curves. Also, note that double-clicking at any point on the canvas causes the Pen tool to finish its work on that particular

line. Using this tool requires a great deal of practice, but with time, even those who are among the graphically challenged can create interesting images like the one shown here.

┼ *Tip*

The Fireworks manual has a detailed description on Bezier curves and their use that describes these powerful tools in more depth than is possible here.

13. Shapes are created by vector paths that are closed, such as circles and rectangles. Since the path is closed, the area defined by the border of the shape is available for a new color application—fills. Create a new document called **shapes_practice.png** so that you have a fresh canvas to practice on.

14. The Shape tool includes a flyout menu that allows you to choose from the Rectangle, Rounded Rectangle, Ellipse, and Polygon tools.

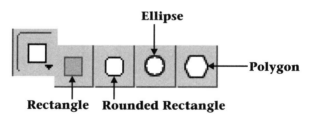

15. Drawing the basic shapes of rectangles and ellipses is a simple matter. Just drag your mouse across the canvas until the shape is the size you want. Change the fill color to a simple solid by accessing the Fill Color option at the bottom of the Tools panel. As with other oval tools, hold down the SHIFT key as you drag an ellipse, and a perfect circle will be drawn.

16. Rounded rectangles include additional options for setting the radius of the corner. To access these options, open the Object panel, shown next, by

13

choosing Window | Object, and move the slider that appears up and down to see the effect of different radius settings on the rectangle.

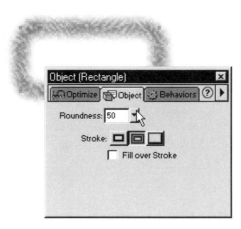

17. The Polygon tool can be used for creating simple polygon shapes based on settings accessed in the Tool Options panel for the tool. Open this panel by double-clicking the icon in the Tools panel, or by choosing Window | Tool Options. To draw a stop sign, set the number of angles to 8 and drag the shape onto the canvas, as shown here.

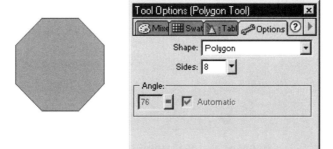

18. One of the coolest things that the Polygon tool can do is create stars. In the Tool Options panel, choose Star from the Shape drop-down list, set Sides to 5, set Angle to 50, then drag your mouse to create a star on the canvas.

19. Have fun with this one. By changing the options in the Options panel for the Polygon tool, you can create some great stars with unusual attributes. When you are finished experimenting, you should be able to duplicate the stars shown here by adjusting the angle of the star and the number of points.

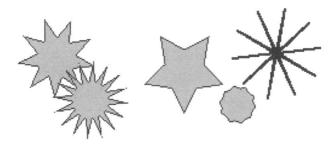

20. Closed paths can be filled with colors, patterns, or gradients to create any number of effects. To create a shape with a simple solid color, set the fill color with the option on the Tools panel and draw your object onto the canvas. You can also change the fill color of an object that is selected or set the fill color to none.

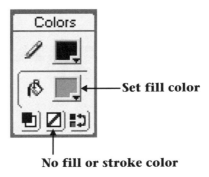

21. The most powerful tool for working with fills though is the Fill panel. Open this panel now by selecting Window I Fill. Much like the Stroke panel, a huge number of options for adjusting an object's filled area are available here, as shown in Figure 13-3.

22. There are almost limitless possibilities for the types of fills and fill combinations that can be applied to an object, and just as with strokes, the Fill panel options change based on the selected category. In addition to simple solid colors, you can create fills that are composed of gradients that you can edit into entirely new color patterns and save for use with another project.

23. Your task as you close out this project is to experiment with the different possibilities that adjusting object fills affords. When you're finished, you should be able to duplicate some of the samples you see in Figure 13-4. To access this file and see which settings were used, open shapes_sample.png from the Exercises folder for this module.

13

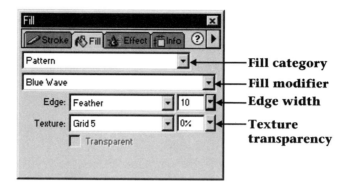

Fill category
Fill modifier
Edge width
Texture transparency

Figure 13-3 Use the Fill panel to set fill colors, textures, and gradient options

Figure 13-4 Use the Fill panel to apply different gradients, patterns, and fills to closed objects such as these basic shapes

1-Minute Drill

● What visual aid is provided to let you know that an object on the canvas
   is selected?

● Which panel is used to modify the attributes of a line?

● Which tool is used for creating complex curved lines?

Project 13-2: Working with Multiple Objects: Arranging, Combining, and Aligning

You have seen how easy it is to create both lines and shapes in Fireworks and
have now had an opportunity to at least begin experimenting with some of
the possibilities that these terrific tools afford. Still, the shapes you have worked
with have been relatively basic, and Fireworks is far more than a tool for
creating stars, even if those stars can be pretty cool. To further extend the
capabilities of what you can do with the software, your next task is to modify
multiple shapes by arranging or combining them in new ways on your canvas.

Step-by-Step

1. Create a new file by choosing File I New and setting the canvas area to 300
   pixels wide by 300 pixels high. Save this file as **multiples_practice.png**.

2. Start by creating four rectangles and placing them near the top of the canvas
   (in two rows with two rectangles). You can duplicate the first rectangle by
   drawing it and then choosing Edit I Copy followed by Edit I Paste, or by using
   the keyboard shortcuts—CTRL-C to copy, and CTRL-V to copy and paste.
   Windows users can also access these functions on the Main toolbar.

3. Next draw one larger rectangle near the bottom of the canvas.

4. Imagine these five rectangles as cards on a table. The first card down will
   always be on the bottom, with succeeding cards stacked on top of it. The
   process of arranging objects on a canvas entails changing the order in which

13

● An object that is selected in Fireworks will appear outlined with a light-blue line and will have blue handles
   designating the points and corners of the object.
● The Stroke panel is used for modifying lines, curves, and the borders of shapes.
● The Pen tool, with its powerful Bezier curve feature, is used to create complex free-form curves.

they are stacked. To see this in action, first drag the smaller rectangles so that they overlap the larger object, as shown here.

5. To change the stacking order arrangement, first select the larger rectangle by clicking it, and then choose Modify | Arrange | Send To Back—moving the selection all the way to the bottom of the stack.

6. The larger rectangle now moves to the bottom of the stack, as shown here, with the smaller rectangles lying on top of it, as if you had reshuffled the cards. This process is simple and easy to learn. Experiment with the different ways that objects can be stacked higher (Bring Forward) and stacked lower (Send Backward) to gain an appreciation for how objects can be arranged on the canvas.

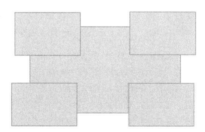

7. The next operation requires a new skill—selecting multiple objects on the canvas. Once again, this is easy to learn. First, delete all the rectangles from the previous operation so that you have a clean canvas, and then draw a circle and a rectangle. Position the objects so they are overlapping slightly.

Tip

Remember that to easily unselect an object, just click anywhere in the negative area of the Document window.

8. To select multiple objects on the canvas, simply choose the Pointer tool and hold the SHIFT key down while clicking on top of the rectangle and circle. Both items will have the blue handles appear, indicating they have been selected.

9. Four options are available for combining objects on the canvas—all accessed by choosing Modify | Combine. Try the first option now—Union—and the two shapes on the canvas will be combined into an entirely new object based on the common points they share along their outside border.

10. Click the Undo button or choose Edit | Undo to return to the original arrangement of a separate circle and rectangle. The next option to explore is Intersect. In this case, only the overlapping areas created where the circle lays on top of the rectangle remains, with the rest of the shapes stripped away.

13

11. Undo the last step and choose Punch from the Combine menu. Using this command causes the object on top to work like a cookie cutter, removing the portion of the object below where they intersect.

12. Finally, you use the Crop command when objects that have different fill and stroke characteristics are to be combined, with the area left behind taking on the attributes of the cropped object. Select the rectangle, change its fill attribute, and then select the circle and set a different fill for it. Next, select both objects and choose Modify | Combine | Crop. The slice that remains will take on the characteristics of the rectangle, as you see here.

13. Figure 13-5 displays different combinations of shapes, all made possible by using multiple objects and then combining them in new ways. See if you can duplicate these examples as you prepare to move on to a new topic.

14. There may be times when you need to align multiple objects on the canvas in nice, neat vertical or horizontal rows. To do this, you'll learn a new selection technique and then align objects on the panel using the Align commands.

15. Start by either creating a new document or deleting all the objects from the previous exercise from your existing canvas. On the canvas, draw five shapes and arrange them with the Pointer tool so that they are distributed randomly.

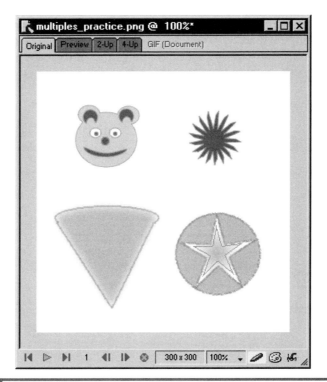

Figure 13-5   Using Combine commands allows new objects to be created from simple shapes

16. Use the Pointer tool to draw a box around all the objects on the canvas, as shown here. Release the mouse button, and Voila!—all the objects are selected at once. This process is known as *marqueeing*, but it should not be confused with the use of the Marquee tool.

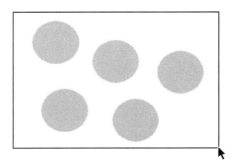

13

17. With all five objects selected, you can now align them in a variety of ways. Choose Modify | Align | Center Vertical and all the objects will retain their horizontal positions but be aligned to the center of the canvas.

18. Undo that alignment, and this time choose Modify | Align | Center Horizontal. All the objects will fall into alignment across the center of the canvas.

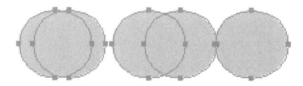

19. Finally, choose Modify | Align | Distribute Heights and Distribute Widths, and the objects will be spaced equally along both the horizontal and vertical axes of the canvas, as shown here.

Tip

You'll achieve the best results by moving objects close to where you want their final position to be before using the Align commands.

20. Just for fun, see if you can duplicate the caterpillar created here by aligning a series of circles and then by adding additional features using the Combine commands. When you are finished, save this document (or not) as you move on to the next topic.

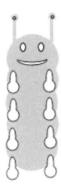

1-Minute Drill

- What combination of actions allows multiple objects to be selected on the canvas?

- Which Combine command causes an object on top of another shape to cut out a section like a cookie cutter?

- What functions on the menu bar allow objects to be arranged on the canvas?

Project 13-3: Transforming Objects

The possibilities for working with vector objects in Fireworks extends well beyond the ability to simply draw objects on a canvas, and even beyond the many possibilities afforded by combining shapes or modifying fills and strokes. With the tools and techniques you'll learn in this project, you will be able to stretch, rotate, distort, and transform objects in entirely new ways. In addition, you'll also learn how a path can be transformed by using a new device, the Subselection tool, to transform individual points along a path. Once again,

13

- Multiple objects on the canvas can be selected by using the Pointer tool while holding down the SHIFT key and then clicking the objects.
- The Punch command takes an object and punches out an area beneath it that matches its shape.
- To arrange objects on the canvas, first select the objects and then choose Modify | Arrange and select one of the options.

the possibilities are almost limitless, because Fireworks provides tools that let you take basic shapes and turn them into entirely new creations.

Step-by-Step

1. Create a new document by choosing File | New and setting the document size to 300 pixels wide by 300 pixels high. Call this new file **transform_practice.png**.

2. Draw a simple rectangle and center it on your canvas. With the rectangle selected, locate the Scale, Skew, and Distort tools on the Tools panel. By default, the Scale tool is visible and the other two are available from a flyout menu.

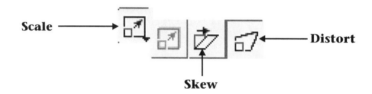

3. Select the Scale tool and try resizing the rectangle by dragging one of the handles that surround the object when this tool is selected. With the Scale tool, you can change the size of any object by changing its height or width, or change both at once by dragging handles from the four corners of the object.

4. Notice that the cursor will change to a curved arrow when it approaches the corner of the selected object. This free rotate option allows you to turn any object by simply holding down the mouse button when the rotate cursor appears and turning the object as you wish.

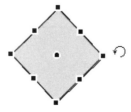

5. Skewing an object with the Skew tool transforms the path along a plane. That is, as you drag the handles, the object will be constrained by a straight line along the border. This is a great method for taking a simple rectangle and building more interesting objects.

6. The final option in the Tools panel allows any object to be twisted freely, allowing for the distortion of the object into entirely new and unusual shapes. Try this with a rectangle, a circle, or even a star.

7. Additional options for transforming objects are available from the Modify menu. For instance, to rotate an item 180 degrees, choose Modify | Transform | Rotate 180° to flip the object over. The options here are easy to understand, and you are invited to explore them on your own.

Tip

Take special note of the Numeric Transform option that lets you specify the exact height and width of an object on the canvas. This is handy if you have limited space—as almost every web page has—and you need to get an object to the exact size that will fit.

8. You'll recall that vector-based objects are composed of a series of points that are connected together by strokes. Paths can be transformed anywhere along the way as long as there is a point to work with. With the Subselection tool, you are able to select an individual point along a path and then alter the appearance of the object by moving that point. That's a wordy description that cries out for an example, so to see the concept in action, start by drawing a five-pointed star on your canvas.

9. Once the star is drawn, choose the Subselection tool at the top of the Tools panel to the right of the pointer. Notice how the handles that define the points of the star seem to change appearance—from solid to hollow. These hollow handles are your clue that the individual point—whether it is in a closed path such as the star or in an open path such as a line—can be moved from its location. Move the individual points of the star around the canvas, and you should be able to transform your star into something like this one.

13

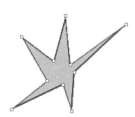

10. To create additional subselection points along a path, the Knife tool is used. By choosing the Knife tool, an object can be sliced into additional paths that then can be modified by the Subselection tool or Pointer tool. Simply drag the Knife tool across any path and a new subselection point will appear where the tool intersects the path. In this example, an ellipse has been sliced in two separate paths and then pulled apart using the Pointer tool.

11. To complete this brief look at the transformation capabilities of Fireworks, duplicate the book that you see here. Create two rectangles and then use the Scale, Skew, and Distort tools to create the front and back cover of the book. Create a third rectangle and scale it to the correct size to be used as the book's spine, and save (or don't) your file when you are finished. While you won't necessarily need this image of a book again, you will be creating one like it in the final project of this module.

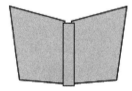

1-Minute Drill

● What three tools are available on the Tools panel for altering the basic size and shape of an object?

● Which option in the Modify menu allows an object to be resized to an exact measurement?

● Which tool is used to modify individual points along a path?

● The three tools on the Tools panel used to alter the shape of an object are the Scale, Skew, and Distort tools.
● To modify an object to a precise measurement, choose Modify | Transform | Numeric Transform.
● The Subselection tool is used for selecting and modifying individual points along a path.

Project 13-4: Working with Live Effects

The sheer number of special effects that can be applied to objects in Fireworks can be a little staggering. After all, with the ability to create 16 different kinds of beveled edges, to use drop shadows, glows, and blurs, and to control each effect precisely with the options available in the Effects panel, you may come to feel a little overwhelmed by all of the possibilities. As usual, employing these effects is a simple matter of understanding the Fireworks interface and then experimenting with the options. Once you get the hang of the basics, you'll quickly be having great fun trying out different settings and exploring all the options here.

Fireworks makes working with effects easier in a number of ways. First, all effects in Fireworks are said to be "live," which means they are automatically applied in the Document window as soon as they are selected. No more choosing an option, clicking OK, and then waiting to see if the effect is really one you like. With Live Effects, you see the effect applied as soon as it is chosen.

Fireworks also summarizes all the effects applied to a particular object and displays them in the Effects panel when the object is selected. You can even save a series of effects that have been applied to an object and use the same settings over and over again. This can be a real time-saver when you are designing for the Web and consistency becomes important for branding the look of your site. Figure 13-6 shows just one possibility for applying Live Effects to a rectangle, and the way that Fireworks summarizes the applied settings in the Effects panel.

Step-by-Step

1. Create a new document by choosing File | New and setting the document size to 300 pixels wide by 300 pixels high. Call this new file **effects_practice.png**.

2. On the canvas, create two objects—a rectangle and an ellipse. Select the rectangle and open the Effects panel by choosing Window | Effects.

3. There are far too many different effects to cover adequately in the short space available here. As a result, this discussion of Live Effects will focus on the most common effects used with images for the Web. You will get additional practice in using and applying effects in succeeding modules.

4. To begin, acquaint yourself with the options available for the application of effects, shown in Figure 13-7. You'll notice right away that this panel is arranged much like the ones you saw when working with the Stroke and Fill panels. And just as with those panels, the available modifiers will change based on the category of effects that is chosen.

13

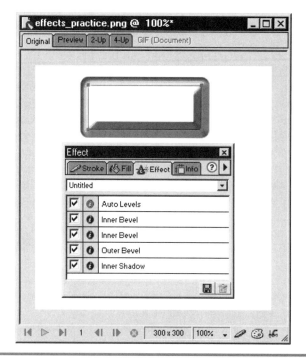

Figure 13-6 The Effects panel lists all Live Effects applied to an object

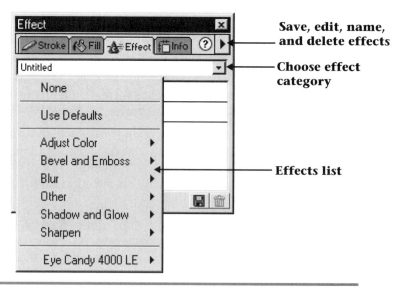

Figure 13-7 The Effects panel includes options for applying a huge variety of Live Effects to an object

5. Choose the Bevel And Emboss category and apply the Inner Bevel option to create the illusion that your rectangle is a button that sticks up from the screen. This type of bevel is considered to be an inner bevel since all of the effects take place within the original borders of the rectangle.

6. The inner bevel that is applied is now listed in the lower portion of the Effects panel in the list area. Fireworks will continue to list all effects applied to this object as you add or delete them. Take particular note of the check box and the information icon that are to the left of the effect name. To turn off the beveled effect, or to turn it back on, simply check or uncheck the box to apply or remove the effect. To make adjustments to the bevel options, click the information icon and you will access the settings, as shown here.

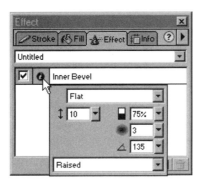

7. At the bottom of the Inner Bevel information panel, take note of the drop-down box that lets you change the settings for the beveled image. Change the setting for this bevel from Raised to Inset and you will create the effect that the button has been pushed in. Have you seen this type of graphic when rollover images were used as links? Now you know how it was done!

8. The other type of bevel that you may use is the outer bevel, which creates a beveled border outside the original object. In this example, an outer bevel was applied to the original rectangle and changed to the Ruffle style in the information panel.

13

9. Try the different options available in the Bevel And Emboss effects category. Be sure to spend some time adjusting the settings for the bevels and embossed areas that you create. Once again, Fireworks makes applying and adjusting special effects to an object a snap.

10. In the same way that bevel and emboss effects are applied, you can add a variety of glows, shadows, and other effects with the Effects panel. Try experimenting with those categories and see if you can re-create the image shown here. Just one hint—this image has five different effects, and a gradient fill applied to it. Still, producing this graphic only took a total of two minutes, and you will quickly be able to create some interesting special visual effects with Fireworks' tools. If you want to see for yourself which effects were used, open effects_sample.png from the exercise files for this module and you'll find this graphic there.

11. Even if you've only spent a few minutes creating the effect, if you had a web site where you needed to reproduce the same effect on a number of buttons and objects, you would want a way to be sure that identical effects were applied. Remember that consistency is one of the key elements of web design. Luckily, Fireworks makes saving a series of applied effects quite easy. To begin, be sure that you have an object with at least one effect applied and selected on the canvas.

12. Open the expansion arrow at the top of the Effects panel and choose Save Effect As.

13. Name the effect in the Save Effect As dialog box that appears. This name should be something that will serve as a reminder to you (for example, "Multiple Bevels and Glows"). This name has no function other than to jog your memory as to the effects that are created when the options are applied to an object.

14. Draw a new object on your canvas and click the drop-down arrow for the effects category. Your saved effect settings will appear in the list of available

options. Simply select the effect by name, and your new object will share matching effects with those that you saved before.

15. Using Fireworks' Live Effects can really unleash your creative streak. This is a great time to experiment with the different options available for further designing interesting shapes and effects. Try the different options available on your practice document, and you'll find that the number of effects that you can create is truly astonishing. Have fun, and as before, you can save or discard this file when you are done.

1-Minute Drill

● What is the difference between an inner bevel and an outer bevel?

● How are effects saved for use with other projects?

Ask the Expert

Question: What are Xtras? Are they similar to Live Effects?

Answer: Xtras are very similar to Live Effects but are used to modify bitmap images—especially JPEG photographs. With Fireworks' Xtras, you can blur an image so that the objects appear to be in the distance, sharpen the edges of objects in a picture, and even make precise adjustments to an image's color properties. Xtras add important capabilities to Fireworks by allowing you to modify bitmap images in very sophisticated ways.

● An inner bevel is created within the boundaries of an object, while an outer bevel creates a new border that is applied outside the object.
● Effects are saved by choosing an object that has effects applied to it and then opening the expansion arrow of the Effects panel and choosing Save Effect As. Give the effect a unique name and it will become available for use on other objects.

13

Project 13-5: Combining Objects and Effects in a Fireworks Document

In the final practice exercise for this module, your task is to re-create the document you see in Figure 13-8. You'll need to use all the tools and techniques that were covered in this module to duplicate the invitation to a special event at the Poinciana Beach Public Library.

Step-by-Step

1. Start by creating a new document 500 pixels wide by 300 pixels high. Save the file as **invitation.png**.

2. Draw a rectangle that fills the entire canvas area and apply a bevel from the Effects panel.

3. Import the text for the invitation by choosing File | Import and browsing to the invitation_text.gif file in the exercise files for this module. Place the cursor in the upper-left corner of the canvas and click once to import the text located in the GIF file.

Figure 13-8 | This invitation was created using the techniques covered in this module

4. Using the skills you have developed, create the caterpillar that you see in Figure 13-8. You will need to create a number of objects, copy and paste them onto the canvas, and then transform them by combining the shapes into new elements. This is meant to be a fun and easy review of the skills you learned in this module. If you are having difficulty completing a particular portion of the caterpillar, review the project that covers the skills needed. In the end, your completed invitation should look at least as good as the one here.

Ask the Expert

Question: Why does my computer take so long to process some of the effects that I apply?

Answer: Remember that Fireworks is a very powerful program, and it takes a good deal of processing power and memory to apply some of the available effects. Macintosh users can choose to allocate more memory to the program and see improved results. Windows users, though, need to understand that their computer should have at least 128MB of memory installed to effectively use the program. Even though Macromedia says that you can run Fireworks with only 64MB of memory, in practice, where you're likely to have Dreamweaver and at least one browser running at the same time you're using Fireworks, you should consider 128MB to be the minimum system requirement.

What to Take Away

In this module, you have been introduced to many of the vector drawing tools available in Fireworks. By combining the basic shapes and lines available in the Tools panel, you can create any number of different basic shapes and paths.

The real power of the software, though, lies in its ability to manipulate objects on the canvas into new and exciting graphics. By using the power to arrange, transform, combine, rotate, and distort objects, a simple series of circles can become a friendly caterpillar. Combine those capabilities with the ability to modify strokes and fills and you will quickly understand why Fireworks has become such a popular image editing software title, particularly when creating images for the Web.

13

✓ Mastery Check

1. What visual aid does Fireworks use to let you know that an object is available for selection?

2. What basic shapes can be drawn using the tools provided in the Tools panel?

3. How are objects freely rotated on the canvas?

4. How does the ability to save effects and apply them to other objects impact web design?

5. How are settings for effects accessed and modified?

Module 14

Working with Text and Text Effects

The Goals of this Module

- Understand the use of text as images
- Explore the Fireworks Text Editor panel
- Modify text for size, orientation, stroke, and fill characteristics
- Understand how text styles are created and saved
- Convert text into vector objects
- Attach text to a vector path

In the first part of this book, you learned a great deal about how the Internet works and how browsers perform the essential task of reading code and displaying text on a web page. You also learned that because of the many differences between browsers and the way they display text, formatting text is often problematic, especially if you want to do something special.

Text that is created in Fireworks does not have that problem. Since it is an image that is converted into a file format read by all common browsers, you can be sure that your audience will see the text you design. Finally! No more limitations! Or are there?

Of course there are—this is the Web after all, a place where nothing seems to come easy—and there is one major decision you must make in the use of text as graphics. When compared to HTML text, text that is a graphic takes up much more space and therefore can significantly slow the loading of a web page. It would be great if you could simply use a graphics program such as Fireworks to enter all the text on a page and publish it as it is. The problem becomes a matter of just how long you want your audience to wait to see your page. A page that is composed of 20 lines of HTML text will load very quickly, while one that contains the same amount of information converted into a graphic will slowly, very slowly, load onto the viewer's screen. In addition, pages that rely too heavily on graphics rather than text often are overlooked by search engines.

Still, the use of text as graphics, and especially the types of dynamic graphics that it is possible to create with Fireworks, can significantly add to the impact of a page's design. Whether the task is to design a logo that becomes a common element throughout the entire web site, or simply eye-catching buttons that include text, Fireworks puts tools at your disposal that are often only found in sophisticated desktop publishing programs.

Project 14-1: Using the Text Editor to Enter and Modify Text

The primary tool for entering and modifying text is the Text Editor that is activated when you click the Text button on the Tools panel. Not only is the Text Editor used for entering text, it is also the place where a wide variety of fonts can be chosen, where you can set other attributes such as colors and alignments, and where you can even fine-tune the spacing between letters with pixel-by-pixel precision. Using the Text Editor often takes a bit of getting used to since it does not behave like a traditional word processor with buttons arrayed in a toolbar, but instead follows the standard Macromedia format of using a floating panel with the modifiers arranged on the panel. You may also find that entering text into a separate panel instead of directly onto a canvas causes you to feel somewhat removed from the creative process. This first project is designed to get you over the initial hurdle of becoming comfortable with the Text Editor and how it is used.

Note

Be sure that you have downloaded the exercise files for this module from www.osborne.com.

Step-by-Step

1. Create a new Fireworks file by selecting File I New. Make the new canvas size 300 pixels wide by 300 pixels high, with a white canvas color, and save the file as **text_practice.png**. Once your file is saved, locate the Text tool on the Tools panel and select it.

2. Text that is entered into a Fireworks document resides in a rectangular area called a text box. When you see the cursor appear as a horizontal *H*, click once and the text box will appear on the canvas, along with the separate Text Editor. As you'll see in a moment, the initial size and position of the text box are not important since it will automatically resize to fit the text that is entered in the Text Editor. For now, simply choose the Text tool and click anywhere on the canvas to create this first text box.

3. Once a text box is created, the Text Editor becomes active, and until you accept the changes you make within the Editor, you cannot use any of the other features of Fireworks. The exception to this rule is the placement of text boxes on the canvas. As you work in the Text Editor, you can reposition text boxes on the canvas. Notice that when you roll your pointer over the text box, the pointer changes to a hand, and by clicking and dragging, the text box can be positioned as you like. Activating the Text Editor to edit or modify existing text is a simple matter of double-clicking the text box on the canvas.

14

4. As previously mentioned, creating text as a graphic image frees you from the font constraints inherent to the Web. Now you can choose from a wide range of font types, sizes, color, and other options. To acquaint yourself with the features of the Text Editor, refer to Figure 14-1.

5. Many people like to set the font type, size, and color before they begin typing text into the work area. However, it is equally easy to select the text inside the work area and then apply your changes. Much as you saw with Live Effects in the last module, Fireworks applies the changes to formatting as you work, as long as the Apply check box is checked in the lower-right corner of the Text Editor. For now, type **A sample of text** in the work area without changing any of the font options. Once the text is in place, use your mouse to select all the text.

6. Click the down arrow next to the font type to access the fonts that are available in Fireworks. The number of font types available is extensive.

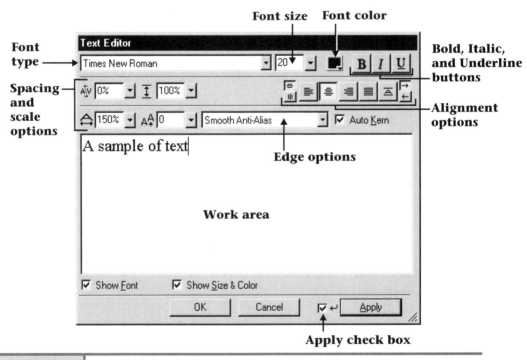

Figure 14-1 The Text Editor includes a huge number of options for formatting text

In addition, with the text selected, Fireworks provides a preview of how it will appear in a particular font type as each is highlighted.

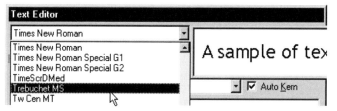

This is a great feature that makes it easy to choose a font that fits your needs. To choose a font, just click the font name, and the text on the canvas will be converted to the new type. You'll also notice that the text box automatically changes its size to fit the font properly. Experiment with a few different font types now before moving on.

7. Font size is set in much the same way that you have changed options previously. You can either type a value directly in the size box or use the slider to make the font larger or smaller to fit your needs. Notice again that as the changes are applied, Fireworks automatically applies the new value to the text in the Text Editor and on the canvas, and the text box expands to accept the new size when you are using the slider. While the slider allows you to change sizes between 8 and 96 points, you can also enter other values manually into the size box—up to 400 points if you need text that large. However, manually entered font sizes do not provide a preview on the canvas.

Note

Fonts are set in points the same way that you would set font sizes in a word processor.

8. Clicking the Color button brings up the familiar Macromedia interface for choosing colors, along with the Eyedropper tool that can be used to select a color anywhere within the Fireworks work area. Take a few moments to experiment with changing the color of your selected text.

9. The basic text styles of bold, italic, and underline are set by selecting text in the work area and then clicking the appropriate button. Again, this is very similar to what you would do in a word processor.

10. Text is aligned within the text box by using the alignment buttons on the right side of the Text Editor. In addition to the basic alignments of left, center, and right, text can also be aligned proportionally (justified) or even stretched. Figure 14-2 shows how these settings affect text.

14

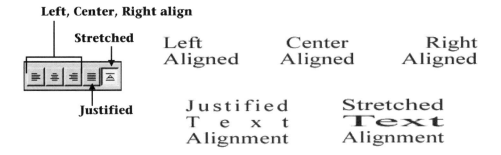

Figure 14-2 Text can be either aligned left, centered, aligned right, justified, or stretched

11. Try typing a few lines of text and experimenting with the alignment features by clicking the different alignment buttons. You will need to press the ENTER key to create new lines of text as you work in the Text Editor.

12. Text can also be changed to flow from the standard left to right to flow from right to left, and then vice versa, by using the two arrow buttons to the right of the alignment buttons. In this example, the text you entered previously has been set to flow backward, or right to left.

txet fo elpmas A

13. The final basic options for changing text are the horizontal and vertical text buttons located to the left of the alignment buttons. If you change the text so that it is oriented vertically, the alignment buttons change to reflect new options based on aligning the text to the top, bottom, or center of the text box.

14. In addition to the basic features of entering text and formatting the font type, size, color, alignment, orientation, and style, Fireworks also includes sophisticated tools for modifying the characteristics of character and line spacing and how the text is arranged on the canvas. Horizontal scale, for instance, enables you to change the basic width of fonts from the standard 100% size to values that make the individual letters either smaller or larger than standard. Other options in this area of the Text Editor include *kerning*, which lets you change spacing between characters, *baseline*, which lets you set text that falls above or below the lower border of the text box, and *leading*, which lets you adjust the amount of space between lines of text. With your sample text selected, try some of these different settings either by using the slider or by entering numbers directly into the value area for each option. You will get additional practice later on, but be sure that you orient yourself to the following options and their functions.

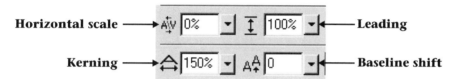

Horizontal scale ⟶ AᵥV `0%` ▼ ↕ `100%` ▼ ⟵ **Leading**

Kerning ⟶ `150%` ▼ AᵃA `0` ▼ ⟵ **Baseline shift**

15. The final option to discuss before you move on to more advanced modification tools is the option for adjusting the anti-aliasing level, found just above the work area of the Text Editor. As discussed in the previous module, anti-aliasing controls the appearance of edges, and in most cases, should be left at the default Smooth Anti-Alias setting.

16. To conclude this project, take some time and try typing your name into the Text Editor and experimenting with the different settings. Remember to press the ENTER key to create a new line for your last name. You should quickly come to appreciate the wide variety of options that Fireworks allows you to access directly in the Text Editor. Once you are done, click OK to accept any changes you've made and close the Text Editor. You can save this file for further practice if you like, or discard it when you are finished.

1-Minute Drill

● What should you consider before deciding to use text as a graphic on a web page?

● What is the primary tool for entering and modifying text in Fireworks?

● What basic styles for text can be applied with the Text Editor?

● Always consider whether or not you could achieve the same impact on your page by using much smaller HTML text as opposed to graphical text. Does the impact justify the added file size?
● The Text Editor is the primary tool for entering and modifying text in Fireworks.
● Bold, italic, and underline styles can be applied to text in the Text Editor.

Project 14-2: Applying Special Effects to Text

As varied as the options are when entering text and modifying it with the Text Editor, you have barely scratched the surface of what Fireworks allows you to do with text. Many of the same options that you saw when working with vector objects, such as shadows and glows, strokes and fills, and others, are available when working with text. By making these choices available, Fireworks lets you create unique high-impact graphics for use on a Web page or even in a printed document. In addition, once Live Effects are created for text, they can be saved as a new style, allowing you to design with the type of consistency that is important when working on the Web.

Step-by-Step

1. Create a new 300×300-pixel document with a white canvas. Save this file as **effects_practice.png**.

2. Create a new text box by selecting the Text tool and clicking the canvas. In the Text Editor, choose a font of your liking and set the font size to approximately 40 points. Type the words **Text Effects**. Click OK to accept the changes and close the Text Editor.

Note

Since Fireworks remembers the last settings that you applied to text, you may need to adjust the text alignment and orientation settings in the Text Editor.

3. Text that is generated in the Text Editor has no stroke by default. The first change you will make to this new block of text, then, is to apply a stroke setting by accessing the Stroke panel. Choose Window | Stroke to open the panel and note that the stroke is initially set to None. To apply a stroke, change None to Pencil and look closely at the results. Notice how a 1-pixel pencil setting leads to a fairly jagged edge around the border of the text. Change the setting to 4-pixels wide and you'll see that the stroke has been smoothed out.

4. The same huge variety of strokes can be applied to text that can be applied to the vector drawings you saw in the last module. Modifying the stroke of text needs to be done with some care though. With large text like the sample you are working on now, strokes can look great. Resize the same text

down to a smaller size, though, and the stroke can quickly overwhelm the fill on the text, making it effectively unreadable. You can try this yourself by double-clicking the text and adjusting the size in the Text Editor. Click OK to accept the size change that you apply to close the Text Editor and to see the effect that resizing has on your text.

5. In general, the larger the text, the more pronounced the impact the use of a custom stroke will have on the appearance of your text. Try experimenting with some of the different stroke settings to see which types of strokes work best with your text. Remember that the text box must be selected before a new stroke effect can be applied. You may also want to review the use of the Stroke panel in Module 13.

6. Fills in text objects are modified in the same way that strokes are changed. By default, Fireworks always makes the fill of a text object a solid color as set in the Text Editor. However, just as with strokes, fills can be modified and applied by using the modification panel. Open the panel by choosing Window I Fill or, if the Stroke panel is already open, by clicking the Fill tab at the top of the panel.

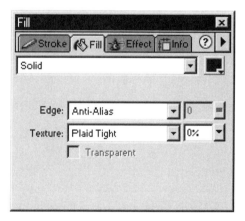

7. Modifying the fill of text can produce some very interesting results, particularly when using the gradient settings. To access the gradients, simply click the down arrow next to the Fill name and choose one of the gradients. Gradients are a great choice when you want to create unique text effects, because they display well in the limited area that text represents.

8. Try some of the other gradients available in the Fill panel and try further modifying them by dragging the gradient alignment handles that appear when the gradient is applied. You can get some very interesting results by

14

changing the center of a gradient and alignment of the pattern, like the metallic "glow" that you see applied to text here.

Gradient starting handle

Gradient ending handle

Gradient width handle

9. Some of the other fill settings that work well include the options available in the Pattern category. However, remember that the smaller the lettering, the less evident some of these fill settings become. There's usually no point in using a modified fill with text that is much smaller than 14 points, since it's unlikely that your audience will be able to see it once it is on your web page.

10. Effects for text are set by choosing Window | Effects or by clicking the Effects tab at the top of the same panel that contains fill and stroke settings. Open this panel and try applying an inner bevel to the text in your text box, and you'll see that Fireworks generates a nicely rounded effect to the text that makes it appear to be raised above the canvas.

Text Effects

11. One of the most common effects applied to text is the drop shadow effect that creates a further illusion that the text is floating above the canvas. With the text selected, choose the Shadow And Glow category from the drop-down box for effects and select the Drop Shadow setting. Your final results should appear as you see here.

12. In addition to the standard drop shadow, you can also use the Knock Out
setting available on the Info panel for drop shadows. Click the information
icon in the Effect panel to access the settings for the shadow, and check the
box that applies the Knock Out feature. When you are finished, your text
should appear as shown here, and you should be able to appreciate the
possibilities for using this nifty feature. You'll notice that with this setting
applied, the beveled edges on the lettering are no longer visible.

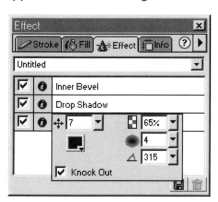 

13. Fireworks includes a special plug-in for the program called Eye Candy
4000LE that lets you further apply some interesting text effects, especially
one known as Motion Trails. Eye Candy is a separate program that extends
Fireworks' capabilities in the same way that a plug-in for a browser makes it
possible to do new things on the Web. With Eye Candy, you can apply a
great effect that makes your text appear to be zooming out of the
background of the canvas and toward the viewer.

14. Select the text box on the canvas and be sure that the Knock Out effect
you applied earlier is disabled. You can do this most easily by unchecking
the Apply box next to the Drop Shadow setting in the Effect panel, or by
repeatedly clicking the Undo button until your text is back to a more
simple setting.

15. Select Eye Candy 4000LE from the Effect panel and choose the Motion
Trail setting.

16. Once Motion Trail is selected, the Eye Candy program presents you with the
Motion Trail dialog box, shown in Figure 14-3, where the different settings
for the effect can be changed by moving the sliders from left to right. You
can change the opacity of the motion trail, change the width of the motion
trail, and even set its orientation on the canvas. Eye Candy will give you a
live preview of each change as it is applied, so move in slow increments as
you are changing the settings so that you can see the effect of each change.

14

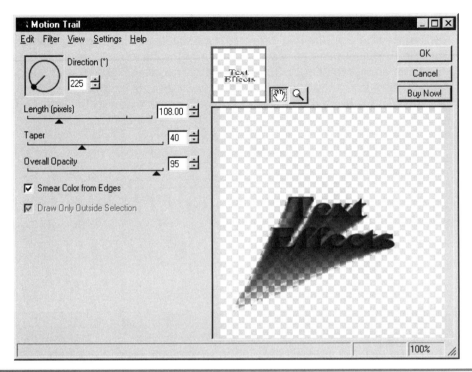

Figure 14-3 The Motion Trail dialog box for Eye Candy lets you change the opacity, width, and orientation of a Motion Trail effect

17. This is a great feature when you want to make an eye-catching text graphic that seems to zoom out of the page at you. Try experimenting with this one and see if you can achieve the effect you see here.

18. Finally, just as you saw when working with vector objects in the last module, a single effect setting or group of settings can be saved for use with text in the same way that you can save effects applied to other objects. First, select

the object that has the settings applied that you want to save, and then click the expansion arrow at the top of the Effect panel. Choose the option to Save Effect As and give the effect a name that is significant to you. Generating additional effects for new objects is a simple matter of finding the effects by name and applying them to your new object.

19. To conclude this activity, try some of the other effects available in the Effect panel. You may even want to experiment with the other two filters available from the Eye Candy plug-in—Marble, and some sophisticated options for beveling text and other options available from the Bevel Boss filter. In the end, you should be able to develop an appreciation for the sheer volume of effects that are possible in Fireworks and be able to see their practical use for yourself.

Note

You will find additional sample files to practice with in the exercise files for this module at www.osborne.com.

1-Minute Drill

● How are Live Effects applied to text?

● Why should stroke settings be applied with caution when working with text?

● How are Live Effects saved for use with other objects?

Project 14-3: Working with Vectors, Paths, and Text

As a sophisticated graphics creation tool, Fireworks can go even further beyond the effects you have created to this point. While the different effects, fills, and strokes you have used allow you to create some unique text effects, the ability to convert text to a vector object and to arrange text so that it follows a vector-based path further extends your capabilities when working with this powerful program.

● Live Effects are applied by accessing the Fill, Stroke, and Effect panels.
● Strokes used with small letters often make the text difficult to read and should be used with caution.
● Effects can be saved by clicking the expansion arrow in the Effect panel and choosing Save Effect As from the options available.

Step-by-Step

1. Create a new 300×300 pixel document with a white canvas. Save this file as **vector_practice.png**.

2. Select the Text tool from the Tools panel and type the letters **A B C** into the Text Editor. Choose a font of your liking and set the size of the font to 40 points or greater.

3. Less sophisticated programs than Fireworks often convert text to a graphic image as soon as it is inserted into a document. Fireworks, on the other hand, keeps the text as text, and this feature is the one that allows you to go back and forth between the Text Editor and the canvas, applying different fonts and font styles, and making other corrections as necessary. The next procedure you will learn will remove that feature, though, which makes it very important that before you convert a text object to a graphic object you are sure that everything (including the spelling) is as it should be.

4. Select the text object on the canvas and choose Text | Convert To Paths to change the letters from text objects to vectors. While you might expect something dramatic to happen, you'll only notice that the selection area changes from a rectangle to four square handles that appear around what used to be the text box.

Tip

The handles that appear around the text indicates that the letters are grouped together. You'll learn more about grouping in the next module. To separate the letters from the grouped arrangement, select Modify | Ungroup.

5. What's really special about converting text to vector-based paths is that they can now be modified with some of the tools that you used in Module 12. Choose the Subselection tool from the Tools panel and click one of the letters, and you will see it light up with paths that can now be moved, modified, and twisted into entirely new letters. You'll notice that the letter A that you see here (magnified to 200 percent) is composed of a large number of vector points along the path that defines the letter.

6. With the Subselection tool, you can modify any point along the path that defines the object. For instance, the letter *A* here can be changed into some dramatic new forms simply by pulling points away from the letter. Or, use the Freeform tool to pull groups of points away from the path to create objects that only retain the hint that they were once letters. Once text is converted to a path, you have complete freedom over its ultimate form and can even use the Punch command and other Combine menu features that are available. Just remember that the process of converting text to paths is irreversible, and that once converted, you will no longer be able to edit the text.

7. In addition to converting text to paths, you can also attach text to paths to create some interesting new effects. This can be a great way to create a logo like the one you see in Figure 14-4. Start by creating a new document that is 300×300 and has a white canvas. Save this new file as **path_practice.png**.

8. Remember from Module 12 that a path is a series of points that are connected by lines. All objects created with vectors are defined by the paths that define their boundaries, and Fireworks gives you the capability of attaching text along one of these defining outlines. To begin the process, use the Ellipse tool to draw a circle on your canvas approximately half the width of the canvas. Don't worry about either the stroke or the fill at this point.

Figure 14-4   Text can be attached to circular paths to create logos, buttons, and other objects

9. Select the Knife tool from the Tools panel and slice the circle in half by dragging a line across its center. Once the circle is "cut" in two, deselect the object by clicking in the negative area of the canvas, and then use the Pointer tool to drag the circle apart. When you are finished, you should have two half-circles.

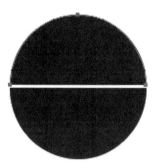

Tip

Hold down the SHIFT key while dragging the Knife tool and you will slice the circle at its exact midpoint.

10. Select the Text tool and place a text box above the upper half of the circle. Type the text **Poinciana Beach Florida** into the Text Editor and set the font size to no greater than 14 points. To attach the text to the path of the upper half-circle, you need to hold down the SHIFT key while selecting both the half-circle and the text box. Both objects must be selected for the final step to work.

11. Finally, select Text | Attach To Path to have the text drape across the top of the circle. Once text is attached to the path, the stroke and fill associated with the path will be removed, leaving only the text arranged in a half circle.

12. If you were to duplicate the preceding steps with the bottom half of the circle, the results would not be as you might expect. Since paths are originally created in a clockwise direction, Fireworks continues to arrange the text the same way, except that this causes the text to display upside down.

13. To achieve the proper effect, the half circle at the bottom of the logo needs to be flipped over before the text is attached to it. This is a simple matter of selecting the lower half-circle and then choosing Modify | Transform | Flip Horizontal to turn the object over on its side. While there is little visible evidence of this step, selecting the half-circle and the text **Chamber of Commerce** and using the Text | Attach To Path command results in exactly the effect desired.

Tip

You can further modify the arrangement of text by choosing Text | Orientation and using the options presented there. Since the text remains editable, you can also double-click it and modify its attributes with the Text Editor.

14. To finish the project and complete this preliminary logo, draw a second circle on the canvas and use the Modify | Arrange command to stack the circle and the text objects in the proper order. You may also want to use the Scale tool to adjust the size of the curved text so that it fits and aligns properly within the circle. Apply a bevel effect to the circle and modify the fill, and your logo will look like the one shown in Figure 14-4.

14

15. Whereas this example uses a circle, because it is one of the most common paths that you may wish to attach text to, text can also be attached to lines or curves. Combine this great feature with some of the other text effects you have seen earlier and you will be able to create some truly unique text-based graphics. When you are finished experimenting, you can save this file for further practice or discard it.

1-Minute Drill

- What happens to the editability of text when it is converted to a vector-based path?

- Which kinds of paths can text be attached to?

- Which objects on the canvas must be selected before text can be attached to a path?

Project 14-4: Creating and Modifying Text Objects

In this Independent Study project, your task is to create a series of buttons that will be used as navigation elements in a web page. The goal is to create two similar images that have some subtle differences that will become apparent when used as a rollover image. To do this, you will need to combine the skills you acquired in this module to create and modify text with those you learned in Module 13 to draw some simple vector objects to act as buttons.

Independent Study Exercise

1. Begin by determining the exact size you want these buttons to be. You may recall from earlier modules that screen real estate is very limited in web pages and that large buttons look amateurish. Create your first file and make the canvas size 100×20 pixels and use a transparent background.

2. Create your first button by drawing a rectangle that is the same size as the canvas. You may want to access the Info panel (with the rectangle selected) to adjust the object to the exact size of the canvas. Arrange the object on the canvas and apply an inner bevel.

- Text that is converted to paths can no longer be edited with the Text Editor.
- Text can be attached to any vector-based path, including rectangles, ellipses, lines, and curves.
- Both the text box and the path must be selected to attach the text to a path.

3. Now enter the text **For Visitors** in the document and arrange its position and color for maximum visibility. You will probably need to keep the font size to a setting of no larger than 14 points.

4. Once the button is created, save it as **visitors_1.png**. Then, use the Pointer tool to marquee both of the objects on the canvas, and copy them to your computer's clipboard by choosing Edit | Copy. Create a new file (Fireworks will automatically use the same 100×20-pixel size you last used) and paste the contents of the clipboard onto the canvas. Once this new document is created, save it as **visitors_2.png** and modify the text so that if these two images were used as a rollover image, the effect would be evident to a viewer.

5. Complete this project by duplicating the buttons and rollovers you saw in the first part of this book—**For Residents**, **For Businesses**, **For Members**, and **Local Events**. Experiment with the different possibilities as you complete this project, being sure to try some of the bevels, glows, inner glows, and shadow settings that are possible with Fireworks. When you are done, you should have received some valuable practice in the use of vector objects, text, and the ways the two can be combined and modified for use on the Web.

What to Take Away

You have learned in this module the many ways that text can be entered into a Fireworks document. You now know that the capabilities of the Text Editor allow you to enter text, modify it, and apply font styles, sizes, and colors to it, all while keeping the text editable so that you can return again and again to perform other modifications as necessary. Since all text in a Fireworks document exists as an editable text object unless it is converted to a vector object, you can repeatedly modify the text by using the Text Editor and can continue modifying the text itself even after applying strokes, fills, and effects.

You have also learned that text can be converted to noneditable vector objects, which makes it possible to modify the text at any point along the path that defines the image. Text that is converted to a vector object can also be combined with other vector objects to create entirely new graphics.

Finally, you saw how text can be attached to a path to create logos and other interesting text effects where you want to move beyond the limitations ssof horizontally or vertically arranged text.

In all, Fireworks provides some outstanding tools for the creation of text for the Web that ensure your text-based graphics have the readability and impact that you desire.

14

✓ Mastery Check

1. What is the major advantage to using text that is converted to graphical images?

2. What is the major disadvantage to using text that is converted to graphical images?

3. What limitations are associated with the use of different font types in Fireworks?

4. What feature in the Text Editor allows you to see the effect of modifications that you make on the canvas as they are made?

5. Which panel contains the options to set a drop shadow, bevel, or glow to text?

Module 15

Creating and Organizing Complex Objects

The Goals of this Module

- Understand how objects are grouped in a Fireworks document
- Combine vectors and bitmaps with the Group function
- Use mask groups to create text effects
- Understand how layers are used for organizing complex images
- Use layers for bitmap and vector editing
- Learn how the Web Layer is used
- Create complex graphics for use on the Web

Fireworks' capabilities as a bitmap-editing and vector-drawing program extend beyond the simple creation and manipulation of singular objects. While you have combined some of the images you have created up to this point, the sophisticated features of Fireworks allow you to group, arrange, and create different interactions between objects in ways that not many programs offer. In addition, Fireworks is unique in its ability to maintain the editability of objects during the design process so that they can be added, deleted, arranged, and ultimately combined in ways that allow a final integrated graphics file to be created for publication to the Web. As always, the main goal of the program is to provide unique high-impact images suitable for use in web pages in ways that other programs simply do not afford. This module takes a look at the tools for creating graphics that will ultimately become a part of a web page, and shows how Fireworks significantly extends your creative freedom through the use of groups, masks, layers, styles, and libraries.

Understanding Groups and Layers

The process of grouping objects can be compared to what happens when six cans of soda are joined together by the plastic holder that changes them from six individual cans to one six-pack of cans. Groups are created in the same way when individual objects on the canvas are joined together so that effects and other operations can be made on the group as a whole. You'll recall that the concluding project of Module 13 had you create a caterpillar from a number of objects that were arranged on the canvas but were independent of each other. Had that same graphic been grouped, however, the effects you see in Figure 15-1 could have been applied to the grouped image.

Layers, on the other hand, are used for defining a particular stack of transparencies that hold images and other information above the canvas, as you see in Figure 15-2. Fireworks allows you to create multiple layers for information so that you can create highly complex graphics while still keeping manageable the editing of the individual objects that are contained on the layer. Layers can be combined and rearranged in a multitude of ways to give you even more flexibility in the creation of graphics for use on the Web or for print. In addition, Fireworks contains a layer that can contain web-specific instructions that are used to create hotspots that act as links when viewed in a browser.

While you may be satisfied with the way that Fireworks has created images up to this point, and the many ways that effects and settings can be applied to

| **Figure 15-1** | Grouping objects allows different Live Effects or Xtras to be applied to the group |

objects, until you are able to understand and employ the advanced capabilities made possible with groups and layers, you will not have discovered the really dynamic features of the program. The exercises in this module are designed to familiarize you with some of the advanced capabilities made possible by these features.

Note

Be sure that you have downloaded the exercise files for this module from www.osborne.com.

Project 15-1: Basic Grouping Operations

Grouping objects is the process of combining and locking separate objects into a single graphical object. Once grouped, these objects can have Live Effects applied and can be modified in ways not possible when the objects remain separate from each other. As the saying goes, the whole is stronger than the parts, and this is certainly true of grouped objects.

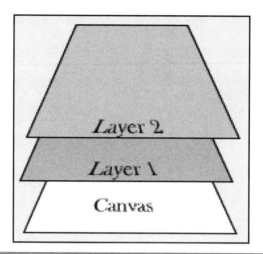

Figure 15-2   Layers are similar to transparencies that are stacked on top of the document's canvas

Step-by-Step

1. To begin understanding groups, create a new file that is 300 pixels wide by 300 pixels high with a white canvas. Name this file **group_practice.png**.

2. Draw a rectangle in the middle of the canvas and insert a text box into the rectangle that contains the words **Grouped Images** (stacked, not side-by-side).

3. The rectangle and the text box are two separate elements of this single image. Grouping the two objects is accomplished by holding down the SHIFT key while using the Pointer tool to select both items. You can also choose Edit I Select All to select all of the objects on a canvas at once, or use the Pointer tool to marquee the objects.

4. Once selected, the command to group the objects is found in the Modify menu. Choose Modify I Group to combine the two separate objects into one. When the grouping is completed, you will see handles appear in the four corners of the area bounded by the rectangle. These are the same handles you saw in the preceding module when working with grouped text. Deselect the grouped object by clicking in the negative area of the Document window, and then try reselecting it by using the Pointer tool. Grouped objects are always denoted by these four handles and the lack of the selection outline that's visible when working with single objects.

Grouped
Images

5. Grouped objects can also be ungrouped at any time. In this case, the text box would need to be ungrouped from the rectangle to modify the text with the Text Editor. To ungroup an object, select Modify | Ungroup, and the objects will return to their separate states.

6. Objects that are grouped can be modified in a variety of ways. For instance, the Skew tool can be used to give this graphic the appearance that it is receding into the distance. Note that the skew effect is applied to both the rectangle and the text at the same time and in the same proportions. Try this now with your document by combining the Scale and Skew tools to nudge the object into place.

7. Groups can also be used with a combination of vector-based objects and bitmap-based images. In this example, the JPEG photograph was grouped with a vector-based ellipse, followed by the application of bevel and shadow effects. The results can often be quite interesting, and with a little practice, you will be able to create these types of effects yourself quickly and easily.

Tip

You can use the JPEG images found in the Module 12 exercise files for additional practice in this technique.

8. The final practical exercise for this project is to open the file named caterpillar.png, located in the exercise files for this module at www.osborne.com. Practice grouping and ungrouping the caterpillar

15

and applying the effects you saw previously in Figure 15-1. For an object like this, use the Edit I Select All sequence to select all the separate objects that were created and combined to make the image of the caterpillar. Once you have the objects grouped, practice on your own by applying different Live Effects to the grouped image.

9. Continue practicing with the process of grouping and ungrouping objects. You can save or discard this practice file when you have finished.

1-Minute Drill

● How are groups created?

● What step should you follow when you want to separate a previously grouped object?

● True or False: Only vector images can be grouped.

Project 15-2: Using Mask Groups to Special Effects

A special type of group is created when Fireworks is instructed to use one object in the group to mask, or partially hide, the other object in the group. You may have seen this effect where mask groups are used to create text effects that cause letters to appear as if they have been cut out of a photograph. Fireworks makes this a very simple task, and once again, the steps to get it done are both easy and fun.

Step-by-Step

1. Create a new file that is 300 pixels wide by 300 pixels high with a white canvas. Name this **file mask_text.png**.

2. The process of creating a mask using text is similar to the way that you combine images using the Punch and Crop commands, as you learned how to do in Module 12. Images are created on a canvas and then arranged in such a way that the object on top controls the appearance of the object underneath it.

● Groups are created when two or more objects in a document are selected and the command Modify I Group is used.
● To separate a grouped object, select Modify I Ungroup.
● False. Bitmaps and vectors can be grouped in any combination.

The primary difference is in the way that the two images interact once the command is given to use the image on top as a mask. In masking, when the object on top is dark, a greater amount of the image below will show through the mask, while lighter mask objects will hide more of the image. Black objects, therefore, will allow the entire masked image to show through, while white objects used as masks will allow none of the underlying image to show. While this may seem backward, keeping that simple rule in mind will let you mask images with ease and create some interesting effects by using patterns and gradients as fills on the masking object. Ultimately, you will be able to create images like the one you see here.

3. Start by importing the beach scene in the exercise files for this module at www.osborne.com. Choose File | Import, locate the file called beach_scene.jpg, and import the image into your blank document. Don't worry about placement of the image for now.

4. Use the Text tool to create a new text box and type the capital letter **B**. Use a large font, such as Elephant or Arial Black, and make the letter 80 points high. Click OK to close the Text Editor and to return to the document. Now, position the letter on top of the girl sitting on the beach. You can even apply a stroke and bevel to the letter for more interesting effects. When you are finished, your Document window should appear as you see in Figure 15-3.

5. To convert these two objects, first make sure that both the letter and the photograph are selected by using the SHIFT key along with the Pointer tool to select them, or choose Edit | Select All. Once that is done, the final creation of the mask group is done by selecting Modify | Group As Mask and letting Fireworks handle the rest. Your masked image will appear as you see here, with the excess parts of the image outside the masking object stripped away. If you don't like the final results, choose Modify | Ungroup, and the letter and photograph will be separated, making it possible to reposition or modify the letter in the usual ways.

15

Figure 15-3 Position the text object to be used as a mask on top of the JPEG image

6. To create the remaining letters, import a new copy of beach_scene.jpg and use the Text tool and Text Editor to insert and modify the text **Gone to the**, and create a second mask group as you previously did. You will not be able to use Edit | Select All for this operation, but instead must use the Pointer tool while holding down the SHIFT key to select these two new objects. Position this new group above the letter *B* on the canvas.

7. Complete the project by typing the letters needed to finish the word "Beach." Experiment with capturing different portions of the JPEG image with the mask. When all of your work is done, the finished product should appear as you see here.

Tip

You can convert text to vectors and then stretch the size of the letters manually to create more space to capture the underlying image. Or, experiment with the kerning settings in the Text Editor to close the space between letters. When using text as masks, you will want to make the text as large as possible to capture the greatest area of the image underneath it.

8. Using text as masks can lead to some really interesting images. However, text is not the only object that can be used as a mask. Other objects can be used as masks as well, and often when you want to create a cropped portion of an existing image, this method is preferable to using the methods described in Module 12, which discussed copying and cropping bitmap images. Masks provide greater creative freedom because of the way that they can be modified with gradients and other fill effects to create unusual and often fascinating effects. Masks are also a terrific way to capture just a portion of an image while leaving the original image intact. Unlike cropping, which effectively destroys part of an image, masks always leave the underlying image intact. To make changes, you need only ungroup the object and reposition and modify the topmost object to adjust your effects.

9. Try this for yourself by creating a new file and importing one of the sample JPEG images you'll find in the exercise files for this module. Draw a simple (or complex) object on top of the JPEG and apply a gradient fill or a solid color with a pattern to the object. Follow the same steps as before by choosing Modify | Group As Mask to group the objects. Experiment with the different effects that the use of Live Effects, strokes, and textures can create. Figure 15-4 shows some of the types of effects you will be able to create by using masks. Save or discard your practice file when you are finished with this project.

1-Minute Drill

● Which color mask object will allow more of the graphic underneath to show—a light mask or a dark mask?

● How are masks created?

● Why is the use of a mask to capture a portion of an image preferable to cropping the image?

● Dark mask objects allow more of the underlying image to show through the mask.
● Mask objects are created when two objects are placed atop each other and the command Modify | Group As Mask is used.
● Masks do not destroy the original image, and it is often easier to ungroup the two objects and modify them than it is to create a new cropped image.

15

Figure 15-4 Masks can be created in almost unlimited varieties by combining objects

Project 15-3: Working with Layers

Another fascinating way to combine objects on a canvas is through use of the layers. You can think of layers as transparent sheets that lie above the canvas where you can insert, stack, and rearrange objects in a variety of ways. In addition to learning about layers in this project, you will also learn how an object's opacity, or transparency, can be set so that once it is on a layer it can be seen or obscured by layers above and below it. Layers are another important addition to the bag of design tricks that Fireworks provides, and with them you will be able to generate some very cool effects.

The Layers panel contains an extensive collection of options, and understanding how each is employed can be a daunting task. Remember that Fireworks is a very powerful software program and that harnessing all of that power often requires that you spend a fair amount of time learning how its tools are accessed and put into play. While this project only touches on some of the possibilities that layers afford, you will need to experiment on your own with these tools before you can become completely comfortable with their use.

Step-by-Step

1. Once again, create a new file that is 300 pixels wide by 300 pixels high with a white canvas. Name this file **layers_practice.png**.

2. Open the Layers panel by choosing Windows I Layers. Figure 15-5 summarizes the different elements of the Layers panel and their use.

3. In a new document, only two layers exist—the layer that by default is called "Layer 1" and a special Web Layer where HTML information about objects such as hotspots is stored. Locate the Add Layer button at the bottom of the panel and click it twice to add two new layers. Notice that Fireworks automatically names them in sequence and places new layers above existing layers in the

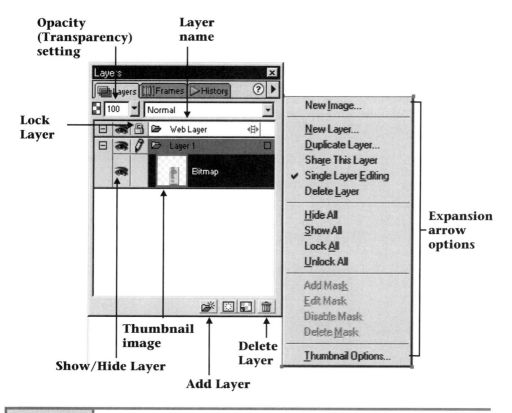

Opacity (Transparency) setting

Layer name

Lock Layer

Thumbnail image

Show/Hide Layer

Add Layer

Delete Layer

Expansion arrow options

Figure 15-5 The Layers panel contains a huge number of options for working with layers

15

"stack" of transparencies. And, just as with transparencies, objects placed on the topmost layer, Layer 3, will hide objects in layers below it. Layer names can be changed by double-clicking the name and typing a new label.

Tip

Give your layers descriptive labels so that you can arrange and modify them more easily. Names such as "background," "shadow text," and "foreground text" make it easier to select the proper layer when you are ready to modify an object.

4. A pencil icon appears to the left of the layer name to indicate that this is the layer where work will take place. To lock a layer to prevent accidentally making changes to the object on the layer, click the pencil icon twice to change it to a lock icon. You can also hide the layer from view by clicking the "eyeball" icon all the way on the left.

5. Use the Text tool and the Text Editor to enter the text **Poinciana Beach** in a font of your choice at about 30 points high in Layer 3. Be sure that the pencil icon appears to the left of the layer name. Once your text is entered, a thumbnail version of the text will appear below the layer name.

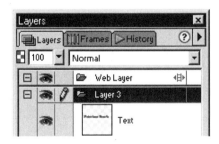

6. With the text in Layer 3 still selected, copy the text to your computer's clipboard by pressing CTRL-C or by choosing Edit | Copy. Lock Layer 3 by clicking the pencil icon twice, and select Layer 2 by clicking its name. Paste

the copy of the text onto the layer by pressing CTRL-V or by choosing Edit |
Paste. The Layers panel will appear as you see here.

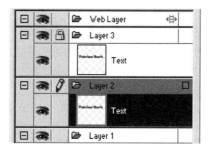

7. Repeat this process to paste a third copy of the text on Layer 1. Now the real
fun can begin.

8. Return to each layer of the document and adjust the properties of the text,
applying Live Effects and changing its position. One example of how your
text might look when you are done is shown here.

9. Layers can be rearranged by dragging the layer up and down in the layers
list. Click and hold on the name of a layer to move it either up or down in
the stack of transparencies. As an object on a layer is repositioned, it
obscures objects below it in the stack.

10. In addition to copying, pasting, and rearranging objects on a layer, this is also
a handy place to change the object's transparency. Select one of the text boxes
on a layer and locate the Opacity setting on the Layers panel, using the slider
to change the transparency of the text to about 50 percent. The image now
changes based on changing the opacity of the topmost text in the stack. This
is a great effect to employ when you want an object to appear out of the
background when making animated GIFs, as you'll do in Module 17.

11. The Web Layer always exists at the top of the stack and cannot be deleted or moved. If a hotspot or other HTML or JavaScript behavior were attached to this image, Fireworks would display a special mask-like image that would overlay the graphic. This is a visual reference only, and while the size and position of the hotspot can be adjusted with the help of the Layers panel, clicking the Hide Layer eyeball icon on the left can just as easily hide it. You will learn more about hotspots and their use in Module 17.

12. Layers provide a level of sophistication well beyond the simple example used in this project. Once your skills develop to the point that you are ready to create more complex graphics that employ the multiple effects that layers provide, you will appreciate the ease with which Fireworks makes the creation of images like the one in Figure 15-6 possible. Once you are done experimenting, you can either discard this file or save it for further practice.

Figure 15-6 Use layers to create complex images with various effects and opacity settings

1-Minute Drill

● How are new layers added to a document?

● How are layers rearranged?

● What is the purpose of the Web Layer?

Project 15-4: Automating Complex Objects with Styles and Symbols

You have probably realized by now that the capabilities of Fireworks as an image-editing program are incredibly deep, and with the advanced features you have seen so far, you can go well beyond creating simple buttons and optimized images for use on the Web. With the incredible number of settings and effects possible when working with both bitmap and vector objects, as well as the sophisticated ways that those objects can be grouped, masked, and layered, it would be easy to get lost in the complexity of the program.

Luckily, Fireworks provides a number of ways to automate the work that you do in order to capture effects and settings so that they can be used repeatedly, saving you the effort of having to redesign every new graphic that you create. In addition to the amount of work this can save you, using styles and symbols can also provide a level of consistency to your graphics that can lead to a more cohesive look and feel for your web site. This project will introduce you to the use of preset styles, explain how to create styles of your own, and describe how to capture images for use throughout your web site through Fireworks' symbols and libraries features.

Step-by-Step

1. Create a new file that is 300 pixels wide by 300 pixels high with a white canvas. Name this file **styles_practice.png**.

● New layers are added to a document by clicking the Add Layer icon at the bottom of the Layers panel.
● Layers are rearranged by clicking and dragging the layer name up or down in the Layers panel.
● The Web Layer contains visual references to any hotspots or behaviors that have been applied to an image.

2. Styles are collections of settings such as strokes, fills, and gradients—combined with effects such as bevels and glows—that have been saved together and appear in the Styles panel, shown in Figure 15-7. Open the Style panel now by selecting Windows | Styles.

3. To see some of these styles in action, first draw a rectangle on the document's canvas. Notice that as you roll your mouse over a style, its name appears in the bottom of the panel. To apply a style, simply click it in the  preview window of the Styles panel. Just that quickly, all of the strokes, fills, bevels, and other effects associated with that particular style are applied, as you can see in this example where Style 17 was applied. Try a few of the styles with this object and with some text that you type in.

4. While there are some great styles included with Fireworks, you can add to your collection at the Macromedia web site, find styles that other designers

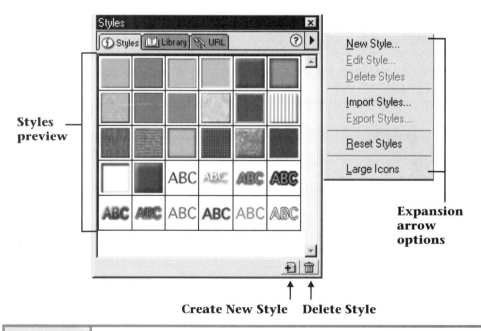

Figure 15-7 The Styles panel contains preset Fireworks styles for use with an object

have posted to the Web, or even create new styles all your own. To make a new style, delete any objects you previously created and draw a new rectangle on the canvas. Apply some new fills, strokes, bevels, or other effects to this new object. When you are finished, make sure the object is selected and choose New Style from the options available with the expansion arrow.

Note

A new object added to the canvas while a style is selected will automatically apply that style. Click in a blank area of the Styles panel to deselect any styles you have been using. You may also find that you need to reset the Effects setting to None, depending on the styles you experimented with.

5. Fireworks now presents the New Style dialog box, shown in Figure 15-8, in which you can choose the settings that you want to be saved and applied with this style. Checking or unchecking the boxes in the dialog box will remove those properties, and Fireworks will present a live preview of the style in the upper-left corner. Choose the style you want to use, give the style a name, and click OK to create the new style.

6. A snapshot of your new style will now be placed in the preview area of the Styles panel. Your only task at this point is to try out your new creation. Draw a few objects of different shapes on the canvas and apply the new style you just created. Incredibly easy and yet equally powerful, styles allow you to define a set of parameters and use them over and over again. Pretty neat stuff!

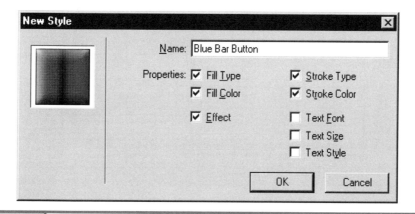

Figure 15-8   Styles are named and defined in the New Style dialog box

15

Tip

If you don't like the way your new style looks, you can choose Edit Style from the expansion arrow options to change it, or delete it entirely by choosing Delete Style.

7. Create a new file that is 300 pixels wide by 300 pixels high with a white canvas. Name this file **symbols_practice.png**.

8. Symbols are copies of images that Fireworks makes accessible in the Library panel. Symbols are just as easy to create as styles, and are particularly useful if you have a graphic that you plan to use over and over again, such as a button or a company logo.

9. Choose Windows | Library to open the Library panel, shown in Figure 15-9.

10. Symbols can be a graphic, an animation, or a special type of graphic that includes an HTML hyperlink, known as a button. To make a new symbol, draw an object on your canvas like the one seen here. You can change the settings and effects for the object manually, or simply apply a style as was done in this example.

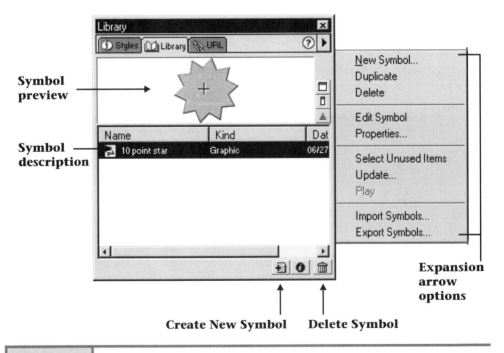

Figure 15-9 The Library panel contains information about symbols that have been created and stored by Fireworks

11. Choose Insert | Convert To Symbol to open the Symbol Properties dialog box, shown in Figure 15-10. Since this is a static graphic, leave the symbol type set to Graphic and click OK after naming the symbol. When you are finished, a preview of the symbol, along with its description, will appear in the Library panel.

12. Once a symbol has been created, multiple copies of the item can be dragged directly from the Library panel and dropped onto the canvas. Each time a symbol is used, Fireworks calls the copy an *instance* of the symbol. In this example, multiple instances of the same symbol have been stacked on the canvas to create a 3-D effect.

13. While this is a great effect, the real power of symbols lies in their ability to automatically be updated whenever the symbol is changed. All you need to do is edit the symbol in the library once, and every file that uses the symbol will automatically be updated when the file is opened. Imagine the time this could save you if you have multiple instances of a particular symbol in use!

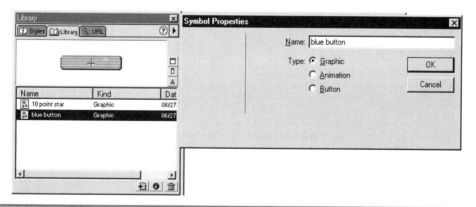

Figure 15-10   Symbols that are defined in the Symbol Properties dialog box will appear in the Library panel

15

14. Choose the symbol you just created by clicking its name in the Library panel. Choose Edit Symbol from the expansion arrow options, and Fireworks will open a special symbol-editing window with a single copy of the symbol on it. The quick and easy way to see this in action is to select the graphic in the symbol-editing window and apply a different style to it. Close the window and return to the document where the symbol was used, and your images will be magically updated to reflect the new settings.

Note

You can create new symbols in the same symbol-editing window that you just saw by selecting Insert | New Symbol. Fireworks will automatically generate a new Document window to work in where you can create the new symbol apart from your primary Document window. You'll learn more about the Symbol Editor in Module 17.

15. Symbols are a great way to not only save yourself the chore of creating a new graphic from scratch every time you need to include a new button or image but also, by using the Library panel, you gain the added (and significant) advantage of having symbols automatically updated any time you edit them. Think back to how you used library items and templates in Dreamweaver, and you will have a good handle on how symbols are used in web design to add consistency to a site's overall style. With the combination of styles and symbols, you will be able to easily and quickly maintain an overall feel to a site that many sites in the rapidly changing world of the Web often lack.

1-Minute Drill

- Define styles.
- Define symbols.

- Styles are collections of settings such as strokes, fills, and gradients—combined with effects such as bevels and glows—that have been saved together and appear in the Styles panel.
- Symbols are copies of images that Fireworks makes accessible in the Library panel.

What to Take Away

In this module, you have seen some of the more powerful features of Fireworks at play as you have learned how to combine objects into groups that can then be further modified by the use of Live Effects. You also learned how mask groups are applied to create stunning new visual effects by combining two objects on a canvas in ways that allow transparencies, patterns, and gradients to interact with bitmaps to enhance their visual impact. In the introduction to layers, you learned how to stack images one on top of the other on virtual transparencies to create even more dynamic effects with your graphics.

With all of the power of those tools at your disposal, the ability to define and apply styles and save and reuse symbols in the Fireworks library becomes even more important. Since modifying and adjusting the effects and settings for individual groups or layered objects can be so time-consuming, the ability to save a set of styles or reuse that perfect button that you labored so hard to get just right is an important method for automating your work. And, as you know from the first part of this book, consistency in web design is a key element in creating a uniform appeal for a site, and can assist in branding your pages in ways that your viewers will find not only appealing, but also helpful when they begin navigating your site.

☑ *Mastery Check*

1. How are grouped objects displayed differently from individual objects in a document when they are selected?

2. Define a mask group.

3. What is the value of using layers in designing an image?

4. Name two methods available for automating design tasks in Fireworks.

Module 16

Optimizing and Exporting Fireworks Files

The Goals of this Module

- Understand the importance of file optimization
- Review appropriate file formats for use on the Web and in print
- Explore options for previewing optimized files
- Apply optimization techniques to GIF and JPEG images
- Understand the features of Export Preview and document previews
- Apply image slicing techniques to large graphics

In Module 6, you learned how images impact web design and encountered some of the challenges presented by their use. In summary, images are read universally by browsers only when they are in the GIF or JPEG formats that all common browsers support. GIF images are superior where a limited range of colors is required, such as the simple styles found in many of the vector shapes and text you have been working with in Fireworks. Photographs, and vector-based images that have fine differences among colors, such as gradients, are more suitable when converted and saved to the JPEG format.

Note

You may wish to review Module 6 for a more thorough discussion of the impact of images and file sizes on web design.

All of the files you have created to this point have been in the Fireworks PNG format. Recognizing that converting these files to web-friendly GIFs and JPEGs would be a major component of a program designed from the ground up to create graphics for the Web, the developers at Macromedia have equipped Fireworks with a number of ways to fine-tune images so they maintain quality while achieving the smallest file sizes possible. This is no mean feat, and until Fireworks came along, most designers working on graphics intended for publication to the Web had to wade through multiple complicated steps to do both. Fireworks takes all of those steps and contains them in the same kind of compact panels and dialog boxes that you are now familiar with, allowing you to quickly minimize the download time of a graphic and convert it to the proper format.

In addition to the standard methods for file optimization available, you will also learn a technique often used when large graphics are required on a web page, called *slicing*. When large images are sliced, they are broken into several smaller graphics that are then reassembled in an HTML table that is inserted into a web page. Before Fireworks, this was an incredibly tedious task that didn't always work out just right, but with the slicing tools that Fireworks provides, optimizing large files so that they download as quickly as possible is a relatively painless operation.

Note

Be sure that you have downloaded the exercise files for this module from www.osborne.com.

Project 16-1: Optimizing Files with the Export Preview Feature

Optimizing and exporting Fireworks PNG files is a four-step process. Every time that you need to prepare an image for use in another program, whether for the Web or for print, you will need to complete these four tasks:

1. Choose the best file format for the image based on the number of colors it contains and how it will be used.

2. Specify the optimization settings for the image by choosing the amount of file compression that most closely maintains the quality of the original image.

3. Adjust the number of colors used in the image.

4. Establish specific export options based on how the graphic is to be used.

While the thought of having to complete four separate steps in order to export a graphic may seem a bit much, Fireworks' ability to accomplish these tasks so easily and consistently is part of the program's appeal for web designers, and a big reason that it has become the leading software application for designing web-specific graphics.

Step-by-Step

1. From the exercise files for this module, open two Fireworks PNG files you will find there—girls_text.png and girls_photo.png. Both images are in the native Fireworks format and must be optimized prior to exporting the files to a format for the Web.

2. Take a good look at the images as they are shown in Figure 16-1. Notice that girls_text.png, while colorful, contains a limited number of colors, and the image overall is relatively flat—making this file suitable for the GIF format. The photograph of the girls, on the other hand, has fine differences in the amount of colors that are displayed, especially soft tones such as the girls' skin and hair colors. The photograph should be exported to a JPEG format.

3. With the many ways that Fireworks is able to modify and apply effects to images, you cannot always assume that every vector-based image is best exported to the GIF format, or that every photograph or scanned image should become a JPEG. In addition to examining how the image looks, you must also decide how it will be used. GIFs, for instance, do a better job of displaying parts of the image transparently, which allows them to more seamlessly blend into the background of a web page. JPEGs, on the other hand, can contain millions of colors, and for those images where you need more than the maximum 216 colors that GIFs allow, a JPEG is the appropriate choice.

Figure 16-1 By closely examining the number of colors and the amount of color gradations, you should be able to decide between the GIF and JPEG formats

4. Fireworks provides two separate ways for you to optimize files and then preview the results: either through a dialog box or by adjusting settings while working "live" on the image in the main Document window. In this first example, you will be introduced to the dialog box method.

5. Select the girls_text.png image that you opened previously. Based on the number of colors in this graphic, it needs to be optimized for the GIF format.

6. In the File menu, you have two choices for optimizing and exporting your file: either the Export Wizard, which will hold your hand while you decide which file format to choose, or Export Preview, which takes you directly to the Export Preview dialog box, shown in Figure 16-2. Make sure that girls_text.png is the active file and choose File | Export Preview.

7. On the left side of the Export Preview dialog box are three tabbed panels that control the settings for file optimization—Options, File, and Animation. Since you will learn about animation in the next module, discussion of that panel will be set aside to focus on the other two.

   The File panel is used to apply final settings for size and numeric cropping of the image. This panel is useful if you have one master graphic that is then used in different images by cropping or resizing the master graphic.

   Contained in the Options panel are those parameters that control how the file is compressed—depending on the format—and additional choices for limiting the number of colors used in the image. Most of your optimization work will take place in this panel.

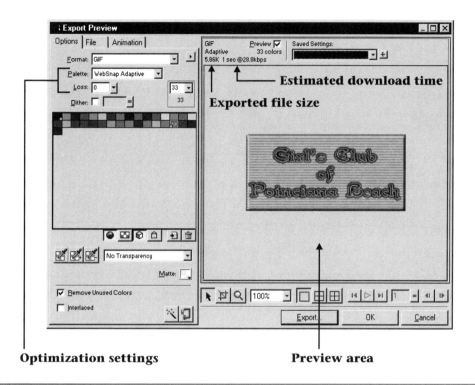

Figure 16-2 The Export Preview dialog box provides multiple options for controlling file sizes and quality

8. The primary means of optimizing a GIF file is to adjust the number of colors that are used in the graphic. Changing the color palette is a simple matter of clicking the expansion arrow and choosing a new set of colors based on the number that will be available. As you do this, watch the file and download sizes change above the preview area.

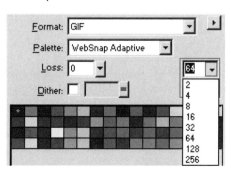

9. In this example, a small file size of only 3.24K has been achieved by setting the number of colors used to only 8, but you'll notice that the quality of the image has suffered as a result.

10. Here, the quality of the image has been improved by adjusting the number of colors in the palette to 128, but the file size has grown to 11.43K as a result.

11. This is the crucial part of optimizing the file—deciding what carries more weight for you and for the goals of your site. If this graphic were one of only a few that were to be inserted into an HTML page, then a larger file size with better quality should not be a problem. On the other hand, if the web page will have many similar, or larger, graphics, then you may need to sacrifice quality to gain download time. Ultimately, you must decide where the right balance is for your site's needs and choose the optimization settings that best meet them.

Tip

Open Dreamweaver and insert the image into a blank page to see the total effect of the graphic on estimated download times. Remember that Dreamweaver also tracks file sizes and displays an estimate of how long it will take a page to load in the toolbar area at the bottom of the Dreamweaver Document window.

12. The Export Preview dialog box includes the ability to change to different file formats and quickly compare file sizes. Try this now by changing the export file type to JPEG. While the image quality improves, the file size jumps to 15.21K. Try the TIFF format, which is recommended for files that will be used in desktop publishing applications, and the size balloons to 60.68K. By using the Format drop-down box, you can quickly switch between the available image formats of GIF, JPEG, BMP, PNG, or TIFF and compare the results.

13. Beyond simply limiting the colors available in the GIF color palette, you can also do some fine-tuning to your image while in the Export Preview dialog box. Dithering, for instance, is the process of automatically replacing one color for another so that colors outside the basic 256-color web palette are simulated. Dithering will improve the look of GIFs that have greater than 256 colors in the source file, but will increase the file size as a result. Dithering is applied by checking the Dither check box, located near the middle of the dialog box. Once the box is checked, you can set the amount of dithering to be applied by using the slider that appears.

14. Interlacing, accessed at the bottom of the panel, is the process of dividing an image into component parts that download more quickly in a browser. The viewer's browser will display a low-resolution version of the graphic almost as soon as the page opens, and then fill in the details as more information is received at the viewer's computer. Interlacing can be a good way to keep viewers interested in how a large image will ultimately display once the entire image is downloaded from the server. To set this option, simply check the Interlaced box.

15. When optimizing a GIF or JPEG that has a transparent element, be sure that the Transparency options have been set. For most images with a transparent canvas or transparent elements, you will want to set this option to Index Transparency. Alpha Transparency gives you more precise options and allows you to set a transparent element within an image, without affecting the transparency of the canvas. Again, this is a simple process of making the selection and letting Fireworks do the rest.

16. Fireworks provides a super option for use with graphics that may need to be used on web pages with different colors. Instead of going back to the original image and changing the color of the canvas, you can simply apply a matte during the optimization process, choosing the color you want applied with the standard Color Chooser. In Figure 16-3, the same graphic has been set to display with four different mattes, and is displayed using the 4-Up preview panel option accessible at the bottom of the dialog box.

17. At the bottom of the Export Preview dialog box, you will find two buttons that will complete the process of optimizing this image. To accept the optimization settings for this file and return to the Fireworks Document window, just click the OK button. You will need to select File | Export Preview to return to the dialog box to make more adjustments, but you will be able to convert the file to its new format by choosing File | Export.

18. Clicking the Export button takes you directly to the Export dialog box, shown in Figure 16-4. For a standard GIF or JPEG format, accept the file type as Images Only, browse to the location on your hard drive where you want

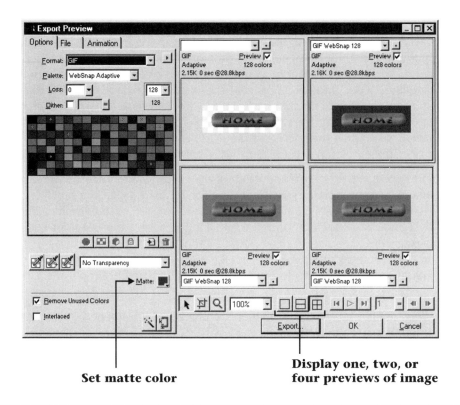

Set matte color

Display one, two, or four previews of image

Figure 16-3	Mattes can be applied in any color to match the background of a web page or other document

the file to be saved, give the file a name, and click OK. That's it! You've optimized and exported your first Fireworks file!

19. Remember that once you export a file, you actually have two images saved—the original Fireworks PNG format with all the original colors and the optimizations settings you have chosen, and a second GIF version of the same image that has been optimized. Close girls_text.png now and save the original file when Fireworks prompts you to do so.

Tip

Keep your original Fireworks PNG files in folders that mirror the file structure of your web site but contain unique names that identify them as the originals, such as "images_png_originals." This will make it easier to find the original when you need to make an adjustment to an optimized file.

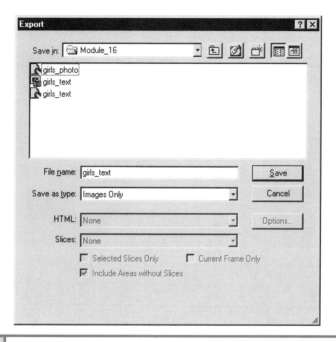

Figure 16-4 Filenames, file types, and file locations for an exported file are set in the Export dialog box

20. With the file girls_photo.png open, choose File | Export Preview and refer to Figure 16-5 during the following discussion of how JPEG images are optimized for export.

21. In the same way that the color palette is restricted for the export of files in the GIF format, JPEG file optimization takes place by limiting the colors available for the image as well. JPEGs, however, use a setting known as Quality that removes colors through a mathematical process. Two standard quality settings are available from the Saved Settings drop-down box above the preview area: JPEG - Better Quality and JPEG - Smaller File. Try both of these settings now while paying close attention to the file size and image quality that results.

22. Image quality settings can also be fine-tuned in the Options panel by choosing the slider that appears when you choose the Quality box. You probably noticed that this image gets very fuzzy when set to the Smaller File option. Instead of using the value of 60 that this preset gives you, try setting the Quality value between 60 and 80 and see if you can find a balance between small file sizes and image quality. Just as with GIFs, choosing between optimal download times and an acceptable image quality is a delicate balancing act.

Optimization presets

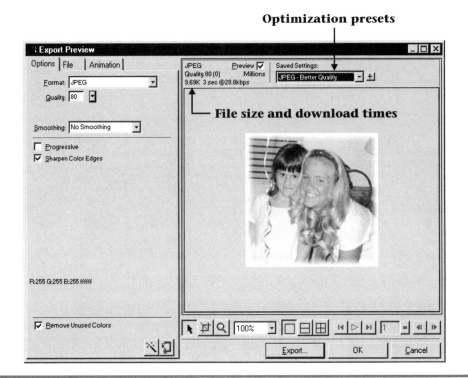

File size and download times

Figure 16-5 Preparing files for export to the JPEG format requires setting options for file quality and smoothing

23. Choosing the Quality setting is the primary way that JPEG files are optimized, just as limiting the color palette allows you to optimize GIFs. In addition to that choice, you can also use the Progressive option, which works in the same way that interlacing works with GIFs—producing a low-resolution image when the page opens and then adding detail as more information is received at the viewer's computer. You may also want to experiment with sharpening color edges to produce crisper images, but with a sacrifice in file size. And, just as with GIFs, a matte can be applied to the canvas when you need the image to match a particular background on a web page.

24. When colors are removed from a JPEG image, the results may look "blocky" if a range of colors similar to one another is taken out of the image. To fine-tune the image, and blend similar colors together, choose one of the Smoothing settings available. With options available from No Smoothing to Maximum

Smoothing and a range of choices in between, smoothing can help improve the overall quality of the image while maintaining smaller file sizes.

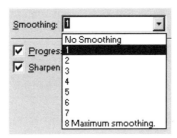

25. The final step to exporting this image is identical to the one you used in step 20. Click the Export button and set the filename and location in the Export dialog box, and your file will be converted to a JPEG image ready for use on your web site. Meanwhile, remember to save the original PNG file for further use in the next project.

1-Minute Drill

- What is the first step in optimizing and exporting Fireworks PNG files?
- What is the primary method for limiting file sizes for the GIF format?
- What is the primary method for limiting file sizes for the JPEG format?

Project 16-2: Optimizing and Exporting Files from the Document Window

While the Export Preview option puts all the tools you need for optimizing and exporting your files in one easy-to-access location, many designers choose to take advantage of the other method for previewing, optimizing, and exporting files that Fireworks provides—working directly in the Document window itself, where optimized versions of files will display "live" while you work on the original. This project will lead you through a discussion of using this option. Ultimately, though, your own preferences will decide whether you work in the Document window or use the Export Preview option.

- The first step in optimizing and exporting Fireworks files is to choose the appropriate export file format.
- The primary method for reducing file size in a GIF format is to limit the number of colors used in the color palette.
- The primary method for reducing file size in a JPEG format is to limit the number of colors used, by adjusting the Quality setting.

Step-by-Step

1. Open the original copy of girls_text.png that you used in the last project and take note of the four tabs across the top of the Document window—Original, Preview, 2-Up, and 4-Up.

2. Click the Preview tab and you will see a GIF version of this image, based on any previously saved export and optimization settings. If you completed the last project and optimized this file, you would see those settings applied in the preview. Fireworks tracks and saves all optimization settings applied to your files and, by default, returns to the settings that were last used when the file was exported.

3. In addition to a single preview, you can also see the original and the optimized version of the file in the preview called 2-Up. Click this tab now and your Document window will appear as you see in Figure 16-6.

4. One of the primary reasons to operate in this preview area is that you will see any changes you make to the original image automatically applied to the preview. This can be a real time-saver when you want to try out new settings or just tweak an image for either better quality or better download time. You can switch between the original and the optimized file simply by clicking in either window and looking for the black border that appears around the active window. In 2-Up preview, the original file will display on the left.

5. Even more previews are available when the 4-Up tab is selected. In this mode, you can set optimization for three versions of the original, and can even switch between GIF and JPEG formats so that you can examine the results of your choices. In 4-Up preview, the original file will display in the upper-left corner of the Document window.

6. Whether you are working in the single, 2-Up, or 4-Up preview, optimization settings are accessed while working in the Document window from a new panel—the Optimize panel. Choose Windows | Optimize to open the Optimize panel, shown in Figure 16-7 for a file set to export as a GIF.

7. Setting the optimization parameters for a GIF file in the Optimize panel is identical to the method you used when working with the Export Preview dialog box. Start by limiting the number of choices available and then fine-tune the image by using options such as dithering, transparency, and background mattes. The primary advantage here is that you can also see a live preview of how the optimized file will appear as you make changes to the original.

Original image   Optimized image

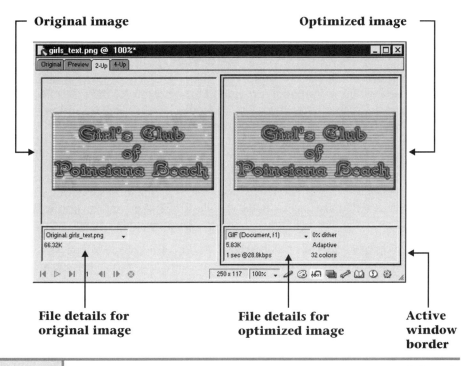

File details for   File details for   Active
original image   optimized image   window
                                                                     border

Figure 16-6 | The 2-Up preview displays original and optimized images side by side

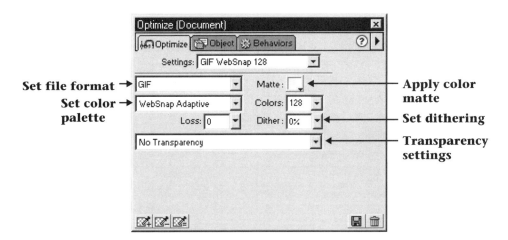

Set file format →

Set color
palette →

                                                        ← Apply color
                                                          matte

                                                        ← Set dithering

                                                        Transparency
                                                        settings

Figure 16-7 | The Optimize panel contains the same optimization settings for GIF
files available in the Export Preview dialog box

8. In the 4-Up preview mode, you can even change the optimization for the three preview images that Fireworks displays. Simply click anywhere in the window of the image that you want to optimize and then change the settings with the Optimize panel. By using this option, you can compare three entirely different sets of optimized images, as shown in Figure 16-8. Take note of the information provided at the bottom of the Document window for each image where Fireworks displays the file size and estimated download time for each version of the graphic.

9. Open girls_photo.png now and choose the 2-Up option in the Document window. The Optimize panel changes to the JPEG options shown in Figure 16-9.

10. Just as with the Export Preview dialog box, the Quality setting for a JPEG image is the primary way to adjust the file size. The higher the Quality setting, the more colors that will be used and the larger the file size will be.

11. Once you have optimized either a GIF or JPEG (or PNG, BMP, or TIFF) file, you are ready to export the image. While you could return to the Export

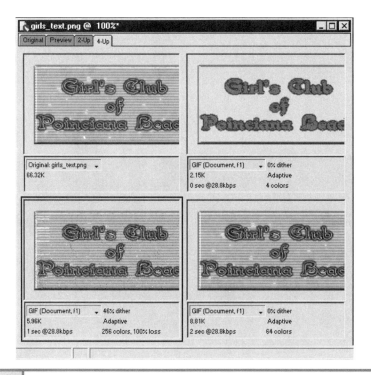

Figure 16-8   Use the 4-Up preview to see how different optimization settings will affect an image's file size and appearance

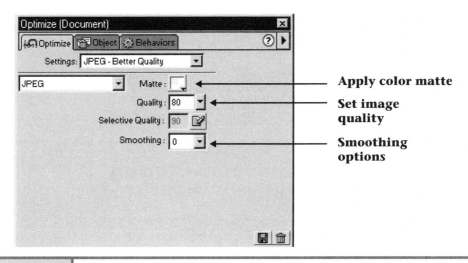

Apply color matte

Set image
quality

Smoothing
options

Figure 16-9   Optimizing JPEG files with the Optimize panel entails establishing
the quality of file to be exported and using other settings to fine-tune
the image

Preview dialog box at this time, the easiest method is to first select the
version of the image that you wish to export by clicking anywhere in the
window of the version you have chosen, and then choose File | Export to
go directly to the Export dialog box. Just as with Export Preview, set the
filename and location, and click OK to have Fireworks convert the file to
the format you have selected.

12. Ultimately, you may find working directly in the Document window to be a
great choice for you, or you may feel restricted by the smaller window size
and prefer to use Export Preview. However, to really appreciate the advantages
of working in this mode, try creating a new image while working in the 2-Up
preview mode. Notice which effects translate well to the GIF format. Do glows,
for instance, take a great deal of file size to display properly? Do they look
better in a JPEG format? The real plus here is being able to try out new things
in a document and then see immediately the effect it has on your image.
Can you afford the additional file size and download time that the cool
effect you're fond of costs you? Working in the preview mode can help
you make that kind of decision and more.

13. To complete this project, experiment with the optimization settings for both
of the sample files. You can save or discard any changes you make to these
files since you will not be using them again here.

1-Minute Drill

● Which Fireworks panel is used for changing file optimization settings?

● Which preview panel is used when you want to see the original version displayed next to a single optimized version of the same graphic?

● How can the preview panels assist you in choosing appropriate effects and colors for use in a graphic?

Project 16-3: Using Image Slicing with Large Graphics

There may be times when the needs of your web site require a particularly large graphic for insertion into a web page. Perhaps you want to create an image map (which you will learn about in Module 18) so that hyperlinks can be embedded in a graphic, or have a need for a large graphic that simply won't have the impact you need if set at a smaller size. Slicing, where an image is literally cut into rectangular pieces, like pieces of a puzzle, and then reassembled in an HTML table, can greatly improve the download time when compared to an unsliced image. In addition, when an image is sliced, the individual slices can have properties of their own, including different file types for export, hotspots that contain hyperlinks, and even rollovers that function inside the image. Slicing has some very sophisticated uses, and in this project, you will get an introduction to how slices are created and some of the special considerations required when they are exported.

Step-by-Step

1. From the exercise files for this module, locate the file named slice_practice.png and open it.

Tip

You may recognize this image as the one that you duplicated in Project 12-5. For additional practice in the use of Fireworks' tools, you may want to work with the file you created in that exercise. After you open the file, create and insert a new symbol, duplicating the buttons you see in Figure 16-10. Use the Arrange features found in the Modify menu to arrange the buttons, and then add the text and group your new buttons.

● The Optimize panel is used for applying the same settings available in the Export Preview dialog box.
● The 2-Up panel displays a copy of the original Fireworks PNG file alongside the optimized version of the graphic.
● Since any work done with the original Fireworks PNG file will automatically display estimated download times in a preview panel, this method is useful for gauging the effect a change will have on overall file size.

16

2. Fireworks contains a great feature that has not been covered to this point. *Guides* are special layout tools that are placed on top of an image to assist you in aligning images or, as in this case, for slicing a large graphic into smaller rectangular images. To create a guide, you must first enable the rulers for your document, which Fireworks will place above and to the left side of your canvas. To turn rulers on, choose View | Rulers, the result of which you see in Figure 16-10.

3. To create a guide, place your pointer anywhere within one of the ruler areas and simply click and drag to "pull" a guide away from the ruler. As your pointer moves away from the ruler, a green line will appear. This is your guide, which can now be positioned anywhere you choose on the canvas with the pointer. Multiple guides can be created, but to keep this project simple, drag one horizontal guide and one vertical guide onto the canvas and position them so they overlap near the center of the image. When you are finished, your image with its two guides should appear as you see in Figure 16-11.

4. These guides will not appear in the image when it is exported to a web format, but they do let you perform some magic during the export process. With just these two simple guides, you can now create four separate documents that Fireworks will put into an HTML document, which in turn can be inserted into

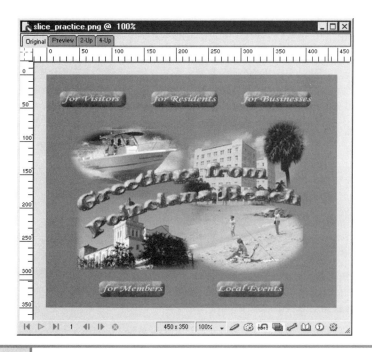

Figure 16-10   Rulers are useful as layout tools and as a way to create guides

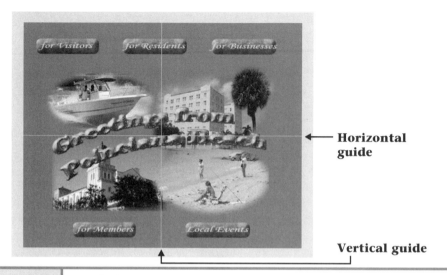

Figure 16-11 Divide the image into four separate rectangles by creating and positioning two guides

a web page. To begin the process, choose File | Export Preview. As with any image, adjust the optimization settings for the image and preview your optimized settings. When you are satisfied that you have achieved the correct balance between file size and image quality, click the Export button.

5. The Export dialog box is where all the real action for a sliced image takes place. As you can see in Figure 16-12, there are a number of settings that are different from those you used with the GIF and JPEG images exported previously.

6. Fireworks is about to create an HTML table that will hold the four rectangular pieces of the image together. Just a few years ago, designers had to do this by hand, but Fireworks makes the process simple, as long as you get the export settings correct. Start by using the Save As Type drop-down box to change from Images Only to HTML And Images. This option must be used so that you can insert the HTML table into a web page.

7. In the HTML options, choose Export HTML File so that Fireworks will create the table to hold the images and save them to your hard drive.

8. Finally, in the Slices area, use the setting Slice Along Guides so that Fireworks will use the guides you placed on the image to slice it into separate rectangles. Your file is almost ready for export now. .

9. With image slices, managing the files that are created is a prime consideration. In this simple exercise, you will be creating five separate documents—the four pieces of the original image plus the HTML file that holds the image

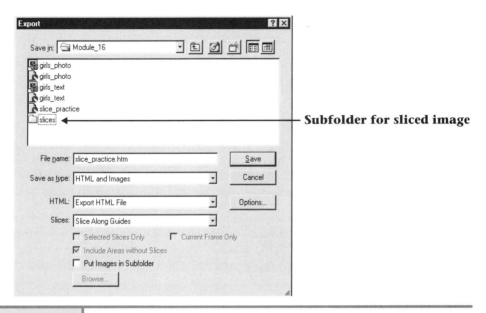

Subfolder for sliced image

Figure 16-12 Special export settings are required when exporting sliced images

together. While five files may not seem like a large number to deal with, it is best to create a new subfolder to hold the images in one storage location. Fireworks will automatically name the five files for you (unless you choose to do it manually), and having them in a separate subfolder will make them easier to find and modify later on.

Note

You must be careful at this point to scrupulously follow the file-naming guidelines for the Web—use only lowercase letters and do not use spaces in your file or folder names. In this case, the name **slices** has been used, but in actual practice, use a subfolder name that identifies the file and its use.

10. Once your subfolder is created and open, just click the Save button, and Fireworks will generate the files for you. If you check your files, you will see that one HTML file and four image files have been created from the one image. You are now ready to insert the image into a web page.

11. Dreamweaver has a terrific way to access the HTML that needs to be inserted to reassemble your image. Open Dreamweaver and create a new document. In the Common category of the Objects panel, locate the Insert Fireworks HTML button.

12. To insert the HTML, browse to the subfolder where you stored the file with the image slices in steps 9 and 10. Remember, the HTML file is what needs to be inserted, not the images. Select the file and click OK to insert it into your practice web page. Almost magically, the image is reassembled and appears in your page as if it had never been cut apart. Preview the completed image in a browser, as has been done in Figure 16-13, and you'll be able to see for yourself how efficiently Fireworks has accomplished the task of slicing and reassembling this image.

13. Image slicing is a great tool for dealing with large images and improving the download time of a large graphic. However, because of the number of images that are created, there are file management issues that should be thought through before you use this technique. For now, you can save or discard the practice images you have been working on, as you conclude this project.

1-Minute Drill

● What objects must be visible in the Document window before a guide can be created?

● Which dialog box is used for setting the options necessary to create sliced images?

● What kind of file is inserted into a web page when a sliced image is used?

What to Take Away

Optimizing and exporting graphics files is a key component of how Fireworks is used, and as software that was designed from the start for use as a web-specific graphics tool, it contains a huge number of options for creating files that download as quickly as possible while maintaining image quality. This optimization process is always necessary for images that are exported for use in other applications, and is especially true when working with images for the Web.

● To create guides, you must first make rulers visible in the Document window.
● The Export dialog box is used to instruct Fireworks to slice along guides and create an HTML table to hold the image together.
● To reassemble a sliced image, the HTML file created when images are sliced is inserted into a web page.

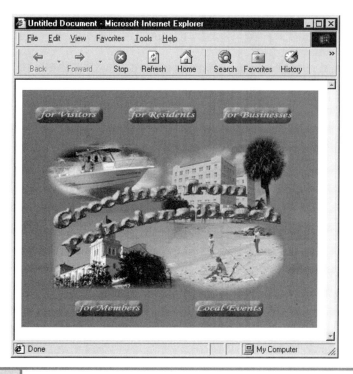

Figure 16-13 Sliced images are reassembled seamlessly for presentation in a browser

Through either the Export Preview dialog box or the use of the preview tabs in the Document window, you now know how to prepare both GIF and JPEG images for export by limiting the number of colors they use, and by adjusting other settings that impact the quality and download time of the graphic. In addition, you have also seen how large images can automatically be sliced into separate pieces that Fireworks and Dreamweaver work together to reassemble into a web page. With the variety of drawing and composing tools that Fireworks includes, coupled with its many options for file optimization, it is easy to see why this program has become a favorite of web designers all over the world.

☑️ Mastery Check

1. What is the primary goal when *optimizing* Fireworks PNG files?

2. What is the primary goal when *exporting* Fireworks PNG files?

3. What two methods does Fireworks provide for viewing and adjusting optimization settings?

4. Describe an image that is best exported to the GIF format.

5. Describe an image that is best exported to the JPEG format.

6. How does the number of colors present in an image affect file size? How is this applied in file optimization?

Module 17

Creating Animated Files with Fireworks

The Goals of this Module

- Understand the principles of animation
- Explore Fireworks' options for creating animations
- Use the Frame panel to animate files
- Create and use animated symbols and instances
- Apply animation techniques to fine-tune an image
- Understand animated file optimization and export options

S ince 1987, animated files on the Internet have been handled by a version of
the GIF format that allows a series of images to be played back in sequence.
More like a miniature filmstrip than a movie, animated GIFs can create the
illusion of movement or perform other animation tricks such as having different
objects fade in or out of an image. Since they are a variation of the GIF format,
these types of files have the same limitations as standard GIFs—colors are
limited to 216 web-safe colors and fine variations in shades and tones do not
display well. And, unlike other animation formats such as Flash, Director, or
QuickTime, animated GIFs cannot contain sounds or provide interactivity for
the viewer. Even though they have these limitations, animated GIFs are the
most common files in use on the Web where the illusion of movement is
needed, because of one factor—they are widely supported by all common
browsers without the need for a plug-in. Fireworks provides all the tools you
need to design and build animations that take full advantage of the format's
possibilities, and helps you to work around its limitations.

In version 4 of Fireworks, a new, and very powerful feature has been added
to the lineup of the program's tools. Animated *symbols* allow you to create a
miniature animation that can be used over and over as part of an animated GIF.
Much like actors on a stage, these animated symbols are provided with movement
and actions they can perform independently as an animation unfolds.

As you would expect where an image contains multiple graphics, file size
and download times are a major issue in the creation of animated GIFs. While
Fireworks provides the usual tools for optimizing and exporting animated files,
it is extremely important that file size be taken into account at every step in the
process of creating animations. The most successful animated GIFs are those
that load quickly and create the visual impact desired in the simplest manner
possible. Techniques such as limiting the colors and effects used, reducing the
number of graphics contained in the image, and animating carefully are all part
of successfully designing animated files.

Fireworks can be used to create animations in one of two ways: either
frame-by-frame animation that is done manually—creating or copying objects
into different frames—or by using the tools that Fireworks provides to make
animation symbols. Frame-by-frame animation is the simpler of the two, and
is useful when you want to make a quick animation to use a single time. Symbols,
on the other hand, while very powerful because of the way they can be combined
and reused, require the use of multiple Fireworks panels and a little more
in-depth work on the part of the designer. Ultimately, you will find yourself

choosing the animation technique that fits your work style best and accomplishes your animation goals with the least amount of effort while achieving the desired result.

Project 17-1: Creating Frame-by-Frame Animations

An animation is essentially a trick; whether it's a Bugs Bunny cartoon, a full-length Disney movie, or an animated computer graphic, animations all function the same way. A series of images are placed on separate canvases, called frames, and then played back in rapid succession. Where there are differences between one frame and the next, the eye translates the change as movement, effectively tricking the mind into believing that the object has moved on the screen. Creating computer animations is the process of designing these separate frames and then arranging them in a manner that creates this illusion.

In Fireworks, the Frames panel is the primary tool for creating, organizing, and working with frames, that when pieced together and played, make objects on the canvas appear to move. "Movement" is a relative term, since, while it can describe an object that actually changes its position on the canvas, an object can also change its transparency, grow or shrink in size, or even rotate around an axis. Animations can be powerful tools for attracting attention to an element of a web page, and if designed and optimized carefully, can add a sophisticated and exciting look to a web page.

Step-by-Step

1. To begin understanding animations, create a new file that is 300 pixels wide by 300 pixels high with a white canvas. Name this file **frames_practice.png**.

2. Open the Frames panel by choosing Windows | Frames and refer to Figure 17-1 for an overview of the main features of the panel. The panel has been positioned on top of the document's canvas for clarity.

3. As you can see, your new file has exactly one frame, called Frame 1, in the Frames panel. To create an animation, the first step is to add frames to the file. To do this, click the expansion arrow and choose the option to Add Frames, which will open the Add Frames dialog box. In the Number text box, type **3** to add three frames to the file, choose the After Current Frame option, and click OK.

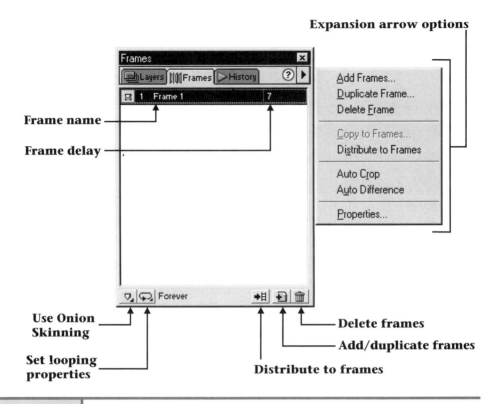

Figure 17-1 The Frames panel allows you to create, delete, organize, and apply properties to animated files

Note

You can also add one frame at a time by clicking the Add Frame button at the bottom of the panel.

4. The Frames panel now contains four frames, and the process of creating your first animation can begin. Select Frame 1 by clicking its name in the Frames panel, and draw a simple vector object on your canvas, such as a circle, in the upper-left corner, as you see here. With the circle selected, choose Edit | Copy to place a copy of the circle on your computer's clipboard.

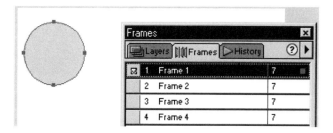

17

Note

When frames are added, the first new frame in the sequence is automatically selected. Be sure that you are working in the correct frame by checking to see that it is highlighted in the Frames panel.

5. Next, select Frame 2 in the Frames panel and choose Edit | Paste to place a copy of the circle from Frame 1 onto the new blank canvas. Position the new circle a little lower than the first one. Complete this process by copying circles in Frames 3 and 4 as well, dropping each circle a little lower on your canvas.

6. Once you have a circle in each frame, you can use a nice feature that Fireworks provides for positioning the different objects. Onion Skinning will create semitransparent versions of each object in the animation sequence and allow you to position or modify them as you wish. To turn on Onion Skinning, locate the button in the bottom of the Frames panel (labeled in Figure 17-1), click it, and select the option Show All Frames from the menu that appears. Once Onion Skinning is enabled, your image will appear as you see here, with the object on the selected frame at full opacity, and the objects on the other frames shown semitransparently.

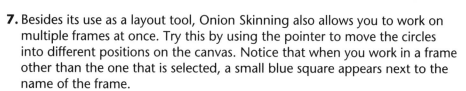

7. Besides its use as a layout tool, Onion Skinning also allows you to work on multiple frames at once. Try this by using the pointer to move the circles into different positions on the canvas. Notice that when you work in a frame other than the one that is selected, a small blue square appears next to the name of the frame.

8. To see your animation in action, use the Play/Stop button at the bottom of the Document window. Just like the buttons on a VCR or CD player, you can play or stop a preview of your animation by using these controls. As each frame plays in sequence, the object appears to move on the canvas, and your first animation is complete.

Tip

Use the 2-Up preview panel to check the file size of this simple animation and to see a preview of how it will look in the animated GIF format.

9. You have now seen how a simple animated sequence is created using the frame-by-frame animation technique. By using the Frames panel, you have added frames and then inserted objects into each frame. Positioning the objects in different areas of the canvas provides the illusion of movement, and your first animation comes to life when it is played.

10. Fireworks has a great feature that allows you to take some of the work out of this simple animation process. Objects that are placed on a canvas can be distributed equally to frames, effectively taking much of the effort out of creating an animated sequence. To see this feature, create a new 300×300-pixel document and name it **frames_practice2.png**.

11. Draw an object on the canvas and choose Edit | Copy to place a copy of the object on your computer's clipboard. Then choose Edit | Paste to create a new copy of the object, but do not add any new frames at this time. As before, move the new object away from the original slightly so the illusion of movement can be created. Complete this process so that you have a total of four objects on your canvas arranged as you see in Figure 17-2.

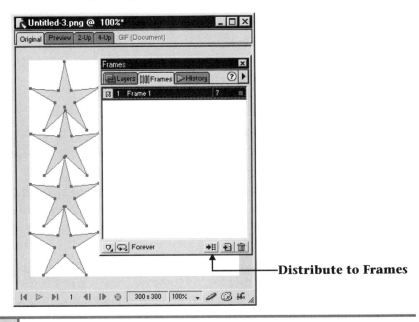

Distribute to Frames

Figure 17-2 Choosing the Distribute To Frames option automatically animates multiple objects

17

12. Choose Edit I Select All so that all four objects are selected, and then click the Distribute To Frames button at the bottom of the Frames panel. Almost magically, three frames are added to the document, and by using the Play button, you can see your new animation in action.

Note

Objects are distributed to frames in the order in which they are created. The original object will be on Frame 1, the first copy on Frame 2, the second on Frame 3, and so on.

13. Frame-by-frame animation can also be used for other techniques that add spice to an animation. To make the object in this animation appear to fade in from the background as it moves, for instance, the opacity settings for objects in each frame can be adjusted manually by using the setting found in the Layers panel.

14. To apply this technique, select Frame 1 in the Frames panel and then select the object. Switch to the Layers panel and adjust the opacity (transparency) setting to around 20 percent, as shown in Figure 17-3. Continue in this way, adjusting the opacity for objects in the remaining frames until you reach the last frame and the opacity setting remains at 100 percent. Play your animation, and your object will appear from out of the background of the canvas.

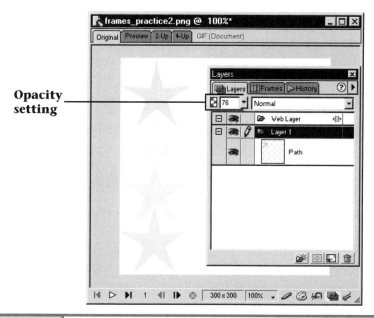

Opacity setting

Figure 17-3 | The opacity setting in the Layers panel is used for manually adjusting the transparency of an object

15. While this effect looks pretty good, adding frames to the document and further adjusting the opacity settings will lead to a smoother animation. Since the file size of an animation can quickly grow quite large, it is best to start with the smallest number of frames that you think will provide a smooth animation, and then add frames as necessary. Select Frame 4 and add four additional frames to this file now by clicking the expansion arrow in the Frames panel and choosing Duplicate Frame. Duplicating the frames will place a copy of any objects on the selected frame, with all their properties intact, onto new frames as specified in the Duplicate Frames dialog box. In the Number text box, type **4** to place four new frames, choose the After Current Frame option, and click OK.

Tip

An object or group of objects that are selected in one frame can also be copied onto other frames by choosing the Copy To Frames option.

16. You can now return to the Frames panel and Layers panel, and working between the two, adjust the opacity setting of the eight objects. The fade-in effect will appear much smoother now that the document has eight frames, but you will also notice that the file size has increased as well when you check the 2-Up preview panel. Just as with optimizing PNG files, you must find the balance between file size and image quality when designing animations.

17. Modifying Live Effects that are applied to objects can be another useful way to create animations. To create text that has an alternating glow effect applied takes only two frames, for instance, and can do a great job of drawing attention to your animation. To see this effect in action, create a new file and name it **frames_practice3.png**. Type any text in the middle of the canvas, and drag the name of the frame in the Frames panel (Frame 1) onto the Add/Duplicate Frames button to make one new frame with a copy of the text in the same position on the canvas.

18. On Frame 2, select the text and open the Effects panel. Simply apply a small glow effect to the object and adjust the color, and your new animation will appear with a flashing glow effect. This is a very quick and easy way to use an animation to draw attention, with the added benefit of maintaining a small file size.

19. In addition to naming and organizing frames, the Frames panel is also the place where you can adjust the amount of time that each frame displays as the animation runs and how many times it will run, or loop.

20. Locate the Frame Delay setting at the far right of the Frames panel for any of the sample animations you have done. Double-clicking this area will open a small window in the Frames panel, shown in Figure 17-4, where you can

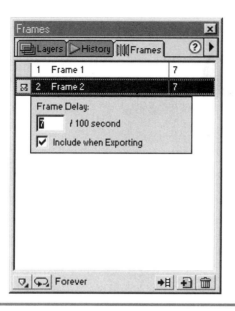

Figure 17-4   Frame timing is adjusted in the Frame Delay portion of the Frames panel

adjust the timing for each individual frame, in increments of 1/100 second. By default, frames play at 7/100 second, but you can just as easily set them to display for one quarter of a second by changing the setting to 25/100 Second, for example, or for three full seconds by making the setting 300/100 Second. As you experiment with animations, you will find that you often need to make adjustments to the frame timing so that important items don't disappear too quickly.

Note

Don't expect your animation timings to be perfectly exact when seen in a browser. Both the version of the browser in use and the speed of the viewer's Internet connection can affect how the animation will replay.

21. Looping determines how many times an animation will run, and should be given careful consideration when you design your animations. Large animations in particular should be set to run only a few times, since the constant animation will undoubtedly distract (and possibly annoy) your viewer. To set looping, click the Looping button in the bottom part of the Frames panel, as shown in Figure 17-5, and set the number of loops to one of the available values.

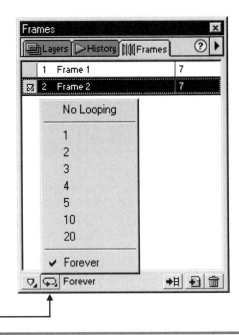

Set looping

Figure 17-5 The Looping setting adjusts the number of times your animation will run

22. Spend some time experimenting with frame-by-frame animation techniques by creating your own practice files. Try different effects, by drawing objects and applying different settings in successive frames. Create a line of text and apply a glow effect in the second frame, or use the Polygon tool to design a star that spins by applying the transform options found in the Modify menu. The variations are almost limitless, and you are sure to find exciting ways to animate your images as you grow more comfortable with Fireworks.

23. Creating animations in this way is fun and relatively easy. For every change that you want to take place in your document, create a new frame in the Frames panel and add, position, or modify the object in the manner you desire. In the end, you will have created an animation by subtly changing objects from one frame to the next, and will have discovered one of the most enjoyable aspects of graphic design—seeing an image that you have created come to life.

Note

You'll find sample files with different kinds of animations in the exercise files for this module at www.osborne.com. Explore the files, paying close attention to how frames are used in conjunction with different settings on the objects within them.

1-Minute Drill

- How are animations created?
- What feature of Fireworks allows you to see and modify multiple objects on different frames?
- How is the Distribute To Frames feature used?

Project 17-2: Animation Techniques with Symbols, Tweening, and Layers

The first project in this module introduced you to the basics of frame-by-frame animation, and in many cases, creating images this way will be perfectly acceptable. Simply create a new file, add objects and frames, and create the illusion of animation by modifying objects on succeeding frames.

As you would expect, Fireworks has additional tools to help in the animation process that allow you to make more complex images than the simple samples you've seen so far, and further assist by letting you work more efficiently. Symbols, tweens, and layers all work together to make you a more productive designer.

Symbols and layers are not new concepts, since they were discussed in Module 15. Tweens (and their use, called tweening) are new, and take a little explanation. The term is one that has been around for some time in the world of animation and describes how a series of important, or key, frames were drawn by the senior animators, while the junior (and lower-paid) animators were given the task of making animations that filled in information *between* the key frames. Their work became known as tweening.

Fireworks provides a similar capability. Using an object, or a symbol, you can define important elements of an animation, such as the symbol's position in a particular frame, and the program will add and fill in additional frames to create the animation. This is a great way to automate some of the animation process, and in this project, you'll learn not only how to apply tweens, but also how symbols and layers are used to further refine your animations.

- Animations are created when a series of images are placed on separate canvases, called frames, and then played back in rapid succession.
- Onion Skinning creates semitransparent versions of each object in the animation sequence and allows you to position or modify them as you wish.
- The Distribute To Frames feature takes individual objects and places one copy of each into a new frame, removing some of the labor from the animation process.

Step-by-Step

1. To begin, create a new file that is 300 pixels wide by 300 pixels high with a white canvas. Name this file **symbols_practice.png**.

2. As you learned in Module 15, symbols are a great way to automate some of the work that you do when creating graphics. With animated graphics, symbols become even more powerful, since placing a symbol into a new frame can be much easier than the duplicating or copying methods you used previously. And, with symbols, if a change needs to be made to an animated object at any time in the future, the process becomes infinitely easier if you only have to modify the symbol, and not every object in your animation. Choose Insert | New Symbol and set the New Symbol dialog box to create a new graphic symbol by typing **smiley** in the Name text box and choosing the Graphic option as the Type.

3. Clicking OK opens the Symbol Editor, which you will use to create an object that will be placed on the canvas in the main document, much like the way that you worked in the Text Editor to create text objects for use in a graphic. In the center of the Symbol Editor are cross hairs that help you to center objects on the canvas and serve as a visual reminder that you are working in the Symbol Editor, and not in the main Document window.

Tip

You can convert any existing object to a symbol by selecting it and choosing Insert | Convert To Symbol.

4. Using your drawing tools, draw a smiley face in the middle of the Symbol Editor, as shown in Figure 17-6. When you are finished, use the Close button (with the ×) in the upper-right corner of the Symbol Editor to close the window and return to the main Document window.

5. When you return to the Document window, a copy of your image will automatically appear with a special indicator of its status that Fireworks provides. The curved arrow in the lower-left corner of the window lets you know that this is a symbol, as you see here. Every time a symbol is placed into a document, it is known as an *instance* of the symbol, or simply as an instance.

6. Now that a symbol is linked to this file, it will appear in the Library panel for this document. Unlike library elements in Dreamweaver, which can be shared throughout an entire site, Fireworks symbols are specific to the

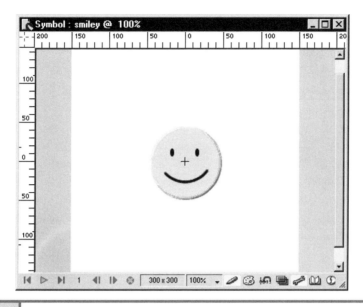

Figure 17-6   New symbols can be created in the Symbol Editor using all of the usual Fireworks tools and effects

document, and can only be shared if they are imported or exported through the Library panel's options, shown in Figure 17-7. Fireworks provides a preview of the symbol at the top of the panel, with its description displayed below.

7. An instance of a symbol is created when you drag the symbol from the Library panel onto your canvas. Once a symbol is created, you can have multiple instances of the same object anywhere you want in a document.

8. The process of tweening is done by placing two instances of a symbol onto the canvas and allowing Fireworks to do the rest. Drag another instance of the smiley face symbol onto the canvas and position the two instances in opposite corners, like you see here. Be sure that both instances of the symbol are selected.

Expansion arrow options

Symbol preview area

Symbol description

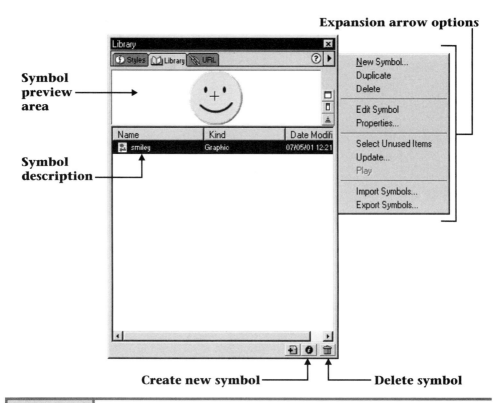

Create new symbol ——— ——— Delete symbol

Figure 17-7 The Library panel stores and displays symbols for each document that contains them

9. Choose Modify I Symbol I Tween Instances to animate the movement of the two objects on the canvas by providing information in the very simple Tween Instances dialog box. Fireworks will create as many new frames as you specify in the Steps text box, and if the Distribute To Frames check box is selected, Fireworks will place each instance on a separate frame. For this example, set Steps to **5**, check the Distribute To Frames box, and click OK.

10. Try the animation by clicking the Play/Stop button at the bottom of the Document window. If your tweens have been applied correctly, the smiley face will slide across the canvas—a complete animation in just a few easy steps!

11. Add more tweens and frames to your animation by selecting the last frame and adding a new instance of the symbol. With both instances selected, use the Modify I Symbol I Tween Instances command to create a complete animation where the smiley face makes one complete lap around the border of your canvas. You can also use Onion Skinning, as has been done in Figure 17-8,

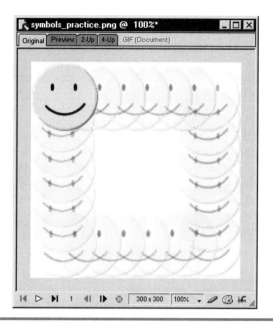

Figure 17-8   Tweening takes much of the work out of animating symbols

to see how your animated object will move around the stage, and then apply further adjustments as needed.

12. Tweening can be applied to the same types of changes that you animated by hand in Project 17-1. The trick to using tweening, though, is to decide what you want the object to look like in the key frames that you are defining, and set those properties *before* you create the tween. In this example, the symbol was first scaled to a smaller size than the original and set to tween after the modifications were in place. Once an object is tweened, you cannot go back and adjust its properties and expect Fireworks to create the animation.

Tip

Tweening works best for animations that change the position, scale, or opacity of an object, or modify a Live Effect. Xtras cannot be tweened without breaking the link that the symbol has to its original in the library. In addition, you cannot tween from one color to another.

13. The last item to discuss in this project is layers. You will recall from Module 15 that layers are particularly useful as an organizational tool since they allow you to stack virtual transparencies one on top of another within a document. Layers are most often used when you want to create a static background that remains fixed in place while the animated objects do their thing. Layers that are to appear in every frame in this way are said to be *shared,* and making this happen is simply a matter of creating the layer that holds the background by using the Layers panel and then choosing Share This Layer from the expansion arrow options. Objects on this shared layer will now appear in every frame of your animation.

14. As you become a more accomplished animator, you will undoubtedly return to symbols and tweening as two of your primary tools for creating and modifying dynamic images. Add the ability to make a background once, and then share it across your entire animation, and you will have a good understanding of how efficient a tool Fireworks is in creating animations for the Web. For now, you can save or discard your practice files as this project draws to a close.

1-Minute Drill

● Which tool is used for creating new symbols?

● How is tweening accomplished?

● List three ways that an object can be tweened.

● The Symbol Editor is used for creating new symbols.
● Tweening is accomplished when two symbols are selected on a canvas and Fireworks is instructed to create frames and modified symbols that fill in the areas between the two key frames.
● Objects can be tweened for position, size (scale), and opacity.

Project 17-3: Creating Animations with Symbols

Prior to version 4 of Fireworks, symbols were a useful tool primarily for making objects that were reused throughout a web site. Since symbols can be easily modified, and changing a symbol automatically changes every copy of the instance of the symbol in use in a document, symbols were used in much the same way as library elements were used in Dreamweaver—as a labor-saving device for creating common objects and as a way to do tweening, as you saw previously. With the revisions included in Fireworks 4, the use of symbols for animated effects has taken a giant leap forward. The capabilities that Fireworks now provides through animated symbols can add more sophistication to an animated file than was possible before and can tremendously reduce the amount of effort required for creating complex animations.

Be forewarned, though. There is a bit of a learning curve involved with using animated symbols, since designing them requires a fair amount of bouncing back and forth between different Fireworks panels, and some special considerations have to be made in the way animations are created. Still, with a little bit of practice, you will be able to successfully create animations that move, fade, spin, and provide the sort of visual impact that these types of files are known for.

Step-by-Step

1. Animated symbols can be created in one of two ways—either from scratch or by converting an existing animation to an animated symbol. To use the Symbol Editor to create an original animation, first create a new 300×300-pixel document with a white canvas. Name this new file **animate_practice.png**.

┤Note ──────

Although most animated files are much smaller than this one, a larger canvas size is being used here for ease of illustration.

2. From the menu bar, choose Insert I New Symbol to open the Symbol Properties dialog box. Name the new symbol **animated_ball** and be sure that the Animation radio button is selected for the Type setting. Click OK to close the dialog box.

3. You'll recall from the previous project that all operations that you can perform in a regular Fireworks Document window can be done in the Symbol Editor, and this is true for animated symbols as well.

4. In the Symbol Editor, draw a small circle in the center of the canvas, centering it on the cross hairs.

5. Animating this symbol begins as an easy-enough process. With the circle still selected, choose Modify I Animate I Animate Selection to open the Animate dialog box, shown in Figure 17-9. What makes this a little intimidating is the sheer number of ways that a symbol can be animated. You can expect to spend a little experimentation time with this dialog box as you become familiar with its capabilities.

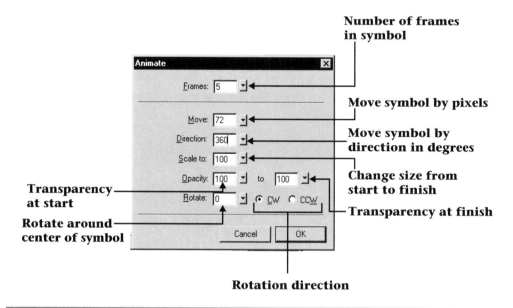

Figure 17-9 The Animate dialog box can be used to set multiple animation effects at once

6. In this case, the goal is to have the ball move across the canvas in five frames. Apply the settings shown in Figure 17-9 to your symbol and click OK.

7. Creating a symbol that has more frames than the document to which it will be attached causes Fireworks to open a dialog box with this warning: "The animation of this symbol extends beyond the last frame of the document. Automatically add new frames?" Click OK to allow the automatic creation of the additional frames that the symbol requires.

8. Now that the animation effects are set for this symbol, you can preview them directly in the Symbol Editor by using the Play/Stop button at the bottom of the window. To add frames or otherwise change the settings for the animation, from the Symbol Editor, select the symbol, and choose Modify | Animate | Settings to reopen the Animate dialog box. Try changing the Opacity setting so that the object fades in as the animation takes place, or experiment with the Scale To option.

9. Fireworks notes that this object is an animated symbol by placing a curved arrow in the lower-left corner of the symbol and two "handles" on the symbol—a green dot that indicates where the animation begins, and a red dot to indicate the end point of the animation. These handles are found in both the Symbol Editor and in the main document after the symbol is inserted from the Library panel.

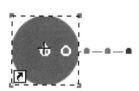

10. The handles for the beginning and end points of an animated symbol can be dragged from their current location and placed wherever you like on the canvas, modifying the motion path that the symbol follows. Try moving the handles into different positions, like those you see in Figure 17-10, and test the effect this has on your animation by using the Play/Stop button.

11. Closing the Symbol Editor causes a rather curious effect. Rather than placing a copy of the animated symbol on your canvas, the program places an instance of a new symbol on the canvas as an indication that an animated symbol is associated with the document. However, this is not the animated symbol you just created, which must be accessed from the Library panel. The "shortcut" instance that initially appears on the canvas can be deleted or positioned as you choose without affecting the animated symbol that you will bring onto the canvas manually.

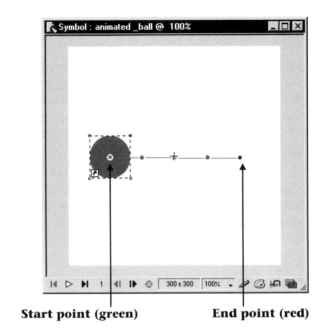

Start point (green)   **End point (red)**

Figure 17-10   The start and end point handles in an animated symbol can be freely positioned in the Symbol Editor

12. The animated symbol is accessed by first finding it by name in the Library panel, shown in Figure 17-11, and then dragging it onto the canvas. Once again, if the document does not have enough frames to support the animation, new frames will be added automatically, as you saw in step 7. Drag the animated ball onto the canvas and add frames as necessary now.

13. Once in the Document window, the animated symbol can be modified in terms of not only its initial position, but also how it moves across the canvas. The same handles that are found in the Symbol Editor reappear here, allowing you to change the position of each instance of the symbol by adjusting the start and end points.

14. Animated symbols like this one are most useful when creating common objects that you may want to reuse either in a single document or in other projects. If you needed a logo that faded in from the background, or wanted to create a spotlight effect by combining symbols on different layers, and these elements were ones that you might expect to use or modify in the future, then taking the time to create them as symbols is definitely worth the effort.

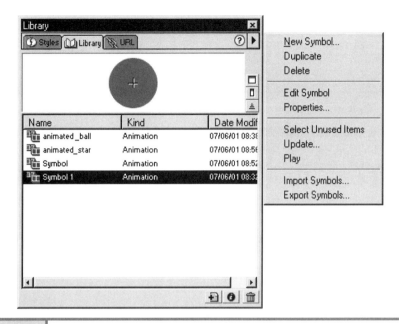

Figure 17-11 Use the Library panel to track and access symbols that you create for a document

15. Accessing animated and graphic symbols is done either by exporting the file to a location that you establish as an archive area for your symbols or by importing them from an existing file. The value in choosing the export method is that you will always know where to find a symbol when you want to use it later on.

16. From the Library panel, open the expansion arrow options and choose Export Symbols to display the Export Symbols dialog box, shown in Figure 17-12. In this panel, you can choose to export the symbol to an existing PNG file or place symbols in an archive file that holds all the symbols you may want to reuse in the future.

─┤*Tip* ──────────────────────────────────────

Hold the SHIFT key down while making your selections to choose multiple symbols.

17. Click the Export button to export the symbol you have selected into a special Fireworks PNG file that contains the symbol and any others that you choose to store there. Using the standard Save As dialog box for your system, you can accept the default Custom Symbols name that Fireworks assigns to the

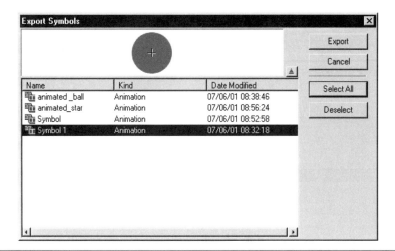

Figure 17-12 Symbols to be exported to an archive file are selected in the Export Symbols dialog box

file, or name it as you wish. Since this technique is useful primarily for saving and accessing common objects that you will want to find some time in the future, give the file a name that will be helpful to you three months down the road when you might not remember where you put that perfect spinning star, for instance. Names like animated_basic_shapes, animated_buttons, or animated_logos are examples of how naming the archive file might make your life easier later on.

18. Importing a file into a document works in much the same way. Open the Library panel, choose Import Symbols, and browse to the Fireworks PNG file that contains the symbol you want to use. Select the symbol from the list that Fireworks provides in the Import Symbol dialog box, and it will be added to the library for the current document. A terrific time- and labor-saving technique!

19. Using animated symbols has its drawbacks, and, as with many new technologies, this new feature added in Fireworks 4 has a few quirks to it. However, if your work requires the repetitive use of the same animated objects, then symbols are definitely worth looking into. With the ability to create symbols and export them to an archive, or to reuse them from existing documents, you may find that using animated symbols becomes one of your favorite design tools.

1-Minute Drill

● Which dialog box allows you to set multiple animation effects at once?

● What devices are used for positioning an animated symbol on the canvas?

● What steps must you take to make an animated symbol available in other documents?

Project 17-4: Exporting Animated GIFs

As noted in Module 16, optimizing and exporting Fireworks PNG files is a mandatory step that must be made before the file becomes available in a web page. Animated GIFs have some additional requirements that need to be tended to, as you'll see in this final look at animated files.

Step-by-Step

1. Any of the practice files that you have created in this module can be used for this exercise. In this case, the file from Project 17-3 will be used—animate_practice.png.

2. You may recall from Module 16 that files can be optimized and exported in one of two ways. One method is to optimize the export settings by using the various panels that allow you to change the file's properties, such as the Frames and Optimize panels. You may find that you prefer to make your changes while working in the main document, and then choose File I Export to convert and save the animated GIF.

3. The preferred method for exporting animations is to use File I Export Preview and make your changes in the Export Preview dialog box. This enables you to adjust not only the usual file optimizations, but also frame timings, and it enables you to see a more realistic preview of how the final version of your file will appear in the Preview panel. Figure 17-13 displays how the dialog box appears when an animated file is chosen. Note the standard Play/Stop button and other controls at the bottom of the preview window that allow you to see your animation in action.

● The Animate dialog box allows you to set options for positioning, opacity, rotation, and scale.
● The start and stop handles that appear with an animated symbol are positioned on the canvas to change the movement of the animation.
● Animated symbols, and other symbols as well, are accessible from an existing document, or may be placed into a special archive file by choosing the Export option from the Library panel.

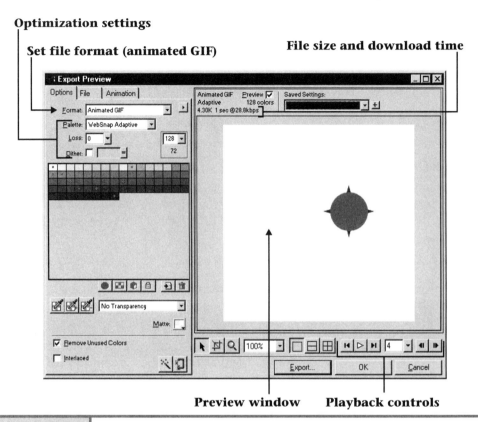

Figure 17-13 The Export Preview dialog box lets you optimize and adjust your animated file before conversion to the animated GIF format

4. Optimization of the file takes place in the usual way in the Options panel. The Animation panel, shown in Figure 17-14, has additional settings for controlling the playback of the animation. Even if you have modified frame delays and set looping values in the Frames panel, it is still a good idea to check those settings here to ensure that the animation sequence is set up properly. Any changes made in the Export Preview dialog box will override previously applied settings in the Frames or Optimize panel.

5. In addition to the standard ways that a file can be modified by changing frame delay and looping, Fireworks provides some other important tools for optimizing the file size of the exported image. Frame disposal, for instance, allows you to specify how you want Fireworks to treat repeated elements in an animation that may not have any effect on the appearance of the

17

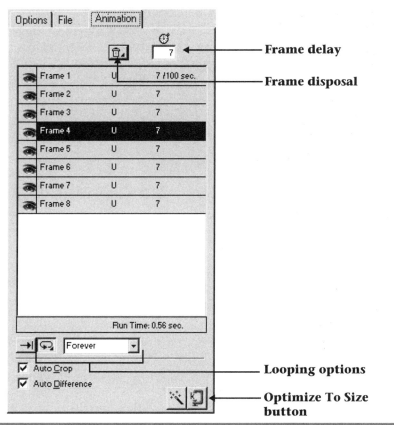

Options | File | Animation |

Frame delay

Frame disposal

	Frame 1	U	7 / 100 sec.
	Frame 2	U	7
	Frame 3	U	7
	Frame 4	U	7
	Frame 5	U	7
	Frame 6	U	7
	Frame 7	U	7
	Frame 8	U	7

Run Time: 0.56 sec.

Forever

☑ Auto Crop
☑ Auto Difference

Looping options

Optimize To Size button

Figure 17-14 Final adjustments to animation settings are made in the Animation panel of the Export Preview dialog box

animation if deleted. A static image that appears in every frame, for instance, may only need to be downloaded once and used repeatedly. In most cases, if you choose to use frame disposal, allow Fireworks to automatically use the best method possible by selecting the Unspecified setting. Be sure to preview any animation that uses frame disposal before it is exported, though, since you may get unexpected results.

6. While in the Export Preview dialog box, you can also choose a target file size for the exported file and let Fireworks take its best shot at meeting your requirements. The Optimize To Size button will open a small window in which you can enter the file size that you'd like to achieve—which is useful when the download time of a web page is growing and you want to see if you can minimize the download time of your new animation.

7. Finally, once you have experimented with the Export Preview settings, click the Export button at the bottom of the window to move on to the Export dialog box. There are no special requirements for exporting an animated file. Just accept the default file type, give your animation a name (Fireworks will use the same name as the source PNG file by default), and choose the location where the file should be stored. You are now ready to insert the animated GIF into a web page, and for that, you should give yourself a big pat on the back!

1-Minute Drill

● What is the recommended method for exporting animated files?

● What is frame disposal?

What to Take Away

Animations are a terrific way to add movement and excitement to a web page, and no program provides the ease of designing animations, combined with superior methods for optimizing the image for the Web, that Fireworks gives you.

In this module, you have been introduced to the way that animations are created by placing a series of images on frames that, when replayed in succession, create the illusion of movement. With the tools that Fireworks provides, you can animate objects by modifying their position, opacity, and rotation, and can even employ Live Effects in animations by using glows and other techniques. You have also seen that many animated effects can be automated by using tweening, where key frames are defined and Fireworks fills in the in-between frames as you specify. Animated symbols, a new feature of Fireworks 4, allow you to create small animated objects that can then be used in other animations by accessing them from an archive file.

In all, no program handles the creation and optimization of animated files with the same ease that Fireworks does. However, just because you now know how to create animations doesn't mean that your web site will be best served by

---

● Final optimization and animation settings should be made in the Export Preview dialog box before exporting an animated GIF.

● Frame disposal is the method that Fireworks uses to delete excess static images from an animated file.

having numerous spinning, fading, and galloping animations on every page. Animations, because of their inherently larger file sizes, should be used in small doses and only in ways that meet the overall goals of your site. If you have a need for a graphic that draws your viewer's attention through the use of an animation, then by all means use one. If, however, your goals can be met by a static image, or even by standard HTML elements, then always stay with the method that produces the fastest download time. Ultimately, your audience will appreciate quick downloads more than clever animations.

✓ *Mastery Check*

1. Why is the animated GIF format used so widely on the Web?

2. What tool allows you to "see" multiple frames of an object at the same time?

3. What technique takes multiple objects in a document and places each one in an individual frame?

4. Where are frame timings adjusted?

5. How is a new animated symbol created?

Part 3

Bringing It All Together

Module 18

Creating Interactive Images

Goals of this Module

- Explore how Fireworks and Dreamweaver work together to create interactive images
- Understand the use of image hotspots and slicing
- Use the Hotspot tool to insert a hyperlink
- Use the Button Editor to create linked images
- Explore options for creating interactive rollovers
- Understand export requirements of image maps
- Use Dreamweaver for simple image maps
- Explore the pop-up menu feature

Between the skills that you have developed in Dreamweaver and Fireworks, you could easily create a highly effective and visually attractive web site without learning any new techniques at all. If you've worked through all the exercises in this book, you now know how to plan and build a web site in Dreamweaver and add visual interest consistently by designing and optimizing your own graphics with Fireworks. No other combination of software programs allows you to do this often-daunting job as easily and seamlessly as the Dreamweaver 4/ Fireworks 4 Studio.

Once you have mastered the basics, though, you may find that you want to take your design capabilities to a higher level. Dreamweaver and Fireworks make this possible by putting the tools in your hands that allow you to create sophisticated images that can contain hyperlinks, rollovers, and even swap images in some fascinating ways. In Fireworks 4, you can even create pop-up windows that will appear as the viewer hovers their mouse over a particular part of an image. *Image maps,* the term by which all interactive images are known, are used widely to add new user interfaces that can make your pages more dynamic.

Note

Macromedia refers to any object containing HTML or JavaScript code that is inserted into an image as a *web object*.

Image maps range from the simple to the incredibly complex—from a simple hyperlink contained in an image, to disjointed rollovers where rolling a mouse pointer over one part of a page will cause another part of the image to display new or additional information. In all, image maps can be a wonderful way to add better usability and more interest to your pages.

As you might expect, creating some of these types of images can be an incredibly complex job, and many designers ultimately decide to learn HTML and JavaScript programming so that they can further extend the capabilities of their image maps. Dreamweaver and Fireworks will do most of the work of creating image maps, as you'll soon learn, but mastering the process can be time- and labor-intensive. Before undertaking the task of designing a complex image map, you should always return to the foremost questions that dominate web design:

● How will the use of this element meet the goals of my site?

● Are image maps necessary if I can create a stimulating site and an effective user interface by using HTML and CSS?

● Will the interface that I am creating with image maps be easy for my intended audience to understand?

If you carefully examine those questions and decide that image maps are something your site needs, then you're ready to see how Dreamweaver and Fireworks pull together to make the creation of interactive images a relatively easy process.

Note

Be sure that you have downloaded the exercise files for this module from www.osborne.com.

Project 18-1: Creating Image Maps with Hotspots

Both Dreamweaver and Fireworks have the capability to insert the simplest type of web object—the hotspot—onto an image. Essentially, a hotspot is an overlay that contains hyperlink information, which is placed over the top of an image. Hotspots add function to an image by making it possible to use the graphic as a link in a web page.

Step-by-Step

1. To learn about interactive images, you will need to have both Fireworks and Dreamweaver running on your computer. Since Fireworks in particular can be a memory-intensive program, it is best to have only these two programs, along with a browser, open when working with image maps.

2. The simplest type of image map to create is a simple image, created in Fireworks, that has interactive hotspots applied in Dreamweaver. To see this in action, create a new Dreamweaver document and choose the Insert Image button from the Object panel. Navigate to the file called hotspots_practice.gif and insert it into the Dreamweaver page. You can choose to save the image into the root folder of your practice site as you wish.

Note

You may want to review Module 6 to brush up on inserting images in Dreamweaver.

3. You'll recognize the practice file you see here as a simple navigation bar created in Fireworks. The buttons in the image were created as Fireworks library items and then arranged on the canvas as you would by using the Modify | Arrange commands in Fireworks when working with other multiple objects. The text was added and the canvas was trimmed to its final dimensions.

4. Applying a hotspot to the separate buttons in the image will add a hyperlink to the URL you specify, and nothing more. Using this method will not allow for any special effects to take place, but simply adding a hotspot to the buttons with Dreamweaver gets the job done in the easiest manner. With the Properties Inspector open, locate the Hotspot tools in the lower-left corner of the panel, shown in Figure 18-1.

5. Locate the Rectangle Hotspot tool in the Properties Inspector (available when an image is selected) and draw a rectangular shaped hotspot directly on top of all the buttons in the image. (Hotspots can also be drawn as circles and polygons by using the other options.)

Tip

Once one hotspot is drawn to the correct size, you can copy and paste duplicate hotspots and position them on top of your other buttons. Each hotspot can contain its own properties, including its own links, as you specify in the Properties Inspector. Just as with other links, you can use either the browse or point-to-file method to specify the URL for the hotspot.

6. An image map such as this, which you may want to share throughout your site, is a perfect candidate for conversion to a Dreamweaver library element. To do so, select the image and all the hotspots by using the pointer while holding down the SHIFT key. Open the Library (choose Windows | Library) and, from the expansion arrow options, choose New Library Item. Give the item a name that will identify it by its use, and update the Library as Dreamweaver instructs you to. Once completed, this simple image map will be available throughout your site by accessing the Assets panel in Dreamweaver.

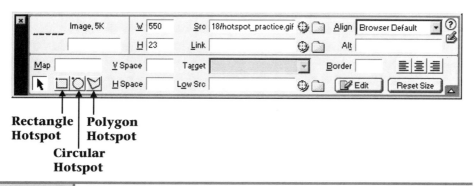

Rectangle | Polygon
Hotspot | Hotspot
Circular
Hotspot

| **Figure 18-1** | The Hotspot tools in the Properties Inspector allow for the easy insertion of a hyperlink in an image |

7. Creating simple image maps in Fireworks is a very similar process to the one you just finished. The Hotspot tool is accessed at the bottom of the Tools panel, shown here, and a simple hotspot is positioned on the image exactly as you have just done in Dreamweaver, with the same options for creating a rectangle, circle, or polygon hotspot. Working now in Fireworks, open the file hotspots_practice.png that you'll find in the exercise files for this module, and position the hotspots over the buttons.

Note

Be sure you open the Fireworks PNG file and not the GIF file used previously.

8. Links for hotspots are entered in either the URL panel or the Object panel. Open both panels now and arrange them below the image. Type a fictitious URL into the Object panel and you will note that the same link is stored in the URL panel for future use in this document, as you can see in Figure 18-2. In addition to the URL, you can also set the alternate text that will appear when the viewer hovers their mouse over the link, when the browser is set not to display images, or the image does not display.

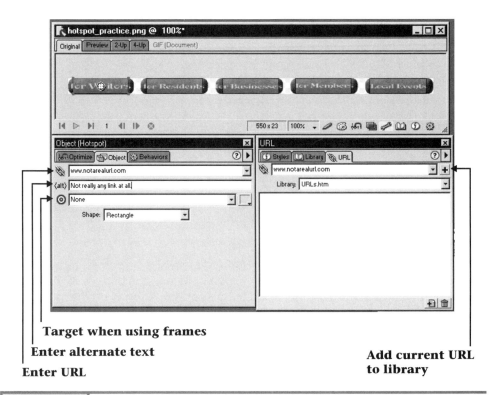

Target when using frames

Enter alternate text

Add current URL
to library

Enter URL

Figure 18-2 Links entered in the Object panel are tracked and organized in the URL panel

9. In addition to automatically tracking URLs in a library, the URL panel is also the place where you can add URLs directly from HTML files. If, for instance, you wanted to have quick access to all the links found in your home page, you would simply open the expansion arrow options in the URL panel and choose Import URLs. Browse to the HTML file that contains the links you want to add, and Fireworks will make all the URLs contained in the page available. This is a great trick when you have multiple links to create with Fireworks hotspots.

10. You'll recall from the module on file optimization that the process of exporting images with web objects (hotspots or slices) is a little different from simply converting the file to a GIF or JPEG format. With hotspots attached, an HTML file needs to be generated to contain any hotspot links you create. It is also important to name this file in a manner consistent with the restrictions for file naming, such as using no spaces in the filename, and using a descriptive name that will allow you to find the file based on its function. Choose File | Export Preview to optimize your file, and then click the Export button. In the Export dialog box, shown in Figure 18-3, be sure that the file type is set to HTML And Images, and that you have carefully considered where the HTML file and the image will be saved. When your export options are set correctly, click OK to finish the process.

11. Inserting the Fireworks HTML in Dreamweaver is a simple process of finding the correct button in the Common category of the Object panel and then browsing to the HTML file you just created. Dreamweaver will import both the hotspot URL information and the image into the page and, what's more, will allow you full access to the hotspots in the image for further modification or conversion to a Dreamweaver library element. This is another example of the wonderful integration that takes place between the two programs.

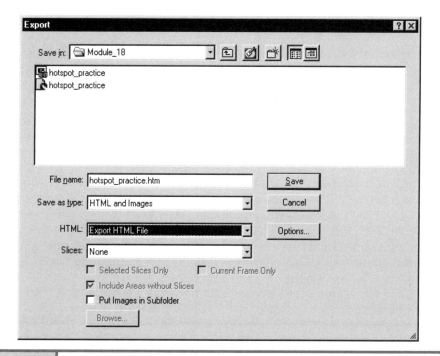

Figure 18-3   Image maps are exported as both an HTML file and an image file

12. Inserting hotspots and entering information about the object's URL are jobs that both Dreamweaver and Fireworks handle equally well. In some cases, you may find it preferable to insert a simple hotspot using Dreamweaver, while in others, you may decide to take advantage of the creative freedom and link-tracking capabilities of Fireworks. Either method handles the task of inserting a simple link into an image, and ultimately you will choose the methods that best suit your needs and your own working style.

1-Minute Drill

● What is the first question you should be able to answer prior to designing image maps?

● Define hotspot.

● Where are Hotspot tools found in Dreamweaver?

Project 18-2: Creating Buttons and Navigation Bars

As easy as hotspots are to include in a graphic, they lack the one thing that many users of the Web expect—a visual clue that a link is present in the image. If you've ever come across a page where the links were not readily apparent, you know that this can be a frustrating experience. Imagine if someone who is not the seasoned Internet expert you have become were to access the same page, and you will be able to understand why rollovers and other effects are used to improve the interface of many web pages.

Fireworks has a number of ways to create sophisticated effects that can be used when interactive images are designed. You already know how to insert simple rollovers in Dreamweaver by creating two images with slight differences in their appearance and inserting them using the Object panel. Working between Fireworks and Dreamweaver, though, you can easily create rollovers that are more sophisticated and have the advantage of being fully editable and reusable. In this exercise, you will learn how to create two types of interactive images—buttons and navigation bars.

● Before creating image maps, you should be able to answer this question: How will the use of this element meet the goals of my site?
● A hotspot is an element that overlays an image and contains links to web pages.
● Hotspot tools in Dreamweaver are found on the Properties Inspector.

Step-by-Step

1. Fireworks provides several ways to create buttons for use in a web page, the easiest of which is the Button Editor. To see this feature in action, create a new Fireworks document that is 300×300 pixels with a white canvas. Name this file **button_practice.png**.

2. Choose Insert | New Button to open a version of the Fireworks' Button Editor, shown in Figure 18-4. Note the tabs across the top of the Document window in the Button Editor, which list the four "states" that a button may be in—Up, Over, Down, and Over While Down—and include a fifth tab, Active Area, for defining the location of the slice that contains the URL information. Select the Up tab before moving to the next step.

3. While working in the Button Editor, you have access to the usual compliment of Fireworks' tools and effects, and you can freely design within the document area of the window. While this example will create a series of rectangular buttons, you could just as easily make buttons that contain only text, contain text combined with an image, or use Live Effects and Styles to subtly change from one image to the other. For now, draw a rectangle in the center of the

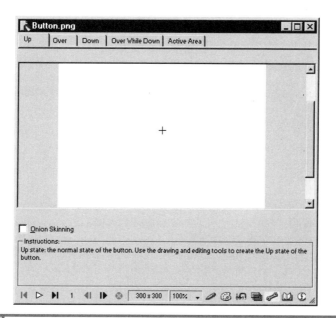

| Figure 18-4 | The Button Editor is used for specifying the appearance of a rollover image |

18

document area of the Button Editor, and use the Text tool to add the word **Home**.

4. Once the basic shape is defined, apply a bevel effect in the Effects panel, set as you see here, to create the impression that the button is waiting to be pressed. This is the Up state—the way a button will appear when the image is first loaded. You will also use this initial drawing to set all of the additional states of the button.

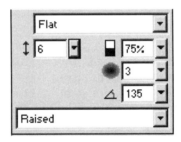

5. Return to the Button Editor and click the Over tab at the top of the window. The Over state is how your button will appear when the viewer hovers their mouse over the top of the button. Locate the Copy Up Graphic button at the bottom of the Editor and click it to place an exact copy of the graphic you made in the Up state onto this canvas.

6. Now, you need simply make a change to the button in some way so that the viewer will know that an active link is contained in the button. Some ways to do this might be to include a glow effect on the text or to change the text color.

7. If you only wanted to create a simple rollover at this point, you could move on to the final steps in the process and assign the slice and hotspot to the image, and complete the process. However, to add even more functions to the button, including the capability to display the effect that the button has been pushed in, you will want to define the Down state as well. Click the Down tab at the top of the window to move on.

8. The Down state is how the button will display after the viewer clicks it. Nothing earth-shattering in that concept, except that Fireworks allows you to apply

some JavaScript magic that will ensure that when the viewer visits the page, if the button that they clicked is there as part of a navigation bar, the Down state will display. This is an effective way to let a viewer know where they are on your site. Locate the check box at the bottom of the Button Editor, and if you want to use this feature, be sure that it is selected.

9. Use the Copy Over Graphic button to bring a copy of the button as it appears in the Over state onto your canvas. Select the rectangle and return to the Effects panel and reset the properties of the bevel from Raised to Inset, as you see here. Fireworks will perfectly create the illusion of a button that has been pressed once this change has been made.

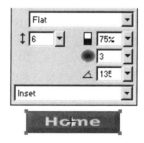

10. In the final tab, Over While Down, you can adjust the properties of the button so that an effect will be created when the viewer moves their mouse over the button, even when it is in the Down state.

11. A simple hotspot would seem like the obvious choice for adding the final functions that are required for this button, and in some ways that would be correct. The difference is that only slices can have the JavaScript behaviors attached to them that will allow the rollovers you have designed to take place. Click the Active Area tab now, and you will see that a slice, along with red slice guides, has been attached to your button. If your button has slices that extend beyond the edges of the button itself, it is very important that the Pointer tool be used to drag the slice area so that it only covers the button. Failing to adjust the slice may lead to conflicts with adjacent buttons or images.

Tip

The Info panel can be used to adjust an object to a precise size. Select the button, note its size in the Info panel, and then adjust the slice to be the exact size of the button.

12. While the slice object enables JavaScript behaviors to take place, such as the rollover effect, the actual URL must still be included for the button to work properly. At this point, you can either exit the Button Editor by clicking the Close button, or use the Link Wizard feature, accessed at the bottom of the Active Area panel, and take care of your optimization and linking tasks at the same time. The Link Wizard contains separate tabs, shown in Figure 18-5, that allow you to choose the file type, provide the same link information that you would provide in the Object panel, and even control how the HTML files and images will be named and saved. Since the Link Wizard is self-explanatory, its use will be left to you to discover on your own. Once you have information entered, click the OK button to return to the Button Editor.

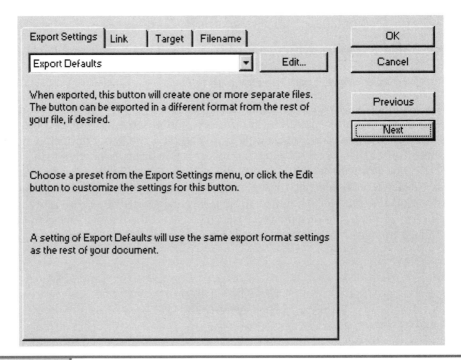

Figure 18-5 Use the Link Wizard to set file types, link URLs, and filenames

13. As with other Fireworks' editors, once you are finished with the creative process, you need only close the Button Editor by closing the window. Do this now to return to the original document, where you will find that a slice labeled Button has been placed in the document, as you see here. To see the button and how it functions, switch to the Preview tab in the main document.

14. You'll also note, by opening the Library panel, that the button appears in the library for this document, ready for reuse here, or for export to a Fireworks archive for use in other documents as well. To modify the button, select the button by name and chose Edit Symbol from the expansion arrow options in the Library panel to return to the Button Editor. Use the tabs to navigate between the different button states, modify the image as you need, and then close the Editor.

15. Using the Button Editor creates a single image on four different frames. In addition to using the method previously described, you can also create an image for the Up state in Frame 1, make a new frame and add the Down state image, and continue this way until you have all four states defined on separate frames. To attach one of the four behaviors that Fireworks includes, first draw a slice on any of the buttons and access the Web Layer in the Layers panel. Once the slice is selected, you will be able to attach a behavior such as a simple rollover, which swaps the image on Frame 1 for the image on Frame 2.

16. The other highly useful technique that can be applied using the Behaviors panel is the creation of a navigation bar. A navigation bar is a collection of links embedded in a series of buttons, and has the unique property of maintaining the Down state for a button when the page that the button is linked to is active. This is similar to the process discussed earlier where a check box was used in the Button Editor to hold a button in the Down state.

17. To work with the navigation bar function, first open the file called navbar_ practice.png, located in the exercise files for this module. In this example, buttons are being used, but as noted before, navigation elements can be text, text plus images, or other objects as you desire. Fireworks gives you a great deal of freedom in creating your navigation elements.

18. The buttons that you see were created by making the buttons, adding text, and then adding frames to hold the Up, Over, Down, and Over While Down states on Frames 1 through 4, respectively.

19. To attach the Nav Bar behavior to the buttons, you must first attach slice objects in Frame 1. Open Frame 1 and, using the Slice tool, draw slices on top of each button, as you see here.

20. Before the buttons can be used as a navigation bar, they must first have a behavior attached that produces the rollover effect. Open the Behaviors panel and choose Add Action by clicking the plus sign in the panel, and set the action to Simple Rollover, as you see in Figure 18-6. Complete this step for all four slices, and your image will now be ready for conversion to a navigation bar.

21. Select all of the slice objects in the graphic by using the SHIFT key with the Pointer tool or by marqueeing the image. Once all the slices are selected, return to the Behaviors panel and click the plus sign to add a new behavior. This time, select Set Nav Bar Image from the available options, which will cause Fireworks to display the Set Nav Bar Image dialog box, shown in Figure 18-7.

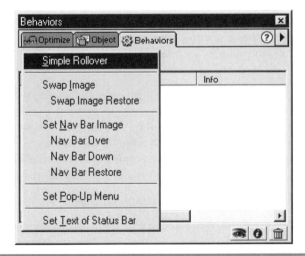

Figure 18-6   The Behaviors panel provides a predefined set of JavaScript behaviors that can be attached to slices

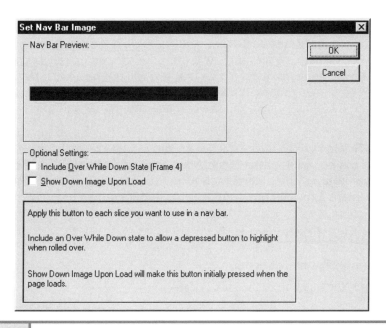

Figure 18-7 Use the Set Nav Bar Image dialog box to finalize the settings for a navigation bar

22. Fireworks will use a small cookie that allows it to track the links that the viewer has selected and display the buttons in their proper state. You can further define how the buttons will appear by using the self-explanatory check boxes at the bottom of the dialog box. Click OK once the navigation bar is set, and you will be returned to the Document window.

23. To see how the navigation bar will appear in a browser, choose the Preview tab in the Document window to see your buttons in action. If all has gone well, your buttons will appear with one item in the Down state, while all others remain in the Up state—a useful tool for letting your viewers know at a glance which page they are on in your site.

24. The final steps in creating a navigation bar include assigning the URL and alternate tags to each slice with the Object panel, and, as with other image maps, using the optimization tools and export features to generate the HTML that will be inserted into the web page. To complete this project, return to Dreamweaver and use the Insert Fireworks HTML button on the Object panel to insert your code, and, if you want to use the navigation bar again, add it to Dreamweaver's library for future use.

25. Remember that creating image maps generates a huge number of files, and you should give some thought to site management as you work with

interactive elements such as this. In the previous exercise, for example, Fireworks actually created 14 files, and if you do not carefully consider how you will manage files such as these, your site can quickly become littered with huge numbers of files that you will not be able to recognize. When using image maps, it is almost always a good idea to create a separate subfolder to hold the sliced image and frames and the HTML that supports them.

26. Using Fireworks to create interactive images can be one of the most satisfying uses of this powerful software tool. When combined with the superb capabilities of Dreamweaver, the suite of tools allows you to quickly and efficiently create image maps for use in one web page, or throughout an entire web site.

1-Minute Drill

● How is the Button Editor organized?

● What is the function of the Link Wizard?

● What web object must be present before a rollover behavior can be attached to an image?

Project 18-3: Creating Disjointed Rollovers

As exciting as button rollovers and navigation bars can be, and as common as they are on the Web, the use of even more sophisticated rollover effects can add even greater visual interest and interactivity to your site. Fireworks includes the ability to create a type of rollover whereby when a viewer moves their mouse over one part of a page, it causes another image to swap with a second image on a different part of the page. While this may sound difficult, the interface that Fireworks uses to make disjointed rollovers has been greatly improved in version 4, and the new interface makes this type of interactive image easy to create.

● The Button Editor contains four tabs for the different states of the button, and a fifth tab for specifying information about the active area of the button.

● The Link Wizard is used to specify information about a button's URL link, alternate tags, and targets, if the button is to be used in a page designed with frames.

● A slice must be present before a rollover behavior can be attached to an image.

Step-by-Step

1. Creating disjointed rollovers is a variation of the work that you completed in the first two projects of this module, and requires the creation and addition of frames and slices to function properly. These are not new concepts, but to save time, a practice file has been provided in which some of the initial groundwork has been done. Navigate to the exercise files for this module and open the file called disjoint_practice.png.

2. The text on the left of the object is known as an *event object*—the area that a viewer will hover their mouse over to trigger the rollover event. Each of the text objects will need a slice placed on top of it to enable the swap image behavior. Do this now by using the Slice tool to draw a slice over each text object, as you see in Figure 18-8.

3. Another slice object is required to enclose the area of the image where the event will take place, known as the *target object.* Draw another slice in the part of the canvas directly below the picture of the boat, and extend it all the way to the bottom edge of the canvas.

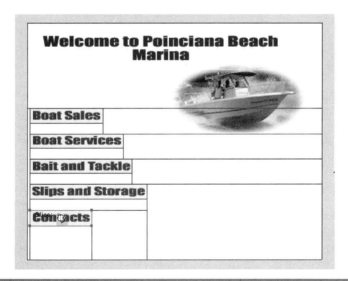

Figure 18-8 Use the Slice tool to draw a slice over each of the text objects to create separate event areas

4. The simplest way to create the swap image behavior is to create new frames that will hold the image that you want to load into the target area when the behavior is activated. In the interest of time, these additional frames have been created for you in the practice file, and by accessing the Frames panel, you'll note that Frames 2 through 6 include text that relates to each of the event objects. In the sample file you are using, the text in Frame 2 relates to the event object for Boat Sales, Frame 3 is associated with the event object for Boat Services, and so on.

5. You can expect to do this type of groundwork whenever you want to use disjointed rollovers. In addition to this method, you can also assign image files to an event object, but using frames is somewhat easier since you can see and modify all of the objects in one Fireworks file.

6. To assign the first behavior to an event object, select the slice that is over the text Boat Sales in Frame 1 and open the Behaviors panel. Click the plus sign to add a behavior, and choose Swap Image from the available options.

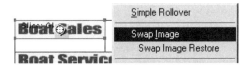

Tip

A quick way to access your slices is to use the Layers panel to find and select the thumbnail version of the slice in the Web Layer.

7. Fireworks will display the Swap Image dialog box, shown in Figure 18-9, in which you will specify the location where the new image is to appear and which frame in the image is to be loaded. In the preview area, select the target area in the lower-right corner of the image, and specify the location where the new image is to be found as Frame 2. You'll also note that Fireworks allows you to restore the image to its original state when the viewer moves their mouse pointer away from the event object (onMouseOut), and will preload all the images when the web page is loaded. In most cases, you will want to leave these check boxes to the default settings. Click OK once your swap image behavior has been set to match the one you see in Figure 18-9.

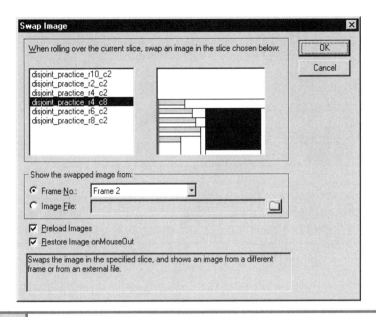

Figure 18-9 The Swap Image dialog box is used to define the area where the swap will take place and where the images are to load from

8. Once you return to the Document window, you'll find that Fireworks has added an annotation to the first event object, a curving line that connects the point-to-file icon in the slice to the target slice. Not only is this a visual clue, but a behavior can also be added by dragging a connection directly from the event object to the target object.

9. Try this method by selecting the second event object located over the text Boat Sales and dragging from the point-to-file icon onto the target. As you do so, Fireworks will display a small dialog box in which you specify the frame number of the image to be swapped. Set the behavior as you see here, and the swap image behavior will be activated. To go to the larger Swap Image dialog box, simply click the More Options button and the regular dialog box will open.

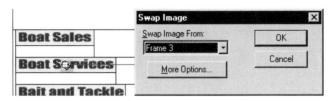

10. Complete your work in this practice file by assigning swap image behaviors to the remaining event objects. To see your creation in action, either switch to the Preview panel or choose File | Preview In Browser. Of course, these images swap nicely, but you would also need to assign URLs to the slices in the Object panel in order for the links to become active.

11. Exporting an image map with a disjointed rollover is performed in the same manner as with all other interactive images. Optimize the file and export the image. Once again, Fireworks will break the image into its separate parts based on how the slices are arranged, and create the HTML table and the JavaScript that Dreamweaver will need to make the image perform properly. Once exported to a new subfolder, you need only return to the Insert Fireworks HTML button in Dreamweaver's Object panel to put your image into a web page.

12. Take a moment to do this now by inserting the image into a new web page, and preview the results in a browser. You'll be surprised at how effective disjointed rollovers can be, and once you've had the chance to practice a little on your own, you will be able to easily create the same types of navigation elements for your pages as well.

1-Minute Drill

● What is an event object?

● What is a target object?

● Which panel is accessed to add a JavaScript action to a slice?

● An event object is the area that a viewer will hover their mouse over to trigger a rollover event.
● The target object is the area of an image where the swap image behavior will take place.
● The Behaviors panel is accessed to add a JavaScript action to a slice.

Project 18-4: Creating Pop-Up Menus

Version 4 of Fireworks also adds a new and exciting feature that allows you to develop a special kind of disjointed rollover that improves on the old HTML drop-down boxes used for site navigation. The new pop-up menus that Fireworks is now capable of producing have generated a great deal of excitement in the Fireworks developers community, and as more people become familiar with this feature, you are sure to see it in use more and more on the Web.

The ability to create pop-up menus was born out of the desire to improve the user interface in large web sites. Web sites have become increasingly complex as time goes by, and designing an interface that is easy for the viewer to understand has become more and more difficult. Pop-up menus can provide a way to create an interface that viewers understand quickly and are able to navigate more efficiently.

Having said all that, you should understand that while the interface for creating pop-ups is fairly straightforward, the menus that are created are not without their problems. Issues such as modifying and adding additional menus, browser compatibility, and positioning pop-ups on web pages make using this technique a little more difficult than others that have been discussed here. Before building your site's entire interface around pop-up menus, you should be sure that you have a good understanding of how they are created, how they function, how they interact with other elements on your pages, and the browser compatibility issues involved. Since those topics are beyond the scope of this book, you'll get some background information now in how pop-ups are designed and how the files that are generated need to be exported.

Step-by-Step

1. As in the previous project, a practice file has been created for you, using simple objects that are easily placed into a Fireworks document. From the exercise files for this module, open the file named popup_practice.htm.

Tip

Use the preview panel to see how this file will appear in a browser, or select File |
Preview In Browser to test the file.

2. Just as with the other interactive elements you've worked with, this image requires that hotspots or slices be in place before a behavior can be attached. The file you are working with contains three slices placed atop the three text objects, as you see here. When you select one of the slices, you'll also notice boxes outlined in blue that are attached to the slice with the same curving line that you saw when working with disjointed rollovers. These are outlines of where the pop-up menus will appear when viewed in a browser, and can be moved freely on the image.

3. With the slice over the text Boat Sales selected, click the point-to-file icon to bring up an option box for attaching a behavior to the slice. Select Add Pop-Up Menu, and you will be taken to the Set Pop-Up Menu dialog box.

Note

In this example, a few links have already been created and placed into the file for you. However, if you were to begin the process of creating a new pop-up menu, the procedures would be exactly the same. You can also add the pop-up menu behavior by accessing the Behaviors panel.

4. Figure 18-10 displays the first of two dialog boxes that will appear when a pop-up menu behavior is to be attached to a web object. In this first dialog box, information is entered and organized that will display in the pop-up menus. To add a new menu item, first type the text **Used Boats** into the Text field of the dialog box and type the link **usedboats.htm** into the Link field. Once the entries are made, click the plus sign to add the link to the list area of the panel.

5. Once links are assigned to a pop-up menu, they can be set as subordinate links of an existing item, as you see with the two links below the Hewes Boats link, or they can be promoted to become a primary link. The presence of subordinate links will create a flyout from the main link in the menu. In addition, links can be dragged up or down in the link list area to move them higher or lower in the menu order.

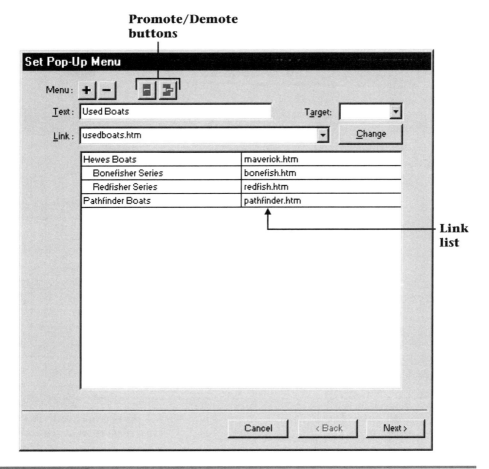

Figure 18-10   Pop-up menu links are inserted and organized in the first window of
the Set Pop-Up Menu dialog box

6. Click the Next button at the bottom of the dialog box to move to the next
window, shown in Figure 18-11, where you will specify information about
the appearance of the menu.

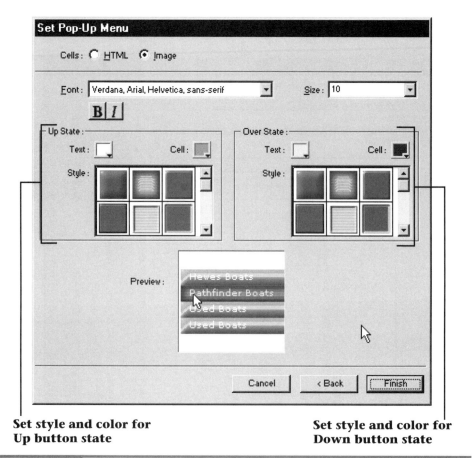

Set style and color for
Up button state

Set style and color for
Down button state

Figure 18-11 Menu styles and appearance are set in the second window of the Set Pop-Up Menu dialog box

7. At the top of the window, you will find two choices for how the text will be displayed—either as an image or as HTML text. Change the options, and you'll notice that Fireworks provides a live preview in the Preview area of the dialog box and changes the available options for the menu's appearance. When HTML is selected, the menu appears as a basic HTML table cell would appear, with background and text color applied.

8. With Image selected, more options are available, including the capability to use the same styles present in the Styles panel. Note that the style applies effects such as textures and bevels, while the color boxes change the color of the

button and the text. Again, as changes are made, a live preview is provided in the Preview area of the dialog box.

9. Once you have finished experimenting with the color and texture selections available, click the Finish button to return to the main Document window. Your first pop-up menu is now set, and you can preview your work in either the Preview panel or in a browser by selecting File | Preview In Browser.

18

Tip

It's often best to test pop-ups immediately in both Internet Explorer and Netscape Navigator as you work.

10. Continue to experiment with the modification of pop-ups in the document by clicking the point-to-file icon and opening the Set Pop-Up Menu dialog box, or by selecting the behavior by name in the Behaviors panel and choosing Edit from the expansion arrow options. You'll likely agree that the creation of pop-up menus not only is easy, but lots of fun as well.

11. Exporting this file takes place in the same way that other image maps are exported, with one very important twist: The HTML file that Fireworks generates *must* be located in the same folder as the page where it will be used. To prepare a pop-up menu for use in a Dreamweaver document, be sure that you have thought through where the page that will use the item will be located in your site structure. To assist with file management, it is a good idea to use the Put Images in Sub-Folder option that Fireworks provides in the Export dialog box that you see here. Click the Browse button, and you'll be able to specify where the images and slices will be stored, or you can allow Fireworks to automatically generate a subfolder.

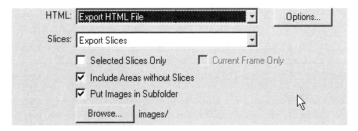

12. It would be wonderful to be able to report that pop-up menus work flawlessly, and that the interactive images you create will appear the same once inserted into a Dreamweaver document as they do in a preview of the image. Using pop-up menus can add a lot to your site if used carefully and tested thoroughly.

Even though precisely positioning pop-ups and dealing with browser compatibility issues make pop-up menus a little more difficult than other types of image maps, the possibilities are so exciting that you can expect to see these types of interactive images more and more as the technology matures.

1-Minute Drill

- What two methods can be used to attach a pop-up menu behavior to a web object?

- How are bevels and textures applied to a pop-up button?

- Where must the HTML file be stored when an image with a pop-up menu is exported?

What to Take Away

Interactive images are often fascinating and frustrating at the same time. Still, the use of image maps can add a certain flair to a web site if designed carefully, tested thoroughly, and used properly. In this module, you have learned how Dreamweaver and Fireworks can be used together to create interactive images that range from simple hotspots that contain links to complex rollovers and pop-up menus that can be used to affect the entire look and feel of a web page.

As with almost everything else that is done for publication to the Web, there are often important considerations to keep in mind when designing image maps. First and foremost is the question of how the use of image maps will affect your viewer's experience when they visit your site. Will using image maps significantly improve the site's interface? Will the longer download times that interactive images often produce be worth the wait for your audience? Do the images load properly and display correctly in all versions of web browsers that your audience may use?

- Pop-up menu behaviors can be attached to a slice by clicking the point-to-file icon or by accessing the Behaviors panel.
- Bevels and textures are applied in the second Set Pop-Up Menu dialog box by selecting a style.
- HTML files generated for pop-up menus must be stored in the same folder as the web page in which the image will be inserted.

18

As with other web technologies, interactive images should be used thoughtfully, but if you decide to employ them, you will have at your disposal the two best programs for the creation of image maps on the market today—the Dreamweaver 4 Fireworks 4 Studio.

☑ Mastery Check

1. What is a web object?

2. What web object can be inserted in both Dreamweaver and Fireworks?

3. What button states can you design when using the Button Editor?

4. Which panel can be accessed to select a thumbnail of a slice?

5. How are links and the appearance of pop-up menus defined?

6. Where must the HTML file be stored when an image with a pop-up menu is exported?

Module 19

Integrating Fireworks and Dreamweaver

The Goals of this Module

- Understand the integration features of Fireworks and Dreamweaver
- Optimize Fireworks graphics from within Dreamweaver
- Edit Fireworks documents from within Dreamweaver
- Working with Dreamweaver Libraries
- Explore additional integration features of the software suite

Fireworks is a terrific graphic design tool for the Web that allows you to create some truly fascinating images quickly and easily. The real strength of Fireworks, though, has always been its ability to work as a graphic design tool for images especially targeted for publication to the Web. While you can certainly use Fireworks in conjunction with other web authoring tools, or even with a simple text editing tool when hand coding web pages, the program really stands out when used in conjunction with the other half of the web design studio—Dreamweaver.

You have already seen how you can create images in Fireworks, apply optimization settings, and even include JavaScript behaviors, and the program will output all the code you need to insert the image into a Dreamweaver document. In this module, you will learn a little more about how the two programs can be used together to maximize your work and allow you to make modifications to images from directly within Dreamweaver's web-authoring environment. As you become a more experienced designer, and your pages become more complex and rich with images, you will quickly come to appreciate how closely integrated the two programs are and how easy it is to move between one program and the other to accomplish your design tasks.

Understanding Dreamweaver/ Fireworks Integration

Installing both Dreamweaver and Fireworks links the two programs together in ways that allow them to assist you in working in both the web design and image design environments. Dreamweaver is programmed to recognize images and code that are imported from Fireworks as being uniquely editable, because of the relationship between the two programs. Fireworks is able to read HTML tables and code generated in Dreamweaver and open an image, for instance, that has been placed into a table. Working between the two programs gives you an incredible amount of flexibility in working with images for the Web.

Project 19-1: Understanding Fireworks/ Dreamweaver Integration Features

No other software combination features the tight integration that the Dreamweaver and Fireworks combination possesses for creating and optimizing graphics for use on the Web. As you have already seen in previous modules, creating graphics that are exported to an HTML file for insertion into a Dreamweaver document is an essential part of what Fireworks does. But what about those times when you just need to make a small adjustment to a graphic, such as resizing it or tweaking the optimization settings so that the file size is reduced? In those cases, Dreamweaver has the capability of launching Fireworks while you are working on a web page, saving you the time and effort that might normally be required to open Fireworks, access the image, modify it as you need, export the image, and reinsert the modified version into your page. Dreamweaver and Fireworks save you all of those additional steps by working closely together to make minor modifications a breeze.

Note

Be sure that you have downloaded the exercise files for this module from www.osborne.com.

Step-by-Step

1. When both Dreamweaver and Fireworks are installed on your computer, the two programs search for each other and make modifications to the preference files for each program that allow them to work together. To be certain that this integration will take place, you should check the preferences for both programs to see that these settings are correct.

2. Begin by opening Dreamweaver and from any open window, choose Edit | Preferences. In the Preferences dialog box, select the File Types/Editors category, as you see in Figure 19-1, and check the Extensions area at the bottom of the window. For PNG, GIF, and JPEG file extensions, be sure that Fireworks is set as the primary editor by finding its name in the Editors listing. If Fireworks is not listed, click the plus sign in the Editors area and browse to the main program file for Fireworks and select it. Use the Make Primary button to set Fireworks as the default editor for those three file types.

3. Fireworks also has preferences that can be set to determine how files will be handled when working in both programs. As you'll recall, almost all images you will use begin as Fireworks PNG files that are optimized and exported to either the GIF or JPEG format. Any time you export a file from Fireworks, information about the original source file is stored in a Design Note that Dreamweaver can access when the file needs modification. Fireworks will allow you to either work on the original source file, or work on the optimized version when making modifications from within Dreamweaver. By default, Fireworks will always ask if you want to work on the source PNG file or only

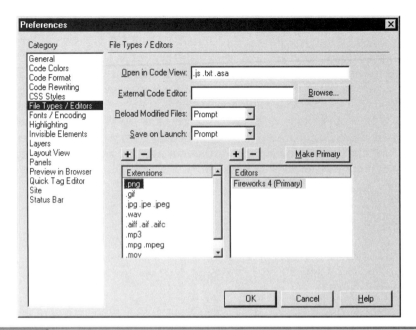

Figure 19-1 Use the Preferences dialog box in Dreamweaver to designate Fireworks as the primary editor for PNG, GIF, and JPEG files

on the exported version when you edit an image from within Dreamweaver. You can change the settings by selecting Edit | Preferences in Fireworks and making adjustments in the Launch and Edit tab.

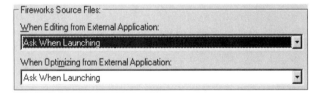

4. With Dreamweaver open, and a new document created, choose the Insert Image button from the Common category of the Objects panel. Select the file named integrate_practice.gif from the exercise files for this module, and insert it into your web page. Be sure that you select the GIF file and not the PNG file. Once the image is inserted into the document, save the Dreamweaver file as **test1.htm**. Dreamweaver will not allow you to perform optimization and editing work in Fireworks until the document is saved.

Note

Dreamweaver will display a warning that the source file needs to be in the same root folder as the web page. Copy the PNG file into the root folder to avoid seeing this error message.

5. If you look at the estimated download time for this page, Dreamweaver has determined that the file will take almost 11 seconds to download over a 28.8K modem. Obviously, this file needs to be further optimized to reduce the download time.

6. To optimize an image directly from within Dreamweaver, right-click the image and choose Optimize In Fireworks.

7. Dreamweaver will display a dialog box asking if you want to work on the original file to optimize the image. Select Yes to open a standard Open dialog box that you use to locate the source file. Browse to the file called integrate_practice.png and click the Open button to open the source file.

8. The window that displays once this process is complete, shown in Figure 19-2, should be very familiar to you by this point, since it is the same Export Preview dialog box that you have used extensively. To optimize the image, modify the settings for the document and click the Update button, and Dreamweaver will automatically apply the new settings and return you to the web page you are working on. Fast and easy, the two programs work amazingly well together to accomplish this common task.

9. Another common issue that you will face as a web designer is the question of image sizes. Editing an image to modify its size and other attributes is just as easy as the process you just completed. Right-click the image and this time select Edit With Fireworks 4 to open Fireworks and be taken directly to the original source file for the image. Fireworks will make an annotation that you are working from within Dreamweaver at the top of the Document window.

10. Modify the image size by choosing Modify I Image Size, and reduce the width of the image to 450 pixels. When your modification is completed, click the Done button, and this special Fireworks window will close.

11. Finally, return to Dreamweaver and, with the image selected, click the Reset Size button in the Properties Inspector. The modification that you made will take effect and the image size will change in the document. Note that the

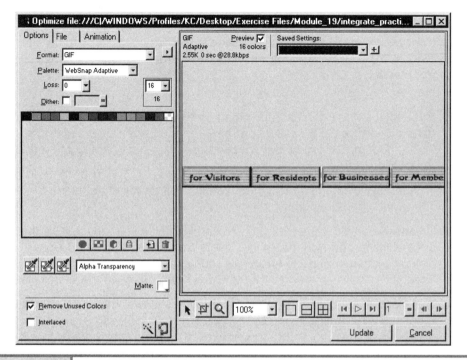

Figure 19-2 Dreamweaver opens a Fireworks Export Preview dialog box to optimize images

Properties Inspector, shown in Figure 19-3, also contains an Edit button that can be used to open the image and modify it in Fireworks.

12. With the close integration between Fireworks and Dreamweaver, you can quickly and easily open, modify, and optimize images created with Fireworks directly in the Dreamweaver environment. When you consider that the

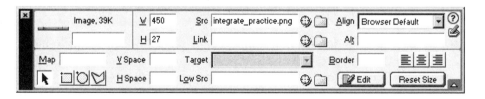

Figure 19-3 The Properties Inspector is used for editing and resetting image sizes

alternative is to open Fireworks, locate the file, modify it, optimize it, and export it, you can appreciate how much easier this method is when you need to fine-tune images in a Dreamweaver document.

1-Minute Drill

- How are images optimized from within Dreamweaver?
- How are images modified from within Dreamweaver?

Project 19-2: Creating Dreamweaver Library Items with Fireworks

As you learned in Module 9, library items are single elements that are inserted into a web page from a central storage location—a special folder within the site that Dreamweaver creates—and that can then be accessed and changed when needed. This allows for the automatic updating of the element throughout the site simply by changing the library item itself, and then letting Dreamweaver do the work of finding every instance of the library item and making the changes as necessary. If you had to do the same job manually, it would mean opening each individual page, making the changes, and then saving the document—an exceptionally tedious task in even a moderately sized web site.

With Fireworks, you have the option of creating an image and exporting it directly into Dreamweaver's Library folder so that you can take advantage of the special features that library items provide. This is another great time saver, and another example of how closely integrated the two programs are.

Step-by-Step

1. With Fireworks open, locate and open the file named library_practice.png from the exercise files for this module.

2. Exporting to a Dreamweaver library item is a relatively straightforward proposition, requiring only a few additional steps to make the file available throughout your site as a reusable element. With the file open, choose File |

- To optimize an image, right-click the image and choose Optimize With Fireworks to be taken to the Export Preview dialog box, in which optimization settings can be changed. ·
- To modify an image, right-click the image and choose Edit With Fireworks 4 to open a special Fireworks Document window in which modifications can take place.

Export Preview to open the Export Preview dialog box. While no additional settings are required here, it is a good practice to always optimize your files, even practice ones, prior to completing the export process.

3. Once you have optimized the image, select Export to go to the Export dialog box, shown in Figure 19-4. Use the Save As Type drop-down list box to change the file format to Dreamweaver Library (.lbi).

4. Dreamweaver requires that all library items be stored in a special folder with the name Library and will prompt you to find and open the proper folder. Click OK to dismiss the warning, and then use the Browse feature to navigate to the location on your hard drive where your practice web site is located. If you don't already have a folder called Library, use your computer's Add Folder feature to create a new folder. Be sure that the folder is named correctly, including the capital *L*, and open the folder so that the file is saved in the proper location, as you see here.

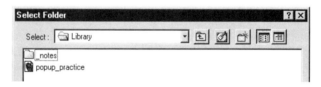

5. With the new (or existing) Library folder open, complete the export process by saving the image as a library item.

6. Return to Dreamweaver and access the items in Dreamweaver's library by opening the Assets panel. Click on the Library icon (the one that looks like a book), and you will find that the Library needs to be updated to include the new item. Click the Refresh button at the bottom of the panel, as shown in Figure 19-5, and the new item will be added to the assets for the site. To insert the item into the page, simply drag it from the Library panel onto the page.

7. Library items can be edited and optimized with Fireworks in the same way that other images can be modified. To edit a library item, select the item by name in the Library panel and choose Edit from the expansion arrow options. Dreamweaver will open a special web page for editing the item, at which point you can right-click and select Edit With Fireworks 4 from the context menu. In this way, you can be sure that you not only always have complete control over the look of regular images in your web pages, but also have the ability to modify and optimize library items. Close this special library item editing window, and Dreamweaver will prompt you to automatically update and save any pages that contain the library item.

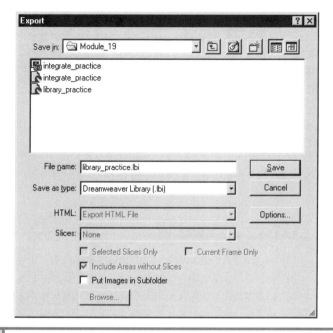

Figure 19-4   Change the file type to Dreamweaver Library in the Export dialog box to create a new library item for use in Dreamweaver

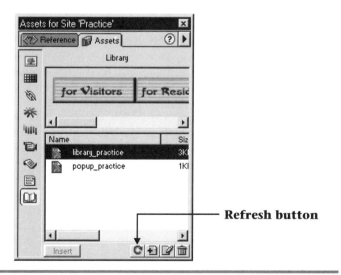

Figure 19-5   The Library panel tracks and organizes images and other assets for your site

8. Library items are a fabulous time-saving device when you have images that are used throughout your web site, such as a navigation bar or company logo. Using Fireworks, you can quickly design and export images for use as library items, taking advantage of the automatic update feature that Dreamweaver provides.

1-Minute Drill

● Where must library items be saved when they are exported from Fireworks?

● Can library items be optimized or modified from within Dreamweaver?

What to Take Away

In this module, you have learned about the two most common ways that Fireworks and Dreamweaver work together in the creation and modification of images for the Web. With the ability to open a Fireworks file directly from within Dreamweaver, you can quickly optimize or modify images as you need. Dreamweaver saves you many unnecessary and tedious steps in the process of getting your images to the exact size you need, while allowing you to also tweak the optimization settings, for the fastest download times possible.

You have also learned how Fireworks makes it possible to design an image and export it directly into the proper Dreamweaver folder so that it can be used repeatedly throughout your web site. Library items can also be modified and optimized from within Dreamweaver, allowing you to make the corrections you need while letting Dreamweaver automatically update all the pages that use the item.

In addition to the techniques discussed here, Fireworks can also output to other file types for use in other applications as well. In the event that you want to capture just the HTML and JavaScript that Fireworks generates for use in some other application, or to share with another person, you need only adjust the export settings and output to the file type you need. In addition, Fireworks HTML is completely editable in Dreamweaver, and if you wish to modify the

---

● Library items must be stored in a folder called Library, located in the same root folder as the files for the web site where it will be used.

● Library items can be modified and optimized by selecting the item in the Library panel, choosing Edit from the expansion arrow options, and modifying the file within the special editing web page that Dreamweaver provides.

underlying code itself to adjust table properties for a sliced image, for instance, then Dreamweaver and Fireworks will collaborate to make that task possible.

As stated before, no other web authoring and graphics design software combination is as closely integrated as Fireworks and Dreamweaver, and the capabilities that the two programs provide when used together continue to keep the designer in mind when it comes to ease of use. It's no wonder, then, that the Dreamweaver 4 Fireworks 4 Studio is the most popular software available on the market for designing high-impact web sites.

19

Mastery Check

1. How are preference settings for Dreamweaver and Fireworks accessed?

2. How are images optimized from within Dreamweaver?

3. What is the primary advantage of using library items in Dreamweaver?

4. Where are Dreamweaver library items stored?

5. How are Dreamweaver library items accessed?

Module 20

Getting It Out There

The Goals of this Module

- Explore web-hosting options
- Review site development and management
- Understand essential file transfer settings in Dreamweaver
- Understand how Dreamweaver accomplishes file transfers
- Use Dreamweaver's file synchronization feature

Well, you've finally done it! You've pushed and pulled and prodded, copied and pasted and exported, inserted and inspected and previewed, and finally your web site is all ready to go. Whew! That's a lot of work!

But for now, the only one who can see all of your hard work is you, and anyone you can drag in front of your computer. It's time to get it out there on the Web where it belongs, and once again, Dreamweaver becomes the primary tool in the web design suite. You may recall that at the very beginning of this book, you learned in some detail how to develop and structure your site, from both a technical and a practical standpoint, and now all that effort is going to pay off. In this module, you will see how Dreamweaver handles the job of transferring an exact copy of your web site from your computer to a web server, where it will be accessible to the world. As this book concludes, you'll also learn how Dreamweaver assists in the task of maintaining your site by allowing you to post new pages as they are created, and update those that you change.

Choosing a Web-Hosting Service

The first step in posting your site to the Internet is already done. You have established a root folder on your hard drive, and you have, at the very least, a file called index.htm in the root folder of your site. If you've followed the steps outlined in Module 2, then your site is ready to go to a server.

But how do you decide where to store your files? How much should it cost? What kinds of services should you look for? This section will provide an overview of some of the web-hosting services available and help you in making the final determination of where your site should be stored.

Types of Web-Hosting Services

Companies that have computers that store web pages and provide the connection to the Internet to make web pages and other Internet services available are called *web hosts*. These companies own the computers to which you will transfer a copy of your site when you want to make it available online to the rest of the world. In general, web-hosting services can be divided into free hosting services, and Internet Service Provider (ISP) hosting services.

Free Hosting Services

The least expensive option for hosting your site, not surprisingly, is one that is completely free. Free hosting services can be found all over the Internet by doing a simple search in a search engine such as www.google.com. Many of them will actually do the things they promise, and some work quite well. Free hosting is an especially viable option if you just want to have a place to store files that you can share with friends or colleagues, or to test a site that you're developing.

Free hosting is not exactly free though. With free hosting, you pay the price of having limited technical support and a site that may be inaccessible during peak times, when traffic to a busy server makes everyone's connections slow down. And, not all free services allow you complete freedom over how your pages will look, while some actually insert ads into your pages that you have no control over. Before committing to a relationship with a free hosting service, be sure that you understand what it will and will not do for you.

Hosting with Your Internet Service Provider

20

Many people choose to post their web sites with the same company that gives them access to the Internet, their ISP. Often, this is an inexpensive option as well, and some ISPs actually provide a limited amount of storage space for free. In most cases, a search of your ISP's customer services section on its web site will reveal the terms and conditions, and instructions for applying for the service. Often, this is a simple online application that you complete, which is followed by an e-mail from the ISP with your account information.

Like free hosting services, though, there may be limitations on the types of things you will be able to do with your site. If you need to be able to process credit cards, or need to have access to the types of cgi-bin scripting that adds more interactivity to your site, the restrictions placed on these low-cost and free hosting services may dictate that you take a step up to a professional web-hosting service.

Dedicated Hosting Services

For professional and business sites, the choice of web hosting becomes simpler—you will want to use a company that has web hosting as one of its primary functions, and has the reliability and support staff to assist you with your site. This doesn't mean that you have to pay an arm and a leg to have your site hosted, since many services cost as little as $20 per month for enough storage to handle a small to medium-sized web site.

The difference is that with a dedicated hosting service, as your site grows, the server will always be available to handle the increased capacity. And perhaps more importantly, as your skills grow and you want to add additional functions to your site, a dedicated service will more than likely have the technical know-how to help you with the process.

Ask the Expert

Question: Do I need my own domain name to post my web site to a server?

Answer: No. In fact, most of the free hosting services, such as Geocities (geocities.yahoo.com/home), will assign a name to your site based on the account name you choose. If you use the name "goober101" for your account name during the sign-up process, your "domain" name as assigned by the free service might look something like www.freehostingservice. com/goober101. Not exactly the same as www.goober101.com (if that's what you're looking for). However, some free hosting services will assist you, for a small fee, with the domain name signup process, and then offer a "virtual" domain that allows the users of the Web to find you by the domain name you register. With dedicated hosting services, your own domain name will almost always be required.

Considerations in Choosing Hosting Services

With so many choices, how do you know which service is right for you? You can get a good idea of the level of service that will be appropriate for your site by keeping the following considerations in mind:

- *Consider the goals of your site.* Are you creating a site that will only be seen by members of your own family? In that case, a free service is probably just fine. Do you want to do some heavy-duty e-commerce, with a virtual online catalog of your products? Then only a dedicated service will give you all the tools you need to meet your goals.

- *How many other sites are stored on the server?* If you want your site to be available 24 hours a day, 7 days a week, then one of the things you will want to know is how jammed up the site might become at peak traffic times. If your hosting service has packed the server with as many sites as it can squeeze in, the connection time to your site may be really slow at times. Ask if there is a limit placed on the number of sites that can be stored on the server you will share.

- *How does the server connect to the Internet?* The faster the service into your server is, the faster the service out to your audience will be. The fastest lines possible are called T3 lines, followed by T1, and then ISDN. Find out what type of connection your service has, especially if you expect to receive lots of traffic.

- *Who do you share the server with?* With the amount of questionable content available on the Internet today, many schools, businesses, and universities employ powerful firewall and web filtering software to be sure this content is not accessible. Often, these services work by blocking access to an entire server, and if your site shares a computer with www.verynaughtythings.com, for instance, then large parts of your intended audience may never see your content.

- *How much space do you get? What about e-mail and other services?* When you use a web-hosting service, the primary thing you are paying for is the storage space on the company's computer—the server—and for access to the Internet. The amount of space you get for your fee should be one of the primary things you use to determine which service to use. But don't forget the other things, too. Does the service provide free CGI scripts for you to use? What is the availability of tech support? How many e-mail accounts do you receive? All of these services, along with the storage space itself, makes up the totality of the service being provided. While it's often true that you get what you pay for, it's equally wise to shop around for the best package of services at the best price.

20

Gathering Essential Information

Now that you're ready to sign up and start using the hosting service, you need to know what information is required so that Dreamweaver will be able to handle file transfer and synchronization for you. Regardless of the hosting service that you ultimately choose, you will need to gather the information, record it in a safe place, record it in another safe place in case you forget where the first safe place is, and then record it again.

Seriously, one of the most common problems people have with any account information they are provided is the tendency to misplace the information. Consider creating a new folder in your e-mail inbox, for instance, that stores information about subscriptions, or about a specific account, and then back that up by writing down somewhere safe, such as the title page of this book, the information you'll need to set up the account.

You can also make a copy of Table 20-1 and use it for storing your account information. Dreamweaver requires the information in Table 20-1 to set up its file transfer functions.

Many times, you will receive the information set forth in Table 20-1 in the form of an e-mail message that is automatically generated by your hosting service during the registration process, especially if you are using a free service. Remember to keep close track of all correspondence with your service, because the information included, especially the login and password, provides the keys to opening up your site and making your files accessible.

Information Required	Description	Your Account Information
FTP host	The most common method for transferring information is known as File Transfer Protocol, or FTP. It is usually in the form of ftp.*yourhostservice*.com.	
Host directory	The subfolder assigned to your files by your service. Often, this field will be blank because the server will automatically give you access to the proper folder based on your login name. If your service requires the information, it will provide it in the form of an Internet address such as http://www.*yourhostingservice*.com/ public/*yourfiles*.	
Login	Your account username that is assigned to you during registration for your account.	
Password	The password that you choose or are assigned. Passwords are usually case-sensitive, so entering the information exactly as it is provided is very important.	
Firewall information	If your computer is on a local area network, your network administrator will need to provide you with information that allows file transfers through the network security system.	
HTTP address	If you have registered a domain name and will use that name for your site, Dreamweaver can help by tracking internal links to your own domain name. If your hosting service offers domain-hosting services, it will be responsible for transferring your site registration information so that computers on the Internet will properly find your files on its server.	

Table 20-1 Required Information when Establishing an Account with a Web-Hosting Service

1-Minute Drill

● What are the three primary options you should explore for web-hosting services?

● What is the first question you should ask when deciding on the appropriate hosting service for your site?

● What is the most common way that files are transferred from your computer to a web server?

Project 20-1: Configuring Dreamweaver for the File Transfer Protocol (FTP)

Dreamweaver provides all the tools you need to transfer your files back and forth to your server through the Site window. With the built-in features of Dreamweaver's file transfer, you will be able to send an entire web site to the server, or work on individual files and let Dreamweaver post only those that have changed. To make use of these features, you will need to properly define your web site in Dreamweaver's Site Definition dialog box.

Step-by-Step

1. To see how site information is entered and organized by Dreamweaver, open the program and, in the Site window, choose Site I Define Sites to bring up the Define Sites dialog box.

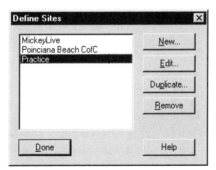

● The three primary options for web-hosting services that you should explore include free hosting services, hosting with your Internet Service Provider, and hosting with a dedicated host service.

● The first question you should ask when deciding on the appropriate hosting service for your site is: What is the goal of my site?

● Files are most commonly transferred between computers using the File Transfer Protocol, or FTP.

2. Highlight an existing web site, such as the Poinciana Beach site that you've been working on throughout this book, or use a site that you have previously defined on your own, and click the Edit button. Alternately, you can click New and create a new site with which to practice setting up file transfers. Remember, to define a site, you must first create a folder on your hard drive where all the site files will be stored, and create at least one HTML file in that folder, called index.htm.

Note

You will see a site called MickeyLive in the Define Sites dialog box shown. As of this writing, Macromedia is providing a free tutorial, called Mickey Live, which includes a free 30-day hosting service for anyone completing the tutorial, allowing you to practice file transfers. To access the tutorial, and the free hosting service, visit www.dreamweaver-tutorial.com.

3. In the first panel of the Site Definition dialog box, you will need to set the parameters for your site, as you see in Figure 20-1. Be sure that your local site is defined properly in the Local Info category, with the root folder defined, and any information about your site's HTTP address entered in the HTTP field.

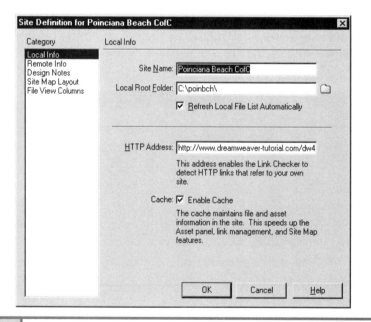

Figure 20-1 Basic information about your site is entered in the Local Info category of the Site Definition dialog box

4. Change the category of the Site Definition dialog box to the Remote Info category by highlighting it in the Category list on the left, as shown in Figure 20-1. In most cases, you will use the FTP function for transferring files, which is selected by choosing it from the drop-down menu in the Access box. If you are accessing your server through some other method, such as a local network, choose that option instead, and provide any firewall information that you need. For sites that you are still working on, this option can remain set to None until you are ready to post the site to a server.

5. The data for the FTP Host, Host Directory (if needed), Login, and Password list boxes is provided by your hosting service, and should be entered now in the appropriate locations. In Figure 20-2, you'll note that the free service that Macromedia provides is being used to practice the transfer of the Poinciana Beach web site.

20

6. The final category to check is the Site Map Layout category. For Dreamweaver to provide a graphic representation of your site in a site map format, Dreamweaver must first know the name of the home page for the site. In most cases, this file will be called index.htm, and must be located in the main root folder for the site, as you see here. While index.htm is the most common name for web site home

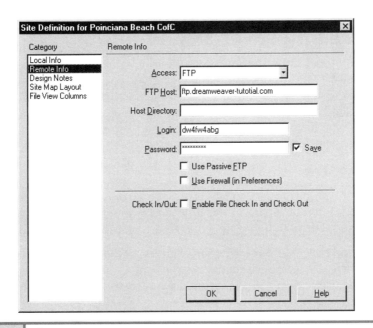

Figure 20-2 | Use the Remote Info category of the Site Definition dialog box to enter information for your hosting service

pages, your service may provide additional information or have other requirements for naming your home page.

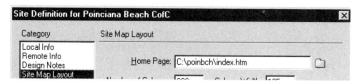

Tip

If you choose the Show File Names option in the middle of the dialog box, you'll have a quick way to check for unnamed documents in the Site Map view of your web site.

7. Once the information has been entered in these three categories, click the OK button and you will be returned to the Define Sites dialog box. Click Done to finish defining sites and return to the Site window. You are now ready to transfer files.

Project 20-2: Transferring Files with the Dreamweaver Site Window

The primary tool for transferring and organizing your files on a web server is Dreamweaver's Site window. In the Site window, you will be able to transfer all of your files to your web-hosting service, and make individual transfers of files as they are added or modified. Dreamweaver handles all of these tasks exceedingly well, and if you have set up your Site properties correctly, you are now ready to post your files to the Web.

Step-by-Step

1. Your first task in transferring files is to open a connection to the Internet. Start your Internet service at this time, and if any browser windows are open, minimize them so that you can concentrate on the transfer process.

2. Locate and click the Connect To Server button at the top of the Site window, shown here. Once you are connected, the light at the center of the button will turn green, letting you know that you have successfully connected to the server.

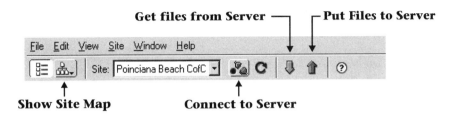

Get files from Server ⎯⎯ ⎡**Put Files to Server**

Show Site Map   **Connect to Server**

3. To send all of your files to the server, locate the arrow that points up—the Put button—and with the root folder highlighted, click the Put button. Dreamweaver will let you know that it is contacting the remote server, and that the file transfer will take place. You will also be asked if you wish to place the entire site onto the server. Click OK to send all of your files, or click Cancel to return to the Site window and choose either individual files or folders to transfer, instead of the entire site.

Note

The Get button is used to retrieve files from your server. If, for instance, a file on your computer becomes corrupted, you can retrieve a copy from the server by highlighting the file in the Remote Info window and clicking the Get button.

4. Depending on the number of files in your site, the size of the documents, and the speed of your Internet connection, uploading your site may take some time. Once your files are successfully put on the server, you will see both the local files that are on your computer in the Local Folder column on the right, and the files stored on the server in the Remote Info column on the left, as shown in Figure 20-3. Your site is now on the Internet!

5. Dreamweaver includes a great feature that lets you find and synchronize files that you have changed or added and compare them with the files on your server. Where Dreamweaver finds new or modified files, the transfer of files from your computer is done automatically.

6. Choose Site I Synchronize to open the Synchronize Files dialog box. Adjust the options in the drop-down menus to meet your needs and then click Preview. In this example, Dreamweaver has been instructed to check the

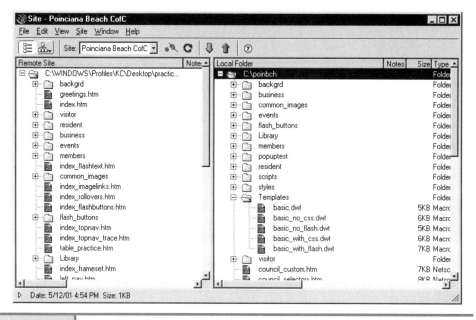

Figure 20-3 The Site window tracks both local files on your computer and files that are stored on a remote computer—your server

entire site, but you can also choose options that synchronize only selected files or folders.

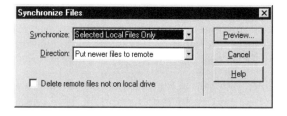

7. Dreamweaver will perform a search and display a listing of all the files that have been added or modified, as shown in Figure 20-4. To synchronize your files, be sure that your Internet connection is open, and that the files selected are the ones that you want to put to the server. Click OK, and Dreamweaver takes care of the rest, automatically updating the files on the server and placing them in their proper folders.

8. That's it! You're done. And what's more, your site is now available for the world to see. Now, your only task is to check out your site by opening your

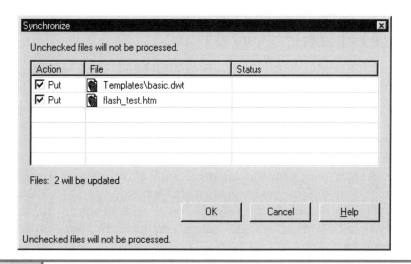

Figure 20-4 | File synchronization allows you to check for new or modified files and automatically put selected files onto the server

favorite browser and seeing how all of your hard work translates when seen on a real live Internet connection. Hopefully, everything will perform exactly as you have planned, and your new web site will be a thing of beauty. Now's the time to start bragging a little. Tell your friends, tell your family, and tell anyone else who you might think will be interested in your site. You've done an incredible amount of work and now is the time to share your work by letting others know about it. Congratulations!

1-Minute Drill

● What three categories in the Site Definition dialog box require data to be entered to enable Dreamweaver to transfer files?

● How do you get information about your login and password for your site?

● What is file synchronization?

● To prepare for the transfer of files to a remote computer, you must provide information in the Local Info, Remote Info, and Site Map Layout categories of the Site Definition dialog box.

● Information about your account's login and password is obtained from the hosting service.

● File synchronization is the process whereby Dreamweaver checks your files on your local computer against the files on the remote computer and automatically puts new files onto the server that have been added or modified.

What to Take Away

If you've worked through all the exercises in this book, you now have a good basic understanding of how to employ the tools that the Dreamweaver 4 Fireworks 4 Studio provides you. You've learned the fundamentals of the Internet, the requirements for establishing and managing your web site, and how to use Dreamweaver to produce web pages and design an entire web site.

You've also learned how Fireworks provides graphic design tools that allow you to add visual spice to your site through the creation of entirely new images, some of which can be quite sophisticated, including animations and pop-up windows.

Finally, in this module you've learned how to take all your work, bundle it properly with Dreamweaver's site management tools, and put your site onto a web server.

Congratulations on taking your first steps on the journey toward becoming a web designer. While this book certainly has put you on the right path, as with any journey, you may decide that you want to continue. If so, then by all means spend time with other books that will help you to develop your design skills even further. Join the web design community, especially the very active one that supports Macromedia products, by visiting the newsgroups that are maintained for Dreamweaver and Fireworks users. Most of all, keep pushing yourself and your skills—the Internet is constantly changing and you will need to make a commitment in time and energy to stay abreast of the latest developments. But most of all, have a good time while you are at it!

☑ *Mastery Check*

1. What is the primary advantage to using a dedicated web-hosting service?

2. What is the fastest connection available between a server and the rest of the Internet called?

3. Where is information about your site and your account entered that allows Dreamweaver to handle file transfers?

4. What is the Put button in the Site window used for?

5. How does Dreamweaver display files and folders that are on your server?

Appendix

Answers to Mastery Checks

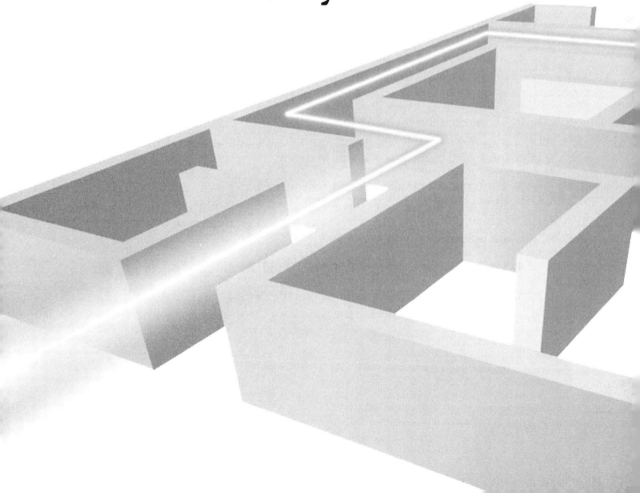

Module 1: Fundamentals of the World Wide Web

1. A web page's address on the Internet is called a universal resource locator (URL).

2. Every web page begins and ends with the <html> tag.

3. The tag inserts a hyperlink to the URL for Osborne.com.

4. Dreamweaver describe its standards-based HTML code as round-trip HTML.

5. A relative link is a link to a page within the same web site. An absolute link is a link to a URL for a page outside the site.

Module 2: Planning and Organizing Your Web Site

1. At the outset of site planning you should be able to answer these two questions: Who exactly do you want to attract to your site? What do you want them to find when they get there?

2. The age of your intended audience may affect decisions about site and page layout, the use of newer technologies, and the overall design of the individual pages that make up your site.

3. The term "root folder" refers to the main folder on a computer that stores all the dependent files and folders. A root folder exists on both the computer where you develop your site and on the server, once your files are uploaded.

4. The Define Sites dialog box is used to add, modify, and delete web sites.

5. Every web site requires a file called index.htm—the page that initially opens when a web site is visited.

Module 3: Understanding the Dreamweaver Interface

1. The Properties Inspector provides detailed information about different elements on your pages—text, graphics, and other elements—and lets you change them to meet your design needs.

2. The Objects panel organizes the different items that can be inserted into a page—everything from simple images to tables to multimedia content—allowing page designers to quickly add these elements.

3. In a new, untitled document, Dreamweaver creates the title and a simple metatag that identifies the HTML specifications used in designing the page.

4. The Tag Selector in the bottom-left corner of the Document window is used to select tags directly by name.

5. Dreamweaver provides updated information regarding the file size and estimated download time in the status bar at the bottom of the Document window.

6. The Layout View button, found at the bottom of the Objects panel, allows designers to switch into layout mode and use tables and cells to lay out their pages.

Module 4: Layouts and Alignments: Building Your First Web Page

1. Only the underscore and dash symbols are permitted in filenames.

2. There are no technical restrictions on title names. However, only limited physical space is available to display your title, so a maximum of 25 characters is a good guide.

3. Background images are tiled on the page—set top to bottom and side to side like floor or wall tiles.

4. Web-safe colors are the 212 colors that have been tested and are known to display accurately regardless of the browser or the computer operating system being used.

5. Reading text on a computer screen requires a good contrast between the text and the background color.

6. The Preview In Browser feature can be activated by clicking the toolbar's Preview icon, by choosing File | Preview In Browser, or by pressing the F12 key.

Module 5: The Printed Word: Working with Text

1. Monospaced type takes the most space on a page, because every letter is given the exact same amount of space in a line.

2. Viewer's have the option of changing their font size by adjusting browser preferences.

3. Font lists are used since only those fonts installed on the viewer's computer are displayed when the page is loaded. Font lists give the page designer a degree of control over their page by setting a family of fonts that are similar in appearance.

4. Many users of the Internet expect links to be in blue, so nonlink text shouldn't appear blue or else users will have trouble determining where the links are located on the page.

5. A relative link is a link to a page within the same web site.

6. An absolute link is a link to a page outside the web site.

Module 6: Adding Visual Interest: Working with Images

1. GIF and JPEG files are the most common image file types in use on the Internet.

2. Macromedia Flash generates images in the SWF file format for use on a web page.

3. A navigation bar is a series of images or text links that lead the viewer to different pages in a web site.

4. The <alt> tag displays alternative text in place of an image. It also generates the small box that appears when the mouse pointer is floated over an image.

5. Alternative methods of site navigation should be included on a page because some viewers turn off the graphics capabilities of their browser to speed download time or use non-graphical browsers that don't display images at all.

6. Image rollovers are created by the JavaScript language.

Module 7: Controlling Page Layout

1. In modern web pages, tables and cells are most commonly used to control page layout.

2. The four principles of page layout that every web designer should be familiar with are alignment, repetition, consistency, and contrast.

3. The Layout View and Standard View buttons appear at the bottom of the Objects panel.

4. Autostretch tables and cells are useful when the designer wants the page content to stretch to fill the window of the viewer's browser regardless of the viewer's particular monitor settings.

5. Tables and cells that contain images that need to remain aligned, like those in a navigation bar, should not be set to Autostretch.

6. Properties for tracing images are set in the Page Properties dialog box.

Module 8: Advanced Page Design: Frames and Cascading Style Sheets

1. Frames reduce the workload for web developers by allowing them to reuse certain elements of a page throughout the site.

2. Frames have problems with bookmarks, with search engines, and with printing. Additionally, their misuse as page layout tools often leads to chopped-up, ugly page designs.

3. Two frames plus the frameset itself means a total of three pages are open when working in a two-frame page.

4. The command File | Save All Frames should always be used when saving pages designed with frames.

5. The formatting standards of CSS were developed to get away from the many formatting problems caused by HTML—a coding language that was never intended for use in page layout.

6. CSS styles have yet to gain wide acceptance due to their lack of support in current versions of Internet browsers.

Module 9: Automating Your Work: Tools for Consistent Content

1. The Assets panel catalogs and tracks all assets in a web site, such as colors, URLS, images, and others.

2. Dreamweaver automatically generates in the root folder of the site new folders called Library and Template to store these items.

3. Templates may be created by choosing File | New Template to start with a blank document, or by choosing File | Save As Template to convert an existing document.

4. Dreamweaver templates are created with the file extension .dwt.

5. The Check Browser behavior checks for the version of a browser installed on the viewer's computer and redirects them to different pages as specified in the Check Browser dialog box.

6. Behaviors must always be attached to HTML tags.

Module 10: Forms and Functions: Interactivity in Web Design

1. Information is processed either at the viewer's computer, client-side processing, or at the server, server-side processing.

2. Using JavaScript for e-mail functions is discouraged because it is not as reliable as using CGI scripts and because of the security warning viewers will see when they submit their information.

3. Dreamweaver indicates the presence of the <form> tag by enclosing the area of the page contained by the tag with a red, dashed line.

4. Form objects require a unique name so that they can interact properly with their supporting script.

5. Dreamweaver extensions are found at the Macromedia Exchange web site—www.macromedia.com/exchange/dreamweaver/.

6. Adobe Acrobat is used to display printed and graphical documents in a form that is easier to read and print than what is possible with HTML.

Module 11: An Introduction to Fireworks 4

1. Fireworks was created with one mission in mind—to produce the best possible images available for use on the Web while maintaining small file sizes that lead to faster downloads.

2. Fireworks files in their native PNG format contain additional information embedded in the image that makes it easier to modify them. This creates larger file sizes that need to be optimized and exported to a standard web format before inserting them in a web page.

3. The tools in the Tools panel are grouped by their function into the categories of selection tools, drawing tools, editing tools, hotspot/slice tools, panning/zooming tools, and color tools.

4. Colors selected with the system Color Chooser may not be web-safe, in which case they will not display properly in a browser.

5. Slices are used when a large image is divided into separate smaller images that are reconstructed by the browser.

Module 12: Working with Bitmap Images

1. The New Document dialog box is used to determine the size, color, and resolution of a new canvas.

2. The negative area around a canvas can be a useful tool when you want to drag images off the canvas so they can be rearranged. Also, whenever you have an object selected on the canvas, a handy way to deselect it is to click in the negative area of the Document window.

3. When using selection tools, edges can be set in the Options panel to Hard, Anti-Alias, or Feathered edges.

4. Lines, shapes, brush strokes, and areas that have been "erased" must be changed by using the Undo function.

5. The Paintbrush tool has the greatest number of options available for adding strokes and objects to the canvas. Options available in the Stroke panel allow brush sizes and shapes to be changed, as well as line colors and special effects.

Module 13: Creating and Modifying Objects with Fireworks Panels

1. As the pointer passes over an object on the canvas, the object becomes outlined in red, letting you know that it is now available to be selected.

2. The Tools panel allows you to draw these shapes—rectangles, rectangles with rounded corners, circles and ellipses, and polygons and stars.

3. To rotate an object on the canvas, select the object and then use either the Scale, Skew, or Distort button to rotate an object by hand.

4. In addition to saving valuable time, the ability to save and reapply effects can also help in creating a consistent look for a web site.

5. Settings for effects can be modified by finding the effect in the list provided in the Effects panel and then clicking the information icon to bring up an options window.

Module 14: Working with Text and Text Effects

1. The major advantage to using text converted to graphical images is that all major browsers will be able to display the images once converted to a bitmap format.

2. The major disadvantage to using text converted to graphical images is that images are larger than HTML and their use increases the file size (and download time) of web pages.

3. Fireworks is only limited by the font types that are installed on your computer. Unlike HTML, there are no further considerations when using text converted to images.

4. The Apply checkbox, when selected, automatically applies modifications to text as they occur.

5. The Effect panel contains options to apply special effects to text, such as bevels, glows, and drop shadows.

Module 15: Creating and Organizing Complex Objects

1. Grouped objects are always denoted by four handles located in the corners of the grouped area and the lack of the selection outline that's visible when working with single objects.

2. A special type of group is created when Fireworks is instructed to use one object in the group to mask, or partially hide, the other object or objects in the group.

3. Layers provide a great deal of control over items such as object transparency and placement and are an excellent way to lay out complex images.

4. Design tasks can be automated by creating and saving styles and by designing and saving symbols.

Module 16: Optimizing and Exporting Fireworks Files

1. The primary goal when optimizing Fireworks PNG files is to minimize the file's download time by adjusting the quality of the graphic. Optimization entails maintaining image quality while limiting file sizes.

2. The primary goal when exporting Fireworks PNG files is to choose the appropriate format that maintains image quality while limiting file size.

3. Fireworks PNG files can be previewed and optimized either in the Export Preview dialog box or by using the preview tabs in the Document window.

4. Images suitable for the GIF format are those files that contain a limited number of primarily solid colors, with few subtle differences between colors.

5. Images suitable for the JPEG format are those files that contain many different colors, with subtle shades and variations of colors.

6. Fewer colors in an image leads to a smaller file size. GIF files are optimized by limiting the available colors in the color palette. JPEG images are optimized through the use of the Quality setting, which limits the available colors for that file format.

Module 17: Creating Animated Files with Fireworks

1. The animated GIF format is the most widely used file format for animations because of its (almost) universal acceptance by web browsers.

2. Onion Skinning allows multiple frames to display at the same time, and is enabled in the Frames panel.

3. Multiple objects on a document's canvas can be placed in separate frames by choosing the Distribute To Frames option found at the bottom of the Frames panel.

4. Frame timings can be adjusted directly in the Frames panel, or by making final adjustments in the Export Preview dialog box.

5. A new animated symbol is created by choosing Insert | New Symbol, setting the symbol type to animation, and using the Animate dialog box while in the Symbol Editor to animate the object.

Module 18: Creating Interactive Images

1. A web object is an item inserted into an image that contains HTML or JavaScript code. Hotspots and slices are web objects.

2. Both Dreamweaver and Fireworks can insert a hotspot into an image.

3. The Button Editor allows you to define the appearance of the Up, Over, Down, and Over While Down button states.

4. Slices can be selected by opening the Layers panel, choosing the Web Layer, and locating the thumbnail of the slice.

5. The Set Pop-Up Menu dialog has two separate pages where links and the appearance of pop-up menus are defined.

6. HTML files generated for pop-up menus must be stored in the same folder as the web page in which the image will be inserted.

Module 19: Integrating Fireworks and Dreamweaver

1. Preferences for Dreamweaver and Fireworks are both accessed by choosing Edit | Preferences.

2. To optimize an image, right-click the image and choose Optimize With Fireworks to be taken to the Export Preview dialog box, in which optimization settings can be changed.

3. Library items allow for the automatic updating of the element throughout the site simply by changing the library item itself, and then letting Dreamweaver do the work of finding every instance of the library item and making the changes as necessary.

4. Library items are stored in a folder called Library, located in the same root folder as the files for the web site where it will be used.

5. Library items are accessed by opening the Assets panel and choosing the Library category.

Module 20: Getting It Out There

1. Dedicated web-hosting services are likely to have better connection speeds, more reliable service, and offer better technical support than free or low-cost hosting services.

2. The fastest connection to the Internet appropriate for web servers is through a T-3 line, followed by a T-1 line, with an ISDN line providing the slowest service.

3. All the information that Dreamweaver needs to make file transfers is located in the Site Definition dialog box.

4. The Put button in the Site window is used for transferring files up to a web server, also called uploading.

5. Files that are on your server are displayed in the Remote Info panel, on the left side of the Site window.

Glossary

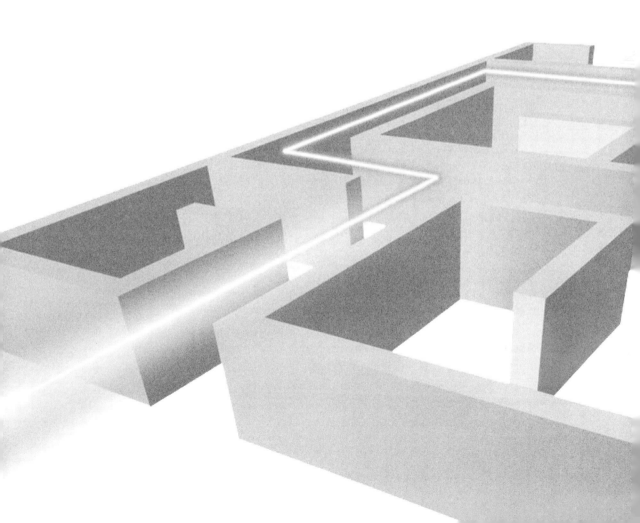

absolute URL   A hyperlink that contains the full web address of a web page, such as http://www.osborne.com.

action   A response triggered by an event initiated by the viewer of a web page, such as rolling their mouse pointer across imbedded code that results in a rollover effect.

active link   A hyperlink that is currently selected by a viewer of a web page.

ActiveX   Technology developed by Microsoft to add functionality to web pages. The functional equivalent of a plug-in.

address   The unique location of an individual web page on the Internet. See **Universal Resource Locator** (**URL**).

alignment   The way text or another object is placed within a table or page layout.

alt text   Short for *alternative text*; additional information that is displayed in a text box when the viewer rolls their mouse over an element on a web page. Typically used with images.

anchor (named anchor)   A navigational element of a web page that allows the viewer to jump to a particular point on the page.

animated GIF   An image file that plays a series of frames, creating the illusion of movement.

applet   A small program that adds unique features by running on a viewer's computer. Usually written in the Java programming language.

Assets panel   A panel in Dreamweaver containing all the elements in use in a particular web site, such as templates, library items, URLs, and colors.

attribute   Instructions that modify the appearance of HTML tags, by adding information such as color and size.

background   A color or image that covers the area behind a web page.

bandwidth   The amount of data that can be transferred from one computer to another. Higher bandwidth translates to faster data transfer.

baseline   An imaginary line used to organize text along a horizontal plane.

Behaviors panel   In both Dreamweaver and Fireworks, the panel used to insert or modify JavaScript behaviors.

bitmap   An image format in which individual elements of the graphic are stored in a grid formation, with each block of the grid filled with a particular color.

Bookmark   Feature of Netscape Navigator that allows you to store a web site's location for future use. Called "Favorites" in Microsoft Internet Explorer.

browser (web browser)   Program used to access and view web pages stored on the World Wide Web. The two most popular browsers are Internet Explorer and Netscape Navigator.

bulleted list   A list of items preceded by a marker, called a bullet.

button   An individual graphic that contains a hyperlink.

Button Editor   The editor used in Fireworks to designate appearance, effects, and hyperlinks to a button.

cache   The area of computer memory that stores information about web pages that have been visited previously.

canvas   The work area in a Fireworks document.

cascading style sheets (CSS)   A series of styles applied to HTML elements that redefine the basic HTML tag and can be used to control its appearance and position on a web page.

cell   The individual box that is created by the intersection of a row and a column in an HTML table.

cgi-bin   The most common storage location (folder/directory) on a server for keeping programs designed for interactivity with CGI scripts.

client   A computer that requests information from another computer, such as when a browser accesses information stored on a server.

closing tag   An HTML tag that denotes the end of a block of code. Closing tags are preceded by the symbol </.

Code view   In Dreamweaver, the option that displays the HTML code contained in a web page.

Common Gateway Interface (CGI)   The interface that allows interactive programs such as forms to run through a web browser and web server.

cookie   A small piece of information that is collected about your computer by your browser when a web page is visited. Cookies allow the web server to track and update information about your use of the server.

dependent files   Files that are linked to a web page, such as images.

Design view   In Dreamweaver, the option that displays a web page in a graphical format.

dithering   The process of mixing colors in an image to create the illusion that another color is present.

Document window   The work area in both Dreamweaver and Fireworks.

domain name   A unique name assigned to a company, individual, or organization that identifies their web site, such as www.osborne.com.

download   The act of retrieving information stored on a remote computer and copying it to a local computer.

editable region   In a Dreamweaver template, the area of the page that is unlocked and can be changed.

Effects panel   The panel in Fireworks where effects such as bevels, glows, and shadows are applied to an image.

event   An action that occurs within a web page, often triggered by the viewer, such as the "event" of passing a mouse pointer across an object. Coupled with actions to create a particular JavaScript behavior.

extensions   Enhancements added to Dreamweaver that add functions to the program. Accessed through the Extensions Manager.

File Transfer Protocol (FTP)   The most common method for transferring files through the Internet from one computer to another.

Fill panel   The panel used in Fireworks to assign options to the inside of a closed object, such as a circle or rectangle.

firewall   A security feature that protects computers on a network. Often used by a network system administrator to block access to certain web pages.

flyout menu   Used in Fireworks to denote additional tool options in the Tools panel.

font   A text style.

font size   The height of a particular font style. Set in the Properties Inspector in Dreamweaver, and in the Text Editor in Fireworks.

form   A part of a web page where information can be entered by the viewer. Forms require additional code or scripts for processing.

form method   The method used to pass information contained in a form to a server, such as GET and POST. Different form methods require different supporting code to process the form.

frame   A feature that allows web developers to design separate HTML documents that load into a browser at the same time.

frameset   The controlling HTML document that defines and contains the other pages that load simultaneously into a browser window.

Frames panel   Used in Dreamweaver to display the frameset and the individual pages that are loaded into it. In Fireworks, the panel that is used for defining and controlling animated files.

Graphics Interchange Format (GIF)   Common image file format in use on the Web, popular because of the typically small file size that the format generates. GIFs are limited to 256 colors.

History panel   In both Dreamweaver and Fireworks, the panel that is used to track changes made to a document.

hotspot   An overlay applied to an image in both Dreamweaver and Fireworks that contains a hyperlink.

HTML element   The combination of the opening and closing tags, and all the information contained between the two, such as a table.

HTML Styles panel   The panel in Dreamweaver that applies HTML styles to fonts.

HTML tag   See closing tag and opening tag.

hyperlink   An object in a web page that takes the viewer to another web page, causes a file to download from the web server, or causes some other action to be performed such as playing a sound file.

Hypertext Markup Language (HTML)   Computer coding language that allows web browsers to read information through the use of tags and attributes that define the document.

Hypertext Transfer Protocol (HTTP)   The standard method for transferring information between a web server and a web browser.

image map   An image that contains JavaScript or HTML information that creates hyperlinks or adds additional functions such as rollovers.

image slicing   A technique used in Fireworks for breaking a large graphic into smaller images that are contained by an HTML table.

Internet   The world-wide collection of interconnected computers that are capable of passing information in the form of text and images.

Java   Computer coding language that adds functions to web pages through the use of an applet.

JavaScript   Computer coding language that is embedded in an HTML document to add additional functions to the page. In Dreamweaver, JavaScript functions are added through the use of the Behaviors panel.

Joint Photographic Experts Group (JPEG)   Image file format used for graphics that can display millions of colors and fine distinctions in shading and contrast. Used primarily for photographs.

jump menu   A list of selections with URLs attached. Selecting the item from the list causes the browser to load the specified URL.

kerning   The spacing between text characters.

Launcher   The Dreamweaver panel that provides access to commonly used panels and inspectors.

layer   A web page element that allows objects to be stacked on different layers and hidden, revealed, or animated. In Fireworks, layers act as transparencies that can be stacked to combine and organize complex objects. Both programs access layers through the Layers panel.

leading   The amount of spacing between different lines of text.

library item   An element that is shared among different web pages within a web site in Dreamweaver. Accessed through the Assets panel.

Library panel   The panel in Fireworks that allows objects such as buttons to be stored and reused.

link   See hyperlink.

Main toolbar   The toolbar in Fireworks that allows access to common operations such as copying and pasting.

Modification toolbar   The toolbar in Fireworks that provides access to operations for placing, grouping, and aligning objects on the canvas.

navigation bar   A set of hyperlinks organized to improve the viewer's ability to access other portions of a web site. Usually a set of graphical buttons.

nonbreaking space   An HTML element that creates a space, providing a workaround for the standard HTML rule that only one space can exist between objects.

Objects panel   The primary tool, organized by category, used in Dreamweaver for inserting objects into a web page. In Fireworks, the panel is used to set characteristics such as transparency.

opacity   The relative transparency assigned to an object in Fireworks.

opening tag   An HTML tag that denotes the beginning of a block of HTML code.

Optimize panel   The panel used in Fireworks to prepare images for conversion to the web-friendly image formats of GIF, JPEG, and PNG.

path   The lines or curves that connect points in a vector-based object.

plug-in   A program that extends the basic capabilities of a browser to make specialized functions possible, such as displaying a movie (QuickTime), a document (Adobe Acrobat Reader), or streaming audio (RealPlayer).

Portable Network Graphic (PNG)   The native file format used by Fireworks. Fireworks PNG files must be optimized and converted to a GIF, JPEG, or standard PNG format before they are used in a web page.

Properties Inspector   The primary tool in Dreamweaver that displays the selected object's properties and allows them to be modified.

relative URL   A URL that links to a web page or file within a web site.

rollover   A JavaScript behavior that causes an image to change when the viewer passes their mouse pointer over it.

server   The controlling computer on a network that stores files and serves the computers connected to it. A web server stores web pages and makes them accessible across the Internet.

site map   A graphical display that shows how a web site is organized.

Site window   The primary tool in Dreamweaver that provides for the organization and display of all the files associated with a web site.

Stroke panel   The tool in Fireworks that is used to modify lines created with vector-based paths in Fireworks.

Styles panel   The panel used in Fireworks to display predefined or custom styles that can be applied to objects, such as color, fill, and stroke characteristics.

symbol   An object stored for reuse in Fireworks.

synchronize   A feature built into Dreamweaver that allows files to be checked on both the local computer and web server and provides for the automatic updating of files.

table   An element of HTML that organizes information into rows and columns.

template   A preformatted web page that is used for creating new documents based on its layout. Templates in Dreamweaver are located in the Assets panel for a site.

Text Editor   The editor used in Fireworks for entering and formatting text.

Timeline panel   A feature used in Dreamweaver for controlling animations.

title   The name that is displayed in the browser's title bar when a page is viewed.

Tool Options panel   The panel used in Fireworks for specifying options for a particular drawing or selection tool.

Tools panel   The primary panel used in Fireworks for accessing drawing and selection tools.

tracing image   An image that is used in Dreamweaver as a template for how the completed page will appear.

tweening   An animation technique used in Fireworks to automatically draw images that complete an animation sequence.

Universal Resource Locator (URL)   The exact address of a web page as it is stored on a web server, such as http://www.osborne.com.

uploading   The act of sending information to a remote computer from a local computer.

URL panel   The panel in Fireworks where a library of links is stored.

vector graphic   An graphic created by mathematical formulas that describe the position and color of points and lines in an image.

web page   A single HTML document, including any supporting files, that displays on a browser.

web-safe colors   Colors that will display correctly when viewed in any browser, and in both the Macintosh and Windows operating systems.

web site   A collection of web pages organized and stored under one domain name on a web server.

World Wide Web Consortium (W3C)   The organization responsible for maintaining and creating HTML standards.

Index

T

INTERNATIONAL CONTACT INFORMATION

AUSTRALIA
McGraw-Hill Book Company Australia Pty. Ltd.
TEL +61-2-9417-9899
FAX +61-2-9417-5687
http://www.mcgraw-hill.com.au
books-it_sydney@mcgraw-hill.com

CANADA
McGraw-Hill Ryerson Ltd.
TEL +905-430-5000
FAX +905-430-5020
http://www.mcgrawhill.ca

GREECE, MIDDLE EAST,
NORTHERN AFRICA
McGraw-Hill Hellas
TEL +30-1-656-0990-3-4
FAX +30-1-654-5525

MEXICO (Also serving Latin America)
McGraw-Hill Interamericana Editores S.A. de C.V.
TEL +525-117-1583
FAX +525-117-1589
http://www.mcgraw-hill.com.mx
fernando_castellanos@mcgraw-hill.com

SINGAPORE (Serving Asia)
McGraw-Hill Book Company
TEL +65-863-1580
FAX +65-862-3354
http://www.mcgraw-hill.com.sg
mghasia@mcgraw-hill.com

SOUTH AFRICA
McGraw-Hill South Africa
TEL +27-11-622-7512
FAX +27-11-622-9045
robyn_swanepoel@mcgraw-hill.com

UNITED KINGDOM & EUROPE
(Excluding Southern Europe)
McGraw-Hill Education Europe
TEL +44-1-628-502500
FAX +44-1-628-770224
http://www.mcgraw-hill.co.uk
computing_neurope@mcgraw-hill.com

ALL OTHER INQUIRIES Contact:
Osborne/McGraw-Hill
TEL +1-510-549-6600
FAX +1-510-883-7600
http://www.osborne.com
omg_international@mcgraw-hill.com